Algorithms for Convex Optimization

In the last few years, algorithms for convex optimization have revolutionized algorithm design, both for discrete and continuous optimization problems. For problems such as maximum flow, maximum matching, and submodular function minimization, the fastest algorithms involve essential methods such as gradient descent, mirror descent, interior point methods, and ellipsoid methods. The goal of this self-contained book is to enable researchers and professionals in computer science, operations research, data science, and machine learning to gain an in-depth understanding of these algorithms. The text emphasizes how to derive key algorithms for convex optimization from first principles and how to establish precise running time bounds. This modern text explains the success of these algorithms in problems of discrete optimization, as well as how these methods have significantly pushed the state of the art of convex optimization itself.

NISHEETH K. VISHNOI is A. Bartlett Giamatti Professor of Computer Science at Yale University. His research areas include theoretical computer science, optimization, and machine learning. He is a recipient of the Best Paper Award at IEEE FOCS in 2005, the IBM Research Pat Goldberg Memorial Award in 2006, the Indian National Science Academy Young Scientist Award in 2011, and the Best Paper Award at ACM FAccT in 2019. He was elected an ACM Fellow in 2019. He obtained a bachelor's degree in computer science and engineering from IIT Bombay and a PhD in algorithms, combinatorics, and optimization from Georgia Institute of Technology.

Algorithms for Convex Optimization

NISHEETH K. VISHNOI
Yale University

CAMBRIDGE
UNIVERSITY PRESS

University Printing House, Cambridge CB2 8BS, United Kingdom

One Liberty Plaza, 20th Floor, New York, NY 10006, USA

477 Williamstown Road, Port Melbourne, VIC 3207, Australia

314–321, 3rd Floor, Plot 3, Splendor Forum, Jasola District Centre,
New Delhi – 110025, India

103 Penang Road, #05–06/07, Visioncrest Commercial, Singapore 238467

Cambridge University Press is part of the University of Cambridge.

It furthers the University's mission by disseminating knowledge in the pursuit of
education, learning, and research at the highest international levels of excellence.

www.cambridge.org
Information on this title: www.cambridge.org/9781108482028
DOI: 10.1017/9781108699211

© Nisheeth K. Vishnoi 2021

First published 2021

A catalogue record for this publication is available from the British Library.

Library of Congress Cataloging-in-Publication Data
Names: Vishnoi, Nisheeth K., 1976– author.
Title: Algorithms for convex optimization / Nisheeth K. Vishnoi.
Description: New York : Cambridge University Press, [2021] |
Includes bibliographical references and index.
Identifiers: LCCN 2020052071 (print) | LCCN 2020052072 (ebook) |
ISBN 9781108482028 (hardback) | ISBN 9781108741774 (paperback) |
ISBN 9781108699211 (epub)
Subjects: LCSH: Mathematical optimization. | Convex functions. |
Convex programming.
Classification: LCC QA402.5 .V57 2021 (print) | LCC QA402.5 (ebook) |
DDC 515/.882–dc23
LC record available at https://lccn.loc.gov/2020052071
LC ebook record available at https://lccn.loc.gov/2020052072

ISBN 978-1-108-48202-8 Hardback
ISBN 978-1-108-74177-4 Paperback

Dedicated to Maya and Vayu

Contents

Preface

Convex optimization studies the problem of minimizing a convex function over a convex set. Convexity, along with its numerous implications, has been used to come up with efficient algorithms for many classes of convex programs. Consequently, convex optimization has broadly impacted several disciplines of science and engineering.

In the last few years, algorithms for convex optimization have revolutionized algorithm design, both for discrete and continuous optimization problems. The fastest-known algorithms for problems such as maximum flow in graphs, maximum matching in bipartite graphs, and submodular function minimization involve an essential and nontrivial use of algorithms for convex optimization such as gradient descent, mirror descent, interior point methods, and cutting plane methods. Surprisingly, algorithms for convex optimization have also been used to design counting problems over discrete objects such as matroids. Simultaneously, algorithms for convex optimization have become central to many modern machine learning applications. The demand for algorithms for convex optimization, driven by larger and increasingly complex input instances, has also significantly pushed the state of the art of convex optimization itself.

The goal of this book is to enable a reader to gain an in-depth understanding of algorithms for convex optimization. The emphasis is to derive key algorithms for convex optimization from first principles and to establish precise running time bounds in terms of the input length. Given the broad applicability of these methods, it is not possible for a single book to show the applications of these methods to all of them. This book shows applications to fast algorithms for various discrete optimization and counting problems. The applications selected in this book serve the purpose of illustrating a rather surprising bridge between continuous and discrete optimization.

The structure of the book. The book has roughly four parts. Chapters 3, 4, and 5 provide an introduction to convexity, models of computation and notions of efficiency in convex optimization, and duality. Chapters 6, 7, and 8 introduce first-order methods such as gradient descent, mirror descent and the multiplicative weights update method, and accelerated gradient descent, respectively. Chapters 9, 10, and 11 present Newton's method and various interior point methods for linear programming. Chapters 12 and 13 present cutting plane methods such as the ellipsoid method for linear and general convex programs. Chapter 1 summarizes the book via a brief history of the interplay between continuous and discrete optimization: how the search for fast algorithms for discrete problems is leading to improvements in algorithms for convex optimization.

Many chapters contain applications ranging from finding maximum flows, minimum cuts, and perfect matchings in graphs, to linear optimization over 0-1-polytopes, to submodular function minimization, to computing maximum entropy distributions over combinatorial polytopes.

The book is self-contained and starts with a review of calculus, linear algebra, geometry, dynamical systems, and graph theory in Chapter 2. Exercises posed in this book not only play an important role in checking one's understanding; sometimes important methods and concepts are introduced and developed entirely through them. Examples include the Frank-Wolfe method, coordinate descent, stochastic gradient descent, online convex optimization, the min-max theorem for zero-sum games, the Winnow algorithm for classification, bandit optimization, the conjugate gradient method, primal-dual interior point method, and matrix scaling.

How to use this book. This book can be used either as a textbook for a stand-alone advanced undergraduate or beginning graduate-level course, or as a supplement to an introductory course on convex optimization or algorithm design. The intended audience includes advanced undergraduate students, graduate students, and researchers from theoretical computer science, discrete optimization, operations research, statistics, and machine learning. To make this book accessible to a broad audience with different backgrounds, the writing style deliberately emphasizes the intuition, sometimes at the expense of rigor.

A course for a theoretical computer science or discrete optimization audience could cover the entire book. A course on convex optimization can omit the applications to discrete optimization and can, instead, include applications as per the choice of the instructor. Finally, an introductory course on convex optimization for machine learning could include material from Chapters 2 to 7.

Beyond convex optimization? This book should also prepare the reader for working in areas beyond convex optimization, e.g., nonconvex optimization and geodesic convex optimization, which are currently in their formative years.

Nonconvex optimization. One property of convex functions is that a "local" minimum is also a "global" minimum. Thus, algorithms for convex optimization, essentially, find a local minimum. Interestingly, this viewpoint has led to convex optimization methods being very successful for nonconvex optimization problems, especially those that arise in machine learning. Unlike convex programs, some of which can be **NP**-hard to optimize, most interesting classes of nonconvex optimization problems are **NP**-hard. Hence, in many of these applications, we define a suitable notion of local minimum and look for methods that can take us to one. Thus, algorithms for convex optimization are important for nonconvex optimization as well; see the survey by Jain and Kar (2017).

Geodesic convex optimization. Sometimes, a function that is nonconvex in a Euclidean space turns out to be convex if we introduce a suitable Riemannian metric on the underlying space and redefine convexity with respect to the "straight lines" – geodesics – induced by the metric. Such functions are called geodesically convex and arise in optimization problems over Riemannian manifolds such as matrix Lie groups; see the survey by Vishnoi (2018). The theory of efficient algorithms for geodesic convex optimization is under construction, and the paper by Bürgisser et al. (2019) presents some recent progress.

Acknowledgments

The contents of this book have been developed over several courses – for both undergraduate and graduate students – that I have taught, starting in Fall 2014 and is closest to that of a course taught in Fall 2019 at Yale. I am grateful to all the students and other attendees of these courses for their questions and comments that have made me reflect on the topic and improve the presentation. I am thankful to Slobodan Mitrovic, Damian Straszak, Jakub Tarnawski, and George Zakhour for being some of the first to take this course and scribing my initial lectures on this topic. Special thanks to Damian for scribing a significant fraction of my lectures, sometimes adding his own insights. I am indebted to Somenath Biswas, Elisa Celis, Yan Zhong Ding, and Anay Mehrotra for carefully reading a draft of this book and giving numerous valuable comments and suggestions.

Finally, this book has been influenced by several classic works: *Geometric Algorithms and Combinatorial Optimization* by Grötschel et al. (1988), *Convex Optimization* by Boyd and Vandenberghe (2004), *Introductory Lectures on Convex Optimization* by Nesterov (2014), and *The Multiplicative Weights Update Method: A Meta-algorithm and Applications* by Arora et al. (2012).

Notation

Numbers and sets:

- The set of natural numbers, integers, rationals, and real numbers are denoted by $\mathbb{N}$, $\mathbb{Z}$, $\mathbb{Q}$, and $\mathbb{R}$, respectively. $\mathbb{Z}_{\geq 0}$, $\mathbb{Q}_{\geq 0}$, and $\mathbb{R}_{\geq 0}$ denote the set of nonnegative integers, rationals, and reals, respectively.
- For a positive integer n, we denote by $[n]$ the set $\{1, 2, \ldots, n\}$.
- For a set $S \subseteq [n]$, we use $1_S \in \mathbb{R}^n$ to denote the indicator vector of S defined as $1_S(i) = 1$ for all $i \in S$ and $1_S(i) = 0$ otherwise.
- For a set $S \subseteq [n]$ of cardinality k, we sometimes write $\mathbb{R}^S$ to denote $\mathbb{R}^k$.

Vectors, matrices, inner products, and norms:

- Vectors are denoted by x and y. A vector $x \in \mathbb{R}^n$ is a column vector but is usually written as $x = (x_1, \ldots, x_n)$. The transpose of a vector x is denoted by $x^\top$.
- The standard basis vectors in $\mathbb{R}^n$ are denoted by $e_1, \ldots, e_n$, where e_i is the vector whose ith entry is one and the remaining entries are zero.
- For vectors $x, y \in \mathbb{R}^n$, by $x \geq y$, we mean that $x_i \geq y_i$ for all $i \in [n]$.
- For a vector $x \in \mathbb{R}^n$, we use $\mathrm{Diag}(x)$ to denote the $n \times n$ matrix whose (i, i)th entry is x_i for $1 \leq i \leq n$ and is zero on all other entries.
- When it is clear from context, 0 and 1 are also used to denote vectors with all 0 entries and all 1 entries, respectively.
- For vectors x and y, their inner product is denoted by $\langle x, y \rangle$ or $x^\top y$.
- For a vector x, its ℓ_2 or Euclidean norm is denoted by $\|x\|_2 := \sqrt{\langle x, x \rangle}$. We sometimes also refer to the ℓ_1 or Manhattan distance norm $\|x\|_1 := \sum_{i=1}^n |x_i|$. The ℓ_∞-norm is defined as $\|x\|_\infty := \max_{i=1}^n |x_i|$.
- The outer product of a vector x with itself is denoted by $xx^\top$.
- Matrices are denoted by capitals, e.g., A and L. The transpose of A is denoted by $A^\top$.

- The trace of an $n \times n$ matrix A is $\text{Tr}(A) := \sum_{i=1}^{n} A_{ii}$. The determinant of an $n \times n$ matrix A is $\det(A) = \sum_{\sigma \in S_n} \text{sgn}(\sigma) \prod_{i=1}^{n} A_{i\sigma(i)}$. Here S_n is the set of all permutations of n elements and $\text{sgn}(\sigma)$ is the number of transpositions in a permutation σ, i.e., the number of pairs $i < j$ such that $\sigma(i) > \sigma(j)$.

Graphs:

- A graph G has a vertex set V and an edge set E. All graphs are assumed to be undirected unless stated otherwise. If the graph is weighted, there is a weight function $w : E \rightarrow \mathbb{R}_{\geq 0}$.
- A graph is said to be simple if there is at most one edge between two vertices and there are no edges whose endpoints are the same vertex.
- Typically, n is reserved for the number of vertices $|V|$ and m for the number of edges $|E|$.

Probability:

- $\mathbb{E}_{\mathcal{D}}[\cdot]$ denotes the expectation and $\text{Pr}_{\mathcal{D}}[\cdot]$ denotes the probability over a distribution $\mathcal{D}$. The subscript is dropped when clear from context.

Running times:

- Standard big-O notation is used to describe the limiting behavior of a function. $\tilde{O}$ denotes that potential poly-logarithmic factors have been omitted, i.e., $f = \tilde{O}(g)$ is equivalent to $f = O(g \log^k(g))$ for some constant k.

1

Bridging Continuous and Discrete Optimization

A large part of algorithm design is concerned with problems that optimize or enumerate over discrete structures such as paths, trees, cuts, flows, and matchings in objects such as graphs. Important examples include the following:

(i) Given a graph $G = (V, E)$, a source $s \in V$, a sink $t \in V$, find a **flow** on the edges of G of maximum value from s to t while ensuring that each edge has at most one unit flow going through it.

(ii) Given a graph $G = (V, E)$, find a **matching** of maximum size in G.

(iii) Given a graph $G = (V, E)$, count the number of **spanning trees** in G.

Algorithms for these fundamental problems have been sought for more than a century due to their numerous applications. Traditionally, such algorithms are **discrete** in nature, leverage the rich theory of **duality** and **integrality**, and are studied in the areas of algorithms and combinatorial optimization; see the books by Dasgupta et al. (2006), Kleinberg and Tardos (2005), and Schrijver (2002a). However, classic algorithms for these problems have not always turned out to be fast enough to handle the rapidly increasing input sizes of modern-day problems.

An alternative, **continuous** approach for designing faster algorithms for discrete problems has emerged. At a very high level, the approach is to first formulate the problem as a convex program and then develop continuous algorithms such as gradient descent, the interior point method, or the ellipsoid method to solve it. The innovative use of convex optimization formulations coupled with algorithms that move in geometric spaces and leverage linear solvers has led to faster algorithms for many discrete problems. This pursuit has also significantly improved the state of the art of algorithms for convex optimization. For these improvements to be possible, it is often crucial to abandon an entirely combinatorial viewpoint; simultaneously, fast convergence of continuous algorithms often leverage the underlying combinatorial structure.

1

1.1 An Example: The Maximum Flow Problem

We illustrate the interplay between continuous and discrete optimization through the $s - t$-maximum flow problem on undirected graphs.

The maximum flow problem. Given an undirected graph $G = (V, E)$ with $n := |V|$ and $m := |E|$, we first define the **vertex-edge incidence matrix** $B \in \mathbb{R}^{n \times m}$ associated to it. Direct each edge $i \in E$ arbitrarily and let i^+ denote the head vertex of i and i^- denote its tail vertex. For every edge i, the matrix B contains a column $b_i := e_{i^+} - e_{i^-} \in \mathbb{R}^n$, where $\{e_j\}_{j \in [n]}$ are the standard basis vectors for $\mathbb{R}^n$.

Given $s \neq t \in V$, an $s - t$-flow in G is an assignment $x : E \to \mathbb{R}$ that satisfies the following **conservation of flow** property: For all vertices $j \in V \setminus \{s, t\}$, we require that the **incoming** flow is equal to the **outgoing** flow, i.e.,

$$\langle e_j, Bx \rangle = 0.$$

An $s - t$-flow is said to be **feasible** if

$$|x_i| \leq 1$$

for all $i \in E$, i.e., the magnitude of the flow in each edge respects its capacity (1 here). The objective of the $s - t$-maximum flow problem is to find a feasible $s - t$-flow in G that maximizes the flow out of s, i.e., the value

$$\langle e_s, Bx \rangle.$$

The $s - t$-maximum flow problem was not only used to encode various real-world routing and scheduling problems; also many fundamental combinatorial problems such as finding a maximum matching in bipartite graph were shown to be its special cases; see Schrijver (2002a,b) for an extensive discussion.

Combinatorial algorithms for the maximum flow problem. An important fact about the $s - t$-maximum flow problem is that there always exists an **integral** flow that maximizes the objective function. As it will be explained later in this book, this is a consequence of the fact that the matrix B is **totally unimodular**: Every square submatrix of B has determinant 0, 1, or -1. Thus, we can restrict

$$x_i \in \{-1, 0, 1\}$$

for each $i \in E$, making the search space for the optimal $s - t$-maximum flow discrete. Because of this, the problem has been traditionally viewed as a combinatorial optimization problem.

One of the first combinatorial algorithms for the $s - t$-maximum flow problem was presented in the seminal work by Ford and Fulkerson (1956). Roughly speaking, the **Ford-Fulkerson method** starts by setting $x_i = 0$ for all edges i and checks if there is a path from s to t such that the capacity of each edge on it is 1. If there is such a path, the method adds 1 to the flow value of the edges that point (from head to tail) in the direction of this path and subtracts 1 from the flow values of edges that point in the opposite direction. Given the new flow value on each edge, it constructs a **residual graph** where the capacity of each edge is updated to reflect how much additional flow can still be pushed through it, and the algorithm repeats. If there is no path left between s and t in the residual graph, it stops and outputs the current flow values.

The fact that the algorithm always outputs a maximum $s - t$-flow is nontrivial and a consequence of **duality** – in particular, of the **max-flow min-cut theorem** that states that the maximum amount of flow that can be pushed from s to t is equal to the minimum number of edges in G whose deletion leads to disconnecting s from t. This latter problem is referred to as the $s - t$-minimum cut problem and is the **dual** of the $s - t$-maximum flow problem. Duality gives a way to certify that we are at an optimal solution and, if not, suggests a way to improve the current solution.

It is not hard to see that the Ford-Fulkerson method generalizes to the setting of nonnegative and integral capacities: Now the flow values are

$$x_i \in \{-U, \ldots, -1, 0, 1, \ldots, U\}$$

for some $U \in \mathbb{Z}_{\geq 0}$. However, the running time of the Ford-Fulkerson method in this general capacity case depends linearly on U. As the number of bits required to specify U is roughly $\log U$, this is not a polynomial time algorithm.

Following the work of Ford and Fulkerson (1956), a host of combinatorial algorithms for the $s - t$-maximum flow problem were developed. Roughly, each of them augments the flow in the graph iteratively in an increasingly faster, but combinatorial, manner. The first polynomial time algorithms were by Dinic (1970) and by Edmonds and Karp (1972), who used breadth-first search to augment flows. This line of work culminated in an algorithm by Goldberg and Rao (1998) that runs in $\tilde{O}\left(m \min\left\{n^{2/3}, m^{1/2}\right\} \log U\right)$ time. Note that unlike the Ford-Fulkerson method, these latter combinatorial algorithms are polynomial time: They find the exact solution to the problem and run in time that depends polynomially on the number of bits required to describe the input. However, since the result of Goldberg and Rao (1998), there was no real progress on improving the running times for algorithms for the $s - t$-maximum flow problem until 2011.

Convex programming-based algorithms. Starting with the paper by Christiano et al. (2011), the last decade has seen striking progress on the $s - t$-maximum flow problem. One of the keys to this success has been to abandon combinatorial approaches and view the $s - t$-maximum flow problem through the lens of continuous optimization. At a very high level, these approaches still maintain a vector $x \in \mathbb{R}^m$ which is updated in every iteration, but this update is dictated by continuous and geometric quantities associated to the graph and is not constrained to be a feasible $s - t$-flow in the intermediate steps of the algorithm. Here, we outline one such approach for the $s - t$-maximum flow problem from the paper by Lee et al. (2013).

For this discussion, assume that we are also given a value F and that we would like to find a feasible $s - t$-flow of value F.[1] Lee et al. (2013) start with the observation that the problem of checking if there is a feasible $s - t$-flow of value F in G is equivalent to determining if the intersection of the sets

$$\{x \in \mathbb{R}^m : Bx = F(e_s - e_t)\} \cap \{x \in \mathbb{R}^m : |x_i| \leq 1, \forall i \in [m]\} \qquad (1.1)$$

is nonempty. Moreover, finding a feasible $s - t$-flow of value F is equivalent to finding a point in this intersection. Note that the first set in Equation (1.1) is the set of all $s - t$-flows (a linear space) and the second set is the set of all vectors that satisfy the capacity constraints, in this case the ℓ_∞-ball of radius one, denoted by B_∞, which is a polytope.

Their main idea is to reduce this nonemptiness testing problem to a convex optimization problem. To motivate their idea, suppose that we have convex sets K_1 and K_2 and the goal is to find a point in their intersection (or assert that there is none). One way to formulate this problem as a convex optimization problem is as follows: Find a point $x \in K_1$ that minimizes the distance to K_2. As K_1 is convex, for this formulation to be a convex optimization problem, we need to find a convex function that captures the distance of a point x to K_2. It can be checked that the squared Euclidean distance has this property. Alternatively, one could consider the convex optimization problem where we switch the roles of K_1 and K_2: Find a point $x \in K_2$ that minimizes the distance to K_1. Note here that, while the squared Euclidean distance to a set is a convex function, it is nonlinear. Thus, at this point it may seem like we are heading in the wrong direction. We started off with a combinatorial problem that is a special type of a linear programming problem, and here we are with a nonlinear optimization formulation for it.

---

[1] Using a solution to this problem, we could solve the $s - t$-maximum flow problem by performing a binary search over F.

Thus the following questions arise: Which formulation should we choose? And why should this convex optimization approach lead us to faster algorithms?

Lee et al. (2013) considered the following convex optimization formulation for the $s - t$-maximum flow problem:

$$\min_{x \in \mathbb{R}^m} \quad \text{dist}^2(x, B_\infty)$$
$$\text{such that} \quad Bx = F(e_s - e_t), \tag{1.2}$$

where $\text{dist}(x, B_\infty)$ is the Euclidean distance of x to the set $B_\infty := \{y \in \mathbb{R}^m : \|y\|_\infty \leq 1\}$. As the optimization problem above minimizes a convex function over a convex set, it is indeed a convex program. The choice of this formulation, however, comes with a foresight that relies on an understanding of algorithms for convex optimization.

A basic method to minimize a convex function is **gradient descent**, which is an iterative algorithm that, in each iteration, takes a step in the direction of the negative gradient of the function it is supposed to minimize. While gradient descent does so in an attempt to optimize the function locally, the convexity of the objective function implies that a local minimum of a convex function is also its global minimum. Gradient descent only requires oracle access to the gradient, or first derivative of the objective function and is, thus, called a **first-order** method. It is really a meta-algorithm and, to instantiate it, one has to fix its parameters such as the step-size and must specify a starting point. These parameters, in turn, depend on various properties of the program including estimates of smoothness of the objective function and those of the closeness of the starting point to the optimal point.

For the convex program in Equation (1.2), the objective function has an easy-to-compute first-order oracle. This follows from the observation that it decomposes into a sum of squared-distances, one for each coordinate, and each of these functions is quadratic. Moreover, the objective function is **smooth**: The change in its gradient is bounded by a constant times the change in its argument; one can visually inspect this in Figure 1.1.

One problem with the application of gradient descent is that the convex program in (1.2) has constraints $\{x \in \mathbb{R}^m : Bx = F(e_s - e_t)\}$ and, hence, the direction gradient descent asks us to move can take us out of this set. A way to get around this is to project the gradient of the objective function onto the subspace $\{x \in \mathbb{R}^m : Bx = 0\}$ at every step and move in the direction of the projected gradient. However, this projection step requires solving a least squares problem that, in turn, reduces to the numerical problem of solving a linear system of equations. While one can appeal to the Gaussian elimination

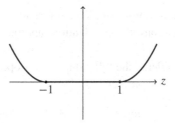

Figure 1.1 The function $\mathrm{dist}^2(z, [-1, 1])$.

method for this latter task, it is not fast enough to warrant improvements over combinatorial algorithms mentioned earlier. Here, a major result discovered by Spielman and Teng (2004) implies that such a projection can, in fact, be computed in time $\widetilde{O}(m)$. This is achieved by noting that the linear system that arises when projecting a vector onto the subspace $\{x \in \mathbb{R}^m : Bx = 0\}$ is the same as solving **Laplacian systems** that are of the form $BB^\top y = a$ (for a given vector a), where B is a vertex-edge incidence matrix of the given graph. Such a result is not known for general linear systems and (implicitly) relies on the combinatorial structure of the graph that gets encoded in the matrix B.

Thus, roughly speaking, in each iteration the projected gradient descent algorithm takes a point x_t in the space of all $s - t$-flows of value F, moves toward the set B_∞ along the negative gradient of the objective function, and then projects the new point back to the linear space; see Figure 1.2 for an illustration. While each iterate is an $s - t$-flow, it is not a feasible flow.

A final issue is that such a method may not lead to an exact solution but only an approximate solution. Moreover, in general, the number of iterations depends inverse polynomially on the quality of the desired approximation. Lee et al. (2013) proved the following result: There is an algorithm that, given an $\varepsilon > 0$, can compute a feasible $s - t$-flow of value $(1 - \varepsilon)F$ in time $\widetilde{O}(mn^{1/3}\varepsilon^{-2/3})$. If we ignore the ε in their bound, this improved the result of Goldberg and Rao (1998) mentioned earlier.

We point out that the combinatorial algorithm of Goldberg and Rao (1998) has the same running time even when the input graph is directed. It is not clear how to generalize the gradient descent–based algorithm for the $s - t$-maximum flow problem presented above to run for directed graphs.

The results of Christiano et al. (2011) and Lee et al. (2013) were further improved using increasingly sophisticated ideas from continuous optimization and finally led to a nearly linear time algorithm for the undirected $s - t$-maximum flow problem in a sequence of work by Sherman (2013), Kelner et al. (2014), and Peng (2016). Remarkably, while these improvements

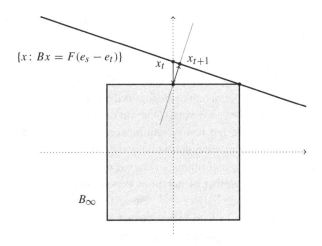

Figure 1.2 An illustration of one step of the projected gradient descent in the algorithm by Lee et al. (2013).

abandoned discrete approaches and used algorithms for convex optimization, beating the running times of combinatorial algorithms leveraged the underlying combinatorial structure of the $s - t$-maximum flow problem.

The goal of this book is to enable a reader to gain an in-depth understanding of algorithms for convex optimization in a manner that allows them to apply these algorithms in domains such as combinatorial optimization, algorithm design, and machine learning. The emphasis is to derive various convex optimization methods in a principled manner and to establish precise running time bounds in terms of the input length (and not just on the number of iterations). The book also contains several examples, such as the one of $s - t$-maximum flow presented earlier, that illustrate the bridge between continuous and discrete optimization. Laplacian solvers are not discussed in this book. The reader is referred to the monograph by Vishnoi (2013) for more on that topic.

The focus of Chapters 3–5 is on basics of convexity, computational models, and duality. Chapters 6–8 present three different first-order methods: gradient descent, mirror descent and multiplicative weights update method, and **accelerated gradient descent.** In particular, the discussion here is presented in detail as an application in Chapter 6. In fact, the fastest version of the method of Lee et al. (2013) uses the accelerated gradient method. Chapter 7 also draws a connection between **mirror descent** and the **multiplicative weights update** method and shows how the latter can be used to design a fast (approximate) algorithm for the bipartite maximum matching problem. We remark that the algorithm of Christiano et al. (2011) relies on the multiplicative weights update method.

Beyond approximate algorithms? The combinatorial algorithms for the $s-t$-maximum flow problem, unlike the first-order convex optimization–based algorithms described above, are exact. One can convert the latter approximate algorithms to exact ones, but it may require setting a very small value of ε making the overall running time non-polynomial. The remainder of the book is dedicated to developing algorithms for convex optimization – **interior point** and **ellipsoid** – whose number of iterations depend **poly-logarithmically** on ε^{-1} as opposed to polynomially on ε^{-1}. Thus, if we use such algorithms, we can set ε to be small enough to recover exact algorithms for combinatorial problems at hand. These algorithms use deeper mathematical structures and more sophisticated strategies (as explained later). The advantage in learning these algorithms is that they work more generally – for linear programs and even convex programs in a very general form. Chapters 9–13 develop these methods, their variants, and exhibit applications to a variety of discrete optimization and counting problems.

1.2 Linear Programming

The $s-t$-maximum flow problem on undirected graphs is a type of linear program: a convex optimization problem where the objective function is a linear function and all the constraints are either linear equalities or inequalities. In fact, the objective function is to maximize the flow value $F \geq 0$ constrained to the set of feasible $s-t$-flows of value F; see Equation (1.1).

A linear program can be written in many different ways and we consider its **standard form**, where one is given a matrix $A \in \mathbb{R}^{n \times m}$, a constraint vector $b \in \mathbb{R}^m$, and a cost vector $c \in \mathbb{R}^n$, and the goal is to solve the following optimization problem:

$$\max_{x \in \mathbb{R}^m} \langle c, x \rangle$$

$$\text{such that } Ax = b,$$

$$x \geq 0.$$

Typically we assume $n \leq m$ and, hence, the rank of A is at most n. Analogous to the $s-t$-maximum flow problem, linear programming has a rich duality theory, and in particular the following is the **dual** of the above linear program:

$$\min_{y \in \mathbb{R}^n} \langle b, y \rangle$$

$$\text{such that } A^\top y \geq c.$$

Note that the dual is also a linear program and has n variables.

Linear programming duality asserts that if there is a feasible solution to both the linear program and its dual, then the optimal values of these two linear programs are the same. Moreover, it is often enough to solve the dual if one wants to solve the primal and vice versa. While duality has been known for linear programming for a very long time (see Farkas [1902]), a polynomial time algorithm for linear programming was discovered much later. What was special about the $s - t$-maximum flow problem that led to a polynomial time algorithm for it before linear programming?

As mentioned earlier, one crucial property that underlies the $s - t$-maximum flow problem is integrality. If one encodes the $s - t$-maximum flow problem as a linear program in the standard form, the matrix A turns out to be totally unimodular: Determinants of all square submatrices of A are $0, 1$, or -1. In fact, in the case of the $s - t$-maximum flow problem, A is just the vertex-edge incidence matrix of the graph G (which we denoted by B) that can be shown to be totally unimodular. Because of linearity, one can always assume without loss of generality that the optimal solution is an extreme point, i.e., a **vertex** of the polyhedra of constraints (not to be confused with the vertex of a graph). Every such vertex arises as a solution to a system of linear equations involving a subset of rows of the matrix A. The total unimodularity of A, then, along with Cramer's rule from linear algebra, implies that each vertex of the polyhedra of constraints has integral coordinates.

While duality and integrality do not directly imply a polynomial time algorithm for the $s - t$-maximum flow problem, the mathematical structure that enables these properties is relevant to the design of efficient algorithms for this problem. It is worth mentioning that these ideas were generalized in a major way by Edmonds (1965a,b) who figured out an integral polyhedral representation for the **matching problem** and gave a polynomial time algorithm for optimizing linear functions over this polyhedron.

For general linear programs, however, integrality does not hold. The reason is that for a general matrix A, the determinants of submatrices that show up in the denominator of the vertices of the associated polyhedra may not be 1 or -1. However, for A with integer entries, these determinants cannot be more than $\text{poly}(n, L)$ in magnitude, where L is the number of bits required to encode A, b and c. This is a consequence of the fact that determinant of a matrix with integer entries bounded by 2^L is no more than $n! \, 2^{nL}$. While there was a

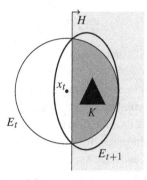

Figure 1.3 Illustration of one step of the ellipsoid method for the polytope K.

combinatorial algorithm for linear programming, e.g., the **simplex method** of Dantzig (1990) that moved from one vertex to another, none was known to run in polynomial time (in the bit complexity) in the worst case.

Ellipsoid method. In the late 1970s, a breakthrough occurred and a polynomial time algorithm for linear programming was discovered by Khachiyan (1979, 1980). The ellipsoid method is a geometric algorithm that checks if a given linear program is feasible or not. As in the case of the $s - t$-maximum flow problem, solving this feasibility problem implies an algorithm to optimize a linear function via a binary search argument.

In iteration t, the ellipsoid method approximates the feasible region of the linear program with an **ellipsoid** E_t and outputs the center (x_t) of this ellipsoid as its guess for a feasible point. If this guess is incorrect, it requires a **certificate** – a hyperplane H that separates the center from the feasible region. It uses this **separating hyperplane** to find a new ellipsoid (E_{t+1}) that encloses the intersection of E_t and the halfspace of H in which the feasible region lies; see Figure 1.3. The key point is that the update ensures that the volume of the ellipsoid reduces at a fast enough rate and only requires solving a linear system of equations to find the new ellipsoid from the previous one. If the **volume** of the ellipsoid becomes so small that it cannot contain any feasible point, we can safely assert the infeasibility of the linear program.

The ellipsoid method belongs to the larger class of **cutting plane methods** as, in each step, the current ellipsoid is cut by an affine halfspace and a new ellipsoid that contains this intersection is determined. The final running time of Khachiyan's ellipsoid method was a polynomial in n, L and, importantly, in $\log \frac{1}{\varepsilon}$: The algorithm output a point $\hat{x}$ in the feasible region such that

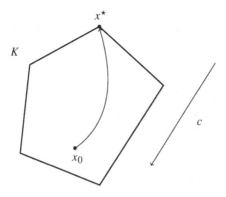

Figure 1.4 Illustration of the interior point method for the polytope K.

$$\langle c, \hat{x} \rangle \leq \langle c, x^\star \rangle + \varepsilon.$$

This implied that one can handle an error as small as $2^{-\text{poly}(n, L)}$, and this is all we need for linear programming to be in polynomial time. While this put linear programming in the complexity class **P** for the first time, the resulting algorithm, when specialized for combinatorial problems such as the $s - t$-maximum flow problem, was far from competitive in terms of running time.

Interior point methods. In 1984, another continuous polynomial time algorithm to solve linear programs was discovered by Karmarkar (1984): This time the idea was to move in the interior of the feasible region until one reaches the optimal solution; see Figure 1.4. Karmarkar's algorithm had its roots in the barrier method from nonlinear optimization. The barrier method is one way to convert a constrained optimization problem to an unconstrained one by choosing a **barrier function** for the constraint set. Roughly speaking, a barrier function for a convex set is a function that is finite only in the interior of it and increases to infinity as one approaches the boundary of the feasible region. Once we have a barrier function for a constraint set, we can add it to the objective function to penalize any violation of the constraints. For such a function to be algorithmically useful, it is desirable that it is a convex a function and also has certain smoothness properties (as explained later in this book).

Renegar (1988) combined the barrier approach with **Newton's method** for root finding to improve upon Karmarkar's method. Unlike gradient descent, which was based on the first-order approximation of the objective function, Renegar's algorithm, following Newton's method, considered a **quadratic**

approximation to the objective function around the current point and optimized it to find the next point. His method took roughly $\widetilde{O}\left(\sqrt{m}\,L\right)$ iterations to find a solution to the given linear program. Here L is the bit complexity of the input (A, b, c). Further, each iteration just had to solve a linear system of equations of size $m \times m$.

While one way to view Newton's method is as a second-order method, an equivalent way is to view it as performing steepest descent in a geometric space where the inner product and the norm change depending on the current location of the algorithm: At a point x, the inner product between vectors u and v is defined as $u^{\top} \nabla^2 F(x) v$ for a barrier function F. As F is convex, this gives rise to a **local norm** and is an example of a **Riemannian metric**.

However, unlike the ellipsoid method that just needs a separating hyperplane, interior point methods require the constraints explicitly in order to compute the Hessian of the barrier function for the constraint set. In Chapter 9, we derive Newton's method both as a quadratic approximation and as a steepest descent on a Riemannian manifold and present its analysis using local norms. In Chapter 10, we introduce barrier functions and present Renegar's path-following interior point method for linear programming.

1.3 Fast and Exact Algorithms via Interior Point Methods

Despite the remarkable effort that went into improving interior point methods in the late 1980s, they could still not compete with combinatorial algorithms for problems such as the $s - t$-maximum flow problem. A key obstacle was the fact that solving a linear system of equations (a primitive used at each step of ellipsoid and interior point method) required roughly $O(m^{2.373})$ time.

Vaidya (1990) observed that the combinatorial structure of the problem manifests in the linear systems that arise, and this structure could be used to speed up certain linear programs. For instance, and as mentioned earlier, for the $s - t$-maximum flow problem, the linear systems that arise correspond to **Laplacian systems**. Vaidya presented some initial results for such linear systems that gave hope for improving the per-iteration cost. His program was completed by Spielman and Teng (2004), who gave an $\widetilde{O}(m)$ time algorithm to solve Laplacian systems. And, using this (and a few more ideas), Daitch and Spielman (2008) gave an exact interior point method for the maximum flow problem that runs in time $\widetilde{O}(m^{1.5} \log U)$, matching the performance of the algorithm by Goldberg and Rao (1998) when $m = O(n)$. In fact, their method could also solve the more general $s - t$-minimum cost flow problem in $\widetilde{O}(m^{1.5}\log U)$ time and improved upon all prior algorithms by a factor of about $\widetilde{O}(n/m^{1/2})$. This is presented in Chapter 11 and was the first sign that general-purpose convex optimization methods can be specialized to be comparable to or even beat combinatorial algorithms.

Beyond log-barrier functions. Meanwhile, in a sequence of papers, Vaidya (1987, 1989a,b) introduced the **volumetric barrier** as a generalization of Karmarkar's barrier function and obtain modest improvements on the number of iterations while ensuring that each iteration of his interior point method for linear programming still just required multiplying two $m \times m$ matrices.

Nesterov and Nemirovskii (1994) abstracted the essence of barrier functions and introduced the notion of **self-concordance**. They introduced the **universal barrier** function and showed that the number of iterations in an interior point method that uses their universal barrier function is $\sqrt{n}$, where n is the dimension of the feasible region. They also showed that this bound cannot, in general, go below $\sqrt{n}$. Computing the barrier function that achieved this, however, was not easier than solving the linear programming problem itself.

Finally, Lee and Sidford (2014), building upon the ideas of Vaidya, gave a new barrier function for interior point methods that not only came sensationally close to the bound of $O(\sqrt{n})$ of Nesterov and Nemirovskii (1994), but each iteration of their method just solves a small number of linear systems. Using these ideas, Lee and Sidford (2014) gave an exact algorithm for the $s - t$-maximum flow problem that runs in $\widetilde{O}(m\sqrt{n}\log^2 U)$ time, the first improvement since Goldberg and Rao (1998). Their method also gave an algorithm that runs in the same time for the $s - t$-minimum cost flow problem, improving upon the results of Daitch and Spielman (2008) and Goldberg and Tarjan (1987). Chapter 11 outlines the methods of Vaidya, Nesterov-Nemirovskii, and Lee-Sidford.

1.4 Ellipsoid Method beyond Succinct Linear Programs

As mentioned earlier, an advantage of the ellipsoid method over interior point methods was the fact that they just needed a **separation oracle** to the polytope to optimize a linear function over it. A separation oracle for a convex set is an algorithm that, given a point, either asserts that the point is in the convex set or outputs a hyperplane that separates the point from the convex set. This fact was exploited by Grötschel et al. (1981) to show that the ellipsoid method can also be used to perform linear optimization over combinatorial polytopes that do not have a succinct linear description. Prominent examples include the matching polytope for general graphs and various matroid polytopes.

Chapter 12 presents the general framework of cutting plane methods, derives the ellipsoid method of Khachiyan, and applies it to the problem of linear optimization over combinatorial **0-1-polytopes** for which we only have a separation oracle. Thus, the ellipsoid method may, sometimes, be the only way one can obtain polynomial time algorithms for combinatorial problems.

Grötschel et al. (1981, 1988) noticed something more about the ellipsoid method: It can be extended to **general convex programs** of the form

$$\min_{x \in K} f(x), \tag{1.3}$$

where both f and K are convex. Their method outputs a point $\hat{x}$ such that

$$f(\hat{x}) \leq \min_{x \in K} f(x) + \varepsilon$$

in time, roughly, $\text{poly}\left(n, \log \frac{R}{\varepsilon}, T_f, T_K\right)$, where R is such that K is contained in a ball of radius R, time T_f is required to compute the gradient of f, and time T_K is required to separate a point from K. Thus, this settled the problem of designing algorithms for convex optimization in its most generality. However, we emphasize that this result does not imply that any convex program of the form (1.3) is in **P**. The reason is that sometimes it may be impossible to get an efficient gradient oracle for f, an efficient separation oracle for K, or a good enough bound on R.

In Chapter 13, we present an algorithm to minimize a convex function over a convex set and prove the guarantee mentioned above. Subsequently, we show how this can be used to give a polynomial time algorithm for another combinatorial problem – **submodular function minimization** – given just an evaluation oracle to the function. A submodular function $f : 2^{[m]} \to \mathbb{R}$ has the **diminishing returns** property: For sets $S \subseteq T \subseteq [m]$, the marginal gain of adding an element not in T to S is at least the marginal gain of adding it to T, i.e., for all $i \notin T$:

$$f(S \cup \{i\}) - f(S) \geq f(T \cup \{i\}) - f(T).$$

The ability to minimize submodular set functions allows us to obtain separation oracles for matroid polytopes. Submodular functions arose in discrete optimization and have recently also appeared as objective functions of machine learning tasks such as data summarization.

Finally, in Chapter 13, we consider convex programs that have been recently used for designing various counting problems over discrete sets, such as spanning trees. Given a graph $G = (V, E)$, let $\mathcal{T}_G$ denote the set of spanning trees

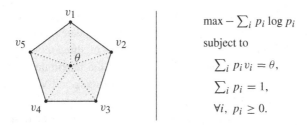

$$\max - \sum_i p_i \log p_i$$

subject to

$$\sum_i p_i v_i = \theta,$$

$$\sum_i p_i = 1,$$

$$\forall i, \ p_i \geq 0.$$

Figure 1.5 The maximum entropy problem and its convex program.

in G and let P_G denote the **spanning tree polytope**, i.e., the convex hull of indicator vectors of all the spanning trees in $\mathcal{T}_G$. Each vertex of P_G corresponds to a spanning tree in G. The problem that we consider is the following: Given a point $\theta \in P_G$, find a way to write θ as a convex combination of the vertices of the polytope P_G so that the probability distribution corresponding to this convex combination maximizes **Shannon entropy**; see Figure 1.5. To see what this problem has to do with counting spanning trees, the reader is encouraged to check that if we let θ be the average of all the vertex vectors of P_G, the value of this optimization problem is exactly $\log |\mathcal{T}_G|$.

As stated, this is an optimization problem where there is a variable corresponding to each vertex of the polytope, the constraints on these variables are linear, and the objective function maximizes a concave function; see Figure 1.5. Thus, this is a convex program. Note, however, that $|\mathcal{T}_G|$ can be exponential in the number of vertices in G; the complete graph on n vertices has n^{n-2} spanning trees. Thus, the number of variables can be exponential in the input size, and it is not clear how to solve this problem. Interestingly, if one considers the dual of this convex optimization problem, the number of variables becomes the number of edges in the graph.

However, there are obstacles to applying the general convex optimization method to this setting, and this is discussed in detail in Chapter 13. In particular, Chapter 13 presents a polynomial time algorithm for the **maximum entropy problem** over polytopes due to Singh and Vishnoi (2014) and Straszak and Vishnoi (2019). Such algorithms have been used to design very general **approximate counting** algorithms for discrete problems by Anari and Oveis Gharan (2017) and Straszak and Vishnoi (2017), and have enabled breakthrough results for the **traveling salesman problem** by Oveis Gharan et al. (2011) and Karlin et al. (2020).

Curiously, nature – via evolution – has developed continuous algorithms to solve discrete problems. An example is the organism *Physarum polycephalum*, a slime mold, that uses a continuous-time dynamical system to solve the shortest path problem in a maze; see the papers by Nakagaki et al. (2000) and Bonifaci et al. (2012). Interestingly, the dynamics of slime mold has served as an inspiration to new continuous algorithms for the maximum flow problem and for linear programming; see the papers by Straszak and Vishnoi (2016a,b, 2021) and Exercises 9.11 and 11.8. Another striking example is a work by Chastain et al. (2014), which argues that the mathematical description of sexual evolution is equivalent to the multiplicative weight updates algorithm. Thus, the bridge between continuous and discrete optimization transcends the artificial world.

In summary, the last few years have seen dramatic progress in approximate and exact algorithms for discrete problems. This progress is a result of viewing discrete problems through the powerful lens of continuous methods and has been fueled by major advances in algorithms for convex optimization. The examples presented here hint at how continuous formulations allow algorithms to harness geometric and analytic structures absent in the discrete world. However, much remains to be done: from discovering even faster algorithms, to conceptually simplifying the existing ones, to explaining the effectiveness of continuous methods for discrete problems.

2

Preliminaries

We review the mathematical preliminaries required for this book. These include some standard notions and facts from multivariate calculus, linear algebra, geometry, topology, dynamical systems, and graph theory.

2.1 Derivatives, Gradients, and Hessians

We start with the definition of the derivative of a univariate function.

Definition 2.1 (Derivative). For $g \colon \mathbb{R} \to \mathbb{R}$ and $t \in \mathbb{R}$, consider the following limit:

$$\lim_{\delta \to 0} \frac{g(t + \delta) - g(t)}{\delta}.$$

The function g is said to be **differentiable** if this limit exists for all $t \in \mathbb{R}$, and this limit is called the derivative of g at t. We denote it by

$$\frac{d}{dt}g(t) \quad \text{or} \quad \dot{g}(t) \quad \text{or} \quad g'(t).$$

A function is said to be **continuously differentiable** if its derivative is also continuous. The central objects of study are functions $f \colon \mathbb{R}^n \to \mathbb{R}$. For such multivariate functions, we can use the definition of the derivative to define gradients. But first, we need the definition of a directional derivative.

Definition 2.2 (Directional derivative). For $f \colon \mathbb{R}^n \to \mathbb{R}$ and $x \in \mathbb{R}^n$, given $h_1, \ldots, h_k \in \mathbb{R}^n$, define $D^k f(x) \colon (\mathbb{R}^n)^k \to \mathbb{R}$ as

$$D^k f(x)[h_1, \ldots, h_k] := \left. \frac{d}{dt_1} \cdots \frac{d}{dt_k} f(x + t_1 h_1 + \cdots + t_k h_k) \right|_{t_1 = \cdots = t_k = 0}.$$

17

$D^k f(x)$ is called the directional derivative as we can evaluate it for any k-tuple of directions $h_1, \ldots, h_k$.

$D^1 f(x)[\cdot]$ is denoted by $Df(x)[\cdot]$ and is also known as the **differential** of f at x. When the kth directional derivative of a function f exists for all arguments to $D^k f(\cdot)[\cdot, \cdots, \cdot]$, we say that f is differentiable up to order k. For $k = 1, 2$ we call such a function differentiable or twice differentiable. Unless otherwise stated, we assume that the functions are sufficiently differentiable. In this case, we can talk about the gradient and the Hessian of f.

Definition 2.3 (Gradient). For a differentiable function $f : \mathbb{R}^n \to \mathbb{R}$ and an $x \in \mathbb{R}^n$, the gradient of f at x is defined as the unique vector $g(x) \in \mathbb{R}^n$ such that

$$\langle g(x), y \rangle = Df(x)[y]$$

for all $y \in \mathbb{R}^n$. When $y = e_i$, the ith standard basis vector in $\mathbb{R}^n$, $Df(x)[e_i]$ is denoted by $\frac{\partial}{\partial x_i} f(x)$. We denote the gradient $g(x)$ by $\nabla f(x)$ or $Df(x)$ and we write it as:

$$\nabla f(x) = \left[\frac{\partial f}{\partial x_1}(x), \ \frac{\partial f}{\partial x_2}(x), \ldots, \ \frac{\partial f}{\partial x_n}(x) \right]^\top.$$

Definition 2.4 (Hessian). For a twice differentiable function $f : \mathbb{R}^n \to \mathbb{R}$, its Hessian at $x \in \mathbb{R}^n$ is defined as the unique linear function $H(x) : \mathbb{R}^n \to \mathbb{R}^n$ such that for all $x, h_1, h_2 \in \mathbb{R}^n$ we have

$$h_1^\top H(x) h_2 = D^2 f(x)[h_1, h_2].$$

The Hessian is often denoted by $\nabla^2 f(x)$ or $D^2 f(x)$ and can be represented as the following matrix whose element at row i and column j is

$$(\nabla^2 f(x_1, x_2, \ldots, x_n))_{ij} = \frac{\partial^2 f}{\partial x_i \partial x_j}(x).$$

In other words, $\nabla^2 f(x)$ is the following $n \times n$ matrix:

$$\begin{bmatrix} \frac{\partial^2 f}{\partial x_1^2} & \frac{\partial^2 f}{\partial x_1 \partial x_2} & \cdots & \frac{\partial^2 f}{\partial x_1 \partial x_n} \\ \frac{\partial^2 f}{\partial x_2 \partial x_1} & \frac{\partial^2 f}{\partial x_2^2} & \cdots & \frac{\partial^2 f}{\partial x_2 \partial x_n} \\ \vdots & \vdots & \ddots & \vdots \\ \frac{\partial^2 f}{\partial x_n \partial x_1} & \frac{\partial^2 f}{\partial x_n \partial x_2} & \cdots & \frac{\partial^2 f}{\partial x_n^2} \end{bmatrix}.$$

The Hessian is symmetric, as the order of i and j does not matter in differentiation. The definitions of gradient and Hessian presented here easily generalize to the setting where the function is defined on a subdomain of $\mathbb{R}^n$; see Chapter 11. As a generalization of the notation used for gradient and Hessian, we sometimes also use the notation $\nabla^k f(x)$ instead of $D^k f(x)$.

2.2 Fundamental Theorem of Calculus

We now show that differentiation in the multivariate setting can be expressed in terms of integrals of univariate functions. It relies on the following (part II of the) fundamental theorem of calculus.

Theorem 2.5 (Fundamental theorem of calculus, part II). *Let $f : [a,b] \to \mathbb{R}$ be a continuously differentiable function. Then*

$$\int_a^b \dot{f}(t)\, dt = f(b) - f(a).$$

The proof of the following useful lemma is left as an exercise (Exercise 2.2).

Lemma 2.6 (Integral representations of functions). *Let $f : \mathbb{R}^n \to \mathbb{R}$ be a continuously differentiable function. For $x, y \in \mathbb{R}$, let $g : [0,1] \to \mathbb{R}$ be defined as*

$$g(t) := f(x + t(y - x)).$$

Then, the following are true:

(i) $\dot{g}(t) = \langle \nabla f(x + t(y - x)), y - x \rangle$, *and*
(ii) $f(y) = f(x) + \int_0^1 \dot{g}(t)\, dt$.

If, in addition, f has a continuous Hessian, then the following are also true:

(i) $\ddot{g}(t) = (y - x)^\top \nabla^2 f(x + t(y - x))(y - x)$, *and*
(ii) $\langle \nabla f(y) - \nabla f(x), y - x \rangle = \int_0^1 \ddot{g}(t)\, dt$.

2.3 Taylor Approximation

It is often useful to consider a linear or quadratic approximation of a function $f : \mathbb{R}^n \to \mathbb{R}$ around a certain point $a \in \mathbb{R}^n$.

Definition 2.7 (Taylor series and approximation). Let $f: \mathbb{R}^n \to \mathbb{R}$ be a function that is infinitely differentiable. The Taylor series expansion of f around a, whenever it exists, is given by:

$$f(x) = f(a) + \langle \nabla f(a), x - a \rangle + \frac{1}{2}(x - a)^\top \nabla^2 f(a)(x - a)$$

$$+ \sum_{k \geq 3} \nabla^k f(a)[x - a, \dots, x - a].$$

The **first-order (Taylor) approximation** of f around a is denoted by

$$f(a) + \langle \nabla f(a), x - a \rangle$$

and the **second-order (Taylor) approximation** of f around a is denoted by

$$f(a) + \langle \nabla f(a), x - a \rangle + \frac{1}{2}(x - a)^\top \nabla^2 f(a)(x - a).$$

In many interesting cases, one can prove that whenever x is close enough to a, then the higher-order terms do not contribute much to the value of $f(x)$ and, hence, the second-order (or even first-order) approximation gives a good estimate of $f(x)$.

2.4 Linear Algebra, Matrices, and Eigenvalues

For a given set of vectors $S = \{v_1, \dots, v_k\} \in \mathbb{R}^n$, their **linear span** or **linear hull** is the following set:

$$\text{span}(S) := \left\{ \sum_{i=1}^{k} \alpha_i v_i : \alpha_1, \dots, \alpha_k \in \mathbb{R} \right\}.$$

Similarly, a set of the form

$$\left\{ \alpha_0 + \sum_{i=1}^{k} \alpha_i v_i : \alpha_0, \alpha_1, \dots, \alpha_k \in \mathbb{R} \right\}$$

is called an **affine span** or **affine hull** of S. A set of vectors $\{v_1, \dots, v_k\}$ is said to be **affinely independent** if their affine hull is $k - 1$-dimensional, i.e., the vectors $\{v_2 - v_1, \dots, v_k - v_1\}$ are linearly independent.

Let $\mathbb{R}^{m \times n}$ denote the set of all $m \times n$ matrices over the real numbers. In many cases, the matrices we work with are square, i.e., $m = n$, and symmetric, i.e., $M^\top = M$ (here $\top$ denotes the transpose). The identity matrix of size n is a square matrix of size $n \times n$ with ones on the main diagonal and zero everywhere else. It is denoted by I_n. If the dimension is clear from the context, we drop the subscript n.

Definition 2.8 (Image, nullspace/kernel, and rank). Let $A \in \mathbb{R}^{m \times n}$.

(i) The image of A is defined as $\text{Im}(A) := \{Ax : x \in \mathbb{R}^n\}$.

(ii) The nullspace or kernel of A is defined as $\text{Ker}(A) := \{x \in \mathbb{R}^n : Ax = 0\}$.

(iii) The column rank of A is defined to be the maximum number of linearly independent columns of A and the row rank the maximum number of rows of A. It turns out that the row rank of a matrix is the same as its column rank – called the rank of a matrix – and the rank of A cannot be more than $\min\{m, n\}$. When the rank of A is equal to $\min\{m, n\}$, it is said to have full rank.

Note that both $\text{Im}(A)$ and $\text{Ker}(A)$ are vector spaces.

Definition 2.9 (Inverse). Let $A \in \mathbb{R}^{n \times n}$. A is said to be invertible if its rank is n. In other words, if for each vector y in the image of A, there is exactly one x such that $y = Ax$. In this case we use the notation A^{-1} for the inverse of A.

Sometimes, a matrix A may be square but not of full rank, or A may be full rank but not square. In both cases, we can extend the notion of inverse.

Definition 2.10 (Pseudoinverse). For $A \in \mathbb{R}^{m \times n}$, a pseudoinverse of A is defined as a matrix $A^+ \in \mathbb{R}^{n \times m}$ satisfying all of the following criteria:

(i) $AA^+A = A$,

(ii) $A^+AA^+ = A^+$,

(iii) $(AA^+)^\top = AA^+$, and

(iv) $(A^+A)^\top = A^+A$.

The pseudoinverse can be shown to always exist. Moreover, if A has linearly independent columns, then

$$A^+ = (A^\top A)^{-1}A^\top$$

and, if A has linearly independent rows, then

$$A^+ = A^\top(AA^\top)^{-1},$$

see Exercise 2.5.

Let $V \subseteq \mathbb{R}^n$ be a linear space. Given a point $x \in \mathbb{R}^n$, its **orthogonal projection** onto V is defined as the point $p(x)$ in V that minimizes the Euclidean distance to x. It can be shown that the mapping $p : \mathbb{R}^n \to \mathbb{R}^n$ is linear and can be described by an $n \times n$ real and symmetric matrix P (i.e., $p(x) = Px$) that has the property that $P^2 = P$; see Exercise 2.6.

An important subclass of symmetric matrices are positive semidefinite matrices, as defined below.

Definition 2.11 (Positive semidefinite matrix). A real symmetric matrix M is said to be positive semidefinite (PSD) if for all $x \in \mathbb{R}^n$, $x^\top M x \geq 0$. This is denoted by:

$$M \succeq 0.$$

M is said to be positive definite (PD) if $x^\top M x > 0$ holds for all nonzero $x \in \mathbb{R}^n$. This is denoted by:

$$M \succ 0.$$

For instance, the identity matrix I is PD, while the diagonal 2×2 matrix with a 1 and a -1 on the diagonal is not PSD. As another example, let $M :=$ $\begin{pmatrix} 2 & -1 \\ -1 & 1 \end{pmatrix}$, then

$$\forall x \in \mathbb{R}^2, \quad x^\top M x = 2x_1^2 - 2x_1 x_2 + x_2^2 = x_1^2 + (x_1 - x_2)^2 \geq 0,$$

hence M is PSD and in fact PD. Occasionally, we make use of the following convenient notation: For two symmetric matrices M and N, we write $M \preceq N$ if and only if $N - M \succeq 0$. It is not hard to prove that $\preceq$ defines a partial order on the set of symmetric matrices. An $n \times n$ real PSD matrix M can be written as

$$M = B B^\top$$

where B is an $n \times n$ real matrix with possibly dependent rows. B is sometimes called the **square root** of M and denoted by $A^{1/2}$. If M is PD, then the rows of such a B are linearly independent (Exercise 2.9).

We now review the notion of eigenvalues and eigenvectors of square matrices.

Definition 2.12 (Eigenvalues and eigenvectors). $\lambda \in \mathbb{R}$ and $u \in \mathbb{R}^n$ is an eigenvalue-eigenvector pair of the matrix $A \in \mathbb{R}^{n \times n}$ if $Au = \lambda u$ and $u \neq 0$.

Geometrically speaking, this means that eigenvectors are vectors that, under the transformation A, preserve the direction of the vector scaled by λ (the corresponding eigenvalue).

Note that for each eigenvalue λ of a matrix A with an eigenvector u, the vector cu is also an eigenvector with eigenvalue λ for any $c \in \mathbb{R} \setminus \{0\}$. An alternate characterization of eigenvalues of a square matrix is that they are zeros of the polynomial equation $\det(A - \lambda I) = 0$ in λ. Thus, it follows from the fundamental theorem of algebra that if $A \in \mathbb{R}^{n \times n}$, then it has n (possibly repeated and complex) eigenvalues. The set of eigenvalues $\{\lambda_1, \ldots, \lambda_n\}$ of a matrix $A \in \mathbb{R}^{n \times n}$ is sometimes referred to as the **spectrum** of A. When A is symmetric, all of its eigenvalues are real (Exercise 2.10). Moreover, if A is

PSD, then all its eigenvalues are nonnegative (Exercise 2.11). Further, in this case, the eigenvectors corresponding to different eigenvalues can be chosen to be orthogonal to each other.

Definition 2.13 (Matrix norm). For an $n \times m$ real-valued matrix A, its $2 \to 2$, or spectral norm, is defined as

$$\|A\|_2 := \sup_{x \in \mathbb{R}^m} \frac{\|Ax\|_2}{\|x\|_2}.$$

Theorem 2.14 (Norm of a symmetric matrix). *When A is an $n \times n$ real symmetric matrix A with eigenvalues $\lambda_1(A) \le \lambda_2(A) \le \cdots \le \lambda_n(A)$, its norm is*

$$\|A\|_2 = \max\{|\lambda_1(A)|, |\lambda_n(A)|\}.$$

If A is a symmetric PSD matrix, $\|A\|_2 = \lambda_n(A)$.

2.5 The Cauchy-Schwarz Inequality

The following basic inequality is used frequently in this book.

Theorem 2.15 (Cauchy-Schwarz inequality). *For every $x, y \in \mathbb{R}^n$,*

$$\langle x, y \rangle \le \|x\|_2 \|y\|_2. \tag{2.1}$$

Intuitively, this inequality can be explained very simply: The two vectors x and y form together a subspace of dimension at most 2 that can be thought of as $\mathbb{R}^2$. Furthermore, assuming $x, y \in \mathbb{R}^2$, we know that $\langle x, y \rangle = \|x\|_2 \|y\|_2 \cos\theta$. Since $\cos\theta \le 1$, the inequality holds. Nevertheless, the following is a formal proof.

Proof: The inequality can be equivalently written as

$$|\langle x, y \rangle|^2 \le \|x\|_2^2 \|y\|_2^2.$$

Let us form the following nonnegative polynomial in z:

$$\sum_{i=1}^{n} (x_i z + y_i)^2 = \left(\sum_{i=1}^{n} x_i^2\right) z^2 + 2\left(\sum_{i=1}^{n} x_i y_i\right) z + \sum_{i=1}^{n} y_i^2 \ge 0.$$

Since this degree two polynomial is nonnegative, it has at most one real zero and its discriminant must be less than or equal to zero, implying that

$$\left(\sum_{i=1}^{n} x_i y_i\right)^2 - \sum_{i=1}^{n} x_i^2 \sum_{i=1}^{n} y_i^2 \le 0,$$

thus completing the proof. ∎

2.6 Norms

So far we have talked about the ℓ_2 (Euclidean) norm and proved the Cauchy-Schwarz inequality for this norm. We now present the general notion of a norm and give several examples used throughout this book. We conclude with a generalization of Cauchy-Schwarz inequality for general norms.

Geometrically, a norm is a way to tell how long a vector is. However, not any function is a norm, and the following definition formalizes what it means to be a norm.

Definition 2.16 (Norm). A norm is a function $\| \cdot \| : \mathbb{R}^n \to \mathbb{R}$ that satisfies, for every $u, v \in \mathbb{R}^n$ and $c \in \mathbb{R}$,

(i) $\|c \cdot u\| = |c| \cdot \|u\|$,
(ii) $\|u + v\| \le \|u\| + \|v\|$, and
(iii) $\|u\| = 0$ if and only if $u = 0$.

An important class of norms are the ℓ_p-norms for $p \ge 1$. Given a $p \ge 1$, for $u \in \mathbb{R}^n$, define

$$\|u\|_p := \left(\sum_{i=1}^{n} |u_i|^p \right)^{1/p}.$$

It can be seen that this is a norm for $p \ge 1$. Another class of norms are those induced by PD matrices. Given an $n \times n$ real PD matrix A and $u \in \mathbb{R}^n$, define

$$\|u\|_A := \sqrt{u^\top A u}.$$

This can also be shown to be a norm.

Definition 2.17 (Dual norm). Let $\| \cdot \|$ be a norm in $\mathbb{R}^n$, then the dual norm, denoted by $\| \cdot \|^*$, is defined as

$$\|x\|^* := \sup_{y \in \mathbb{R}^n : \|y\| \le 1} \langle x, y \rangle.$$

It is an exercise to show that for all $p, q \ge 1$, $\| \cdot \|_q$ is a dual norm of $\| \cdot \|_p$ whenever $\frac{1}{p} + \frac{1}{q} = 1$. Since $p = q = 2$ satisfies the equality above, $\| \cdot \|_2$ is the dual norm of itself. Another important example of dual norms is $p = 1$ and $q = \infty$. One can also see that, for a PD A, the dual norm corresponding to $\|u\|_A$ is $\|u\|_{A^{-1}}$. We conclude with a generalization of the Cauchy-Schwarz inequality.

Theorem 2.18 (Generalized Cauchy-Schwarz inequality). *For every pair of dual norms* $\|\cdot\|$ *and* $\|\cdot\|^*$, *the following general version of the Cauchy-Schwarz inequality holds:*

$$\langle x, y \rangle \leq \|x\| \, \|y\|^*.$$

Unless stated otherwise in this book, $\|\cdot\|$ will denote $\|\cdot\|_2$, the Euclidean norm.

2.7 Euclidean Topology

We are concerned with $\mathbb{R}^n$ along with natural topology induced on it. An **open ball** centered at a point $x \in \mathbb{R}^n$ and of radius $r > 0$ is the following set:

$$\{y \in \mathbb{R}^n : \|x - y\|_2 < r\}.$$

An open ball generalizes the concept of an open interval over real numbers. A set $K \subseteq \mathbb{R}^n$ is said to be **open** if every point in K is the center of an open ball contained in K. A set $K \subseteq \mathbb{R}^n$ is said to be **bounded** if there exists an $0 \leq r < \infty$ such that K is contained in an open ball of radius r. A set $K \subseteq \mathbb{R}^n$ is said to be **closed** if $\mathbb{R}^n \setminus K$ open. A closed and bounded set $K \subseteq \mathbb{R}^n$ is also sometimes referred to as **compact**. A point $x \in \mathbb{R}^n$ is a **limit point** of a set K if every open set containing x contains at least one point of K different from x itself. It can be shown that a set is closed if and only if it contains all of its limit points. The **closure** of a set K consists of all points in K along with all limit points of K. A function $f : \mathbb{R}^n \to \mathbb{R}$ is said to be closed if it maps every closed set $K \subseteq \mathbb{R}^n$ to a closed set.

A point $x \in K \subseteq \mathbb{R}^n$ is said to be in the **interior** of K if some ball of positive radius containing x is contained in K. For a set $K \subseteq \mathbb{R}^n$, let ∂K denote its **boundary:** It is the set of all points x in the closure of K that are not in the interior of K. The point $x \in K$ is said to be in the **relative interior** of K if K contains the intersection of a ball of positive radius centered at x with the smallest affine space containing K (also called the **affine hull** of K).

2.8 Dynamical Systems

Many algorithms introduced in this book are best viewed as dynamical systems. Dynamical systems typically belong to two classes: continuous-time and discrete-time. Both of them consist of a domain Ω and a "rule" according to which a point moves in the domain. The difference is that in a discrete-time dynamical system, the time at which the point moves is discrete $t = 0$, $1, 2, \ldots$, while in the continuous-time dynamical system it is continuous, i.e., $t \in [0, \infty)$.

Definition 2.19 (Continuous-time dynamical system). A continuous-time dynamical system consists of a domain $\Omega \subseteq \mathbb{R}^n$ and a function $G \colon \Omega \to \mathbb{R}^n$. For any point $s \in \Omega$, we define a solution (a trajectory) originating at s to be a curve $x \colon [0, \infty) \to \Omega$ such that

$$x(0) = s \quad \text{and} \quad \frac{d}{dt} x(t) = G(x(t)) \quad \text{for } t \in (0, \infty).$$

For brevity, the differential equation in the definition above is often written as $\dot{x} = G(x)$. The definition essentially says that a solution to a dynamical system is any curve $x \colon [0, \infty) \to \Omega$ that is tangent to $G(x(t))$ at $x(t)$ for every $t \in (0, \infty)$, thus $G(x)$ gives a direction to be followed at any given point $x \in \Omega$.

Definition 2.20 (Discrete-time dynamical system). A discrete-time dynamical system consists of a domain Ω and a function $F \colon \Omega \to \Omega$. For any point $s \in \Omega$, we define a solution (a trajectory) originating at s to be the infinite sequence of points $\{x^{(k)}\}_{k \in \mathbb{N}}$ with $x^{(0)} = s$ and $x^{(k+1)} = F(x^{(k)})$ for every $k \in \mathbb{N}$.

Sometimes we derive our algorithms by first defining a continuous-time dynamical system and then discretizing it. There is no standard way to do this, and sometimes the discretization can be very creative. The simplest way, however, is the Euler discretization.

Definition 2.21 (First-order Euler discretization). Consider a dynamical system given by $\dot{x} = G(x)$ on some domain Ω. Then, given a step size $h \in (0, 1)$, its first-order Euler discretization is a discrete-time dynamical system (Ω, F), where

$$F(x) = x + h \cdot G(x).$$

This is perfectly compatible with the intuition that a continuous dynamical system at x is basically moving "just a little bit" along $G(x)$. Note that formally the above definition is not quite correct, as $F(x)$ might land outside of Ω – this is a manifestation of the "existence of solution" issue for discrete systems – sometimes in order to achieve existence one has to take h very small, and in some cases it might not be possible at all.

2.9 Graphs

An **undirected** graph $G = (V, E)$ consists a finite set of **vertices** V and a set of **edges** E. Each edge $e \in E$ is a two element subset of V. A vertex v is said to be **incident** to e if $v \in e$. A loop is an edge for which both endpoints are the same. Two edges are said to be parallel if their endpoints are identical. A graph without loops and parallel edges is said to be **simple**. A simple, undirected graph that has an edge between every pair of vertices is called the **complete** graph and is denoted by K_V or K_n where $n := |V|$. For a vertex $v \in V$, $N(v)$ denotes the set of vertices u such that $\{u, v\}$ is an edge in E. The **degree** of a vertex v is denoted by $d_v := |N(v)|$. A **subgraph** of a graph $G = (V, E)$ is simply a graph $H = (U, F)$ such that $U \subseteq V$ and $F \subseteq E$, where the edges in F are only incident to vertices in U.

A graph $G = (V, E)$ is said to be **bipartite** if the vertex set V can be partitioned into two parts V_1 and V_2 and all edges contain one vertex from V_1 and one vertex from V_2. If there is an edge between every vertex in V_1 to every vertex in V_2, G is called a complete bipartite graph and denoted by K_{n_1, n_2}, where $n_1 := |V_1|$ and $n_2 := |V_2|$.

A **directed** graph is one where the edges $E \subseteq V \times V$ are 2-tuples of vertices. We denote an edge by $e = (u, v)$, where u is the "tail" of the edge e and v is its "head." The edge is "outgoing" at u and "incoming" at v. When the context is clear, we sometimes use $e = uv = \{u, v\}$ (undirected) or $e = uv = (u, v)$ (directed) to denote an edge.

2.9.1 Structures in Graphs

A **path** in a graph is a nonempty subgraph with vertex set $v_0, v_1, \ldots, v_k$ and edges $\{v_0 v_1, v_1 v_2, \ldots, v_{k-1} v_k\}$. Since a path is defined to be a subgraph, vertices cannot repeat in a path. A **walk** is a sequence of vertices connected by edges without any restriction on repetition. A **cycle** in a graph is a nonempty subgraph with vertex set $v_0, v_1, \ldots, v_k$ and edges $\{v_0 v_1, v_1 v_2, \ldots, v_{k-1} v_k, v_k v_0\}$. A graph is said to be **connected** if there is a path between every two vertices, and **disconnected** otherwise.

A **cut** in a graph is subset of edges such that if one removes them from the graph, the graph is disconnected. For a graph $G = (V, E)$ and $s \neq t \in V$, an $s - t$ cut in a graph is a set of edges whose removal leaves no path between s and t.

A graph is said to be **acyclic** if it does not contain any cycle. A connected acyclic graph is called a **tree**. A **spanning** tree of a graph $G = (V, E)$ is a subgraph that is a tree with vertex set V. Check that a spanning tree contains exactly $|V| - 1$ edges.

An $s - t$ **flow** in an undirected $G = (V, E)$ for $s \neq t \in V$ is an assignment $f : E \to \mathbb{R}$ that satisfies the following properties. For all vertices $u \in V \setminus \{s, t\}$, we require that the "incoming" flow is equal to the "outgoing" flow:

$$\sum_{v \in V} f(v, u) = 0.$$

As a convention, we extend f from E to $V \times V$ as a skew-symmetric function on the edges: If the edge $e = uv$, we let $f(v, u) := -f(u, v)$.

A **matching** M in an undirected graph $G = (V, E)$ is a subset M of edges such that for every $e_1, e_2 \in M$, $e_1 \cap e_2 = \emptyset$. A matching is said to be **perfect** if $\cup_{e \in M} e = V$.

2.9.2 Matrices Associated to Graphs

Two basic matrices associated with a simple, undirected graph $G = (V, E)$, indexed by its vertices, are its **adjacency** matrix A and its **degree** matrix D.

$$A_{u,v} := \begin{cases} 1 & \text{if } uv \in E, \\ 0 & \text{otherwise,} \end{cases}$$

and

$$D_{u,v} := \begin{cases} d_v & \text{if } u = v, \\ 0 & \text{otherwise.} \end{cases}$$

The adjacency matrix is symmetric. The graph **Laplacian** of G is defined to be

$$L := D - A.$$

Given an undirected graph $G = (V, E)$, consider an arbitrary orientation of its edges. Let $B \in \{-1, 0, 1\}^{n \times m}$ be the matrix whose columns are indexed by the edges and rows by the vertices of G, where the entry corresponding to (v, e) is 1 if a vertex v is the tail of the directed edge corresponding to e, is -1 if i is the head of the directed edge e, and is zero otherwise. B is called the **vertex-edge incidence matrix** of G. The Laplacian can now be expressed in terms of B. While B depends on the choice of the directions to the edges, the Laplacian does not.

Lemma 2.22 (Laplacian and incidence matrix). *Let G be a simple, undirected graph with (arbitrarily chosen) vertex-edge incidence matrix B. Then, $BB^\top = L$.*

Proof: For the diagonal elements of $BB^\top$, $(BB^\top)_{v,v} = \sum_e B_{v,e} B_{v,e}$. The terms are nonzero only for those edges e that are incident to v, in which case the product is 1 and, hence, this sum gives the degree of vertex v in the undirected graph. For other entries, $(BB^\top)_{u,v} = \sum_e B_{u,e} B_{v,e}$. The product terms are nonzero only when the edge e is shared by u and v. In either case, the product is -1. Hence, $(BB^\top)_{u,v} = -1$, for all $u \neq v, uv \in E$. Hence, $BB^\top = L$. ∎

Observe that $L1 = 0$ where 1 is the all-ones vector. Thus, the Laplacian does not have full rank. However, if $G = (V, E)$ is connected, then the Laplacian has rank $|V| - 1$ (check) and, in the space orthogonal to the all-ones vector, we can define an inverse of the Laplacian and denote it by L^+.

A **weighted**, undirected graph $G = (V, E, w)$ has a function $w \colon E \to \mathbb{R}_{>0}$ that gives weights to edges. For such graphs, we define the Laplacian as

$$L := BWB^\top,$$

where W is the diagonal $|E| \times |E|$ matrix with $W_{e,e} = w(e)$ and 0 otherwise.

2.9.3 Polytopes Associated to Graphs

For a graph $G = (V, E)$, let $\mathcal{F} \subseteq 2^E$ denote a family of subsets of its edges. For each $S \in \mathcal{F}$, let $1_S \in \{0, 1\}^E$ denote the indicator vector of the set S. Consider the polytope $P_{\mathcal{F}} \subseteq [0, 1]^E$ that is defined as the convex hull of the vectors $\{1_S\}_{S \in \mathcal{F}}$. When $\mathcal{F}$ is the set of all spanning trees in G, the corresponding polytope is called the **spanning tree polytope** of G. When $\mathcal{F}$ is the set of all matchings in G, the corresponding polytope is called the **matching polytope** of G.

2.10 Exercises

2.1   For each of the following functions, compute the gradient and the Hessian, and write the second-order Taylor approximation.

(a) $f(x) = \sum_{i=1}^m (a_i^\top x - b_i)^2$ for $x \in \mathbb{Q}^n$, where $a_1, \ldots, a_m \in \mathbb{Q}^m$ and $b_1, \ldots, b_m \in \mathbb{Q}$.

(b) $f(x) = \log\left(\sum_{j=1}^m e^{\langle x, v_j \rangle}\right)$, where $v_1, \ldots, v_m \in \mathbb{Q}^n$.

(c) $f(X) = \text{Tr}(AX)$, where A is a symmetric $n \times n$ matrix and X runs over symmetric matrices.

(d) $f(X) = -\log \det X$, where X runs over positive definite matrices.

2.2   Prove Lemma 2.6.

2.3   Prove that, for a function $f \colon \mathbb{R}^n \to \mathbb{R}$, its differential $Df(x) \colon \mathbb{R}^n \to \mathbb{R}^n$ at a point $x \in \mathbb{R}^n$ is a linear function.

2.4   Prove that the row rank of a matrix is equal to its column rank.

2.5   For $A \in \mathbb{R}^{m \times n}$, prove that its pseudoinverse always exists. Moreover, prove that, if A has linearly independent columns, then

$$A^+ = (A^\top A)^{-1} A^\top$$

and, if A has linearly independent rows, then

$$A^+ = A^\top (A A^\top)^{-1}.$$

2.6   Consider a real $m \times n$ matrix A with $n \le m$ and a vector $b \in \mathbb{R}^m$. Let $p(x) := \arg\min_{x \in \mathbb{R}^n} \|Ax - b\|_2^2$. Assuming that A is of full rank, derive a formula for $p(x)$ in terms of A and b.

2.7   Prove that, given $A \in \mathbb{R}^{n \times n}$, it holds that λ is an eigenvalue of A if and only if $\det(A - \lambda I) = 0$.

2.8   Given an $n \times n$ PD matrix H and a vector $a \in \mathbb{R}^n$, prove that $H \succeq a a^\top$ if and only if $1 \ge a^\top H^{-1} a$.

2.9   Prove that if M is an $n \times n$ real symmetric matrix that is PD, then

$$M = B B^\top$$

where B is an $n \times n$ real matrix with linearly independent rows.

2.10   Prove that if A is an $n \times n$ real symmetric matrix, then all of its eigenvalues are real.

2.11   Prove that every eigenvalue of a PSD matrix is nonnegative.

2.12   Prove that $\|u\|_p := \left(\sum_{i=1}^n |u_i|^p \right)^{1/p}$ is a norm for $p \ge 1$. Is it also a norm for $0 < p < 1$?

2.13   Given an $n \times n$ real PD matrix A and $u \in \mathbb{R}^n$, show that

$$\|u\|_A := \sqrt{u^\top A u}$$

is a norm. What aspect of being a norm for $\|u\|_A$ breaks down when A is just guaranteed to be PSD (and not PD)? And when A has negative eigenvalues?

2.14   Prove that for all $p, q \ge 1$, the norm $\| \cdot \|_q$ is the dual norm of $\| \cdot \|_p$ whenever $\frac{1}{p} + \frac{1}{q} = 1$.

2.15   Prove Theorem 2.18.

2.16   Prove Theorem 2.14.

2.17   Prove that the intersection of any family of closed sets in $\mathbb{R}^n$ is also closed.

2.18   Prove that the closure of $K \subseteq \mathbb{R}^n$ is exactly the set of the limits of all converging sequences of elements of K.

2.19   Find the solution to the following one-dimensional continuous time dynamical system

$$\frac{dx}{dt} = -\alpha x^2 \text{ with } x(0) = \beta.$$

2.20 Let $l_1 = L - 1$ and $l_2 = L$ for some $L > 1$. Fix $h \in (0, 1)$. Consider the discrete-time dynamical system below. Consider the solution $x_1^{(k)}, x_2^{(k)}$ to this dynamical system. Prove that this solution converges to a pair of numbers as $k \to \infty$ and derive the pair of numbers it converges to.

$$\begin{cases} x_1^{(k+1)} = x_1^{(k)} \left((1-h) + h \cdot \frac{l_2}{x_1^{(k)} \cdot l_2 + x_2^{(k)} \cdot l_1} \right) \\ x_2^{(k+1)} = x_2^{(k)} \left((1-h) + h \cdot \frac{l_1}{x_1^{(k)} \cdot l_2 + x_2^{(k)} \cdot l_1} \right) \\ x_1^{(0)} = x_2^{(0)} = 1. \end{cases} \quad (2.2)$$

2.21 For a simple, connected, and undirected graph $G = (V, E)$, let

$$\Pi = B^\top L^+ B,$$

where B is any vertex-edge incidence matrix associated to G. Prove the following:

(a) Π is symmetric.
(b) $\Pi^2 = \Pi$.
(c) The eigenvalues of Π are all either 0 or 1.
(d) The rank of Π is $|V| - 1$.
(e) Let T be a spanning tree chosen uniformly at random from all spanning trees in G. Prove that the probability that an edge e belongs to T is given by

$$\Pr[e \in T] = \Pi(e, e).$$

2.22 Let $G = (V, E)$ (with $n := |V|$ and $m := |E|$) be an undirected, connected graph with a weight vector $w \in \mathbb{R}^E$. Consider the following algorithm for finding a maximum weight spanning tree in G.

• Sort the edges in nondecreasing order:

$$w(e_1) \le w(e_2) \le \cdots \le w(e_m).$$

• Set $T = E$.
• For $i = 1, 2, \ldots, m$

    – If the graph $(V, T \setminus \{e_i\})$ is connected, set $T := T \setminus \{e_i\}$.

• Output T.

Is the algorithm correct? If yes prove its correctness, otherwise provide a counterexample.

2.23 Let $T = (V, E)$ be a tree on n vertices V and let L denote its Laplacian. Given a vector $b \in \mathbb{R}^n$, design an algorithm for solving linear systems of the form $Lx = b$ in time $O(n)$. *Hint:* Use Gaussian elimination, but carefully consider the order in which you eliminate variables.

2.24 Let $G = (V, E, w)$ be a connected, weighted, undirected graph. Let $n := |V|$ and $m := |E|$. We use L_G to denote the corresponding Laplacian. For any subgraph H of G, we use the notation L_H to denote its Laplacian.

(a) Let $T = (V, F)$ be a connected subgraph of G. Let P_T be any square matrix satisfying

$$L_T^+ = P_T P_T^\top.$$

Prove that

$$x^\top P_T^\top L_G P_T x \geq x^\top x$$

for all $x \in \mathbb{R}^n$ satisfying $\langle x, 1 \rangle = 0$.

(b) Prove that

$$\mathrm{Tr}\left(L_T^+ L_G\right) = \sum_{e \in G} w_e b_e^\top L_T^+ b_e,$$

where b_e is the column of B corresponding to the edge e.

(c) Now let $T = (V, F)$ be a spanning tree of G. For an edge $e \in G$, write an explicit formula for $b_e^\top L_T^+ b_e$.

(d) The weight of a spanning tree $T = (V, F)$ of $G = (V, E, w)$ is defined as

$$w(T) := \sum_{e \in F} w_e.$$

Prove that if T is the maximum weight spanning tree of G, then $\mathrm{Tr}\left(L_T^+ L_G\right) \leq m(n - 1)$.

(e) Deduce that if T is a maximum weight spanning tree of G and P_T is any matrix such that $P_T P_T^\top = L_T^+$, then the **condition number** of the matrix $P_T L_G P_T^\top$ is at most $\leq m(n - 1)$. The condition number of $P_T L_G P_T^\top$ is defined as

$$\frac{\lambda_n(P_T L_G P_T^\top)}{\lambda_2(P_T L_G P_T^\top)}.$$

Here $\lambda_n(P_T L_G P_T^\top)$ denotes the largest eigenvalue $P_T L_G P_T^\top$ and $\lambda_2(P_T L_G P_T^\top)$ is the smallest nonzero eigenvalue of $P_T L_G P_T^\top$. How large can the condition number of L_G be?

2.25 Let $G = (V, E)$ (with $n := |V|$ and $m := |E|$) be a connected, undirected graph and L be its Laplacian. Take two vertices $s \neq t \in V$. Let $\chi_{st} := e_s - e_t$ (where e_v is the standard basis vector for a vertex v) and let $x \in \mathbb{R}^n$ such that $Lx = \chi_{st}$. Define the distance between two vertices $s, t \in V$ as

$$d(s, t) := x_s - x_t.$$

For $s = t$, we set $d(s, t) = 0$. Let k be the value of the minimum $s - t$ cut, i.e., the minimum number of edges one needs to remove from G to disconnect s from t. Prove that

$$k \leq \sqrt{\frac{m}{d(s, t)}}.$$

2.26 A matrix is said to be **totally unimodular** if each of its square submatrices has determinant 0, $+1$, or -1. Prove that, for a graph $G = (V, E)$, any of its vertex-edge incidence matrices B is totally unimodular.

2.27 Prove that the matching polytope of a bipartite graph $G = (V, E)$ can be equivalently written as

$$P_M(G) = \left\{ x \in \mathbb{R}^E : x \geq 0, \ \sum_{e: \, v \in e} x_e \leq 1 \ \forall v \in V \right\}.$$

Hint: Write $P_M(G) = \{x \in \mathbb{R}^E : Ax \leq b\}$, and prove that resulting A is a totally unimodular matrix.

Notes

The content presented in this chapter is classic and draws from several textbooks. For a first introduction to calculus, including a proof of the fundamental theorem of calculus (Theorem 2.5), see the textbook by Apostol (1967a). For an advanced discussion on multivariate calculus, the reader is referred to the textbook by Apostol (1967b). For an introduction to real analysis (including introductory topology), the reader is referred to the textbook by Rudin (1987). Linear algebra and related topics are covered in great detail in the textbook by Strang (2006). See also the paper by Strang (1993) for an accessible treatment of the fundamental theorem of algebra. The Cauchy-Schwarz inequality has a wide range of applications; see the book by Steele (2004). For a formal discussion on dynamical systems, refer to the book by Perko (2001). The books by Diestel (2012) and Schrijver (2002a) provide in-depth introductions to graph theory and combinatorial optimization, respectively.

3

Convexity

We introduce convex sets, notions of convexity, and show the power that comes along with convexity: Convex sets have separating hyperplanes, subgradients exist, and locally optimal solutions of convex functions are globally optimal.

3.1 Convex Sets

We start by introducing the notion of a convex set.

Definition 3.1 (Convex set). A set $K \subseteq \mathbb{R}^n$ is said to be convex if for every pair of points $x, y \in K$ and for every $\lambda \in [0, 1]$, we have

$$\lambda x + (1 - \lambda)y \in K.$$

In other words, a set $K \subseteq \mathbb{R}^n$ is convex if for every two points in K, the line segment connecting them is contained in K. Common examples of convex sets are:

(1) **Hyperplanes:** sets of the form

$$\{x \in \mathbb{R}^n : \langle h, x \rangle = c\}$$

for some $h \in \mathbb{R}^n$ and $c \in \mathbb{R}$.

(2) **Halfspaces:** sets of the form

$$\{x \in \mathbb{R}^n : \langle h, x \rangle \leq c\}$$

for some $h \in \mathbb{R}^n$ and $c \in \mathbb{R}$.

(3) **Polytopes:** For a set of vectors $X \subseteq \mathbb{R}^n$ its **convex hull** $\mathrm{conv}(X) \subseteq \mathbb{R}^n$ is
defined as the set of all convex combinations

$$\sum_{j=1}^{r} \alpha_j x_j$$

for $x_1, x_2, \ldots, x_r \in X$ and $\alpha_1, \alpha_2, \ldots, \alpha_r \geq 0$ such that $\sum_{j=1}^{r} \alpha_j = 1$.
When the set X has a finite cardinality, $\mathrm{conv}(X)$ is called a polytope and
is convex by definition. X is said to be **full-dimensional** if the linear span
of the points defining it is all of $\mathbb{R}^n$.

(4) **Polyhedra:** sets of the form $K = \{x \in \mathbb{R}^n : \langle a_i, x \rangle \leq b_i$ for $i = 1,$
$2, \ldots, m\}$, where $a_i \in \mathbb{R}^n$ and $b_i \in \mathbb{R}$ for $i = 1, 2, \ldots, m$. A polyhedron
that is bounded can be shown to be a polytope (Exercise 3.6).

(5) ℓ_p-**balls:** for $p \geq 1$, sets of the form $B_p(a, 1) := \{x \in \mathbb{R}^n :$
$\|x - a\|_p \leq 1\}$, where $a \in \mathbb{R}^n$ is a vector.

(6) **Ellipsoids:** sets of the form $\{x \in \mathbb{R}^n : x = T(B) + a\}$, where B is the
n-dimensional unit ℓ_2-ball centered at the origin, $T : \mathbb{R}^n \to \mathbb{R}^n$ is an
invertible linear transformation, and $a \in \mathbb{R}^n$. This is seen to be equivalent
to $\{x \in \mathbb{R}^n : (x - a)^\top A(x - a) \leq 1\}$, where $A \in \mathbb{R}^{n \times n}$ is a PD matrix.
When $a = 0$, this set is also the same as the set of all x with $\|x\|_A \leq 1$.

3.2 Convex Functions

We define convex functions and present two ways to characterize them, which
apply depending on their smoothness.

Definition 3.2 (**Convexity**). A function $f : K \to \mathbb{R}$, defined over a convex set
K, is convex if for all $x, y \in K$ and $\lambda \in [0, 1]$, we have

$$f(\lambda x + (1 - \lambda)y) \leq \lambda f(x) + (1 - \lambda) f(y). \tag{3.1}$$

Examples of convex functions include:

(1) **Linear functions:** $f(x) = \langle c, x \rangle$ for a vector $c \in \mathbb{R}^n$.
(2) **Quadratic functions:** $f(x) = x^\top A x + b^\top x$ for a PSD matrix $A \in \mathbb{R}^n$
and a vector $b \in \mathbb{R}^n$.
(3) **Negative entropy function:** $f : [0, \infty) \to \mathbb{R}$, $f(x) = x \log x$.

Sometimes when working with convex functions f defined over a certain
subset $K \subseteq \mathbb{R}^n$ we extend them to the whole $\mathbb{R}^n$ by setting $f(x) = +\infty$ for all

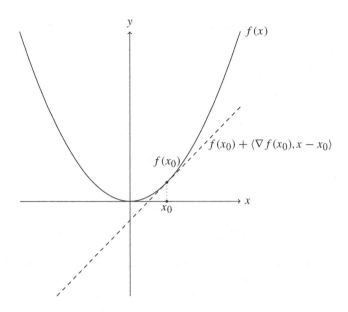

Figure 3.1 The first-order convexity condition at the point x_0. Note that in this one-dimensional case, the gradient of f is just its derivative.

$x \notin K$. One can check that f is then still convex (on $\mathbb{R}^n$) when the arithmetic operations on $\mathbb{R} \cup \{+\infty\}$ are interpreted in the only reasonable way. A function f is said to be **concave** if $-f$ is convex.

For a function $f \colon \mathbb{R}^n \to \mathbb{R}$, its c-sublevel set is defined as

$$\{x \colon f(x) < c\},$$

If f is convex, then all its sublevel sets are convex; see Exercise 3.3.

We now provide two different characterizations of convexity that might be more convenient to apply in certain situations. They require additional smoothness conditions on f (differentiability or twice-differentiability, respectively).

Theorem 3.3 (First-order notion of convexity). *A differentiable function* $f \colon K \to \mathbb{R}$ *over a convex set K is convex if and only if*

$$f(y) \geq f(x) + \langle \nabla f(x), y - x \rangle, \quad \forall x, y \in K. \tag{3.2}$$

In other words, any tangent to a convex function f lies below the function f as illustrated in Figure 3.1. Similarly, any tangent to a concave function lies above the function.

Proof: Suppose f is convex as in Definition 3.2. Fix any $x, y \in K$. Then, from (3.1), for every $\lambda \in (0, 1)$, we have

$$(1 - \lambda)f(x) + \lambda f(y) \geq f((1 - \lambda)x + \lambda y) = f(x + \lambda(y - x)).$$

Subtracting $(1 - \lambda)f(x)$ and dividing by λ yields

$$f(y) \geq f(x) + \frac{f(x + \lambda(y - x)) - f(x)}{\lambda}.$$

Taking the limit as $\lambda \to 0$, the second term on the right converges to the directional derivative of f in the direction $y - x$, hence

$$f(y) \geq f(x) + \langle \nabla f(x), y - x \rangle.$$

Conversely, suppose the function f satisfies (3.2). Fix $x, y \in K$ and $\lambda \in [0, 1]$. Let $z := \lambda x + (1 - \lambda)y$ be some point in the convex hull. Note that the first-order approximation of f around z underestimates both $f(x)$ and $f(y)$. Thus, the two underestimates are

$$f(x) \geq f(z) + \langle \nabla f(z), x - z \rangle, \tag{3.3}$$
$$f(y) \geq f(z) + \langle \nabla f(z), y - z \rangle. \tag{3.4}$$

Multiplying (3.3) by λ and (3.4) by $(1 - \lambda)$, and summing both inequalities, we obtain

$$(1 - \lambda)f(x) + \lambda f(y)) \geq f(z) + \langle \nabla f(z), \lambda x + (1 - \lambda)y - z \rangle$$
$$= f(z) + \langle \nabla f(z), 0 \rangle$$
$$= f((1 - \lambda)x + \lambda y). \qquad \blacksquare$$

A convex function can be shown to be continuous (Exercise 3.10), but it does not have to be differentiable; take for example the function $f(x) := |x|$. In some of the examples considered in this book, the function f will be convex but may not be differentiable everywhere. In such cases, the following notion of a subgradient turns out to be helpful.

Definition 3.4 (Subgradient). For a convex function f defined over a convex set K, a vector v is said to be a subgradient of f at a point $x \in K$ if for any $y \in K$,

$$f(y) \geq f(x) + \langle v, y - x \rangle.$$

The set of subgradients at x is denoted by $\partial f(x)$.

It follows from the definition that the set $\partial f(x)$ is always a convex set, even when f is not convex (Exercise 3.11). In Section 3.3.2 we show that a subgradient of a convex function at any point in its domain always exists, even when it is not differentiable. Subgradients are useful, especially in linear or nonsmooth optimization, and Theorem 3.3 holds in the nondifferentiable case if we replace $\nabla f(x)$ with any $v \in \partial f(x)$.

Before we go into the second-order convexity conditions, we prove the lemma below that is necessary for their proof.

Lemma 3.5. *Let $f : K \to \mathbb{R}$ be a continuously differentiable function over a convex set K. The function f is convex if and only if for all $x, y \in K$,*

$$\langle \nabla f(y) - \nabla f(x), y - x \rangle \geq 0. \tag{3.5}$$

Proof: Let f be convex. Then from Theorem 3.3, we have

$$f(x) \geq f(y) + \langle \nabla f(y), x - y \rangle \text{ and } f(y) \geq f(x) + \langle \nabla f(x), y - x \rangle.$$

Summing both inequalities and rearranging yields (3.5).

Let us now assume that (3.5) holds for all $x, y \in K$. For $\lambda \in [0, 1]$, let $x_\lambda :=
x + \lambda(y - x)$. Then, since ∇f is continuous, we can apply Lemma 2.6 to obtain

$$f(y) = f(x) + \int_0^1 \langle \nabla f(x + \lambda(y - x)), y - x \rangle \, d\lambda$$

$$= f(x) + \langle \nabla f(x), y - x \rangle + \int_0^1 \langle \nabla f(x_\lambda) - \nabla f(x), y - x \rangle \, d\lambda$$

$$= f(x) + \langle \nabla f(x), y - x \rangle + \int_0^1 \frac{1}{\lambda} \langle \nabla f(x_\lambda) - \nabla f(x), x_\lambda - x \rangle \, d\lambda$$

$$\geq f(x) + \langle \nabla f(x), y - x \rangle.$$

Here, the first equality comes from Lemma 2.6 and the last inequality comes from the application of (3.5) in the integral. ∎

The following second-order notion of convexity generalizes the second derivative test of convexity for the one-dimensional case that the readers might already be familiar with.

Theorem 3.6 (Second-order notion of convexity). *Suppose K is convex and open. If $f : K \to R$ is twice continuously differentiable, then it is convex if and only if*

$$\nabla^2 f(x) \succeq 0, \quad \forall x \in K.$$

Proof: Suppose $f : K \to \mathbb{R}$ is twice continuously differentiable and convex. For any $x \in K$ and any $s \in \mathbb{R}^n$, since K is open, there is some $\tau > 0$ such that $x_\tau := x + \tau s \in K$. Then, from Lemma 3.5, we have

$$0 \leq \frac{1}{\tau^2} \langle \nabla f(x_\tau) - \nabla f(x), x_\tau - x \rangle$$
$$= \frac{1}{\tau} \langle \nabla f(x_\tau) - \nabla f(x), s \rangle$$
$$= \frac{1}{\tau} \int_0^\tau \langle \nabla^2 f(x + \lambda s)s, s \rangle \, d\lambda,$$

where the last equality is from the second part of Lemma 2.6. We can conclude the result by letting $\tau \to 0$.

Conversely, suppose that for all $x \in K$, $\nabla^2 f(x) \succeq 0$. Then, for any $x, y \in K$, we have

$$f(y) = f(x) + \int_0^1 \langle \nabla f(x + \lambda(y - x)), y - x \rangle \, d\lambda$$

$$= f(x) + \langle \nabla f(x), y - x \rangle + \int_0^1 \langle \nabla f(x + \lambda(y - x)) - \nabla f(x), y - x \rangle \, d\lambda$$

$$= f(x) + \langle \nabla f(x), y - x \rangle$$
$$+ \int_0^1 \int_0^\lambda \underbrace{(y - x)^\top \nabla^2 f(x + \tau(y - x))(y - x)}_{\geq 0} \, d\tau \, d\lambda$$

$$\geq f(x) + \langle \nabla f(x), y - x \rangle.$$

The first and third equality come from Lemma 2.6 and the last inequality uses the fact that $\nabla^2 f$ is PSD. ∎

For some functions, the inequalities in the notions of convexity mentioned above can be strict everywhere, and the following definitions capture this phenomena.

Definition 3.7 (Strict convexity). A function $f \colon K \to \mathbb{R}$, defined over a convex set K, is said to be strictly convex if for all $x \neq y \in K$ and $\lambda \in (0, 1)$, we have

$$\lambda f(x) + (1 - \lambda) f(y) > f(\lambda x + (1 - \lambda) y). \tag{3.6}$$

It can be shown that if the function is differentiable, then it is strictly convex if and only if for all $x \neq y \in K$,

$$f(y) > f(x) + \langle \nabla f(x), y - x \rangle;$$

see Exercise 3.12. If the function is also twice differentiable and

$$\nabla^2 f(x) \succ 0, \quad \forall x \in K,$$

then f is strictly convex. The converse is not true; see Exercise 3.13.

We now introduce the notion of strong convexity that makes the notion of strict convexity quantitative.

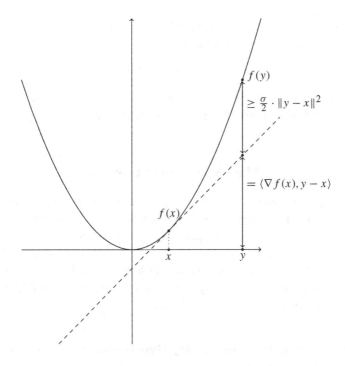

Figure 3.2 Illustration of strong convexity.

Definition 3.8 (Strong convexity). For $\sigma > 0$ and a norm $\|\cdot\|$, a differentiable function $f\colon K \to \mathbb{R}$, defined over a convex set K, is said to be σ-strongly convex with respect to a norm $\|\cdot\|$ if

$$f(y) \geq f(x) + \langle \nabla f(x), y - x \rangle + \frac{\sigma}{2} \cdot \|y - x\|^2.$$

Note that a strongly convex function is also strictly convex, but not vice versa. Both strict and strong convexity can be defined for nondifferentiable functions if the gradient is replaced by the subgradient. If f is twice continuously differentiable and $\|\cdot\| = \|\cdot\|_2$ is the ℓ_2-norm, then strong convexity is implied by the condition

$$\nabla^2 f(x) \succeq \sigma I$$

for all $x \in K$. Intuitively, strong convexity means that there exists a quadratic lower bound on

$$f(y) - (f(x) + \langle \nabla f(x), y - x \rangle);$$

see Figure 3.2 for an illustration. The quantity $f(y) - (f(x) + \langle \nabla f(x), y - x \rangle)$ is important enough to have a name.

Definition 3.9 (Bregman divergence). The Bregman divergence of a function $f \colon K \to \mathbb{R}$ at $u, w \in K$ is defined to be:

$$D_f(u, w) := f(w) - (f(u) + \langle \nabla f(u), w - u \rangle).$$

Note that, in general, the Bregman divergence is not symmetric in u and w, i.e., $D_f(u, w)$ is not necessarily equal to $D_f(w, u)$ (Exercise 3.18).

3.3 The Usefulness of Convexity

In this section, we prove some fundamental results about convex sets and convex functions. For instance, one can always "separate" a point that is not in a convex set from the set by a "simple" object – a hyperplane. This enables us to provide a "certificate" of when a given point is not in a convex set. And, for a convex function, a local minimum also has to be a global minimum. These properties illustrate why convexity is so useful and plays a key role in the design of algorithms for convex optimization.

3.3.1 Separating and Supporting Hyperplanes for Convex Sets

For some $h \in \mathbb{R}^n$ and $c \in \mathbb{R}$, let

$$H := \{x \in \mathbb{R}^n : \langle h, x \rangle = c\}$$

denote the hyperplane defined by h and c. Recall that for a set $K \subseteq \mathbb{R}^n$, ∂K denotes its boundary.

Definition 3.10 (Separating and supporting hyperplane). Suppose $K \subseteq \mathbb{R}^n$ is convex. A hyperplane H defined by h and c is said to **separate** $y \in \mathbb{R}^n$ from K if

$$\langle h, x \rangle \leq c \tag{3.7}$$

for all $x \in K$, but

$$\langle h, y \rangle > c.$$

If $y \in \partial K$, then H is said to be a **supporting** hyperplane for K containing y if (3.7) holds and

$$\langle h, y \rangle = c.$$

The first consequence of convexity is that for a closed convex set, a "proof" of non-membership of a point – a separating hyperplane – always exists.

Theorem 3.11 (Separating and supporting hyperplane theorem). *Let $K \subseteq \mathbb{R}^n$ be a nonempty, closed, and convex set. Then, given a $y \in \mathbb{R}^n \setminus K$, there is an $h \in \mathbb{R}^n \setminus \{0\}$ such that*

$$\forall x \in K \quad \langle h, x \rangle < \langle h, y \rangle.$$

If $y \in \partial K$, then there exists a supporting hyperplane containing y.

Proof: Let $x^\star$ be the unique point in K that minimizes the Euclidean distance to y, i.e.,

$$x^\star := \operatorname*{argmin}_{x \in K} \|x - y\|.$$

The existence of such a minimizer requires that K is nonempty, closed, and convex (Exercise 3.19). Since K is convex, any point $x_t := (1 - t)x^\star + tx$ is in K for all $t \in [0, 1]$ and for all $x \in K$. Thus, by optimality of $x^\star$,

$$\|x_t - y\|^2 \geq \|x^\star - y\|^2.$$

On the other hand, for small enough t,

$$\|(1 - t)x^\star + tx - y\|^2 = \|x^\star - y + t(x - x^\star)\|^2$$
$$= \|x^\star - y\|^2 + 2t\langle x^\star - y, x - x^\star \rangle + O(t^2).$$

Taking the limit $t \to 0$, we obtain

$$\langle x^\star - y, x - x^\star \rangle \geq 0 \quad \text{for all} \ x \in K. \tag{3.8}$$

Now, we can let

$$h := y - x^\star.$$

Note that, in the case $y \notin K$, $x^\star \neq y$ and, hence, $h \neq 0$. Moreover, observe that for any $x \in K$,

$$\langle h, x \rangle \overset{(3.8)}{\leq} \langle h, x^\star \rangle < \langle h, y \rangle,$$

where the last strict inequality follows from the fact that

$$\langle h, x^\star \rangle - \langle h, y \rangle = -\|h\|^2 < 0.$$

Finally, note that if $y \in \partial K$, then $x^\star = y$ and the the hyperplane corresponding to h and $\langle h, y \rangle$ is a supporting hyperplane for K at y. ∎

3.3.2 Existence of Subgradients

Theorem 3.11 can be used to show the existence of subgradients (see Definition 3.4) of a convex function.

Theorem 3.12 (Existence of subgradients). *For a convex function* $f: K \to \mathbb{R}$, *and an* x *in the relative interior of a convex set* $K \subseteq \mathbb{R}^n$, *there always exists a vector* v *such that for any* $y \in K$,

$$f(y) \geq f(x) + \langle v, y - x \rangle.$$

In other words, $\partial f(x) \neq \emptyset$.

The proof uses the notion of the **epigraph** of a function f (denoted by $\operatorname{epi} f$):

$$\operatorname{epi} f := \{(x, y) \in K \times \mathbb{R} : y \geq f(x)\}.$$

It is an exercise (Exercise 3.4) to prove that, for a function $f: K \to \mathbb{R}$ where $K \subseteq \mathbb{R}^n$ is convex, f is convex if and only if $\operatorname{epi} f$ is convex. Moreover, $\operatorname{epi} f$ is a closed and nonempty set.

Proof: For a given x in the relative interior of K, consider the point $(x, f(x))$ that lies on the boundary of the convex set $\operatorname{epi} f$. Thus, from the "supporting hyperplane" part of Theorem 3.11, we obtain that there is a nonzero vector $(h_1, \ldots, h_n, h_{n+1}) \in \mathbb{R}^{n+1}$ such that

$$\sum_{i=1}^{n} h_i z_i + h_{n+1} y \leq \sum_{i=1}^{n} h_i x_i + h_{n+1} f(x)$$

for all $(z, y) \in \operatorname{epi} f$. Rearranging, we obtain

$$\sum_{i=1}^{n} h_i (z_i - x_i) + h_{n+1}(y - f(x)) \leq 0 \tag{3.9}$$

for all $(z, y) \in \operatorname{epi} f$. Plugging in $z = x$ and $y \geq f(x)$ as a point in $\operatorname{epi} f$, we deduce that $h_{n+1} \leq 0$. Since $(z, f(z)) \in \operatorname{epi} f$, from (3.9) it follows that

$$\sum_{i=1}^{n} h_i (z_i - x_i) + h_{n+1}(f(z) - f(x)) \leq 0.$$

If $h_{n+1} \neq 0$, then by dividing the above by h_{n+1} (and reversing the sign since $h_{n+1} < 0$), we obtain

$$f(z) \geq f(x) - \frac{1}{h_{n+1}} \langle h, z - x \rangle,$$

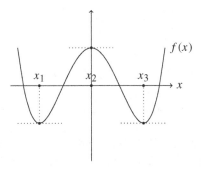

Figure 3.3 A nonconvex function for which $\nabla f(x) = 0$ at points x_1, x_2, x_3.

where $h := (h_1, \ldots, h_n)$. This establishes that $v := -\frac{h}{h_{n+1}} \in \partial f(x)$. On the other hand, if $h_{n+1} = 0$, then we know that $h \neq 0$ and

$$\langle h, z - x \rangle \leq 0$$

for all $z \in K$. This implies that

$$\langle h, z \rangle \leq \langle h, x \rangle$$

for all $z \in K$. However, x is in the relative interior of K and, hence, the above cannot be true. Thus, h_{n+1} must be nonzero and we deduce the theorem. ∎

3.3.3 Local Optima of Convex Functions are Globally Optimum

For simplicity, let us assume that we are in the unconstrained setting, i.e., $K = \mathbb{R}^n$. In general, for a function $f : \mathbb{R}^n \to \mathbb{R}$, the gradient can be zero at many points; see Figure 3.3. However, if f is a convex and differentiable function, this cannot happen.

Theorem 3.13 (A local optimum of a convex function is a global optimum).
If $f : \mathbb{R}^n \to \mathbb{R}$ is a convex and differentiable function, then for a given $x \in \mathbb{R}^n$,

$$f(x) \leq f(y), \quad \forall y \in \mathbb{R}^n$$

if and only if

$$\nabla f(x) = 0.$$

Proof: We start by showing that if x is a global minimizer of f, i.e., it satisfies the first condition of the theorem, then $\nabla f(x) = 0$. Indeed, for every vector $v \in \mathbb{R}^n$ and every $t \in \mathbb{R}$, we have

$$f(x + tv) \geq f(x)$$

and, hence,

$$0 \leq \lim_{t \to 0} \frac{f(x + tv) - f(x)}{t} = \langle \nabla f(x), v \rangle.$$

Since $v \in \mathbb{R}^n$ is chosen arbitrarily, if we let $v := -\nabla f(x)$, we deduce that $\nabla f(x) = 0$.

We proceed with the proof in the opposite direction: If $\nabla f(x) = 0$ for some x, then x is a minimizer for f. First-order convexity (Theorem 3.3) of f implies that for all $y \in \mathbb{R}^n$:

$$f(y) \geq f(x) + \langle \nabla f(x), y - x \rangle$$
$$= f(x) + \langle 0, y - x \rangle$$
$$= f(x).$$

Hence, if $\nabla f(x) = 0$, then $f(y) \geq f(x)$ for all $y \in \mathbb{R}^n$, proving the claim. ∎

Note that, in the constrained setting (i.e., $K \neq \mathbb{R}^n$), Theorem 3.13 does not necessarily hold. However, one can prove the following generalization that holds for all convex functions, differentiable or not.

Theorem 3.14 (Optimality in the constrained setting). *If $f : K \to \mathbb{R}$ is a convex and differentiable function defined on a convex set K, then*

$$f(x) \leq f(y), \quad \forall y \in K$$

if and only if

$$\langle \nabla f(x), y - x \rangle \geq 0, \quad \forall y \in K.$$

The proof of this theorem is left for the reader (Exercise 3.20). We conclude by noting that if $\nabla f(x) \neq 0$, then $-\nabla f(x)$ gives us a supporting hyperplane for ∂K at the point x.

3.4 Exercises

3.1   Is the intersection of two convex sets convex? Is the union of two convex sets convex?

3.2   Prove that the following sets are convex.

(a) **Polyhedra:** sets of the form $K = \{x \in \mathbb{R}^n : \langle a_i, x \rangle \leq b_i$ for $i = 1, 2, \ldots, m\}$, where $a_i \in \mathbb{R}^n$ and $b_i \in \mathbb{R}$ for $i = 1, 2, \ldots, m$.

(b) **Ellipsoids:** sets of the form $K = \{x \in \mathbb{R}^n : x^\top A x \leq 1\}$ where $A \in \mathbb{R}^{n \times n}$ is a PD matrix.

(c) **Unit balls in ℓ_p-norms for $p \geq 1$:** $B_p(a, 1) := \{x \in \mathbb{R}^n : \|x - a\|_p \leq 1\}$, where $a \in \mathbb{R}^n$ is a vector.

3.3 Prove that if $f : \mathbb{R}^n \to \mathbb{R}$ is a convex function, then all its sublevel sets are convex.

3.4 Prove that a function $f : K \to \mathbb{R}$, where $K \subseteq \mathbb{R}^n$ is convex, is convex if and only if epi f is convex.

3.5 For two sets $S, T \subseteq \mathbb{R}^n$, define their **Minkowski sum** to be

$$S + T := \{x + y : x \in S, y \in T\}.$$

Prove that if S and T are convex, then so is their Minkowski sum.

3.6 Prove that a polyhedron $K \subseteq \mathbb{R}^n$ is bounded, i.e., K is contained in an ℓ_2-ball of radius $r < \infty$, then it can be written as a convex hull of finitely many points, i.e., K is also a polytope.

3.7 Prove that the set of $n \times n$ real PSD matrices is convex.

3.8 Prove that if $f : \mathbb{R}^n \to \mathbb{R}$ is convex, $A \in \mathbb{R}^{n \times m}$ and $b \in \mathbb{R}^n$ then $g(y) := f(Ay + b)$ is also convex.

3.9 Prove that the functions in Exercise 2.1 are convex.

3.10 Prove that a convex function is continuous.

3.11 Prove that the set $\partial f(x)$ is always a convex set, even when f is not convex.

3.12 Prove that a differentiable function $f : K \to \mathbb{R}$ is strictly convex if and only if for all $x \neq y \in K$,

$$f(y) > f(x) + \langle \nabla f(x), y - x \rangle.$$

3.13 Prove that if a function $f : K \to \mathbb{R}$ has a continuous and PD Hessian, then it is strictly convex. Prove that the converse is false: The univariate function $f(x) := x^4$ is strictly convex, but its second derivative can be 0.

3.14 Prove that a strictly convex function defined on an open convex set can have at most one minimum.

3.15 Consider a convex function $f : K \to \mathbb{R}$. Let $\lambda_1, \ldots, \lambda_n$ be a set of n non-negative real numbers that sum to 1. Prove that for all $x_1, \ldots, x_n \in K$,

$$f\left(\sum_{i=1}^n \lambda_i x_i\right) \leq \sum_{i=1}^n \lambda_i f(x_i).$$

3.16 Let $B \in \mathbb{R}^{n \times n}$ be a symmetric matrix. Consider the function $f(x) = x^\top B x$. Write the gradient and the Hessian of $f(x)$. When is f convex and when is it concave?

3.17   Prove that if A is an $n \times n$ PD matrix with smallest eigenvalue λ_1, then the function $f(x) = x^\top A x$ is λ_1-strongly convex with respect to the ℓ_2-norm.

3.18   Consider the generalized negative entropy function $f(x) = \sum_{i=1}^n x_i \log x_i - x_i$ over $\mathbb{R}^n_{>0}$.

   (a)   Write the gradient and Hessian of f.
   (b)   Prove f is strictly convex.
   (c)   Prove that f is not strongly convex with respect to the ℓ_2-norm.
   (d)   Write the Bregman divergence D_f. Is $D_f(x,y) = D_f(y,x)$ for all $x, y \in \mathbb{R}^n_{>0}$?
   (e)   Prove that f is 1-strongly convex with respect to ℓ_1-norm when restricted to points in the subdomain $\{x \in \mathbb{R}^n_{>0} : \sum_{i=1}^n x_i = 1\}$.

3.19   Prove that for a nonempty, closed, and convex set K, $\operatorname{argmin}_{x \in K} \|x - y\|$ exists.

3.20   Prove Theorem 3.14.

Notes

The study of convexity is central to a variety of mathematical, scientific, and engineering disciplines. For a detailed discussion on convex sets and convex functions, the reader is referred to the classic textbook by Rockafellar (1970). The textbook by Boyd and Vandenberghe (2004) also provides a comprehensive (and modern) treatment of convex analysis. The book by Barvinok (2002) provides an introduction to convexity with various mathematical applications, e.g., to lattices. The book by Krantz (2014) introduces analytical (real and complex) tools for studying convexity.

4

Convex Optimization and Efficiency

We present the notion of convex optimization and discuss formally what it means to solve a convex program efficiently as a function of the representation length of the input and the desired accuracy.

4.1 Convex Programs

The central object of study is the following class of optimization problems.

Definition 4.1 (Convex program). Given a convex set $K \subseteq \mathbb{R}^n$ and a convex function $f : K \to \mathbb{R}$, a convex program is the following optimization problem:

$$\inf_{x \in K} f(x). \tag{4.1}$$

When f is concave, then maximizing f while constrained to be in K is also referred to as a convex program. We say that a convex program is **unconstrained** when $K = \mathbb{R}^n$, i.e., when we are optimizing over all inputs, and we call it **constrained** when the set K is a strict subset of $\mathbb{R}^n$. Further, when f is differentiable with a continuous derivative, we call (4.1) a **smooth** convex program and **nonsmooth** otherwise. Many of the functions we consider have higher-order smoothness properties, but sometimes we encounter functions that are not smooth in their domains.

Remark 4.2 (Minimum vs. infimum). Consider the case of convex optimization where $f(x) = 1/x$ and $K = (0, \infty)$. In this case,

$$\inf \left\{ \frac{1}{x} : x \in (0, \infty) \right\} = 0,$$

and there is no x that attains this value. However, if $K \subseteq \mathbb{R}^n$ is closed and bounded (compact) then we are assured that the infimum value is attained by a point $x \in K$. In almost all cases presented in this book we are interested in the latter case. Even when $K = \mathbb{R}^n$ is unbounded, the algorithms developed to solve this optimization problem work in some closed and bounded subset. Hence, often we ignore this distinction and use minimum instead of infimum. A similar comment applies to supremum vs. maximum.

4.1.1 Examples of Convex Programs

Several important problems can be encoded as convex programs. Here are two prominent examples.

System of linear equations. Suppose we are given the task to find a solution to a system of linear equations $Ax = b$ where $A \in \mathbb{R}^{m \times n}$ and $b \in \mathbb{R}^n$. The traditional method to solve this problem is via Gaussian elimination. Interestingly, the problem of solving a system of linear equations can also be formulated as the following convex program:

$$\min_{x \in \mathbb{R}^n} \ \|Ax - b\|_2^2 .$$

The objective function is indeed convex as

$$f(x) = x^\top A^\top A x - 2b^\top A x + b^\top b$$

(why?), from which it can be easily calculated that

$$\nabla^2 f(x) = 2A^\top A \succeq 0,$$

hence, by Theorem 3.6, the function f is convex. Therefore solving such a convex program can lead to the solution of a system of equations.

Linear programming. Linear programming is the problem of optimizing a linear objective function subject to being inside a polyhedron. A variety of discrete problems that appear in computer science can be represented as linear programs, for instance, finding the shortest path between two vertices in a graph, or finding the maximum flow in a graph. One way to represent a linear program is as follows. Given $A \in \mathbb{R}^{n \times m}, b \in \mathbb{R}^n, c \in \mathbb{R}^m$:

$$\min_{x \in \mathbb{R}^m} \ \langle c, x \rangle$$
$$\text{subject to} \quad Ax = b \tag{4.2}$$
$$x \geq 0.$$

The objective function $\langle c, x \rangle$ is a linear function that is (trivially) convex. The set of points x satisfying $Ax = b$ and $x \geq 0$ is a polyhedron, which is also a convex set. We now illustrate how the problem of finding the shortest path in a graph between two nodes can be encoded as a linear program.

Shortest path in a graph. Given a directed graph $G = (V, E)$ with a "source" vertex s, a "target" vertex t, and a nonnegative "weight" w_{ij} for each edge $(i, j) \in E$, consider the following program with variables x_{ij}:

$$\min_{x \in \mathbb{R}^E} \quad \sum_{ij \in E} w_{ij} x_{ij}$$

$$\text{subject to} \quad x \geq 0,$$

$$\forall i \in V, \quad \sum_{j \in V} x_{ij} - \sum_{j \in V} x_{ji} = \begin{cases} 1 & \text{if } i = s, \\ -1 & \text{if } i = t, \\ 0 & \text{otherwise.} \end{cases}$$

The intuition behind this formulation is that x_{ij} is an indicator variable for whether the edge (i, j) is part of the minimum weight, or **shortest path:** 1 when it is, and 0 if it is not. We wish to select the set of edges with minimum weight, subject to the constraint that this set forms a walk from s to t (represented by the equality constraint: For all vertices except s and t, the number of incoming and outgoing edges must be equal).

The equality condition can be rewritten in the form $Bx = b$, where B is the **vertex-edge incidence matrix.** In particular, if $e = (i, j)$ is the kth edge, then the kth column of B has value 1 in the jth row, -1 in the ith row, and 0s elsewhere. $b \in \mathbb{R}^V$ has value 1 in the sth row, -1 in the tth row, and 0s elsewhere.

Note that the solution to the above linear program might be "fractional," i.e., it might not give true paths. However, one can still prove that the optimal value is exactly the length of the shortest path, and one can recover the shortest path from an optimal solution to the above linear program.

4.2 Computational Models

Towards developing algorithms to solve convex programs of the kind (4.1), we need to specify a model of computation, explain how we can input a convex set or a function, and what it means for an algorithm to be efficient. The following is by no means a substitute for a background on theory of computing but just a refresher and a reminder that in this book we care about the running time of algorithms from this point of view.

As the model of computation, we first quickly recall the standard notion of a Turing machine (TM) that has a single one-directional infinite tape and works with a finite-sized alphabet and transition function. The "head" of a TM that implements its transitions function encodes the algorithm. A computation on a TM is initialized with a binary input $\sigma \in \{0,1\}^\star$ on its tape and terminates with an output $\tau \in \{0,1\}^\star$ written on it. We measure the running time of such a TM as the *maximum* number of steps performed on an input of a certain length n. Here are some important variations of this standard model that will also be useful:

- **Randomized TMs.** In this model, the TM has access to an additional tape that is an infinite stream of independent and uniformly distributed random bits. We then often allow such machines to be sometimes incorrect (in what they output as a solution), but we require that the probability of providing a correct answer is, say, at least 0.51.[1]
- **TMs with oracles.** For some applications, it is convenient to consider TMs that have access to a black box primitive (called an **oracle**) for answering certain questions or computing certain functions. Formally, such a TM has an additional tape on which it can write a particular input and query the oracle, which then writes the answer to such a query on the same tape. If the size of the output of such an oracle is always polynomially bounded as a function of the input query length, we call it a polynomial oracle.

As it is standard in computational complexity, our notion of efficiency is polynomial time computability, i.e., we would like to design Turing machines (algorithms) that solve a given problem and have (randomized) polynomial running time. We will see that for several convex programs this goal is possible to achieve, while for others it might be hard or even impossible. The reader is referred to the notes for references on computational complexity and time complexity classes such as **P** and its randomized variants such as **RP** and **BPP**.

RAM model. Oftentimes, we (unrealistically) consider the case when each arithmetic operation (addition, multiplication, subtraction, checking equality, etc.) takes exactly 1 time step. This is sometimes called the RAM model of computation. On a TM, adding two numbers takes time proportional to the number of bits required to represent them. If the numbers encountered in the algorithm remain polynomially bounded, this causes only a poly-logarithmic

---

[1] In fact, any number strictly more than 0.5 suffices.

overhead and we do not worry about it. However, sometimes, the numbers to be added/multiplied are itself produced by the algorithm and we have to be careful.

In subsequent sections we analyze several natural computational questions one might ask regarding convex sets and convex functions and formalize further what kind of an input shall we provide and what type of a solution are we really looking for.

4.3 Membership Problem for Convex Sets

Perhaps the simplest computational problem one can consider that is relevant to convex optimization is the **membership** problem in convex sets:

Given a point $x \in \mathbb{R}^n$ and $K \subseteq \mathbb{R}^n$, is $x \in K$?

We now examine some specific instances of this question and understand how to specify the input (x, K) to the algorithm. While for x, we can imagine writing it down in binary (if it is rational), K is an infinite set and we need to work with some kind of finite representation. In this process, we introduce several important concepts that are useful later on.

Example: Halfspaces. Let

$$K := \{y \in \mathbb{R}^n : \langle a, y \rangle \leq b\},$$

where $a \in \mathbb{R}^n$ is a vector and $b \in \mathbb{R}$ is a number. K then represents a halfspace in the Euclidean space $\mathbb{R}^n$. For a given $x \in \mathbb{R}^n$, checking whether $x \in K$ just boils down to verifying whether the inequality $\langle a, x \rangle \leq b$ is satisfied or not. Computing $\langle a, x \rangle$ requires $O(n)$ arithmetic operations and, hence, is computationally efficient.

Let us now try to formalize what an input for an algorithm that checks whether $x \in K$ should be in this case. We need to provide x, a, and b to this algorithm. For this we need to represent these objects exactly using finitely many bits. Hence, we assume that these are rational numbers, i.e., $x \in \mathbb{Q}^n$, $a \in \mathbb{Q}^n$, and $b \in \mathbb{Q}$. If we want to provide a rational number $y \in \mathbb{Q}$ as input, we represent it as an irreducible fraction $y = \frac{y_1}{y_2}$ for $y_1, y_2 \in \mathbb{Z}$ and give these numbers in binary. The **bit complexity** $L(z)$ of an integer $z \in \mathbb{Z}$ is defined to be the number of bits required to store its binary representation, thus

$$L(z) := 1 + \lceil \log(|z| + 1) \rceil,$$

and we overload this notation to rational numbers by defining

$$L(y) := L\left(\frac{y_1}{y_2}\right) := L(y_1) + L(y_2).$$

Further, if $x \in \mathbb{Q}^n$ is a vector of rationals, we define

$$L(x) := L(x_1) + L(x_2) + \cdots + L(x_n).$$

And finally, for inputs that are collections of rational vectors, numbers, matrices, etc., we set

$$L(x, a, b) := L(x) + L(a) + L(b),$$

i.e., the total bit complexity of all numbers involved.

Given this definition, one can now verify that checking whether $x \in K$ for a halfspace K can be done in polynomial time with respect to the input length, i.e., the bit complexity $L(x, a, b)$. It is important to note that the arithmetic operations involved in checking this are multiplication, addition, and comparison, and all of the operations can be implemented efficiently (with respect to the bit lengths of the inputs) on a TM.

Example: Ellipsoids. Consider that case when $K \subseteq \mathbb{R}^n$ is an ellipsoid, i.e., a set of the form

$$K := \{y \in \mathbb{R}^n : y^\top A y \leq 1\}$$

for a PD matrix $A \in \mathbb{Q}^{n \times n}$. As before, the task of checking whether $x \in K$ for an $x \in \mathbb{Q}^n$ can be performed efficiently: Indeed, computing $x^\top A x$ requires $O(n^2)$ arithmetic operations (multiplications and additions) and, thus, can be performed in polynomial time with respect to the bit complexity $L(x, A)$ of the input.

Example: Intersections and polyhedra. Note that being able to answer membership questions about two sets $K_1, K_2 \subseteq \mathbb{R}^n$ allows us to answer questions about their intersection $K_1 \cap K_2$. For instance, consider a polyhedron, i.e., a set of the form

$$K := \{y \in \mathbb{R}^n : \langle a_i, y \rangle \leq b_i \text{ for } i = 1, 2, \ldots, m\},$$

where $a_i \in \mathbb{Q}^n$ and $b_i \in \mathbb{Q}$ for $i = 1, 2, \ldots, m$. Such a K is an intersection of m halfspaces, each of which is easy to deal with computationally. Determining whether $x \in K$ reduces to m such questions, and hence is easy as well; it can be answered in polynomial time with respect to the bit complexity

$$L(x, a_1, b_1, a_2, b_2, \ldots, a_m, b_m).$$

Example: ℓ_1-ball. Consider the case where

$$K := \{y \in \mathbb{R}^n : \|y\|_1 \le r\}$$

for $r \in \mathbb{Q}$. Interestingly, K falls into the category of polyhedra: It can be written as

$$K = \{y \in \mathbb{R}^n : \langle y, s \rangle \le r, \text{ for all } s \in \{-1, 1\}^n\},$$

and one can argue that none of the 2^n (**exponentially** many) different linear inequalities is redundant. Thus, using the method from the previous example, our algorithm would not be efficient. However, in this case one can just check whether

$$\sum_{i=1}^{n} |x_i| \le r.$$

This requires only $O(n)$ arithmetic operations and can be efficiently implemented on a TM.

Example: Polytopes. Recall that, by definition, a polytope $K \subseteq \mathbb{R}^n$ is a convex hull of finitely many points $v_1, \ldots, v_N \in \mathbb{Q}^n$ for some integer N. We know from Exercise 3.6 that a bounded polyhedron is also a polytope. We can choose the above points so that each $v_i \in K$ is also a **vertex** of K. A vertex of a polytope K is a point $x \in K$ that does not belong to $\text{conv}(K \setminus \{x\})$. We can show that if the inequalities and equalities generating the polyhedron contain rational coefficients, then all vertices of K have a rational description, $v_i \in \mathbb{Q}^n$, and the description of each v_i is polynomial in the bit complexity of the defining inequalities. Thus, we can specify a polytope by specifying the list of inequalities and equalities it is supposed to satisfy, or as a list of its vertices. The latter representation, however, can often be much larger. Consider the case of the **hypercube** $[0, 1]^n$: It has 2^n vertices but can be described by $2n$ inequalities, each of which requires $O(n)$ bits. Thus, the polyhedral description, which can be much more succinct, is often preferred. In the polyhedral representation, the membership problem can be easily solved in polynomial time. However, developing a polynomial time algorithm for linear programming problem in this model was a major development and is presented in later parts of the book.

Example: Spanning tree polytope. Given an undirected and simple (no repeated edge or loop) graph $G = (V, E)$ with $n := |V|$ and $m := |E| \le n(n-1)/2$, let $\mathcal{T} \subseteq 2^{[m]}$ denote the set of all **spanning trees** in G. A spanning tree in a graph is a subset of edges such that each vertex has at least one edge incident to it and has no cycles. Define the spanning tree polytope corresponding to G, $P_G \subseteq \mathbb{R}^m$, as follows:

$$P_G := \mathrm{conv}\{1_T : T \in \mathcal{T}\},$$

where conv denotes the convex hull of a set of vectors and $1_T \in \mathbb{R}^m$ is the indicator vector of a set $T \subseteq [m]$.[2] In applications, the input is just the graph $G = (V, E)$ whose size is $O(n + m)$. P_G can have an exponential (in n) number of vertices. Further, it is not easy, but one can show that the number of inequalities describing P_G could also be an exponential in n. Nevertheless, given $x \in \mathbb{Q}^m$ and the graph G, checking whether $x \in P_G$ can be done in polynomial time in the number of bits needed to represent x and G, and is discussed more in the next section.

Example: PSD matrices. Consider now $K \subseteq \mathbb{R}^{n \times n}$ to be the set of all symmetric PSD matrices. Is it algorithmically easy to check whether $X \in K$? In Exercise 3.7 we proved that K is convex. Recall that for a symmetric matrix $X \in \mathbb{Q}^{n \times n}$,

$$X \in K \quad \Leftrightarrow \quad \forall y \in \mathbb{R}^n, \ y^\top X y \geq 0.$$

Thus, K is defined as an intersection of infinitely many halfspaces – one for every vector $y \in \mathbb{R}^n$. Clearly, it is not possible to go over all such y and check them one by one, thus a different approach for checking if $X \in K$ is required. Recall that by $\lambda_1(X)$ we denote the smallest eigenvalue of X (note that because of symmetry, all its eigenvalues are real). It holds that

$$X \in K \quad \Leftrightarrow \quad \lambda_1(X) \geq 0.$$

Recall from basic linear algebra that eigenvalues of X are roots of the polynomial $\det(\lambda I - X)$. Hence, one can just try to compute all of them and check if they are nonnegative. However, computing roots of a polynomial is nontrivial. On the one hand, there are efficient procedures to compute eigenvalues of matrices. However, they are all approximate since eigenvalues are typically irrational numbers and, thus, cannot be represented exactly in binary. More precisely, there are algorithms to compute a sequence of numbers $\lambda_1', \lambda_2', \ldots, \lambda_n'$ such that $|\lambda_i - \lambda_i'| < \varepsilon$ where $\lambda_1, \lambda_2, \ldots, \lambda_n$ are eigenvalues of X and $\varepsilon \in (0, 1)$ is the specified precision. Such algorithms can be made run

---

[2] Recall that the indicator vector $1_T \in \{0,1\}^m$ of a set $T \subseteq [m]$ is defined as $1_T(i) = 1$ for all $i \in T$ and $1_T(i) = 0$ otherwise.

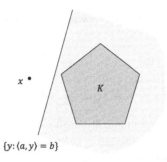

$\{y: \langle a, y \rangle = b\}$

Figure 4.1 A convex set K, a point $x \notin K$, and a hyperplane $\{y: \langle a, y \rangle = b\}$ separating x from K.

in time polynomial in the bit complexity $L(X)$ and $\log \frac{1}{\varepsilon}$. Consequently, we can check whether $X \in K$ "approximately." This kind of approximation often suffices in applications.

4.3.1 Separation Oracles for Convex Sets

When considering the question of whether a point x is in a set K, in the case when the answer is negative one might want to give a "certificate" for that, i.e., a proof that x is outside of K. It turns out that if K is a convex set, such a certificate always exists and is given by a hyperplane separating x from K (see Figure 4.1). More precisely, Theorem 3.11 in Chapter 3 asserts that for any convex and closed set $K \subseteq \mathbb{R}^n$ and $x \in \mathbb{R}^n \setminus K$, there exists a hyperplane separating K from x, i.e., there exists a vector $u \in \mathbb{R}^n$ and a number $b \in \mathbb{R}$ such that $\langle a, y \rangle \leq b$ for all $y \in K$ and $\langle a, x \rangle > b$. In this theorem, the hyperplane separating K from x is $\{y \in \mathbb{R}^n: \langle a, y \rangle = b\}$, as K is on one side of the hyperplane while x is on the other side. The converse of Theorem 3.11 is also true: Every set that can be separated (by a hyperplane) from every point in its complement is convex.

Theorem 4.3 (Converse of separation over convex sets). *Let $K \subseteq \mathbb{R}^n$ be a closed set. If for every point $x \in \mathbb{R}^n \setminus K$ there exists a hyperplane separating x from K, then K is a convex set.*

In other words, a convex set can be represented as a collection of hyperplanes separating it from points outside. For it to be computationally useful, the hyperplane separating x and K must be described using rational numbers. This motivates the following definition.

Definition 4.4 (Separation oracle). A separation oracle for a convex set $K \subseteq \mathbb{R}^n$ is a primitive that:

- given $x \in K$, answers YES,
- given $x \notin K$, answers NO and outputs $a \in \mathbb{Q}^n$, $b \in \mathbb{Q}$ such that the hyperplane $\{y \in \mathbb{R}^n : \langle a, y \rangle = b\}$ separates x from K.

For this primitive to be algorithmically useful, we require that the output of a separation oracle, i.e., a and b, has polynomial bit complexity $L(a, b)$ as a function of $L(x)$. Separation oracles provide a convenient way of "accessing" a given convex set K, as by Theorems 3.11 and 4.3 they provide a complete description of K.

Let us now give some examples and make a couple of remarks regarding separation oracles.

Example: Spanning tree polytope. Recall the spanning tree polytope from the previous section. By definition, to solve the membership problem for this polytope, it is sufficient to construct a polynomial time separation oracle for this polytope. Surprisingly, one can prove that there exists a polynomial time (in the number of bits needed to encode the graph G) for this polytope that only needs access to the graph G – we discuss this and other similar polytopes in Chapter 13.

Example: PSD matrices. We note that the algorithm to check if a matrix X is PSD can be turned into an approximate separation oracle for the set of PSD matrices. Compute an approximation λ to the smallest eigenvalue $\lambda_1(X)$ along with a v such that $Xv = \lambda v$. If $\lambda \geq 0$, output YES. If $\lambda < 0$, output NO along with $vv^\top$. In this case, we know that

$$\langle X, vv^\top \rangle := \mathrm{Tr}(Xvv^\top) = v^\top X v < 0.$$

In both cases we are correct approximately. Here, the quality of the approximation depends on the error in our estimate for $\lambda_1(X)$; we let the reader figure out the details.

Separation vs. optimization. It is known that constructing efficient (polynomial time) separation oracles for a given family of convex sets is equivalent to constructing algorithms to optimize *linear* functions over convex sets in this family. When applying such theorems one has to be careful though, as several technicalities show up related to bit complexity; see the notes of this chapter for references.

Composing separation oracles. Suppose that K_1 and K_2 are two convex sets and that we have access to separation oracles for them. Then we can construct a separation oracle for their intersection $K := K_1 \cap K_2$. Indeed, given a point x we can just check whether x belongs to both of K_1, K_2 and if not, say $x \notin K_1$, then we output the separating hyperplane output by the oracle for K_1. Using a similar idea, we can also construct a separation oracle for $K_1 \times K_2 \subseteq \mathbb{R}^{2n}$.

4.4 Solution Concepts for Optimization Problems

With a better understanding of how to represent convex sets in a computationally convenient way, we now go back to optimizing functions and to a crucial question: What does it mean to solve a convex program of the form (4.1)?

One way of approaching this problem might be to formulate it as a decision problem of the following form:

$$\text{Given } c \in \mathbb{Q}, \text{ is } \min_{x \in K} f(x) = c?$$

While in many important cases (e.g., linear programming) we can solve this problem, even for the simplest of nonlinear convex programs this may not be possible.

Example: Irrational solutions. Consider a simple, univariate convex program of the form

$$\min_{x \geq 1} \frac{2}{x} + x.$$

By a direct calculation one can see that the optimal solution is $x^\star = \sqrt{2}$ and the optimal value $2\sqrt{2}$. Thus, we obtain an irrational optimal solution even though the problem was stated as minimizing a rational function with rational entries. In such a case, the optimal solution cannot be represented exactly using a finite binary expansion and, thus, we are forced to consider approximate solutions.

For this reason, we often cannot hope to obtain the optimal value

$$y^\star := \min_{x \in K} f(x),$$

and we revise the question of asking for an approximation, or in other words, asking for a small interval containing $y^\star$:

$$\text{Given } \varepsilon > 0, \text{ compute } c \in \mathbb{Q}, \text{ such that } \min_{x \in K} f(x) \in [c, c + \varepsilon]. \quad (4.3)$$

Since it requires roughly $\log \frac{1}{\varepsilon}$ bits to store ε, we expect an efficient algorithm to run in time **poly-logarithmic** in $\frac{1}{\varepsilon}$. We elaborate a little more about this issue in the subsequent section.

Optimal value vs. optimal point. Perhaps the most natural way to approach problem (4.3) is to try to find a point $x \in K$ such that $y^\star \le f(x) \le y^\star + \varepsilon$. Then we can simply take $c := f(x) - \varepsilon$. Note that providing such a point $x \in K$ is a significantly stronger solution concept (than just outputting an appropriate c) and provides much more information. The algorithms we consider in this book will typically output both the optimal point as well as the value, but there are examples of methods which naturally compute the optimal value only, and recovering the optimal input for them is rather nontrivial, if not impossible; see notes.

Example: Linear programming. As discussed in the previous subsections, linear programming (or linear optimization) is a special case of convex optimization, and a nontrivial case of it is when one is given a linear objective

$$f(x) = \langle c, x \rangle$$

and a polyhedron

$$K = \{x \in \mathbb{R}^n : Ax \le b\},$$

where $A \in \mathbb{Q}^{m \times n}$ and $b \in \mathbb{Q}^m$. It is not hard to show that whenever $\min_{x \in K} f(x)$ is bounded (i.e., the solution is not $-\infty$), and K has a vertex, then its optimal value is achieved at some vertex of K. Thus, in order to solve a linear program, it is enough to find the minimum value over all its vertices.

It turns out that every vertex $\tilde{x}$ of K can be represented as a solution to $A'x = b$, where A' is some square submatrix of A. In particular, this means that there is a *rational* optimal solution whenever the input data is rational. Moreover, if the bit complexity of (A, b) is L, then the bit complexity of the optimal solution is polynomial in L (and n), and hence a priori, there is no direct obstacle (from the viewpoint of bit complexity) for obtaining efficient algorithms for exactly solving linear programs.

Distance to optimum vs. approximation in value. Consider a convex program that has a unique optimal solution $x^\star \in K$. One can then ask, what is the relation between the following two statements about an $x \in K$:

- being approximately optimal in value, i.e., $f(x) \le f(x^\star) + \varepsilon$,
- being close to optimum, i.e., $\|x - x^\star\| \le \varepsilon$.

It is not hard to see that in general (when f is an arbitrary convex function), neither of these conditions implies the other, even approximately. However, as we see in later chapters, under certain conditions such as *Lipschitzness* or strong convexity, we might expect some such implications to hold.

4.4.1 Representing Functions

Finally, we come to the question of how the objective function f is given to us when trying to solve convex programs of the form (4.1). Below we discuss several possibilities.

Explicit descriptions of functions. There are several important families of functions that we often focus on instead of considering the general, abstract case. These include:

- **Linear and affine functions:** $f(x) = \langle c, x \rangle + b$ for a vector $c \in \mathbb{Q}^n$ and $b \in \mathbb{Q}$.
- **Quadratic functions:** $f(x) = x^\top A x + \langle b, x \rangle + c$ for a PSD matrix $A \in \mathbb{Q}^n$, a vector $b \in \mathbb{Q}^n$, and a number $c \in \mathbb{Q}$.
- **Linear matrix functions:** $f(X) = \text{Tr}(XA)$, where $A \in \mathbb{Q}^{n \times n}$ is a fixed symmetric matrix and $X \in \mathbb{R}^{n \times n}$ is a symmetric matrix variable.

All these families of functions can be described compactly. For instance, a linear function can be described by c and b, and a quadratic function by providing A, b, c.

Black box models. Unlike the examples mentioned above, where f is specified "explicitly," now consider perhaps the most primitive – or **black box** – access that we can hope to have for a function:

$$\text{Given } x \in \mathbb{Q}^n, \text{ output } f(x).$$

Note that such a black box, or **evaluation** oracle, is in fact a complete description of the function, i.e., it hides no information about f. However, if we have no additional analytical handle on f, such a description might be hard to work with. In fact, if we drop the convexity assumption and only assume that f is continuous, then one can show that no algorithm can efficiently optimize f; see notes for a pointer. Under the convexity assumption, the situation improves, but still, typically more information about the local behavior of f around a given point is desired to optimize f efficiently. If the function f is sufficiently smooth, one can ask for gradients, Hessians, and possibly higher-order derivatives of f. We formalize this concept in the definition below.

Definition 4.5 (Function oracle). For a function $f : \mathbb{R}^n \to \mathbb{R}$ and $k \in \mathbb{N}_{\geq 0}$, a kth order oracle for f is the primitive:

$$\text{Given } x \in \mathbb{R}^n, \text{ output } \nabla^k f(x),$$

i.e., the kth order derivative of f.

In particular, the 0-order oracle (same as an evaluation oracle) is simply a primitive which given x outputs $f(x)$, a 1st-order oracle given x outputs the gradient $\nabla f(x)$, and a 2nd-order oracle outputs the Hessian of f. In some cases, we do not need the Hessian per se but, for a vector v, it suffices to have $(\nabla^2 f(x))^{-1} v$. We will see (when discussing the gradient descent method) that even a 1st-order oracle alone is sometimes enough to approximately minimize a convex function (rather) efficiently.

Remark 4.6. We note that in the oracle model, while we are not charged for the time it takes to compute $\nabla^k f(x)$ given x, we do have to account for the bit length of the input x to the oracle and for the bit length of the output of the oracle.

Stochastic models. Another interesting (and practically relevant) way of representing a function is to provide a randomized black box procedure for computing their values, gradients, or higher-order information. To understand this, consider an example of a quadratic loss function that often shows up in machine learning applications. Given $a_1, a_2, \ldots, a_m \in \mathbb{R}^n$, and $b_1, b_2, \ldots, b_m \in \mathbb{R}$, we define

$$l(x) := \frac{1}{m} \sum_{i=1}^{m} \| \langle a_i, x \rangle - b_i \|^2 .$$

Now suppose that $F(x)$ is a randomized procedure that given $x \in \mathbb{Q}^n$, outputs at random one of $\| \langle a_1, x \rangle - b_1 \|^2$, $\| \langle a_2, x \rangle - b_2 \|^2$, $\ldots$, $\| \langle a_m, x \rangle - b_m \|^2$, each with probability $\frac{1}{m}$. Then we have

$$\mathbb{E}[F(x)] = l(x),$$

and, thus, $F(x)$ provides an "unbiased estimator" for the value $l(x)$. One can design a similar unbiased estimator for the gradient $\nabla l(x)$. Note that such "randomized oracles" have the advantage of being more computationally efficient over computing the value or gradient of $l(x)$ – in fact, they run m

times faster than their exact deterministic counterparts. Still, in many cases, one can perform minimization given just oracles of this type – for instance, using a method called *stochastic gradient descent*.

4.5 The Notion of Polynomial Time for Convex Optimization

For decision problems – where the answer is "YES" or "NO" and the input is a string of characters – one defines the class **P** to be all problems that can be solved by algorithms (deterministic Turing machines) that run in time polynomial in the number of bits needed to represent the input. The randomized counterparts to **P** are **RP** and **BPP**. Problems belonging to these classes are also considered efficiently solvable. Roughly speaking, the class **RP** consists of problems for which there exist randomized TMs that run in polynomial time in the input size. In particular, if the correct answer is NO, such a randomized TM will always return NO. If the correct answer is YES, then the randomized TM returns YES with probability at least 2/3 and NO with the remaining probability.

For optimization problems, we can define a concept analogous to a polynomial time algorithm, yet for this we need to take into account the running time as a function of the precision ε. We say that an algorithm runs in **polynomial time** for a class of optimization problems of the form $\min_{x \in K} f(x)$ (for a specific family of sets K and functions f) if the time to find an ε-approximate solution $x \in K$, i.e., such that

$$f(x) \leq y^* + \varepsilon$$

is polynomial in the bit complexity L of the input, the dimension n and $\log \frac{1}{\varepsilon}$. Similarly, we can talk about polynomial time algorithms in the black box model – then the part depending on L is not present; we instead require that the number of oracle calls (to the set K and to the function f) is polynomially bounded in the dimension and, importantly, in $\log \frac{1}{\varepsilon}$.

One might ask why we insist on the dependency on $\frac{1}{\varepsilon}$ to be poly-logarithmic. There are several important applications where a polynomial dependency on $\frac{1}{\varepsilon}$ would be not sufficient. For instance, consider a linear program $\min_{x \in K} \langle c, x \rangle$ with $K = \{x \in \mathbb{R}^n : Ax \leq b\}$, where $A \in \mathbb{Q}^{m \times n}$ and $b \in \mathbb{Q}^m$. For simplicity, assume there is exactly one optimal solution (a vertex) $v^* \in K$ of value $y^* = \langle c, v^* \rangle$. Suppose we would like to find v^* in polynomial time, given an algorithm that provides only approximately optimal answers.

How small an $\varepsilon > 0$ do we need to take to make sure that an approximate solution $\tilde{x}$ (with $\langle c, \tilde{x} \rangle \leq y^\star + \varepsilon$) can be uniquely "rounded" to the optimal vertex $v^\star$? A necessary condition for that is that there is no non-optimal vertex $v \in K$ with

$$y^\star < \langle c, v \rangle \leq y^\star + \varepsilon.$$

Thus, we should ask: What is the minimum nonzero distance in value between two distinct vertices of K? By our discussion on linear programming in Section 4.4, it follows that every vertex is a solution to an $n \times n$ subsystem of $Ax = b$. Thus, one can deduce that a minimal such gap is at least roughly 2^{-L}; see Exercise 4.9. Consequently, our choice of ε should be no bigger than that for the rounding algorithm to work properly.[3] Assuming our rounding algorithm is efficient, to get a polynomial time algorithm for linear programming we need to make the dependence on ε in our approximate algorithm polynomial in $\log \frac{1}{\varepsilon}$ in order to be polynomial in L. Thus, in this example, an approximate polynomial time algorithm for linear programming yields an exact polynomial time algorithm for linear programming.

Finally, we note that such an approximate algorithm with logarithmic dependence on $\frac{1}{\varepsilon}$ indeed exists (and we will learn a couple of such algorithms in this book).

4.5.1 Is Convex Optimization in P or Not?

Given the notion of efficiency in the previous sections one may ask:

Can every convex program be solved in polynomial time?

Even though the class of convex programs is very special and generally believed to have efficient algorithms, the short answer is no.

There are various reasons why this is the case. For instance, not all (even natural examples of) convex sets have polynomial-time separation oracles, which makes the task of optimizing over them impossible (see Exercise 4.10). It may also be sometimes computationally hard to evaluate a function in polynomial time (see Exercise 4.11). Further, it may be information-theoretically impossible (especially in black box models) to design algorithms with logarithmic dependency on the error ε. And finally, being polynomial in the bit complexity L of the input is also often a serious problem, since for

---

[3] Such a rounding algorithm is quite nontrivial, and is based on the lattice basis reduction.

certain convex programs, the bit complexity of all close-to-optimal solutions is exponential in L and, thus, even the space required to output such a solution is already exponential.

Despite these obstacles, there are still numerous interesting algorithms that show that (certain subclasses) of convex programs can be solved efficiently (might not necessarily mean "in polynomial time"). We will see several examples in subsequent chapters.

4.6 Exercises

4.1 Prove that, when A is a full rank $n \times n$ matrix and $b \in \mathbb{R}^n$, the unique minimizer of the function $\|Ax - b\|^2$ over all x is $A^{-1}b$.

4.2 Let $\mathcal{M}$ be a collection of subsets of $\{1, 2, \ldots, n\}$ and $\theta \in \mathbb{R}^n$ be given. For a set $M \in \mathcal{M}$, let $1_M \in \mathbb{R}^n$ be the indicator vector of the set M, i.e., $1_M(i) = 1$ if $i \in M$ and $1_M(i) = 0$ otherwise. Let

$$f(x) := \sum_{i=1}^{n} \theta_i x_i + \ln \sum_{M \in \mathcal{M}} e^{\langle x, 1_M \rangle}.$$

Consider the following optimization problem:

$$\inf_{x \in \mathbb{R}^n} f(x).$$

(a) Prove that, if $\theta_i > 0$ for some i, then the value of the above program is $-\infty$, i.e., it is unbounded from below.

(b) Assume the program attains a finite optimal value. Is the optimal point necessarily unique?

(c) Compute the gradient of f.

(d) Is the program convex?

4.3 Give a precise formula for the number of spanning trees in the complete graph K_n on n vertices.

4.4 For every n, give an example of a polytope that has 2^n vertices but can be described using $2n$ inequalities.

4.5 Prove that, if A is an $n \times n$ full rank matrix with entries in $\mathbb{Q}$ and $b \in \mathbb{Q}^n$, then $A^{-1}b \in \mathbb{Q}^n$.

4.6 Prove that the following algorithm for linear programming when the polytope $K \subseteq \mathbb{R}^n$ is given as a list of vertices $v_1, \ldots, v_N$ is correct: Compute $\langle c, v_i \rangle$ for each $i \in [N]$ and output the vertex with the least cost.

4.7 Find a polynomial time separation oracle for a set of the form $\{x \in \mathbb{R}^n : f(x) \leq y\}$, where $f : \mathbb{R}^n \to \mathbb{R}$ is a convex function and $y \in \mathbb{R}$. Assume that we have zero- and first-order oracle access to f.

4.8 Give bounds on the time complexity of computing the gradients and Hessians of the functions in Exercise 2.1.

4.9 The goal of this problem is to bound bit complexities of certain quantities related to linear programs. Let $A \in \mathbb{Q}^{m \times n}$ be a matrix and $b \in \mathbb{Q}^m$ be a vector, and let L be the bit complexity of (A, b). (Thus, in particular, $L \geq m$ and $L \geq n$.) We assume that $K = \{x \in \mathbb{R}^n : Ax \leq b\}$ is a bounded, full-dimensional polytope in $\mathbb{R}^n$.

(a) Prove that there is an integer $M \in \mathbb{Z}$ and a matrix $B \in \mathbb{Z}^{m \times n}$ such that $A = \frac{1}{M}B$ and the bit complexities of M and every entry in B are bounded by L.

(b) Let C be any square and invertible submatrix of A. Consider the matrix norm $\|C\|_2 := \max_{x \neq 0} \frac{\|Cx\|_2}{\|x\|_2}$. Prove that there exists a constant d such that $\|C\|_2 \leq 2^{O(L \cdot [\log(nL)]^d)}$ and $\|C^{-1}\|_2 \leq 2^{O(nL \cdot [\log(nL)]^d)}$.

(c) Prove that every vertex of P has coordinates in $\mathbb{Q}$ with bit complexity $O(nL \cdot [\log(nL)]^d)$ for some constant d.

4.10 A matrix $M \in \mathbb{R}^{n \times n}$ that is symmetric is said to be **copositive** if for all $x \in \mathbb{R}^n_{\geq 0}$,

$$x^\top M x \geq 0.$$

Let C_n denote the set of all $n \times n$ copositive matrices.

(a) Prove that the set C_n is closed and convex.

(b) Let $G = (V, E)$ be a simple and undirected graph. Prove that the following is a convex program:

$$\min_{t \in \mathbb{R}} \quad t$$
$$\text{subject to} \quad \forall i \in V, \quad M_{ii} = t - 1,$$
$$\forall ij \notin E, \quad M_{ij} = -1,$$
$$M \in C_n.$$

(c) Prove that the value of the above convex program is $\alpha(G)$, where $\alpha(G)$ is size of the largest **independent set** in G: An independent set is a set of vertices such that no two vertices in the set are adjacent.

Since computing the size of the largest independent set in G is **NP**-hard, we have an instance of convex optimization that is **NP**-hard.

4.11 Recall that an undirected graph $G = (V, E)$ is said to be bipartite if the vertex set V has two disjoint parts L, R and all edges go between L and R. Consider the case when $n := |L| = |R|$ and $m := |E|$. A perfect matching in such a graph is a set of n edges such that each vertex has exactly one edge incident to it. Let $\mathcal{M}$ denote the set of all perfect matchings in G. Let $1_M \in \{0, 1\}^E$ denote the indicator vector of the perfect matching $M \in \mathcal{M}$. Consider the function

$$f(y) := \ln \sum_{M \in \mathcal{M}} e^{\langle 1_M, y \rangle}.$$

(a) Prove that f is convex.

(b) Consider the bipartite perfect matching polytope of G defined as

$$P := \mathrm{conv}\{1_M : M \in \mathcal{M}\}.$$

Give a polynomial time separation oracle for this polytope.

(c) Prove that, if there is a polynomial time to evaluate f given the graph G as input, then one can count the number of perfect matchings in G in polynomial time.

Since the problem of computing the number of perfect matchings in a bipartite graph is **#P**-hard, we have an instance of convex optimization that is **#P**-hard.

Notes

For a detailed background on computational complexity, including models of computation and formal definitions of complexity classes such as **P**, **NP**, **RP**, **BPP**, and **#P**, the reader is referred to the textbook by Arora and Barak (2009). For a formal and detailed treatment on oracles for convex functions, see the book by Nesterov (2014). Algorithmic aspects of convex sets are discussed in detail in chapter 2 of the classic book by Grötschel et al. (1988). Chapter 2 of Grötschel et al. (1988) also presents precise details of the results connecting separation and optimization.

For an algorithm on approximately computing eigenvalues, see the paper by Pan and Chen (1999). For more on copositive programs (introduced in Exercise 4.10), the reader is referred to chapter 7 of the book by Gärtner and Matousek (2014). In a seminal result, Valiant (1979) proved that counting the number of perfect matchings in a bipartite graph (introduced in Exercise 4.11) is #**P**-hard. For more on optimization problems where there is a gap between finding the optimal value and the optimal point, see the paper by Feige (2008).

An intriguing type of nonlinear convex program is the so-called **rational convex program**. A rational convex program, defined in the paper by Vazirani (2012), is a nonlinear convex program all of whose parameters are rational numbers and which always admits a rational solution in which the denominators are polynomially bounded. Thus, while being nonlinear, a rational convex program is similar to a linear program as far as the solution set is concerned, and can be solved exactly using algorithms such as the ellipsoid method (which we introduce in Chapters 12 and 13). An example of such a program is the Eisenberg-Gale convex program that arises in the equilibrium computation literature; see Exercise 5.18.

5

Duality and Optimality

We introduce the notion of Lagrangian duality and show that under a mild condition, called Slater's condition, strong Lagrangian duality holds. Subsequently, we introduce the Legendre-Fenchel dual that often arises in Lagrangian duality and optimization methods. Finally, we present Kahn-Karush-Tucker (KKT) optimality conditions and their relation to strong duality.

Consider a general (not necessarily convex) optimization problem of the form

$$\inf_{x \in K} f(x), \tag{5.1}$$

where $f: K \to \mathbb{R}$ and $K \subseteq \mathbb{R}^n$. Let y^* be one of its optimal value. In the process of computing y^*, one often tries to obtain a good upper bound $y_U \in \mathbb{R}$ and a good lower bound $y_L \in \mathbb{R}$, so that

$$y_L \leq y^* \leq y_U,$$

and $|y_L - y_U|$ is as small as possible. However, by inspecting the form of (5.1) it is evident that the problems of producing y_L and y_U seem rather different and the situation is asymmetric. Finding an upper bound y_U may be much simpler, as it boils down to picking an $x \in K$ and taking $y_U = f(x)$, which is trivially a correct upper bound. Giving an (even trivial) lower bound on y^* does not seem to be such a simple task. One can think of duality as a tool to construct lower bounds for y^* in an automatic way that is almost as simple as above – it reduces to plugging in a feasible input to a different optimization problem, called the Lagrangian dual of (5.1).

5.1 Lagrangian Duality

Definition 5.1 (Primal). Consider a problem of the form

$$\inf_{x \in \mathbb{R}^n} \; f(x)$$

$$\text{such that } \; f_j(x) \leq 0 \quad \text{for } j = 1, 2, \ldots, m, \tag{5.2}$$

$$h_i(x) = 0 \quad \text{for } i = 1, 2, \ldots, p.$$

Here $f, f_1, \ldots, f_m, h_1, \ldots, h_p \colon \mathbb{R}^n \to \mathbb{R}$ and need not be convex.[1]

Note that this problem is a special case of (5.1) when the set K is defined by m inequalities and p equalities.

$$K := \{x \in \mathbb{R}^n \colon f_j(x) \leq 0 \; \text{ for } \; j = 1, \ldots, m \; \text{ and}$$

$$h_i(x) = 0 \; \text{ for } \; i = 1, \ldots, p\}.$$

Suppose we would like to obtain a lower bound on the optimal value of (5.2). Towards that, one can apply the general idea of "moving the constraints to the objective." More precisely, introduce m new variables $\lambda_1, \ldots, \lambda_m \geq 0$ for the inequality constraints and p new variables $\mu_1, \ldots, \mu_p \in \mathbb{R}$ for the equality constraints; these are referred to as **Lagrange multipliers.** Then, consider the following **Lagrangian** function:

$$L(x, \lambda, \mu) := f(x) + \sum_{j=1}^{m} \lambda_j f_j(x) + \sum_{i=1}^{p} \mu_i h_i(x). \tag{5.3}$$

One can immediately see that, since $\lambda \geq 0$, whenever $x \in K$ we have that

$$L(x, \lambda, \mu) \leq f(x)$$

and $L(x, 0, 0) = f(x)$. Moreover, for every $x \in \mathbb{R}^n$,

$$\sup_{\lambda \geq 0, \mu} \; L(x, \lambda, \mu) = \begin{cases} f(x) & \text{if } x \in K, \\ +\infty & \text{otherwise.} \end{cases}$$

and for $x \in K$, the supremum is attained at $\lambda = 0$. To see the second equality above, note that when $x \notin K$, then either $h_i(x) \neq 0$ for some i or $f_j(x) > 0$ for some j. Hence, we can set the corresponding Lagrange multiplier μ_i or λ_j appropriately (and the other Lagrange multipliers to 0) to let the Lagrangian go to $+\infty$. Thus, consequently one can write the optimal value $y^\star$ of (5.2) as

$$y^\star := \inf_{x \in K} \sup_{\lambda \geq 0, \mu} L(x, \lambda, \mu) = \inf_{x \in \mathbb{R}^n} \sup_{\lambda \geq 0, \mu} L(x, \lambda, \mu).$$

---

[1] We also allow f to take the value $+\infty$, the discussion in this section is still valid in such a case.

It follows that for every fixed $\lambda \geq 0$ and μ, we have

$$\inf_{x \in \mathbb{R}^n} L(x, \lambda, \mu) \leq y^\star.$$

Thus, every choice of $\lambda \geq 0$ and μ provides us with a *lower bound* for $y^\star$. This is exactly what we were looking for, except that now, our lower bound is a solution to an optimization problem, which is not necessarily easier than the one we started with. This is a valid concern, since we wanted a lower bound that is easy to compute. However, the optimization problem we are required to solve now is at least unconstrained, i.e., the function $L(x, \lambda, \mu)$ is minimized over all $x \in \mathbb{R}^n$. In fact, for numerous important examples of problems of the form (5.2), the value

$$g(\lambda, \mu) := \inf_{x \in \mathbb{R}^n} L(x, \lambda, \mu) \tag{5.4}$$

has a closed-form solution (as a function of λ and μ) and thus allows efficient computation of lower bounds to $y^\star$. We will see some examples soon.

So far, we have constructed a function $g(\lambda, \mu)$ over λ, μ such that for every $\lambda \geq 0$, we have $g(\lambda, \mu) \leq y^\star$. A natural question arises: What is the best lower bound we can achieve this way?

Definition 5.2 (Lagrangian dual). For the primal optimization problem considered in Definition 5.1, the following is referred to as the dual optimization problem of the dual program.

$$\sup_{\lambda \geq 0, \mu} g(\lambda, \mu), \tag{5.5}$$

where $g(\lambda, \mu) := \inf_{x \in \mathbb{R}^n} L(x, \lambda, \mu)$.

From the above considerations we can deduce the following inequality.

Theorem 5.3 (Weak duality).

$$\sup_{\lambda \geq 0, \mu} g(\lambda, \mu) \leq \inf_{x \in K} f(x). \tag{5.6}$$

An important observation is that the dual problem in Definition 5.2 is a convex optimization problem irrespective of whether the primal problem of Definition 5.1 is convex or not. This is because the Lagrangian dual function g is concave because it is a pointwise infimum of linear functions; see Exercise 5.1.

One might ask then: Does equality hold in the inequality (5.6)? It turns out that in the general case, one cannot expect equality to hold. However, there are sufficient conditions that imply equality. An important example is Slater's condition.

Definition 5.4 (Slater's condition). Slater's condition is that there exists a point $\bar{x} \in K$, such that all inequality constraints defining K are strict at $\bar{x}$, i.e., $h_i(\bar{x}) = 0$ for all $i = 1, 2, \ldots, p$, and for all $j = 1, 2, \ldots, m$, we have $f_j(\bar{x}) < 0$.

When a convex optimization problem satisfies Slater's condition, we have the following fundamental theorem.

Theorem 5.5 (Strong duality). *Suppose that the functions* $f, f_1, f_2, \ldots, f_m$ *and* $h_1, h_2, \ldots, h_p$ *are affine and satisfy Slater's condition. Then*

$$\sup_{\lambda \geq 0, \mu} g(\lambda, \mu) = \inf_{x \in K} f(x).$$

In other words, the **duality gap** *is zero.*

We defer the proof of this theorem to later. The proof relies on Theorem 3.11, along with Slater's condition, to show the existence of Lagrange multipliers that achieve strong duality. It has some similarity to the proof of Theorem 3.12 and starts by constructing the following (epigraph-type) convex set related to the objective function and the constraints.

$$\{(w, u) \in \mathbb{R} \times \mathbb{R}^m : f(x) \leq w, \ f_i(x) \leq u_i \ \forall i \in [m], \text{for some } x \in \mathcal{F}\},$$

where $\mathcal{F}$ is the set of points that satisfy all the equality constraints. It is then argued that Lagrange multipliers exist whenever there is a "nonvertical" supporting hyperplane that passes through the point $(y^\star, 0)$ on the boundary of this convex set. Here $y^\star$ is the optimal value to the convex program (5.2), and nonvertical means that the coefficient corresponding to the first coordinate in the hyperplane is nonzero. Such a nonvertical hyperplane can only fail to exist when constraints of the convex program can only be achieved at certain extreme points of this convex set, and Slater's condition ensures that this does not happen.

For now, we present some interesting cases where strong duality holds and some where it does not. We conclude this section by providing two examples: one where strong duality holds even though the primal program is nonconvex and one where strong duality fails to hold, even for a convex program (implying that Slater's condition is not satisfied).

Example: Dual of a linear program in standard form. Consider a linear program of the form

$$\min_{x \in \mathbb{R}^n} \ \langle c, x \rangle$$

$$\text{sush that } \ Ax \geq b,$$

(5.7)

where A is an $m \times n$ matrix and $b \in \mathbb{R}^m$ is a vector. The notation $Ax \leq b$ is a short way to say

$$\langle a_i, x \rangle \geq b_i \quad \text{for all } i = 1, 2, \ldots, m,$$

where $a_1, a_2, \ldots, a_m$ are the rows of A.

To derive its dual, we introduce a vector of dual variables $\lambda \in \mathbb{R}^m_{\geq 0}$ and consider the Lagrangian

$$L(x, \lambda) = \langle c, x \rangle + \langle \lambda, b - Ax \rangle.$$

The next step is to derive $g(\lambda) := \inf_x L(x, \lambda)$. For this, we first rewrite

$$L(x, \lambda) = \langle x, c - A^\top \lambda \rangle + \langle b, \lambda \rangle.$$

From this form, it is easy to see that, unless $c - A^\top \lambda = 0$, the minimum of $L(x, \lambda)$ over all $x \in \mathbb{R}^n$ is $-\infty$. More precisely,

$$g(\lambda) = \begin{cases} \langle b, \lambda \rangle & \text{if } c - A^\top \lambda = 0, \\ -\infty & \text{otherwise.} \end{cases}$$

Consequently, the dual program is

$$\max_{\lambda \in \mathbb{R}^m} \quad \langle b, \lambda \rangle$$
$$\text{such that } A^\top \lambda = c, \tag{5.8}$$
$$\lambda \geq 0.$$

It is known that in the setting of linear programming strong duality holds, i.e., whenever (5.7) has a finite optimal value, then the dual (5.8) is also finite and has the same optimal value.

Example: Strong duality for a nonconvex program. Consider the following univariate optimization problem where $\sqrt{\cdot}$ refers to the positive square root:

$$\inf \quad \sqrt{x}$$
$$\text{such that } \frac{1}{x} - 1 \leq 0. \tag{5.9}$$

Since $x \mapsto \sqrt{x}$ is not a convex function, the above is a nonconvex program. Its optimal value is equal to 1, attained at the boundary $x = 1$.

Verify that the dual program takes the following form:

$$\sup \quad \frac{3}{2}\lambda - \frac{1}{2}\lambda^3$$
$$\text{such that } \lambda \geq 0. \tag{5.10}$$

The above is a convex program as the objective function is concave. Its optimal value is attained at $\lambda = 1$ and is equal to 1, hence strong duality holds. Note that if we replace the constraint $\frac{1}{x} - 1 \leq 0$ by an equivalent, but different constraint $x \geq 1$, we would get a different dual.

Example: Strong duality fails for a convex program. The fact that strong duality can fail for convex programs might be a little disheartening, yet such programs are not commonly encountered in practice. The reason for such behavior is typically an unnatural or redundant description of the domain.

The standard example used to illustrate this is as follows: Consider a function $f : D \to \mathbb{R}$ given by $f(x) := e^{-x}$ and the two-dimensional domain

$$D = \{(x, y) : y > 0\} \subseteq \mathbb{R}^2.$$

The convex program we consider is

$$\inf_{(x,y) \in D} e^{-x}$$
$$\text{such that } \frac{x^2}{y} \leq 0. \tag{5.11}$$

Such a program is indeed convex, as e^{-x} and $\frac{x^2}{y}$ are convex functions over D but we see that its description is rather artificial, as the constraint forces $x = 0$ and hence the y variable is redundant. Still, the optimal value of (5.11) is 1 and we can derive its Lagrangian dual. To this end, we write down the Lagrangian

$$L(x, y, \lambda) = e^{-x} + \lambda \frac{x^2}{y}$$

and derive that

$$g(\lambda) = \inf_{(x,y) \in D} L(x, y, \lambda) = 0$$

for every $\lambda \geq 0$. Thus, $g(\lambda)$ is a lower bound for the optimal value of (5.11), but there is no λ that makes $g(\lambda)$ equal to 1. Hence, strong duality fails in this case.

5.2 The Conjugate Function

We now introduce a notion that is closely related to Lagrangian dual and often useful in deriving duals of optimization problems.

Definition 5.6 (Conjugate function). For a function $f: \mathbb{R}^n \to \mathbb{R} \cup \{+\infty\}$, its conjugate $f^*: \mathbb{R}^n \to \mathbb{R} \cup \{+\infty\}$ is defined as

$$f^*(y) := \sup_{x \in \mathbb{R}^n} \langle y, x \rangle - f(x),$$

for $y \in \mathbb{R}^n$.

When f is a univariate function, the conjugate function has a particularly intuitive geometric interpretation. Suppose for a moment that f is strictly convex and that the derivative of f attains all real values. Then for every value of the angle θ, there exists a unique line that is tangent to the plot of f and has slope θ. The value of $f^*(\theta)$ is then (the negative of) the intersection of this line with the y-axis. One can then think of f^* as an alternative encoding of f using a different coordinate system.

Examples of conjugate functions.

(1) If $f(x) := ax + b$, then $f^*(a) = -b$ and $f^*(y) = \infty$ for $y \neq a$.
(2) If $f(x) := \frac{1}{2}x^2$, then $f^*(y) = \frac{1}{2}y^2$.
(3) If $f(x) := x \log x$, then $f^*(y) = e^{y-1}$.

Recall that a function $g: \mathbb{R}^n \to \mathbb{R}$ is said to be closed if it maps every closed set $K \subseteq \mathbb{R}^n$ to a closed set. For instance $g(x) := e^x$ is not closed as $g(\mathbb{R}) = (0, +\infty)$, while $\mathbb{R}$ is a closed set and $(0, +\infty)$ is not. One property of f^* is that it is closed and convex.

Lemma 5.7 (Conjugate function is closed and convex). *For every function f (convex or not), its conjugate f^* is convex and closed.*

Proof: This follows directly from the definition as f^* is a pointwise supremum of a set of convex (linear) functions, hence it is convex and closed. ∎

Another simple, yet useful conclusion of the definition is the following inequality.

Lemma 5.8 (Young-Fenchel inequality). *Let $f: \mathbb{R}^n \to \mathbb{R} \cup \{+\infty\}$ be any function, then for all $x, y \in \mathbb{R}^n$, we have*

$$f(x) + f^*(y) \geq \langle x, y \rangle.$$

The following fact that explains the name "conjugate" function – the conjugation operation is in fact an involution, and applying it twice brings the original function back. Clearly, this cannot hold in general, as we observed that f^* is always convex, but in fact not much more than convexity is required.

Lemma 5.9 (Conjugate of conjugate). *If* $f : \mathbb{R}^n \to \mathbb{R}^n$ *is a convex and closed function, then* $(f^*)^* = f$.

Finally, we present a lemma that is useful in viewing the gradient of a convex function as a mapping that is invertible.

Lemma 5.10 (The inverse of the gradient map). *Suppose that* f *is closed and convex. Then* $y \in \partial f(x)$ *if and only if* $x \in \partial f^*(y)$.

Proof: Given a $y \in \partial f(x)$, it follows from Definition 3.4 that for all u,

$$f(u) \geq f(x) + \langle y, u - x \rangle. \tag{5.12}$$

Hence,

$$f^*(y) = \sup_u (\langle y, u \rangle - f(u)) = \max_u (\langle y, u \rangle - f(u)) \leq \langle y, x \rangle - f(x). \tag{5.13}$$

The first equality is the definition of f^*, the second equality follows from the fact that f is closed, and the last inequality follows from 5.12 (in fact, it is an equality). However, for any v,

$$f^*(v) \geq \langle v, x \rangle - f(x) = \langle v - y, x \rangle - f(x) + \langle y, x \rangle \geq \langle v - y, x \rangle + f^*(y),$$

where the inequality follows from the definition of f^* and the last inequality follows from (5.13). From Definition 3.4, this implies that $x \in \partial f^*(y)$.

For the other direction, let $g := f^*$. Then, by Lemma 5.7, g is closed and convex. Thus, we can use the above argument for g to deduce that if $x \in \partial g(y)$, then $y \in \partial g^*(x)$. By Lemma 5.9, we know that $g^* = f$ and, hence, the claim follows. ∎

The conjugate function is a fundamental object in convex analysis and optimization. For instance, as we see in some of the exercises, the Lagrangian dual $g(\lambda, \mu)$ can sometimes be expressed in terms of the conjugate of the primal objective function.

5.3 KKT Optimality Conditions

We now introduce the Kahn-Karush-Tucker (KKT) optimality conditions for the pair of primal and dual programs introduced in Definitions 5.1 and 5.2.

Definition 5.11 (KKT conditions). Let $f, f_1, \ldots, f_m, h_1, \ldots, h_p \colon \mathbb{R}^n \to \mathbb{R}$ be functions in variables $x_1, \ldots, x_n$. Let $L(x, \lambda, \mu)$ and $g(\lambda, \mu)$ be functions as defined in Equations (5.3) and (5.4) in dual variables $\lambda_1, \ldots, \lambda_m$ and $\mu_1, \ldots, \mu_p$. Then, $x^\star \in \mathbb{R}^n$, $\lambda^\star \in \mathbb{R}^m$, and $\mu^\star \in \mathbb{R}^p$ are said to satisfy KKT optimality conditions if:

(1) **Primal feasibility:** $f_j(x^\star) \leq 0$ for $j = 1, \ldots, m$ and $h_i(x^\star) = 0$ for $i = 1, \ldots, p$,
(2) **Dual feasibility:** $\lambda^\star \geq 0$,
(3) **Stationarity:** $\partial_x L(x^\star, \lambda^\star, \mu^\star) = 0$, where ∂_x denotes the subgradient set with respect to the x variables, and
(4) **Complementary slackness:** $\lambda_j^\star f_j(x^\star) = 0$ for $j = 1, \ldots, m$.

We now show that strong duality along with primal and dual feasibility are equivalent to the KKT conditions. This is sometimes useful in solving a convex optimization problem.

Theorem 5.12 (Equivalence of strong duality and KKT conditions). *Let $x^\star$ and $(\lambda^\star, \mu^\star)$ be primal and dual feasible points. Then they satisfy the remaining KKT conditions if $f(x^\star) = g(\lambda^\star, \mu^\star)$. In addition, if the functions f and $f_1, \ldots, f_m$ are convex, and the functions $h_1, \ldots, h_p$ are affine, the converse is also true.*

Proof: Assume strong duality holds. Then we have the following:

$$
\begin{aligned}
f(x^\star) &= g(\lambda^\star, \mu^\star) \\
&= \inf_x L(x, \lambda^\star, \mu^\star) \\
&= \inf_x \left(f(x) + \sum_{j=1}^m \lambda_i^\star f_i(x) + \sum_{i=1}^p \mu_i^\star h_i(x) \right) \\
&\leq f(x^\star) + \sum_{j=1}^m \lambda_j^\star f_j(x^\star) + \sum_{i=1}^p \mu_i^\star h_i(x^\star) \\
&\leq f(x^\star).
\end{aligned}
$$

Here, the last inequality follows from primal and dual feasibility. Thus, all of the inequalities above should be equalities. Hence, from the tightness of the first inequality we deduce the stationarity condition, and from the tightness of the second inequality we deduce the complementary slackness condition. The converse is left as an exercise (Exercise 5.15). ∎

5.4 Proof of Strong Duality under Slater's Condition

Here we prove Theorem 5.5, assuming that the convex program (5.2) satisfies Slater's condition and that $y^\star$ is finite. For simplicity, we assume that there are no equality constraints ($p = 0$). Key to the proof is the following set:

$$\mathcal{C} := \{(w, u) \in \mathbb{R} \times \mathbb{R}^m : f(x) \leq w, \ f_i(x) \leq u_i \ \forall i \in [m], \text{for some } x \in \mathbb{R}^n\}.$$

It is straightforward to verify that $\mathcal{C}$ is convex and upwardly closed: For any $(w, u) \in \mathcal{C}$ and any (w', u') such that $u' \geq u$ and $w' \geq w$, we have $(w', u') \in \mathcal{C}$.

Let $y^\star$ be the optimal value to the convex program (5.2) (we assume it is finite). Then, observe that $(y^\star, 0)$ cannot be in the interior of the set $\mathcal{C}$, as otherwise $y^\star$ is not optimal. Thus, $(y^\star, 0)$ is on the boundary of $\mathcal{C}$. Thus, from Theorem 3.11, we obtain that there is a $(\lambda_0, \lambda) \neq 0$ such that

$$\langle (\lambda_0, \lambda), (w, u) \rangle \geq \lambda_0 y^\star \ \forall (w, u) \in \mathcal{C}. \tag{5.14}$$

From this, we deduce that that $\lambda \geq 0$ and $\lambda_0 \geq 0$ as, otherwise, we could make the left-hand side of the inequality above arbitrarily negative, contradicting that $y^\star$ is finite. Now, there are two possibilities:

(1) $\lambda_0 = 0$: Then $\lambda \neq 0$ and, on the one hand,

$$\inf_{(w, u) \in \mathcal{C}} \langle \lambda, u \rangle = 0.$$

On the other hand,

$$\inf_{(w, u) \in \mathcal{C}} \langle \lambda, u \rangle = \inf_x \sum_{i=1}^m \lambda_i f_i(x) \leq \sum_{i=1}^m \lambda_i f_i(\bar{x}) < 0,$$

where in the last inequality we have used the fact that $\lambda \neq 0$ and the existence of a point $\bar{x}$ that satisfies Slater's condition. This gives a contradiction, hence $\lambda_0 > 0$.

(2) $\lambda_0 > 0$: In this case, we can divide (5.14) by λ_0 to obtain

$$\inf_{(w, u) \in \mathcal{C}} \langle \lambda/\lambda_0, u \rangle + w \geq y^\star.$$

Thus, letting $\hat{\lambda} := \lambda/\lambda_0$, we obtain

$$g(\hat{\lambda}) = \inf_x \left\{ f(x) + \sum_i \hat{\lambda}_i f_i(x) \right\} \geq y^\star.$$

Maximizing the left-hand side for all $\hat{\lambda} \geq 0$, we obtain the nontrivial side of strong duality, proving the theorem.

Observe that Slater's condition does not hold for the convex optimization problem 5.11.

5.5 Exercises

5.1   Prove that the dual function g in Definition 5.2 is concave irrespective of whether the primal problem is convex or not.

5.2   **Univariate duality.** Consider the following optimization problem:

$$\min_{x \in \mathbb{R}} \ x^2 + 2x + 4$$

$$\text{such that } x^2 - 4x \leq -3$$

(a) Solve this problem, i.e., find the optimal solution.

(b) Is this a convex program?

(c) Derive the dual problem $\max_{\lambda \geq 0} g(\lambda)$. Find g and its domain.

(d) Prove that weak duality holds.

(e) Is Slater's condition satisfied? Does strong duality hold?

5.3   **Duality for linear programs.** Consider the linear program in the canonical form:

$$\min_{x \in \mathbb{R}^n} \ \langle c, x \rangle$$

$$\text{such that } Ax = b,$$

$$x \geq 0.$$

Derive its Lagrangian dual and try to arrive at the simplest possible form. *Hint:* Represent equality constraints $\langle a_i, x \rangle = b_i$ as $\langle a_i, x \rangle \leq b_i$ and $-\langle a_i, x \rangle \leq -b_i$.

5.4   **Shortest vector in an affine space.** Consider the following optimization problem

$$\min_{x \in \mathbb{R}^n} \ \|x\|^2 \tag{5.15}$$

$$\text{such that } \langle a, x \rangle = b, \tag{5.16}$$

where $a \in \mathbb{R}^n$ is a vector and $b \in \mathbb{R}$. The above represents the problem of finding the (squared) distance from the hyperplane $\{x : \langle a, x \rangle = b\}$ to the origin.

(a) Is this a convex program?

(b) Derive the dual problem.

(c) Solve the dual program, i.e., derive a formula for its optimal solution.

5.5   Prove that the conjugate functions of the following functions are as specified:

(a) If $f(x) := ax + b$, then $f^*(a) = -b$ and $f^*(y) = \infty$ for $y \neq a$.

(b) If $f(x) := \frac{1}{2}x^2$, then $f^*(y) = \frac{1}{2}y^2$.

(c) If $f(x) := x \log x$, then $f^*(y) = e^{y-1}$.

5.6   Fill in the details of the proof of Lemma 5.7.

5.7   Prove Lemma 5.9.

5.8   Let $f(x) := \|x\|$ for some norm $\| \cdot \| \colon \mathbb{R}^n \to \mathbb{R}$. Prove that $f^*(y) = 0$ if $\|y\|^* \le 1$ and ∞ otherwise.

5.9   Write the conjugate dual of the following functions:

(a) $f(x) := |x|$.

(b) For a positive definite matrix X, let $f(X) := \mathrm{Tr}(X \log X)$.

5.10 Given a function $f \colon \mathbb{R} \to \mathbb{R}$ and numbers $\eta \neq 0$ and c, write down the conjugate dual of the function $\eta f + c$.

5.11 Consider the primal problem where $f_j(x) := \langle a_j, x \rangle - b_j$ for some vectors $a_1, \ldots, a_m \in \mathbb{R}^n$ and $b_1, \ldots, b_m \in \mathbb{R}$. Prove that the dual is

$$g(\lambda) = -\langle b, \lambda \rangle - f^*(-A^\top \lambda),$$

where A is the $m \times n$ matrix whose rows are the vectors a_j.

5.12 Write the dual of the primal convex optimization problem over the set real $n \times n$ PD matrices X for $f(X) := -\log \det X$ and $f_j(X) := a_j^\top X a_j$ for $j = 1, \ldots, m$ where $a_j \in \mathbb{R}^n$.

5.13 **Lagrange-Hamilton duality in physics.** Consider a particle with unit mass in one dimension and let $V \colon \mathbb{R} \to \mathbb{R}$ be a potential function. In Lagrangian dynamics, one typically denotes the position of a particle by q and its (generalized) velocity by $\dot{q}$, as it is normally a time derivative of the position. The **Lagrangian** of the particle is defined as

$$L(q, \dot{q}) := \frac{1}{2}\dot{q}^2 - V(q).$$

The **Hamiltonian**, on the other hand, is defined with respect to a momentum variable, denoted by p as

$$H(q, p) := V(q) + \frac{1}{2}p^2.$$

Prove that the Hamiltonian is the Legendre-Fenchel dual of the Lagrangian:

$$H(q, p) = \max_{\dot{q}} \langle \dot{q}, p \rangle - L(q, \dot{q}).$$

5.14 **Polars and convexity.** For a set $S \subseteq \mathbb{R}^n$, define its *polar* S° as

$$S^\circ := \{ y \in \mathbb{R}^n \colon \langle x, y \rangle \le 1, \text{ for all } x \in S \}.$$

(a) Prove that $0 \in S^\circ$ and S° is convex, whether S is convex or not.

(b) Write the polar of a halfspace $S = \{x \in \mathbb{R}^n : \langle a, x \rangle \leq b\}$.

(c) Write the polar of $S = \{x \in \mathbb{R}^n : x_1, x_2, \ldots, x_n \geq 0\}$ (the positive orthant) and the polar of the set of PSD matrices.

(d) What is the polar of a polytope $S = \text{conv}\{x_1, x_2, \ldots, x_m\}$? Here $x_1, x_2, \ldots, x_m \in \mathbb{R}^n$.

(e) Prove that if S contains the origin along with a ball of radius $r > 0$ around it, then S° is contained in a ball of radius $\frac{1}{r}$.

(f) Let S be a closed convex subset of $\mathbb{R}^n$, and suppose we have access to an oracle, which given $c \in \mathbb{Q}^n$ outputs[2] $\text{argmin}_{x \in S} \langle c, x \rangle$. Construct an efficient separation oracle for S°.[3]

5.15 Prove the converse direction in Theorem 5.12.

5.16 Consider the primal problem where $f, f_1, \ldots, f_m : \mathbb{R}^n \to \mathbb{R}$ are convex and there are no equality constraints. Suppose $x^\star$ and $\lambda^\star$ satisfy the KKT conditions. Prove that

$$\langle \nabla f(x), x - x^\star \rangle \geq 0$$

for all feasible x (Theorem 3.14).

5.17 ℓ_1-**minimization.** For a matrix $A \in \mathbb{R}^{m \times n}$ and a vector $b \in \mathbb{R}^m$, consider the following convex program:

$$\min_{Ax=b} \|x\|_1 . \tag{5.17}$$

Prove that, if for a feasible solution $z \in \mathbb{R}^n$ (i.e., $Az = b$), there exists a $\lambda \in \mathbb{R}^m$ such that

(a) $(A^\top \lambda)_i = \text{sgn}(z_i)$ for all i such that $z_i \neq 0$, and

(b) $|(A^\top \lambda)_i| \leq 1$ for all i such that $z_i = 0$,

then z is the optimal solution to the program in Equation (5.17). Furthermore, prove that if the columns of A corresponding to the nonzero entries of z are linearly independent, and if the inequalities in (b) are strict, then z is the unique optimum.

5.18 **Eisenberg-Gale convex program.** Let G be a finite set of *divisible goods* and B be a finite set of *buyers*. For $j \in G$ and $i \in B$, let $U_{ij} \geq 0$ denote the *utility* derived by buyer i on obtaining a unit amount of good j. Assume that for every $i \in B$ there is a $j \in G$ such that $U_{ij} > 0$,

---

[2] We assume that the output of this oracle is always a vector with rational entries, and the bit complexity of the output is polynomial in the bit complexity of c. Such oracles exist in particular for certain important classes of polytopes with rational vertices.

[3] As we will see later in the book, the converse of this theorem is also true.

and similarly, for every $j \in G$ there is an $i \in B$ such that $U_{ij} > 0$. Consider the following nonlinear convex program with *allocation variables* $x_{ij} \geq 0$ for $i \in B$ and $j \in G$:

$$\max_{x \in \mathbb{R}_{\geq 0}^{B \times G}} \sum_{i \in B} \log \sum_{j \in G} U_{ij} x_{ij}$$

$$\text{such that } \sum_{i \in B} x_{ij} \leq 1, \qquad \forall j \in G.$$

For $j \in G$, let $p_j \geq 0$ denote the Lagrangian dual variable corresponding to the jth inequality constraint (the *price* of the jth good) in the program above.

(a) Prove that strong duality holds for the Eisenberg-Gale convex program.

(b) Prove that the corresponding KKT conditions are as follows:

(1) $\forall i \in B$ and $\forall j \in G$, $x_{ij} \geq 0$,

(2) $\forall j \in G$, $p_j \geq 0$,

(3) $\forall j \in G$, if $p_j > 0$, then $\sum_{i \in B} x_{ij} = 1$,

(4) $\forall i \in B$ and $\forall j \in G$, $\dfrac{U_{ij}}{\sum_{k \in G} U_{ik} x_{ik}} \leq p_j$, and

(5) $\forall i \in B$ and $\forall j \in G$, if $x_{ij} > 0$, then $\dfrac{U_{ij}}{\sum_{k \in G} U_{ik} x_{ik}} = p_j$.

(c) Let $x^\star$ and $p^\star$ be such that they satisfy the KKT conditions. Prove that

(1) $p_j^\star > 0$, for all $j \in G$, and

(2) $\sum_{j \in G} p_j^\star x_{ij}^\star = 1$, for all $i \in B$.

(d) Prove that if $U_{ij} \in \mathbb{Q}_{\geq 0}$ for all $j \in G$ and $i \in B$, then $x^\star$ and $p^\star$ can be chosen to have rational entries as well. Thus, the Eisenberg-Gale convex program is an example of a rational convex program (see the notes in Chapter 4 for a definition).

Notes

The book by Boyd and Vandenberghe (2004) provides a thorough treatment of Lagrangian duality, conjugate functions, and KKT optimality conditions. The reader looking for additional examples and exercises is referred this book.

Chapter IV in the book by Barvinok (2002) discusses polarity and convexity (introduced in Exercise 5.14) in detail.

Exercise 5.18 is from the paper by Eisenberg and Gale (1959). See the papers by Devanur et al. (2016) and Garg et al. (2013) for a wider class of nonlinear convex programs that appear in the area of equilibrium computation.

6

Gradient Descent

The remainder of the book is devoted to the design and analysis of algorithms for convex optimization. We start by presenting the gradient descent method and show how it can be viewed as a steepest descent. Subsequently, we prove a convergence time bound on the gradient descent method when the gradient of the function is Lipschitz continuous. Finally, we use the gradient descent method to come up with a fast algorithm for a discrete optimization problem: computing maximum flow in an undirected graph.

6.1 The Setup

We first consider the problem of unconstrained minimization

$$\min_{x \in \mathbb{R}^n} f(x),$$

when only a first-order oracle to a convex function f is given, i.e., we can query the gradient of f at any point; see Definition 4.5. Let $y^\star$ be the optimal value for this function and assume that $x^\star$ is a point that achieves this value: $f(x^\star) = y^\star$. Our notion of a solution is an algorithm (could be randomized), which, given access to f and given $\varepsilon > 0$, outputs a point $x \in \mathbb{R}^n$ such that

$$f(x) \leq f(x^\star) + \varepsilon.$$

Recall that one measures the running time of such an algorithm as a function of the number of bits required to represent ε and the number of oracle calls to the gradient of f. We note that while we are not charged for the time it takes to compute $\nabla f(x)$ given x, the running time depends on the bit length of x and that of $\nabla f(x)$. While we normally regard such an algorithm as a polynomial time algorithm if its total running time is polynomial in $\log \frac{1}{\varepsilon}$ and it outputs the right answer with high probability, in this chapter we present algorithms with running times proportional to some polynomial in $\frac{1}{\varepsilon}$.

6.2 Gradient Descent

Gradient descent is not a single method but a general framework with many possible realizations. We describe some concrete variants and present guarantees on their running times. The performance guarantees that we are going to obtain depend on the assumptions that we make about f. We first describe the core ideas of the gradient descent methods in the unconstrained setting, i.e., $K := \mathbb{R}^n$. In Section 6.3.2, we discuss the constrained setting.

The general scheme of gradient descent is summarized below.

(1) Choose a starting point $x_0 \in \mathbb{R}^n$.
(2) For some $t \geq 0$, suppose $x_0, \ldots, x_t$ have already been computed. Choose x_{t+1} as a linear combination of x_t and $\nabla f(x_t)$.
(3) Stop once a certain stopping criterion is met and output the last iterate.

Let x_t denote the point chosen in Step 2 of this algorithm at the tth iteration and let T be the total number of iterations performed. T is usually given as a part of the input, but it could also be implied by a given stopping criteria. The running time for the algorithm is $O(T \cdot M)$, where M is an upper bound on the time of each update, including that of finding the starting point. Normally, the update time M is something that cannot be optimized below a certain level (for a fixed function f) and, hence, the main goal is to design methods with T as small as possible.

6.2.1 Why Descend along the Gradient?

In what follows we motivate one possible method for choosing the next iteration point x_{t+1} from x_t. Since the process we are about to describe can use only the local information about f, it makes sense to pick a direction that locally maximizes the rate of decrease of the function value – the direction of **steepest descent** (Figure 6.1). More formally, we would like to pick a unit vector u for which the rate at which f decreases is maximized. Such a direction is captured by the following optimization problem:

$$\max_{\|u\|=1} \left[\lim_{\delta \to 0} \frac{f(x) - f(x + \delta u)}{\delta} \right].$$

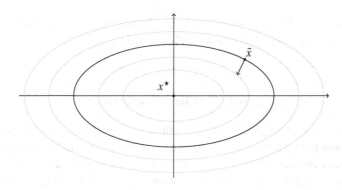

Figure 6.1 The steepest descent direction for the function $x_1^2 + 4x_2^2$ at $\tilde{x} = (\sqrt{2}, \sqrt{2})$.

The expression inside the limit is simply the negative directional derivative of f at x in direction u and, thus, we obtain

$$\max_{\|u\|=1} \left(-Df(x)[u]\right) = \max_{\|u\|=1} \left(-\langle \nabla f(x), u \rangle\right). \tag{6.1}$$

We claim that the above is maximized at

$$u^\star := -\frac{\nabla f(x)}{\|\nabla f(x)\|}.$$

Indeed, consider any point u with norm 1. From the Cauchy-Schwarz inequality (Theorem 2.15), we have

$$-\langle \nabla f(x), u \rangle \leq \|\nabla f(x)\| \, \|u\| = \|\nabla f(x)\|,$$

and the equality is attained at $u = u^\star$. Thus, the negative of the gradient at the current point is the direction of steepest descent. This instantaneous direction at each point x gives rise to a continuous-time dynamical system (Definition 2.19) called the **gradient flow** of f:

$$\frac{dx}{dt} = -\frac{\nabla f(x)}{\|\nabla f(x)\|}.$$

However, to implement the strategy in an algorithm, we should consider discretizations of the differential equations above. Since we assume first-order access to f, a natural discretization is the so-called Euler discretization (Definition 2.19):

$$x_{t+1} = x_t - \alpha \frac{\nabla f(x_t)}{\|\nabla f(x_t)\|}, \tag{6.2}$$

where $\alpha > 0$ is the "step length," i.e., how far we move along $u^\star$. Since $\frac{1}{\|\nabla f(x_t)\|}$ is only a normalization factor, we can omit it and arrive at the gradient descent update rule

$$x_{t+1} = x_t - \eta \nabla f(x_t), \tag{6.3}$$

where, again, $\eta > 0$ is a parameter – the step length (which we might also make depend on the time t or the point x_t). In machine learning, η is often called the **learning rate.**

6.2.2 Assumptions on the Function, Gradient, and Starting Point

While moving in the direction of the negative gradient is a good instantaneous strategy, it is far from clear how big a step to take. Ideally, we would like to take big steps, hoping for a smaller number of iterations, but there is also a danger. The view we have of the function at the current point is local and implicitly assumes the function is linear. However, the function can change or bend quite dramatically, and taking a long step can lead to a large error. This is one of many issues that can arise.

To bypass this and related problems, it is customary to make assumptions on the function in terms of parameters such as the **Lipschitz constant** of the function f or its gradient. These are natural measures of how "complicated" f is, and thus how hard to optimize f could be, using a first-order oracle. Therefore, these "regularity parameters" often show up in the running time guarantees for the optimization algorithms we develop. Moreover, when designing methods with oracle access to f only, it is natural to provide as input an additional point $x_0 \in \mathbb{R}^n$ that is not "too far" from an optimal solution, as otherwise, it is not even clear where such an algorithm should start its search. More formally, we list the kind of assumptions that show up in the theorems below. We begin with a definition.

Definition 6.1 (Lipschitz continuity). For a pair of arbitrary norms $\|\cdot\|_a$ and $\|\cdot\|_b$ on $\mathbb{R}^n$ and $\mathbb{R}^m$, respectively, and an $L > 0$, a function $g : \mathbb{R}^n \to \mathbb{R}^m$ is said to be L-Lipschitz continuous if for all $x, y \in \mathbb{R}^n$,

$$\|g(x) - g(y)\|_b \le L\|x - y\|_a.$$

L is called the corresponding Lipschitz constant.

The Lipschitz constant of the same function can vary dramatically with the choice of the norms. Unless specified, we assume that both the norms are $\|\cdot\|_2$.

(1) **Lipschitz continuous gradient.** Suppose f is differentiable, and for every $x, y \in \mathbb{R}^n$, we have

$$\|\nabla f(x) - \nabla f(y)\| \leq L \|x - y\|,$$

where $L > 0$ is a possibly large but finite constant.

This is also sometimes referred to as the L-**smoothness** of f. This condition ensures that around x, the gradient changes in a controlled manner and, thus, the gradient flow trajectories can only "bend" in a controlled manner. The smaller the L is, the larger the step size we can think of taking.

(2) **Bounded gradient.** For every $x \in \mathbb{R}^n$, we have

$$\|\nabla f(x)\| \leq G,$$

where $G \in \mathbb{Q}$ is a possibly large but finite constant.[1] It is an exercise to show that this condition implies that f is a G-Lipschitz continuous function (Exercise 6.1). This quantity essentially controls how quickly the function can go towards infinity. The smaller G is, the slower this growth is.

(3) **Good initial point.** A point $x_0 \in \mathbb{Q}^n$ is provided such that $\|x_0 - x^\star\| \leq D$, where $x^\star$ is some optimal solution to (4.1).[2]

We now state the main result that we prove in this chapter.

Theorem 6.2 (Guarantees on gradient descent for Lipschitz continuous gradient). *There is an algorithm that, given first-order oracle (see Definition 4.5) access to a convex function $f: \mathbb{R}^n \to \mathbb{R}$, a bound L on the Lipschitz constant of its gradient, an initial point $x_0 \in \mathbb{R}^n$, value D such that $\max\{\|x - x^\star\| : f(x) \leq f(x_0)\} \leq D$ (where $x^\star$ is an optimal solution to $\min_{x \in \mathbb{R}^n} f(x)$), and an $\varepsilon > 0$, outputs a point $x \in \mathbb{R}^n$ such that $f(x) \leq f(x^\star) + \varepsilon$. The algorithm makes $T = O\left(\frac{LD^2}{\varepsilon}\right)$ queries to the first-order oracle for f and performs $O(nT)$ arithmetic operations.*

We note that while in this chapter we only prove the theorem in the above variant, one can alternatively use a weaker condition, $\|x_0 - x^\star\| \leq D$, to arrive at the same conclusion. In Chapter 7, we prove a similar result that gives an

---

[1] We assume here that the bound on the gradient is valid for all $x \in \mathbb{R}^n$. One might often relax it to just x over a suitably large set $X \subseteq \mathbb{R}^n$, which contains x_0 and an optimal solution $x^\star$. This requires one to prove that the algorithm "stays in X" for the whole computation.

[2] There might be more than just one optimal solution; here it is enough that the distance to any one of them is small.

algorithm that can compute an ε-approximate solution under the condition that the gradient is bounded by G and makes $T = O\left(\left(\frac{DG}{\varepsilon}\right)^2\right)$ queries to the first-order oracle for f.

Before going any further, one might wonder if it is reasonable to assume knowledge of parameters such as G, L, and D of the function f in Theorem 6.2, especially when the access to the function is black box only. While for D it is often possible to obtain sensible bounds on the solution, finding G or L might be more difficult. However, one can often try to set these values adaptively. As an example, it is possible to start with a guess G_0 (or equivalently L_0) and update the guess given the outcome of the gradient descent. Should the algorithm "fail" (the gradient at the point at the end of the gradient descent algorithm is not small enough) for this value of G_0, we can double the constant $G_1 = 2G_0$. Otherwise, we can halve the constant $G_1 = \frac{1}{2}G_0$ and so on.

In practice, especially in machine learning applications, these quantities are often known up to a good precision and are often considered to be constants. Under such an assumption, the number of oracle calls performed by the respective algorithms are $O\left(\frac{1}{\varepsilon^2}\right)$ and $O\left(\frac{1}{\varepsilon}\right)$ and do not depend on the dimension n. Therefore, such algorithms are often referred to as **dimension-free,** their convergence rate, as measured in the number of **iterations** (as clarified later) does not depend on n but only on certain regularity parameters of f. In theoretical computer science applications, an important aspect is to find formulations where these quantities are small, and this is often the key challenge.

6.3 Analysis When the Gradient Is Lipschitz Continuous

This section is devoted to proving Theorem 6.2. We start by stating an appropriate variant of the gradient descent algorithm and, subsequently, provide its analysis. In Algorithm 1, the values D and L are as in the statement of Theorem 6.2.

Before we present the proof of Theorem 6.2, we need to establish an important lemma that shows how to upper bound the Bregman divergence (Definition 3.9), using our assumption on the gradient of f.

Lemma 6.3 (Upper bound on the Bregman divergence for L-smooth functions). *Suppose that $f \colon \mathbb{R}^n \to \mathbb{R}$ is a differentiable function that satisfies*

Algorithm 1: Gradient descent when the gradient is Lipschitz continuous

Input:
- First-order oracle for a convex f
- A bound $L \in \mathbb{Q}_{>0}$ on the Lipschitz constant of the gradient of f
- A bound $D \in \mathbb{Q}_{>0}$ on the distance to optimal solution D
- A starting point $x_0 \in \mathbb{Q}^n$
- An $\varepsilon > 0$

Output: A point x such that $f(x) - f(x^\star) \leq \varepsilon$

Algorithm:
1: Set $T := O\left(\frac{LD^2}{\varepsilon}\right)$
2: Set $\eta := \frac{1}{L}$
3: **for** $t = 0, 1, \ldots, T - 1$ **do**
4:     $x_{t+1} = x_t - \eta \nabla f(x_t)$
5: **end for**
6: **return** x_T

$\|\nabla f(x) - \nabla f(y)\| \leq L \|x - y\|$ *for every* $x, y \in \mathbb{R}^n$. *Then, for every* $x, y \in \mathbb{R}^n$, *it holds that*

$$f(y) - f(x) - \langle \nabla f(x), y - x \rangle \leq \frac{L}{2} \|x - y\|^2. \tag{6.4}$$

We note that this lemma does not assume that f is convex. However, if f is convex, then the distance in the left-hand side of Equation (6.4) is nonnegative. See Figure 6.2 for an illustration. Moreover, when f is convex, (6.4) is equivalent to the condition that the gradient of f is L-Lipschitz continuous; see Exercise 6.2.

Proof: For fixed x and y, consider a univariate function

$$g(\lambda) := f((1 - \lambda)x + \lambda y)$$

for $\lambda \in [0, 1]$. We have $g(0) = f(x)$ and $g(1) = f(y)$. Since g is differentiable, from the fundamental theorem of calculus we have

$$\int_0^1 \dot{g}(\lambda) d\lambda = f(y) - f(x).$$

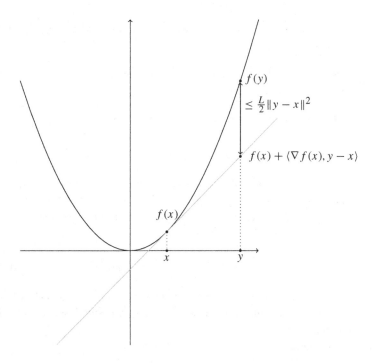

Figure 6.2 for a convex function f, the gap at y between the value of f and the first-order approximation of f at x is nonnegative and bounded from above by a quadratic function $\frac{L}{2}\|x - y\|^2$ when the gradient of f is L-Lipschitz continuous.

Since $\dot{g}(\lambda) = \langle \nabla f((1 - \lambda)x + \lambda y), y - x \rangle$ (using the chain rule), we have that

$$f(y) - f(x)$$

$$= \int_0^1 \langle \nabla f((1 - \lambda)x + \lambda y), y - x \rangle \, d\lambda$$

$$= \int_0^1 \langle \nabla f(x), y - x \rangle \, d\lambda + \int_0^1 \langle \nabla f((1 - \lambda)x + \lambda y) - \nabla f(x), y - x \rangle \, d\lambda$$

$$\leq \langle \nabla f(x), y - x \rangle + \int_0^1 \|\nabla f((1 - \lambda)x + \lambda y) - \nabla f(x)\| \, \|y - x\| \, d\lambda$$

$$\leq \langle \nabla f(x), y - x \rangle + \|x - y\| \int_0^1 L \, \|\lambda(y - x)\| \, d\lambda$$

$$\leq \langle \nabla f(x), y - x \rangle + \frac{L}{2} \|x - y\|^2,$$

where we have used the Cauchy-Schwarz inequality and the L-Lipschitz continuity of the gradient of f.   ∎

Proof of Theorem 6.2: Let us examine the evolution of the error as we iterate. We first use Lemma 6.3 to obtain

$$f(x_{t+1}) - f(x_t) \le \langle \nabla f(x_t), x_{t+1} - x_t \rangle + \frac{L}{2} \|x_{t+1} - x_t\|^2$$

$$= -\eta \|\nabla f(x_t)\|^2 + \frac{L\eta^2}{2} \|\nabla f(x_t)\|^2 .$$

Since we wish to maximize the drop in the function value $(f(x_t) - f(x_{t+1}))$, we should choose η to be as large as possible. The right-hand side is a convex function of η, and a simple calculation shows that it is minimized when $\eta = \frac{1}{L}$. Substituting it, we obtain

$$f(x_{t+1}) - f(x_t) \le -\frac{1}{2L} \|\nabla f(x_t)\|^2 . \tag{6.5}$$

Intuitively, (6.5) suggests that if the norm of the gradient $\|\nabla f(x_t)\|$ is large, we make good progress. On the other hand, if $\|\nabla f(x_t)\|$ is small, we are already close to the optimum.

Let us now denote

$$R_t := f(x_t) - f(x^\star),$$

which measures how far the current objective value is from the optimal value. Note that R_t is nonincreasing, and we would like to find the smallest t for which it is below ε. Let us start by noting that $R_0 \le LD^2$. This is because

$$R_0 \le \|\nabla f(x_0)\| \cdot \|x_0 - x^\star\| \le D \|\nabla f(x_0)\| . \tag{6.6}$$

The first inequality in (6.6) follows from the first-order characterization of convexity of f and the second inequality follows (vacuously) from the definition of D. The optimality of $x^\star$ (Theorem 3.13) implies that $\nabla f(x^\star) = 0$. Therefore, by the L-smoothness of f, we obtain

$$\|\nabla f(x_0)\| = \|\nabla f(x_0) - \nabla f(x^\star)\| \le L\|x_0 - x^\star\| \le LD. \tag{6.7}$$

Combining (6.6) and (6.7), we obtain that $R_0 \le LD^2$.

Further, from (6.5) we know that

$$R_t - R_{t+1} \ge \frac{1}{2L} \|\nabla f(x_t)\|^2 .$$

Again, by convexity of f and the Cauchy-Schwarz inequality, we obtain

$$R_t \le f(x_t) - f(x^\star) \le \langle \nabla f(x_t), x_t - x^\star \rangle \le \|\nabla f(x_t)\| \cdot \|x_t - x^\star\| .$$

Note that we can bound $\|x_t - x^\star\|$ by D (by the assumption in the theorem) since $f(x_t)$ is a nonincreasing sequence in t and, hence, always at most $f(x_0)$. Hence, we obtain

$$\|\nabla f(x_t)\| \geq \frac{R_t}{D},$$

and, by (6.5),

$$R_t - R_{t+1} \geq \frac{R_t^2}{2LD^2}. \tag{6.8}$$

Thus, to bound the number of iterations to reach ε, we need to solve the following calculus problem: Given a sequence of numbers $R_0 \geq R_1 \geq R_2 \geq \cdots \geq 0$, with $R_0 \leq LD^2$ and satisfying the recursive bound (6.8), find a bound on T for which $R_T \leq \varepsilon$.

Before we give a formal proof that T can be bounded by $O\left(\frac{LD^2}{\varepsilon}\right)$, let us provide some intuition by analyzing a continuous time analogue of recursion (6.8) – it gives rise to the following dynamical system:

$$\frac{d}{dt} R(t) = -\alpha R(t)^2,$$

where $R: [0,\infty) \to \mathbb{R}$ with $R(0) = LD^2$ and $\alpha = \frac{1}{LD^2}$. To solve it, first rewrite the above as

$$\frac{d}{dt}\left[\frac{1}{R(t)}\right] = \alpha,$$

and hence we obtain

$$R(t) = \frac{1}{R(0)^{-1} + \alpha t}.$$

From this we deduce that to reach $R(t) \leq \varepsilon$, we need to take

$$t \geq \frac{1 - \frac{\varepsilon}{R(0)}}{\varepsilon \alpha} \approx \Theta\left(\frac{LD^2}{\varepsilon}\right).$$

To formalize this argument in the discrete setting (where $t = 0, 1, 2, \ldots$), the idea is to first estimate the number of steps for R_0 to drop below $R_0/2$, then to go from $R_0/2$ to $R_0/4$, then from $R_0/4$ to $R_0/8$ and so on, until we reach ε.

Given (6.8), to go from R_t to $R_t/2$ it suffices to make k steps, where

$$k \cdot \frac{(R_t/2)^2}{2LD^2} \geq R_t/2.$$

In other words, k needs to be at least $\left\lceil \frac{4LD^2}{R_t} \right\rceil$. Let $r := \left\lceil \log \frac{R_0}{\varepsilon} \right\rceil$. By repeatedly halving r times to get from R_0 to ε, the required number of steps is at most

$$\sum_{i=0}^{r} \left\lceil \frac{4LD^2}{R_0 \cdot 2^{-i}} \right\rceil \le r+1+\sum_{i=0}^{r} 2^i \frac{4LD^2}{R_0}$$

$$\le (r+1)+2^{r+1}\frac{4LD^2}{R_0}$$

$$= O\left(\frac{LD^2}{\varepsilon}\right). \qquad\blacksquare$$

6.3.1 A Lower Bound

One can ask whether the gradient descent algorithm proposed in the previous section, which performs $O(\varepsilon^{-1})$ iterations, is optimal. Consider now a general model for first-order black box minimization that includes gradient descent and many related algorithms. The algorithm is given $x_0 \in \mathbb{R}^n$ and access to a gradient oracle for a convex function $f : \mathbb{R}^n \to \mathbb{R}$. It produces a sequence of points $x_0, x_1, \ldots, x_T$ such that

$$x_t \in x_0 + \text{span}\{\nabla f(x_0), \ldots, \nabla f(x_{t-1})\}, \tag{6.9}$$

i.e., the algorithm can move only in the subspace spanned by the gradients at previous iterations. Note that gradient descent clearly follows this scheme, as

$$x_t = x_0 - \sum_{j=0}^{t-1} \eta \nabla f(x_j).$$

We do not restrict the running time of one iteration of such an algorithm; in fact we allow it to do an arbitrarily long calculation to compute x_t from $x_0, \ldots, x_{t-1}$ and the corresponding gradients. In this model we are interested only in the number of iterations. The lower bound is as follows.

Theorem 6.4 (Lower bound). *Consider any algorithm for solving the convex unconstrained minimization problem $\min_{x \in \mathbb{R}^n} f(x)$ in the model as in (6.9), when the gradient of f is Lipschitz continuous (with a constant L) and the initial point $x_0 \in \mathbb{R}^n$ satisfies $\|x_0 - x^\star\| \le D$. There is a function f such that for any $1 \le T \le \frac{n}{2}$, it holds that*

$$\min_{0 \le t \le T-1} f(x_t) - \min_{x \in \mathbb{R}^n} f(x) \ge \Omega\left(\frac{LD^2}{T^2}\right).$$

The above theorem translates to a lower bound of $\Omega\left(\frac{1}{\sqrt{\varepsilon}}\right)$ iterations to reach an ε-optimal solution. This lower bound does not quite match the upper bound of $\frac{1}{\varepsilon}$ established in Theorem 6.2. Therefore one can ask: *Is there a method that matches the above* $\frac{1}{\sqrt{\varepsilon}}$ *iterations bound?* And, surprisingly, the answer is yes. This can be achieved using the so-called **accelerated gradient descent.** This is the topic of Chapter 8. We also prove Theorem 6.4 in Exercise 8.4.

6.3.2 Projected Gradient Descent for Constrained Optimization

So far, we have discussed the unconstrained optimization problem, however, the same method can be also extended to the constrained setting, when we would like to solve

$$\min_{x \in K} f(x)$$

for a convex subset $K \subseteq \mathbb{R}^n$.

When applying the gradient descent method, the next iterate x_{t+1} might fall outside of the convex body K. In this case, we need to project it back onto K: Find the point in K with the minimum Euclidean distance to x, denoted by $\text{proj}_K(x)$. Formally, for a closed set $K \subseteq \mathbb{R}^n$ and a point $x \in \mathbb{R}^n$,

$$\text{proj}_K(x) := \underset{y \in K}{\text{argmin}} \, \|x - y\|.$$

We take the projected point to be our new iterate, i.e.,

$$x_{t+1} = \text{proj}_K \left(x_t - \eta_t \nabla f(x_t) \right).$$

This is called the **projected gradient descent** method. The convergence rate of this method remains the same (the proof carries over to this new setting by noting that $\|\text{proj}_K(x) - \text{proj}_K(y)\| \leq \|x - y\|$ for all $x, y \in \mathbb{R}^n$). However, depending on K, the projection may or may not be difficult (or computationally expensive) to perform. More precisely, as long as the algorithm has access to an oracle that, given a query point x, returns the projection $\text{proj}_K(x)$ of x onto K, we have the following analogue of Theorem 6.2.

Theorem 6.5 (Projected gradient descent for Lipchitz gradient). *There is an algorithm that, given first-order oracle access to a convex function* $f: K \to \mathbb{R}$, *access to the projection operator* $\text{proj}_K: \mathbb{R}^n \to K$, *a bound L on the Lipschitz constant of its gradient, an initial point* $x_0 \in \mathbb{R}^n$, *a value D such that* $\max \{\|x - x^\star\| : f(x) \leq f(x_0)\} \leq D$ *(where $x^\star$ is an optimal solution to* $\min_{x \in K} f(x)$), *and an $\varepsilon > 0$, outputs a point $x \in K$ such that* $f(x) \leq f(x^\star) + \varepsilon$. *The algorithm makes* $T = O\left(\frac{LD^2}{\varepsilon}\right)$ *queries to the first-order oracle for f and the projection operator* proj_K *and performs $O(nT)$ arithmetic operations.*

6.4 Application: The Maximum Flow Problem

As an application of the algorithms developed in this chapter, we present an algorithm to solve the problem of computing the $s - t$-maximum flow in an undirected graph. This is our first nontrivial example of a discrete optimization problem for which we first present a formulation as a linear program and then show how we can use continuous optimization – in this case, gradient descent – to solve the problem.

6.4.1 The $s - t$-Maximum Flow Problem

We first formally define the $s - t$-maximum flow problem. The input to this problem consists of an undirected, simple, and unweighted graph $G = (V, E)$ with $n := |V|$ and $m := |E|$, two special vertices $s \neq t \in V$, where s is the "source" and t is the "sink," and "capacities" $\rho \in \mathbb{Q}_{\geq 0}^m$. Let $B \in \mathbb{R}^{n \times m}$ denote the vertex-edge incidence matrix of the graph introduced in Section 2.9.2.

Recall also the definition of an $s - t$-flow in G from Sections 1.1 and 2.9.1. An $s - t$-flow in G is an assignment $x \colon E \to \mathbb{R}$ that satisfies the following properties.[3] For all vertices $u \in V \setminus \{s, t\}$, we require that the "incoming" flow is equal to the "outgoing" flow:

$$\langle e_u, Bx \rangle = 0.$$

An $s - t$-flow satisfies the given capacities if for all $i \in [m]$, $|x_i| \leq \rho_i$ for all $i \in [m]$. The goal is to find such a flow in G that is feasible and maximizes the flow

$$\langle e_s, Bx \rangle$$

out of s. Let $F^\star$ denote this maximum flow value.

Then, the following linear program encodes the $s - t$-maximum flow problem:

$$\max_{x \in \mathbb{R}^E, \, F \geq 0} \quad F$$
$$\text{such that} \quad Bx = Fb, \tag{6.10}$$
$$|x_i| \leq \rho_i, \quad \forall i \in [m],$$

where $b := e_s - e_t$.

---

[3] As mentioned earlier, we extend x from E to $V \times V$ as a skew-symmetric function on the edges. If the ith edge went between u and v and $b_i = e_u - e_v$, we let $x(v, u) := -x(u, v)$. If we do not wish to refer to the direction of the ith edge, we use the notation x_i.

From now on, we assume that all the capacities are one, i.e., $\rho_i = 1$ for all $i \in [m]$, and hence the last constraint in (6.10) simplifies to $\|x\|_\infty \leq 1$. The approach presented here can be extended to the general capacity case.

It is important to note that $F^\star \geq 1$ if in G there is at least one path from s to t; we assume this (we can check this property in $\widetilde{O}(m)$ time using breadth-first search). Moreover, since each edge has capacity 1, $F^\star \leq m$. Thus, not only is feasibility not an issue, but we know that $1 \leq F^\star \leq m$.

6.4.2 The Main Result

Theorem 6.6 (Algorithm for the $s - t$-maximum flow problem). *There is an algorithm, which given an undirected graph G with unit capacities, two vertices s,t and an $\varepsilon > 0$, finds an $s - t$-flow of value at least $(1 - \varepsilon)F^\star$ in time $\widetilde{O}\left(\varepsilon^{-1} \frac{m^{5/2}}{F^\star}\right).$*[4]

We do not give a fully detailed proof of the above but rather present the main steps and leave certain steps as exercises.

6.4.3 A Formulation as an Unconstrained Convex Program

The first key idea is to reformulate (6.10) as an unconstrained convex optimization problem. Note that it is already convex (in fact linear), however, we would like to avoid complicated constraints such as "$\|x\|_\infty \leq 1$." To this end, note that instead of maximizing F, we might just make a guess for F and ask if there is a flow x with value F obeying the capacity constraints. If we could solve such a decision problem efficiently, then we could solve (6.10) up to good precision by performing a binary search over F. Thus it is enough, for a given $F \in \mathbb{Q}_{\geq 0}$, to solve the following problem:

$$\text{Find} \quad x \in \mathbb{R}^m$$
$$\text{such that} \quad Bx = Fb, \tag{6.11}$$
$$\|x\|_\infty \leq 1.$$

If we denote

$$H_F := \{x \in \mathbb{R}^m : Bx = Fb\}$$

and

$$B_{m,\infty} := \{x \in \mathbb{R}^m : \|x\|_\infty \leq 1\},$$

---

[4] The notation $\widetilde{O}(f(n))$ means $O(f(n) \cdot \log^k f(n))$ for some constant $k > 0$.

then the set of solutions above is the intersection of these two convex sets, and hence the problem really asks the following question for the convex set $K := H_F \cap B_{m,\infty}$:

Is $K \neq \emptyset$? If so, find a point in K.

As we would like to use the gradient descent framework, we need to first state the above problems as a minimization problem. We have two choices to this problem as a convex optimization problem:

(1) minimize the distance of x from $B_{m,\infty}$ while constraining it to be in H_F, or
(2) minimize the distance of x from H_F while constraining it to be in $B_{m,\infty}$.

It turns out that the first formulation has the following advantage over the second: For a suitable choice of the distance function, the objective function is convex, has an easily computable first-order oracle, and, importantly, the Lipschitz constant of its gradient is $O(1)$. Thus, we reformulate (6.11) as minimizing the distance of x to $B_{m,\infty}$ over $x \in H_F$. Towards that, let P be the orthogonal projection operator $P \colon \mathbb{R}^m \to B_{m,\infty}$, given as

$$P(x) := \operatorname{argmin}\left\{\|x - y\| : y \in B_{m,\infty}\right\}.$$

The final form of (6.10) we would like to consider is

$$\min_{x \in \mathbb{R}^E} \quad \|x - P(x)\|^2 \tag{6.12}$$
$$\text{such that} \quad Bx = Fb.$$

One might be concerned about the constraint $Bx = Fb$, as so far we have mostly talked about unconstrained optimization over $\mathbb{R}^m$ – however, as it is an affine subspace of $\mathbb{R}^m$, one can easily prove that as long as we, in every step, project the gradient onto $\{x \colon Bx = 0\}$, then the conclusion of Theorem 6.2 still holds.[5] We will see later that this projection operator has a fast $\widetilde{O}(m)$ oracle.

Further, since we expect to solve (6.12) approximately, we need to show how to deal with errors that might occur in this step and how they affect solving (6.10) given a solution to (6.12); we refer to Section 6.4.6 for a discussion on this.

---

[5] For that, one can either consider projected gradient descent – see Theorem 6.5, or just repeat the proof of Theorem 6.2 over a linear subspace.

6.4.4 Bounding Parameters for Gradient Descent

To apply the gradient descent algorithm to problem (6.12) and estimate its running time, we need to perform the following steps:

(1) Prove that the objective $f(x) := \|x - P(x)\|^2$ is convex on $\mathbb{R}^m$.
(2) Prove that f has a Lipschitz continuous gradient and find the Lipschitz constant.
(3) Find a "good starting point" $x_0 \in \mathbb{R}^m$.
(4) Estimate the running time of a single iteration, i.e., how quickly can we compute the gradient.

We now discuss these steps one by one.

Step 1: Convexity. In general, for every convex set $S \subseteq \mathbb{R}^n$, the function $x \mapsto \text{dist}^2(x, S)$ is convex; see Exercise 6.9. Here

$$\text{dist}(x, S) := \inf_{y \in S} \|x - y\|.$$

Step 2: Lipschitz continuous gradient. One has to compute the gradient of f first to analyze its properties. For that, we first observe that the projection operator on the hypercube is described rather simply by the following:

$$P(x)_i = \begin{cases} x_i & \text{if } x_i \in [-1, 1], \\ -1 & \text{if } x_i < -1, \\ 1 & \text{if } x_i > 1. \end{cases} \tag{6.13}$$

Hence,

$$f(x) = \sum_{i=1}^{n} h(x_i),$$

where $h \colon \mathbb{R} \to \mathbb{R}$ is the function $\text{dist}^2(z, [-1, 1])$, i.e.,

$$h(z) = \begin{cases} 0 & \text{if } z \in [-1, 1], \\ (z + 1)^2 & \text{if } z < -1, \\ (z - 1)^2 & \text{if } z > 1. \end{cases}$$

Thus, in particular,

$$\left[\nabla f(x)\right]_i = \begin{cases} 0 & \text{if } x_i \in [-1, 1], \\ 2(x_i + 1) & \text{if } x_i < -1, \\ 2(x_i - 1) & \text{if } x_i > 1. \end{cases}$$

Such a function $(\nabla f(x))$ is easily seen to be Lipschitz continuous, with a Lipschitz constant $L = 2$ with respect to the Euclidean norm.

Step 3: Good starting point. We need to provide a flow $g \in H_F$ that is as close as possible to the "cube" $B_{m,\infty}$. For that, we can just find the flow $g \in H_F$ with smallest Euclidean norm. In other words, we can project the origin onto the affine subspace H_F to obtain a flow g (we discuss the time complexity of this task in Step 4). Note that if $\|g\|^2 > m$ then the optimal value of (6.12) is nonzero, which is enough to conclude that $F^\star < F$. Indeed, if there was a flow $x \in B_{m,\infty}$ such that $Bx = Fb$, then x would be a point in H_F of Euclidean norm

$$\|x\|^2 \le m \, \|x\|^2_\infty \le m,$$

and hence, we would arrive at a contradiction with the choice of g. Such a choice of $x_0 = g$ implies that $\|x_0 - x^\star\| \le 2\sqrt{m}$, thus we have $D = O(\sqrt{m})$.

Step 4: The complexity of computing gradients. In Step 2 we have already derived a formula for the gradient of f. However, since we are working in a constrained setting, such a vector $\nabla f(x)$ needs to be projected onto the linear subspace $H := \{x \in \mathbb{R}^m : Bx = 0\}$. In Exercise 6.10 we show that if we let

$$\Pi := B^\top (BB^\top)^+ B,$$

where $(BB^\top)^+$ is the pseudoinverse of $BB^\top$ (the Laplacian of G), then the matrix $I - \Pi : \mathbb{R}^m \to \mathbb{R}^m$ corresponds to the operator proj_H. Thus, in every step t of the projected gradient descent algorithm, we need to compute

$$(I - \Pi)\nabla f(x_t).$$

While $\nabla f(x_t)$ is easy to compute in linear time given the formulas derived previously, computing its projection might be quite expensive. In fact, even if we precomputed Π (which would take roughly $O(m^3)$ time), it would still take $O(m^2)$ time to apply it to the vector $\nabla f(x_t)$. To the rescue comes an important and nontrivial result that such a projection can be computed in time $\widetilde{O}(m)$. This is achieved by noting that this problem trivially reduces to solving Laplacian systems of the form $BB^\top y = a$.

6.4.5 Running Time Analysis

Given the above discussion, we can bound the running time of the gradient descent–based algorithm to find an δ-approximate max-flow. By Theorem 6.5, the number of iterations to solve (6.12) up to an error of δ is $O\left(\frac{LD^2}{\delta}\right) = O\left(\frac{m}{\delta}\right)$, and the cost of every iteration (and of finding x_0) is $\widetilde{O}(m)$. Thus, in total, this requires $\widetilde{O}\left(\frac{m^2}{\delta}\right)$ time.

To recover a flow of value $F^\star(1 - \varepsilon)$ from a solution to (6.12), we need to solve (6.12) up to precision $\delta := \frac{F^\star \varepsilon}{\sqrt{m}}$ (see Section 6.4.6). Thus, we obtain a running time bound of $\widetilde{O}\left(\varepsilon^{-1}\frac{m^{2.5}}{F^\star}\right)$. The binary search over F to find $F^\star$ up to a good precision incurs only a logarithmic factor in m (since $1 \leq F^\star \leq m$) and, hence, does not significantly affect the running time. This completes the proof of Theorem 6.6.

6.4.6 Dealing with Approximate Solutions

A concern that arises when dealing with the formulation (6.12) is that in order to solve (6.11), we need to solve (6.12) exactly, i.e., with error $\varepsilon = 0$ (we need to know whether the optimal solution is zero or nonzero), which is not really possible using gradient descent. This is dealt with using the following lemma.

Lemma 6.7 (From approximate to exact flows). *Let $g \in \mathbb{R}^m$ be an $s - t$-flow of value F in the graph G, i.e., $Bg = Fb$. Suppose that g overflows a total of F_{ov} units of flow (formally $F_{ov} := \|g - P(g)\|_1$) on all edges. There is an algorithm that, given g, finds a flow g' that does not overflow any edge (i.e., $g' \in B_{m,\infty}$) of value $F' \geq F - F_{ov}$. The algorithm runs in time $O(m \log n)$.*

The lemma says that any error we incur in solving (6.12) can be efficiently turned into an error in the original objective of (6.10). More precisely, if we solve (6.12) up to an error of $\delta > 0$, then we can efficiently recover a flow of value at least $F - \sqrt{m}\delta$. Thus, for the flow to be of value at least $F(1 - \varepsilon)$, we need to set $\delta := \frac{\varepsilon F}{\sqrt{m}}$.

6.5 Exercises

6.1   Let $f : \mathbb{R}^n \to \mathbb{R}$ be a differentiable function. Prove that if $\|\nabla f(x)\| \leq G$ for all $x \in \mathbb{R}^n$ and some $G > 0$, then f is G-Lipschitz continuous, i.e.,

$$\forall x, y \in \mathbb{R}^n, \ |f(x) - f(y)| \leq G.$$

Is the converse true? (See Exercise 7.1.)

6.2   Suppose that a differentiable function $f : \mathbb{R}^n \to \mathbb{R}$ has the property that for all $x, y \in \mathbb{R}^n$,

$$f(y) \le f(x) + \langle y - x, \nabla f(x) \rangle + \frac{L}{2} \|x - y\|^2. \qquad (6.14)$$

Prove that if f is twice-differentiable and has a continuous Hessian, then (6.14) is equivalent to $\nabla^2 f(x) \preceq LI$. Further, prove that if f is also convex, then (6.14) is equivalent to the condition that the gradient of f is L-Lipschitz continuous, i.e.,

$$\forall x, y \in \mathbb{R}^n, \quad \|\nabla f(x) - \nabla f(y)\| \le L \|x - y\|.$$

6.3   Let $\mathcal{M}$ be a nonempty family of subsets of $\{1, 2, \ldots, n\}$. For a set $M \in \mathcal{M}$, let $1_M \in \mathbb{R}^n$ be the indicator vector of M, i.e., $1_M(i) = 1$ if $i \in M$ and $1_M(i) = 0$ otherwise. Consider a function $f : \mathbb{R}^n \to \mathbb{R}$, given by

$$f(x) := \log \left(\sum_{M \in \mathcal{M}} e^{\langle x, 1_M \rangle} \right).$$

Prove that the gradient of f is L-Lipschitz continuous for some $L > 0$ that depends polynomially on n with respect to the Euclidean norm.

6.4   Prove Theorem 6.5.

6.5   **Gradient descent for strongly convex functions.** In this problem, we analyze a gradient descent algorithm for minimizing a twice-differentiable convex function $f : \mathbb{R}^n \to \mathbb{R}$, which satisfies for every $x \in \mathbb{R}^n$, one has $mI \preceq \nabla^2 f(x) \preceq MI$ for some $0 < m \le M$.

The algorithm starts with some $x_0 \in \mathbb{R}^n$ and at every step $t = 0, 1, 2, \ldots$ it chooses the next point

$$x_{t+1} := x_t - \alpha_t \nabla f(x_t),$$

where α_t is chosen to minimize the value $f(x_t - \alpha \nabla f(x_t))$ over all $\alpha \in \mathbb{R}$ while fixing x_t. Let $y^\star := \min\{f(x) : x \in \mathbb{R}^n\}$.

(a)   Prove that

$$\forall x, y \in \mathbb{R}^n, \quad \frac{m}{2} \|y - x\|^2 \le f(y) - f(x) + \langle \nabla f(x), x - y \rangle$$

$$\le \frac{M}{2} \|y - x\|^2.$$

(b)   Prove that

$$\forall x \in \mathbb{R}^n, \quad f(x) - \frac{1}{2m} \|\nabla f(x)\|^2 \le y^\star \le f(x) - \frac{1}{2M} \|\nabla f(x)\|^2.$$

(c)   Prove that for every $t = 0, 1, 2, \ldots$

$$f(x_{t+1}) \le f(x_t) - \frac{1}{2M} \|\nabla f(x_t)\|^2.$$

(d) Prove that for every $t = 0, 1, 2, \ldots$

$$f(x_t) - y^\star \leq \left(1 - \frac{m}{M}\right)^t \left(f(x_0) - y^\star\right).$$

What is the number of iterations t required to reach
$f(x_t) - y^\star \leq \varepsilon$?

(e) Consider a linear system $Ax = b$, where $b \in \mathbb{R}^n$ is a vector and
$A \in \mathbb{R}^{n \times n}$ is a symmetric positive definite matrix such that
$\frac{\lambda_n(A)}{\lambda_1(A)} \leq \kappa$ (where $\lambda_1(A)$ and $\lambda_n(A)$ are the smallest and the
largest eigenvalues of A, respectively). Use the above framework
to design an algorithm for approximately solving the system
$Ax = b$ with logarithmic dependency on the error $\varepsilon > 0$ and
polynomial dependency on κ. What is the running time?

6.6   **Subgradient descent for nonsmooth functions.** Consider the function
$R: \mathbb{R}^n \to \mathbb{R}$ where $R(x) := \|x\|_1$.

(a) Show that $R(x)$ is convex.

(b) Show that $R(x)$ is not differentiable everywhere.

(c) Recall that we say that $g \in \mathbb{R}^n$ is a subgradient of $f : \mathbb{R}^n \to \mathbb{R}$ at a
point $x \in \mathbb{R}^n$ if

$$\forall y \in \mathbb{R}^n, \quad f(y) \geq f(x) + \langle g, y - x \rangle.$$

Let $\partial f(x)$ denote the set of all subgradient of f at x. Describe
$\partial R(x)$ for every $x \in \mathbb{R}^n$.

(d) Consider the following optimization problem:

$$\min \left\{ \|Ax - b\|^2 + \frac{1}{\eta} R(x) : x \in \mathbb{R}^n \right\}$$

where $A \in \mathbb{R}^{m \times n}$, $b \in \mathbb{R}^m$, and $\eta > 0$. The objective is not
differentiable, hence we cannot apply gradient descent directly.
Use subgradients to handle the nondifferentiability of R. State the
update rule and derive the corresponding running time.

6.7   **Coordinate descent for smooth functions.** Let $f : \mathbb{R}^n \to \mathbb{R}$ be a
convex, twice-differentiable function with $\frac{\partial^2 f}{\partial^2 x_i} \leq \beta_i$ (for every $i =
1, 2, \ldots, n$) and let $B := \sum_{i=1}^n \beta_i$.

(a) Let $x \in \mathbb{R}^n$ and let

$$x' := x - \frac{1}{\beta_i} \frac{\partial f(x)}{\partial x_i} e_i,$$

where $i \in \{1, 2, \ldots, n\}$ is chosen at random from the distribution given by $p_i := \frac{\beta_i}{B}$. Prove that

$$\mathbb{E}\left[f(x')\right] \leq f(x) - \frac{1}{2B} \|\nabla f(x)\|^2.$$

(b) Use the above randomized update rule to design a randomized gradient descent–like algorithm, which after T steps satisfies

$$\mathbb{E}\left[f(x_t) - f(x^*)\right] \leq \varepsilon,$$

whenever $T = \Omega\left(\frac{BD^2}{\varepsilon}\right)$, where $D := \max\{\|x - x_0\| : f(x) \leq f(x_0)\}$.

6.8   **Frank-Wolfe method.** Consider the following algorithm for minimizing a convex function $f : K \to \mathbb{R}$ over a convex domain $K \subseteq \mathbb{R}^n$.

- Initialize $x_0 \in K$,
- For each iteration $t = 0, 1, 2, \ldots, T$:

    - Define $z_t := \operatorname{argmin}_{x \in K} \{f(x_t) + \langle \nabla f(x_t), x - x_t \rangle\}$
    - Let $x_{t+1} := (1 - \gamma_t)x_t + \gamma_t z_t$, for some $\gamma_t \in [0, 1]$

- Output x_T.

(a) Prove that if the gradient of f is L-Lipschitz continuous with respect to a norm $\|\cdot\|$, $\max_{x,y} \|x - y\| \leq D$ and γ_t is taken to be $\Theta\left(\frac{1}{t}\right)$, then

$$f(x_T) - f(x^*) \leq O\left(\frac{LD^2}{T}\right),$$

where x^* is any minimizer of $\min_{x \in K} f(x)$.

(b) Show that one iteration of this algorithm can be implemented efficiently when given a first-order oracle access to f and the set K is any of

- $K := \{x \in \mathbb{R}^n : \|x\|_\infty \leq 1\}$,
- $K := \{x \in \mathbb{R}^n : \|x\|_1 \leq 1\}$,
- $K := \{x \in \mathbb{R}^n : \|x\|_2 \leq 1\}$.

6.9   Recall that for a nonempty subset $K \subseteq \mathbb{R}^n$, we can define the distance function $\operatorname{dist}(\cdot, K)$ and the projection operator $\operatorname{proj}_K : \mathbb{R}^n \to K$ as

$$\operatorname{dist}(x, K) := \inf_{y \in K} \|x - y\| \quad \text{and} \quad \operatorname{proj}_K(x) := \operatorname{arginf}_{y \in K} \|x - y\|.$$

(a) Prove that proj_K is well-defined when K is a closed and convex set, i.e., show that the minimum is attained at a unique point.

(b) Prove that for all $x, y \in \mathbb{R}^n$,

$$\|\text{proj}_K(x) - \text{proj}_K(y)\| \leq \|x - y\|.$$

(c) Prove that for any set $K \subseteq \mathbb{R}^n$, the function $x \mapsto \text{dist}^2(x, K)$ is convex.

(d) Prove correctness of the explicit formula (given in Equation (6.13) in this chapter) for the projection operator proj_K when $K = B_{m,\infty} = \{x \in \mathbb{R}^m : \|x\|_\infty \leq 1\}$.

(e) Prove that the function $f(x) := \text{dist}^2(x, K)$ has a Lipschitz continuous gradient with Lipschitz constant equal to 2.

6.10 Let $G = (V, E)$ be an undirected graph with n vertices and m edges. Let $B \in \mathbb{R}^{n \times m}$ be the vertex-edge incidence matrix of G. Assume that G is connected, and let $\Pi := B^\top (BB^\top)^+ B$. Prove that, given a vector $g \in \mathbb{R}^m$, if we let $x^\star$ denote the projection of g on the subspace $\{x \in \mathbb{R}^m : Bx = 0\}$ (as defined in Exercise 6.9), then it holds that

$$x^\star = g - \Pi g.$$

6.11 **$s - t$-minimum cut problem.** Recall the $s - t$-maximum flow problem from this chapter.

(a) Prove that the dual of the formulation (6.11) presented earlier in this chapter is equivalent to the following:

$$\min_{y \in \mathbb{R}^n} \quad \sum_{ij \in E} |y_i - v_j| \tag{6.15}$$

$$\text{such that} \quad y_s - y_t = 1.$$

(b) Prove that the optimal value of (6.15) is equal to $\text{MinCut}_{s,t}(G)$: the minimum number of edges one needs to remove from G to disconnect s from t. This latter problem is known as the $s - t$-minimum cut problem.

(c) Reformulate (6.15) as follows:

$$\min_{x \in \mathbb{R}^m} \quad \|x\|_1$$

$$\text{such that} \quad x \in \text{Im}(B^\top), \tag{6.16}$$

$$\langle x, z \rangle = 1$$

for some $z \in \mathbb{R}^m$ that depends on G and s, t. Write an explicit formula for z.

(d) Apply gradient descent to solve the program (6.16). Estimate
     all relevant parameters and provide a complete analysis. What
     is the running time to reach a point with value at most
     $\text{MinCut}_{s,t}(G) + \varepsilon$?

     Hint: To make the objective smooth (have Lipschitz continuous
     gradient) replace $\|x\|_1$ by $\sum_{i=1}^{m} \sqrt{x_i^2 + \mu^2}$. Then pick μ
     appropriately to make the error incurred by this approximation
     small compared to ε.

Notes

While this chapter focuses on one version of gradient descent, there are several
variants of the gradient descent method and the reader is referred to the book
by Nesterov (2004) and the monograph by Bubeck (2015) for a discussion of
more variants. For more on the Frank-Wolfe method (introduced in Exercise
6.8), see the paper by Jaggi (2013). The lower bound (Theorem 6.4) was first
established in a paper by Nemirovski and Yudin (1983).

The $s - t$-maximum flow problem is one of the most well-studied problems
in combinatorial optimization. Early combinatorial algorithms for this problem
included those by Ford and Fulkerson (1956), Dinic (1970), and Edmonds and
Karp (1972)) leading to an algorithm by Goldberg and Rao (1998) that runs in
$\tilde{O}\left(m \min\left\{n^{2/3}, m^{1/2}\right\} \log U\right)$ time.

A convex optimization–based approach for the $s - t$-maximum flow problem was initiated in a paper by Christiano et al. (2011), who gave an algorithm
for the $s-t$-maximum flow problem that runs in time $\tilde{O}(mn^{1/3}\varepsilon^{-11/3})$. Section
6.4 is based on a paper by Lee et al. (2013). We refer the reader to Lee et al.
(2013) for a stronger version of Theorem 6.6 that achieves a running time of
$\tilde{O}\left(\frac{m^{1.75}}{\sqrt{\varepsilon F^\star}}\right)$ by applying the accelerated gradient descent method (discussed in
a Chapter 8) instead of the version we use here; also see Exercise 8.5. By
further optimizing the trade-off between these parameters, one can obtain an
$\tilde{O}\left(mn^{1/3}\varepsilon^{-2/3}\right)$ time algorithm for the $s - t$-maximum flow problem. Nearly
linear time algorithms for the $s - t$-maximum flow problem were discovered in
papers by Sherman (2013), Kelner et al. (2014), and Peng (2016). All of these
algorithms used techniques from convex optimization. See Chapter 11 for a
different class of continuous algorithms for maximum flow problems whose
dependence on ε is $\text{polylog}(\varepsilon^{-1})$.

All of the above results rely on the availability of fast Laplacian solvers. A nearly linear time algorithm for Laplacian solvers were first discovered in a seminal paper of Spielman and Teng (2004). To read more about Laplacian systems and their applications to algorithm design, see the surveys by Spielman (2012) and Teng (2010), and the monograph by Vishnoi (2013).

7

Mirror Descent and the Multiplicative Weights Update

We derive our second algorithm for convex optimization – called the mirror descent method – via a regularization viewpoint. First, the mirror descent algorithm is developed for optimizing convex functions over the probability simplex. Subsequently, we show how to generalize it and, importantly, derive the multiplicative weights update (MWU) method from it. This latter algorithm is then used to develop a fast approximate algorithm to solve the bipartite matching problem on graphs.

7.1 Beyond the Lipschitz Gradient Condition

Consider a convex program

$$\min_{x \in K} f(x), \tag{7.1}$$

where $f : K \to \mathbb{R}^n$ is a convex function over a convex set. In Chapter 6 we introduced the (projected) gradient descent algorithm and proved that when f satisfies the Lipschitz gradient condition, then it can solve the problem (7.1) up to an additive error of ε in a number of iterations that are proportional, roughly, to $\frac{1}{\varepsilon}$. As we have seen, several classes of functions, e.g., quadratic functions $f(x) = x^\top A x + x^\top b$ and squared distances to convex sets $f(x) = \mathrm{dist}^2(x, K')$ (for some convex $K' \subseteq \mathbb{R}^n$), satisfy the bounded Lipschitz gradient condition.

In Chapter 6, we also introduced the **bounded gradient** condition. It states that there exists a $G > 0$ such that for all $x \in K$,

$$\|\nabla f(x)\|_2 \leq G. \tag{7.2}$$

Using the fundamental theorem of calculus (as in the proof of Lemma 6.3), this condition can be shown to imply the condition that f is G-Lipschitz, i.e.,

$$|f(x) - f(y)| \leq G \|x - y\|_2$$

for all $x, y \in K$; see Exercise 6.1. Moreover, if f is also convex, then these two conditions are equivalent; see Exercise 7.1. Note, however, that the Lipschitz continuous gradient condition may not imply the bounded gradient condition. For instance, it may be the case that $G = O(1)$, but there is no such bound on the Lipschitz constant of the gradient of f; see Exercise 7.2. In this case, one can prove the following theorem.

Theorem 7.1 (Guarantee for gradient descent when the gradient is bounded). *There is a gradient descent-based algorithm that, given a first-order oracle access to a convex function $f : \mathbb{R}^n \to \mathbb{R}$, a number G such that $\|\nabla f(x)\|_2 \leq G$ for all $x \in \mathbb{R}^n$, an initial point $x^0 \in \mathbb{R}^n$ and D such that $\|x^0 - x^\star\|_2 \leq D$, and an $\varepsilon > 0$, outputs a sequence of points $x^0, \ldots, x^{T-1}$ such that*

$$f\left(\frac{1}{T}\sum_{t=0}^{T-1} x^t\right) - f(x^\star) \leq \varepsilon$$

where

$$T = \left(\frac{DG}{\varepsilon}\right)^2$$

Note that the dependence on ε, as compared to the Lipschitz continuous gradient case (Theorem 6.2), has become worse: from $\frac{1}{\varepsilon}$ to $\frac{1}{\varepsilon^2}$. Moreover, note that the definition of bounded gradient (7.2) is in terms of the Euclidean norm. Sometimes we might find ourselves in a setting where $\|\nabla f\|_\infty = O(1)$, and a naive bound would only give us $\|\nabla f\|_2 = O(\sqrt{n})$. We see in this chapter how to deal with such a situation by a generalization of this version of the gradient descent that can exploit the bounded gradient property in different norms.

We introduce the mirror descent method: a powerful method that can be, on the one hand, viewed through the lens of gradient descent in a "dual" space through an appropriate conjugate function, and on the other hand viewed as a **proximal** method in the "primal" space. It turns out that these are equivalent, and we show that as well.

Remark 7.2 (Notation change in this chapter). Just in this chapter, we index vectors using upper-indices: $x^0, x^1, \ldots$ This is to avoid confusion with the coordinates of these vectors that are often referred to, i.e., the ith coordinate of vector x^t is denoted by x_i^t. Also, since the results of this chapter generalize to arbitrary norms, we are careful about the norm. In particular, $\| \cdot \|$ refers to a general norm, and the Euclidean norm is explicitly denoted by $\| \cdot \|_2$.

7.2 A Local Optimization Principle and Regularizers

To construct an algorithm for optimizing functions with bounded gradients, we first introduce a general idea – **regularization**. Our algorithm is iterative: Given points $x^0, x^1, \ldots, x^t$ it finds a new point x^{t+1} based on its history. How do we choose the next point x^{t+1} to converge to the minimizer $x^\star$ quickly? An obvious choice would be to let

$$x^{t+1} := \underset{x \in K}{\text{argmin}} \, f(x).$$

It certainly converges to $x^\star$ quickly (in one step), yet clearly it is not very helpful because then x^{t+1} is **hard to compute**. To counter this problem, one might try to construct a function f_t – a "simple model" of f – that **approximates** f in a certain sense and is **easier to minimize**. Then the update rule of our algorithm becomes

$$x^{t+1} := \underset{x \in K}{\text{argmin}} \, f_t(x).$$

If the approximation f_t of f becomes more and more accurate with increasing t near x^t, then intuitively, the sequence of iterates should converge to the minimizer $x^\star$.

One can view the gradient descent method for the Lipschitz continuous gradient case we introduced in Chapter 6 to be in this class of algorithms, with

$$f_t(x) := f(x^t) + \langle \nabla f(x^t), x - x^t \rangle + \frac{L}{2} \left\| x - x^t \right\|_2^2.$$

To see this, observe that f_t is convex and, hence, its minimum occurs at a point x^{t+1} where $\nabla f_t(x^{t+1}) = 0$. And,

$$0 = \nabla f_t(x^{t+1}) = \nabla f(x^t) + L(x^{t+1} - x^t),$$

which implies that

$$x^{t+1} = x^t - \frac{1}{L} \nabla f(x^t). \tag{7.3}$$

If the gradient of f is L-Lipschitz continuous, then $f(x) \leq f_t(x)$ for all $x \in K$ and, moreover, $f_t(x)$ is a good approximation of $f(x)$ for x in a small neighborhood around x^t. In this setting (as proved in Chapter 6), such an update rule guarantees convergence of x^t to the global minimizer.

In general, when the functions we deal with do not have Lipschitz continuous gradients, we might not be able to construct such good quadratic approximations. However, we might still use first-order approximations of f at x^t (using subgradients if we have to): Convexity of f implies that if we define

$$f_t(x) := f(x^t) + \langle \nabla f(x^t), x - x^t \rangle,$$

then

$$\forall x \in K, \quad f_t(x) \leq f(x)$$

and, moreover, we expect f_t to be a decent approximation of f in a small neighborhood around x^t. Thus, one could try to apply the resulting update rule as follows:

$$x^{t+1} := \underset{x \in K}{\arg\min} \left\{ f(x^t) + \langle \nabla f(x^t), x - x^t \rangle \right\}. \tag{7.4}$$

A downside of the above is that it is very aggressive – in fact, the new point x^{t+1} could be very far from x^t. This is easily illustrated by an example in one dimension, when $K = [-1, 1]$ and $f(z) = z^2$. If started at 1, and updated using (7.4), the algorithm jumps indefinitely between -1 and 1. This is because one of these two points is always a minimizer of a linear lower bound of f over K. Thus, the sequence $\{x^t\}_{t \geq 0}$ never reaches 0 – the unique minimizer of f. The reader is encouraged to check the details.

The situation is even worse when the domain K is unbounded: The minimum is not attained at any finite point and, hence, the update rule (7.4) is not well defined. This issue can be easily countered when the function is σ-strongly convex (see Definition 3.8) for some $\sigma > 0$, since then we can use a stronger quadratic lower bound on f at x^t, i.e.,

$$f_t(x) = f(x^t) + \langle \nabla f(x^t), x - x^t \rangle + \frac{\sigma}{2} \|x - x^t\|_2^2.$$

Then, the minimizer of $f_t(x)$ is always attained at the following point (using the same calculation leading to (7.3)):

$$x^{t+1} = x^t - \frac{1}{\sigma} \nabla f(x^t),$$

which can be made close to x^t by choosing a large σ. For the case of $f(z) = z^2$ over $[-1, 1]$,

$$x^{t+1} = \frac{\sigma - 2}{\sigma} x^t,$$

which converges to 0.

This observation leads to the following idea: Even if the gradient of f is not Lipschitz continuous, we can still add a function to f_t, to make it smoother. Specifically, we add a term involving a "distance" function $D \colon K \times K \to \mathbb{R}$ that does not allow the new point x^{t+1} to land far away from the previous point x^t; D is referred to as a **regularizer**.[1] More precisely, instead of minimizing $f_t(x)$, we minimize $D(x, x^t) + f_t(x)$. To vary the importance of these two terms we also introduce a positive parameter $\eta > 0$ and write the revised update as:

$$x^{t+1} := \underset{x \in K}{\operatorname{argmin}} \left\{ D(x, x^t) + \eta \left(f(x^t) + \langle \nabla f(x^t), x - x^t \rangle \right) \right\}.$$

Since the above is an argmin, we can ignore terms that depend only on x and simplify it as

$$x^{t+1} = \underset{x \in K}{\operatorname{argmin}} \left\{ D(x, x^t) + \eta \langle \nabla f(x^t), x \rangle \right\}. \tag{7.5}$$

Note that by picking large η, the significance of the regularizer $D(x, x^t)$ is reduced, and thus it does not play a big role in choosing the next step. By picking η to be small, we force x^{t+1} to stay in a close vicinity of x^t.[2] However, unlike gradient descent, the value of the function does not have to decrease: $f(x^t)$ may be more than $f(x^{t+1})$, hence, it is not clear how to analyze progress of this method; we explain it later.

Before we go any further with these general considerations, let us consider one important example, where the "right" choice of the distance function $D(\cdot, \cdot)$ for a simple convex set already leads to a very interesting algorithm – exponential gradient descent. This algorithm can then be generalized to the setting of an arbitrary convex set K.

7.3 Exponential Gradient Descent

Consider a convex optimization problem

$$\min_{p \in \Delta_n} f(p), \tag{7.6}$$

---

[1] This D should not be confused with a bound on the distance of the starting point to the optimal point.

[2] A slightly different, yet related way to ensure that the next point x^{t+1} does not move too far away from x^t is to first compute a candidate $\tilde{x}^{t+1}$ according to the rule (7.4) and then to make a small step from x^t towards $\tilde{x}^{t+1}$ to obtain x^{t+1}. This is the main idea of the Frank-Wolfe algorithm; see Exercise 6.8.

where $f: \Delta_n \to \mathbb{R}$ is a convex function over the (closed and compact) n-dimensional **probability simplex**

$$\Delta_n := \left\{ p \in [0,1]^n : \sum_{i=1}^n p_i = 1 \right\},$$

i.e., the set of all probability distributions over n elements. From the discussion in the previous section, the general form of an algorithm we would like to construct is

$$p^{t+1} := \operatorname*{argmin}_{p \in \Delta_n} \left\{ D(p, p^t) + \eta \left\langle \nabla f(p^t), p \right\rangle \right\}, \tag{7.7}$$

where D is a certain distance function on Δ_n. The choice of D is up to us, but ideally it should allow efficient computation of x^{t+1} given x^t and $\nabla f(x^t)$ and should be a "natural" metric that is compatible with the geometry of the feasible set Δ_n so as to guarantee quick convergence. For the probability simplex, one choice of such a metric is the relative entropy, called the Kullback-Leibler (KL) divergence. The appropriateness of this metric will be explained later.

Definition 7.3 (Kullback-Leibler divergence over Δ_n). For two probability distributions $p, q \in \Delta_n$, their Kullback-Leibler divergence is defined as

$$D_{KL}(p,q) := -\sum_{i=1}^n p_i \log \frac{q_i}{p_i}.$$

For this definition to make sense, whenever $q_i = 0$, we require that $p_i = 0$. When $p_i = 0$ the corresponding term is set to 0 as $\lim_{x \to 0^+} x \log x = 0$.

While not being symmetric, D_{KL} satisfies several natural distance-like properties. For instance, from convexity it follows that $D_{KL}(p,q) \geq 0$. The reason it is called a **divergence** is because it can also be seen as the Bregman divergence (Definition 3.9) corresponding to the function

$$h(p) := \sum_{i=1}^n p_i \log p_i.$$

Recall that for a convex function $F: K \to \mathbb{R}$ that is differentiable over a convex subset K of $\mathbb{R}^n$, the Bregman divergence corresponding to F at x with respect to y is defined as

$$D_F(x, y) := F(x) - F(y) - \langle \nabla F(y), x - y \rangle.$$

$D_F(x, y)$ measures the error in approximating $F(x)$ using the first-order Taylor approximation of F at y. In particular, $D_F(x, y) \geq 0$ and $D_F(x, y) \to 0$ when x is fixed and $y \to x$. In the next section, we derive several other properties of D_{KL}.

When specialized to this particular distance function D_{KL}, the update rule takes the form

$$p^{t+1} := \operatorname*{argmin}_{p \in \Delta_n} \left\{ D_{KL}(p, p^t) + \eta \langle \nabla f(p^t), p \rangle \right\}. \qquad (7.8)$$

As we prove in the lemma below, the vector p^{t+1} can be computed using an explicit formula involving only p^t and $\nabla f(p^t)$. It is useful to extend the notion of KL-divergence to $\mathbb{R}^n_{\geq 0}$ by introducing the generalized KL-divergence D_H: It is the Bregman divergence corresponding to the function

$$H(x) := \sum_{i=1}^{n} x_i \log x_i - x_i.$$

Thus, for $x, y \in \mathbb{R}^n_{\geq 0}$,

$$D_H(x, y) = -\sum_{i=1}^{n} x_i \log \frac{y_i}{x_i} + \sum_{i=1}^{n} (y_i - x_i),$$

where, as before, whenever $y_i = 0$, we require that $x_i = 0$, and when $x_i = 0$, the corresponding term is set to 0 as $\lim_{x \to 0^+} x \log x = 0$. Note that $D_H(x, y) = D_{KL}(x, y)$ when $x, y \in \Delta_n$, and we often use D_{KL} to denote D_H for all nonnegative vectors (even outside of the simplex).

With the choice of the regularizer being D_H, the following lemma gives a characterization of the argmin in (7.5) for $D = D_H$ and $K = \mathbb{R}^n_{\geq 0}$ and Δ_n, respectively. In the lemma below, we rename $q := x^t$, $g := \nabla f(x^t)$ and $w = x$ from (7.5).

Lemma 7.4 (Projection under KL-divergence). *Consider any vector $q \in \mathbb{R}^n_{\geq 0}$ and a vector $g \in \mathbb{R}^n$.*

(1) *Let $w^\star := \operatorname{argmin}_{w \geq 0} \{D_H(w, q) + \eta \langle g, w \rangle\}$, then $w_i^\star = q_i \exp(-\eta g_i)$ for all $i = 1, 2, \ldots, n$.*

(2) *Let $p^\star := \operatorname{argmin}_{p \in \Delta_n} \{D_H(p, q) + \eta \langle g, p \rangle\}$, then $p^\star = \frac{w^\star}{\|w^\star\|_1}$ for all $i = 1, 2, \ldots, n$.*

Proof: In the first part, we are given an optimization problem of the form

$$\min_{w \geq 0} \sum_{i=1}^{n} w_i \log w_i + \sum_{i=1}^{n} w_i (\eta g_i - \log q_i - 1) + q_i. \qquad (7.9)$$

The above problem is in fact convex, hence, one just needs to find a zero of the gradient with respect to w to find the minimum. By computing the gradient, we obtain the optimality condition

$$\log w_i = -\eta g_i + \log q_i,$$

and, hence,

$$w_i^\star = q_i \exp(-\eta g_i).$$

For the second part, we use ideas developed in Chapter 5. To incorporate the constraint $\sum_{i=1}^n p_i = 1$, we introduce a Lagrange multiplier $\mu \in \mathbb{R}$ and obtain

$$\min_{p \geq 0} \quad \sum_{i=1}^n p_i \log p_i + \sum_{i=1}^n p_i (\eta g_i - \log q_i) + \mu \left(\sum_{i=1}^n p_i - 1 \right). \qquad (7.10)$$

Then, the optimality condition becomes

$$p_i = q_i \exp(-\eta g_i - \mu)$$

and, thus, we just need to pick μ so that $\sum_{i=1}^n p_i = 1$, which gives

$$p^\star = \frac{w^\star}{\|w^\star\|_1}. \qquad \blacksquare$$

Algorithm 2: Exponential gradient descent (EGD)

Input:
- First order oracle for a convex function $f : \Delta_n \to \mathbb{R}$
- An $\eta > 0$
- An integer $T > 0$

Output: A point $\bar{p} \in \Delta_n$

Algorithm:

1: Set $p^0 := \frac{1}{n} \mathbf{1}$ (the uniform distribution)
2: **for** $t = 0, 1, \ldots, T - 1$ **do**
3:     Obtain $g^t := \nabla f(p^t)$
4:     $w_i^{t+1} := p_i^t \exp(-\eta g_i^t)$
5:     $p_i^{t+1} := \frac{w_i^{t+1}}{\sum_{j=1}^n w_j^{t+1}}$
6: **end for**
7: **return** $\bar{p} := \frac{1}{T} \sum_{t=0}^{T-1} p^t$

7.3.1 Main Theorem on Exponential Gradient Descent

We now have all the background necessary to describe the exponential gradient descent (EGD) algorithm (Algorithm 2). In this algorithm, we introduce an auxiliary (weight) vector w^t at every iteration. While it is not necessary to state the algorithm, it is useful for us to refer to w^t in the proof of the convergence guarantee of the algorithm.

Note one interesting difference between EGD and the variant of gradient descent studied in Chapter 6: The output of EGD is the **average** of all iterates $\bar{p}$, not the **last** iterate p^{T-1}. It is a research problem to find conditions under which one can get a similar theorem with p^{T-1} instead of $\bar{p}$.

To illustrate the problem, note that if $f(x) = |x|$, then the gradient at every point is either 1 or -1.[3] Hence, by knowing that the gradient at a certain point x is 1, we still have no clue whether x is close to the minimizer (0) or very far from it. Thus, as opposed to the Lipschitz gradient case, the gradient at a point x does not provide us with a certificate that $f(x)$ is close to optimal. Therefore one naturally needs to gather more information by visiting multiple points and averaging them in some manner.

Theorem 7.5 (Guarantees for EGD). *Suppose that* $f : \Delta_n \rightarrow \mathbb{R}$ *is a convex function that satisfies* $\|\nabla f(p)\|_\infty \leq G$ *for all* $p \in \Delta_n$. *If we let* $\eta := \Theta\left(\frac{\sqrt{\log n}}{\sqrt{T}G}\right)$, *then, after* $T = \Theta\left(\frac{G^2 \log n}{\varepsilon^2}\right)$ *iterations of the EGD algorithm, the point* $\bar{p} := \frac{1}{T}\sum_{t=0}^{T-1} p^t$ *satisfies*

$$f(\bar{p}) - f(p^\star) \leq \varepsilon,$$

where $p^\star$ *is any minimizer of* f *over* Δ_n.

7.3.2 Properties of Bregman Divergence

We present several important properties of KL-divergence that are useful in the proof of Theorem 7.5. Many of these are more general and hold for Bregman divergence.

We start with a simple, yet useful identity involving the Bregman divergence.

Lemma 7.6 (Law of cosines for Bregman divergence). *Let* $F : K \rightarrow \mathbb{R}$ *be a convex, differentiable function and let* $x, y, z \in K$. *Then*

$$\langle \nabla F(y) - \nabla F(z), y - x \rangle = D_F(x, y) + D_F(y, z) - D_F(x, z).$$

---

[3] Except from the point $x = 0$, which is very unlikely to be hit by an iterative algorithm, hence, we can ignore it.

The proof of the above identity is a direct calculation (Exercise 7.7). Note that for the case when $F(x) = \|x\|_2^2$, the above says that for three points $a, b, c \in \mathbb{R}^n$, we have

$$2 \langle a - c, b - c \rangle = \|b - c\|_2^2 + \|a - c\|_2^2 - \|b - a\|_2^2,$$

which is the familiar **law of cosines** in the Euclidean space.

Perhaps the simplest property of D_F is the fact that it is strictly convex in the first argument, i.e., the mapping

$$x \mapsto D_F(x, y)$$

is strictly convex. This ensures, for instance, the existence and uniqueness of a point $u \in S$ that minimizes the divergence $D_F(u, x)$ for a point x from a closed and convex set S. This is useful in the following generalization of the Pythagoras theorem.

Theorem 7.7 (Pythagorean theorem for Bregman divergence). *Let $F : K \to \mathbb{R}$ be a convex, differentiable function and let $S \subseteq K$ be a closed, convex subset of K. Let $x, y \in S$ and $z \in K$ such that*

$$y := \operatorname*{argmin}_{u \in S} D_F(u, z),$$

then

$$D_F(x, y) + D_F(y, z) \le D_F(x, z).$$

It is an instructive exercise to consider the special case of this lemma for $F(x) = \|x\|_2^2$. It says that if we project z onto a convex set S and call the projection y, then the angle between the vectors $x - y$ and $z - y$ is obtuse (larger than 90 degrees).

Proof: Let x, y, z be as in the statement of the lemma. By the optimality condition for the optimization problem $\min_{u \in S} D_F(u, z)$ at the minimizer y (Theorem 3.14), we obtain that, for every point $w \in S$, if we let

$$g(u) := D_F(u, z),$$

then

$$\langle \nabla g(y), w - y \rangle \ge 0,$$

which translates to

$$\langle \nabla F(y) - \nabla F(z), w - y \rangle \ge 0.$$

By plugging in $w = x$ and using the Lemma 7.6, we obtain

$$D_F(x, y) + D_F(y, z) - D_F(x, z) \leq 0. \qquad \blacksquare$$

Finally, we state the following inequality that asserts that the negative entropy function is 1-strongly convex with respect to the ℓ_1-norm, when restricted to the probability simplex Δ_n (Exercise 3.18).

Lemma 7.8 (Pinsker's inequality). *For every $x, y \in \Delta_n$ we have*

$$D_{KL}(x, y) \geq \frac{1}{2} \|x - y\|_1^2.$$

7.3.3 Convergence Proof of EGD

Given the properties of KL-divergence stated in the previous section, we are ready to proceed with the proof of Theorem 7.5. We show that for any $p \in \Delta_n$, it holds that

$$f(\bar{p}) - f(p) \leq \varepsilon$$

where $\bar{p} = \frac{1}{T} \sum_{t=0}^{T-1} p^t$, provided the conditions of the theorem are satisfied; therefore in particular, the result holds for the minimizer $p^\star$.

Proof of Theorem 7.5:

Step 1: Bounding $f(\bar{p}) - f(p)$ by gradients $\frac{1}{T} \sum_{t=0}^{T-1} \langle g^t, p^t - p \rangle$. Start by noting that a simple consequence of convexity of f (used twice below) is that

$$
\begin{aligned}
f(\bar{p}) - f(p) &\leq \left(\frac{1}{T} \sum_{t=0}^{T-1} f(p^t) \right) - f(p) \\
&= \frac{1}{T} \sum_{t=0}^{T-1} \left(f(p^t) - f(p) \right) \\
&\leq \frac{1}{T} \sum_{t=0}^{T-1} \langle \nabla f(p^t), p^t - p \rangle \\
&= \frac{1}{T} \sum_{t=0}^{T-1} \langle g^t, p^t - p \rangle.
\end{aligned}
\tag{7.11}
$$

Thus, from now on, we focus on the task of providing an upper bound on the sum $\sum_{t=0}^{T-1} \langle g^t, p^t - p \rangle$.

Step 2: Writing $\langle g^t, p^t - p \rangle$ in terms of KL-divergence. Fix $t \in \{0, \dots, T-1\}$. First, we provide an expression for g^t in terms of w^{t+1} and p^t. Note that since

$$w_i^{t+1} = p_i^t \exp(-\eta g_i^t)$$

for all $i \in \{1, 2, \dots, n\}$, we have

$$g_i^t = \frac{1}{\eta} \left(\log p_i^t - \log w_i^{t+1} \right).$$

This can be also written in terms of the gradient of the generalized negative entropy function $H(x) = \sum_{i=1}^{n} x_i \log x_i - x_i$ as follows:

$$g^t = \frac{1}{\eta} \left(\log p^t - \log w^{t+1} \right) = \frac{1}{\eta} \left(\nabla H(p^t) - \nabla H(w^{t+1}) \right), \qquad (7.12)$$

where the log is applied coordinate-wise to the appropriate vectors. Thus, using Lemma 7.6 (law of cosines), we obtain that

$$\begin{aligned} \langle g^t, p^t - p \rangle &= \frac{1}{\eta} \left\langle \nabla H(p^t) - \nabla H(w^{t+1}), p^t - p \right\rangle \\ &= \frac{1}{\eta} \left(D_H(p, p^t) + D_H(p^t, w^{t+1}) - D_H(p, w^{t+1}) \right). \end{aligned} \qquad (7.13)$$

Step 3: Using the Pythagorean theorem to get a telescoping sum. Now, since p^{t+1} is the projection with respect to D_H of w^{t+1} onto Δ_n (see Lemma 7.4), the generalized Pythagorean theorem (Theorem 7.7) says that

$$D_H(p, w^{t+1}) \geq D_H(p, p^{t+1}) + D_H(p^{t+1}, w^{t+1}).$$

Thus, we can bound the expression $\sum_{t=0}^{T-1} \langle g^t, p^t - p \rangle$ as follows:

$$\begin{aligned} \eta \sum_{t=0}^{T-1} \langle g^t, p^t - p \rangle &= \sum_{t=0}^{T-1} D_H(p, p^t) + D_H(p^t, w^{t+1}) - D_H(p, w^{t+1}) \\ &\leq \sum_{t=0}^{T-1} D_H(p, p^t) + D_H(p^t, w^{t+1}) \\ &\qquad - \left[D_H(p, p^{t+1}) + D_H(p^{t+1}, w^{t+1}) \right] \end{aligned}$$

$$= \sum_{t=0}^{T-1} \left[D_H(p, p^t) - D_H(p, p^{t+1}) \right]$$

$$+ \left[D_H(p^t, w^{t+1}) - D_H(p^{t+1}, w^{t+1}) \right]$$

$$\le D_H(p, p^0) + \sum_{t=0}^{T-1} \left[D_H(p^t, w^{t+1}) - D_H(p^{t+1}, w^{t+1}) \right].$$

$$(7.14)$$

In the last step, we used the fact that the first term of the sum is telescoping to $D_H(p, p^0) - D_H(p, p^T)$ and that $D_H(p, p^T) \ge 0$.

Step 4: Using Pinsker's inequality and bounded gradient to bound the remaining terms. To bound the second term, we first apply the law of cosines:

$$D_H(p^t, w^{t+1}) - D_H(p^{t+1}, w^{t+1}) = \left\langle \nabla H(p^t) - \nabla H(w^{t+1}), p^t - p^{t+1} \right\rangle$$

$$- D_H(p^{t+1}, p^t)$$

$$= \eta \left\langle g^t, p^t - p^{t+1} \right\rangle - D_H(p^{t+1}, p^t).$$

$$(7.15)$$

And finally, we apply Pinsker's inequality (Lemma 7.8) to obtain

$$D_H(p^t, w^{t+1}) - D_H(p^{t+1}, w^{t+1}) \le \eta \left\langle g^t, p^t - p^{t+1} \right\rangle - \frac{1}{2} \left\| p^{t+1} - p^t \right\|_1^2,$$

$$(7.16)$$

where we use the fact that D_H restricted to both arguments in Δ_n is the same as D_{KL}. Further, since $\left\langle g^t, p^t - p^{t+1} \right\rangle \le \| g^t \|_\infty \| p^t - p^{t+1} \|_1$ we can write

$$D_H(p^t, w^{t+1}) - D_H(p^{t+1}, w^{t+1}) \le \eta \| g^t \|_\infty \left\| p^t - p^{t+1} \right\|_1 - \frac{1}{2} \left\| p^{t+1} - p^t \right\|_1^2$$

$$\le \eta G \left\| p^{t+1} - p^t \right\|_1 - \frac{1}{2} \left\| p^{t+1} - p^t \right\|_1^2$$

$$\le \frac{(\eta G)^2}{2}, \qquad (7.17)$$

where the last inequality follows by simply maximizing the quadratic function $z \mapsto \eta G z - \frac{1}{2} z^2$.

Step 5: Conclusion of the proof. By combining (7.14) with the summation of (7.17) over all t, we obtain

$$\sum_{t=0}^{T-1} \langle g^t, p^t - p \rangle \leq \frac{1}{\eta} \left(D_H(p, p^0) + T \frac{(\eta G)^2}{2} \right).$$

By observing that

$$D_H(p, p^0) = D_{KL}(p, p^0) \leq \log n$$

and optimizing the choice of η, the theorem follows. ∎

7.4 Mirror Descent

In this section, we take inspiration from the exponential gradient descent algorithm to derive a general method for convex optimization called mirror descent.

7.4.1 Generalizing the EGD Algorithm and the Proximal Viewpoint

The main idea follows the intuition provided at the very beginning of the chapter. Recall that our update rule is (7.5), i.e., at a given point x^t we construct a linear lower bound

$$f(x^t) + \langle \nabla f(x^t), x - x^t \rangle \leq f(x)$$

and move to the next point, which is the minimizer of this lower bound "regularized" by a distance function $D(\cdot, \cdot)$, thus we get (7.5)

$$x^{t+1} := \underset{x \in K}{\operatorname{argmin}} \left\{ D(x, x^t) + \eta \langle \nabla f(x^t), x \rangle \right\}.$$

When deriving the exponential gradient descent algorithm, we used the generalized KL-divergence $D_H(\cdot, \cdot)$.

Mirror descent is defined with respect to $D_R(\cdot, \cdot)$ for any convex regularizer $R \colon \mathbb{R}^n \to \mathbb{R}$. In general, by denoting the gradient at step t by g^t, we have

$$\begin{aligned}
x^{t+1} &= \underset{x \in K}{\operatorname{argmin}} \left\{ D_R(x, x^t) + \eta \langle g^t, x \rangle \right\} \\
&= \underset{x \in K}{\operatorname{argmin}} \left\{ \eta \langle g^t, x \rangle + R(x) - R(x^t) - \langle \nabla R(x^t), x - x^t \rangle \right\} \qquad (7.18) \\
&= \underset{x \in K}{\operatorname{argmin}} \left\{ R(x) - \langle \nabla R(x^t) - \eta g^t, x \rangle \right\},
\end{aligned}$$

where in the last step we have ignored the terms that do not depend on x. Let w^{t+1} be a point such that

$$\nabla R(w^{t+1}) = \nabla R(x^t) - \eta g^t.$$

It is not clear under what conditions such a point w^{t+1} should exist, and we address this later; for now, assume such a w^{t+1} exists. This corresponds to the same w^{t+1} as we had in the EGD algorithm (the "unscaled" version of p^{t+1}). We then have

$$
\begin{aligned}
x^{t+1} &= \operatorname*{argmin}_{x \in K} \left\{ R(x) - \left\langle \nabla R(w^{t+1}), x \right\rangle \right\} \\
&= \operatorname*{argmin}_{x \in K} \left\{ R(x) - R(w^{t+1}) + \left\langle \nabla R(w^{t+1}), x \right\rangle \right\} \quad (7.19) \\
&= \operatorname*{argmin}_{x \in K} \left\{ D_R(x, w^{t+1}) \right\}.
\end{aligned}
$$

Note again the analogy with the EGD algorithm: There, p^{t+1} was obtained as a KL-divergence projection of w^{t+1} onto the simplex $\Delta_n = K$, exactly as above. This is also called the **proximal** viewpoint of mirror descent, and the calculations above establish the equivalence of the regularization and the proximal viewpoints.

7.4.2 The Mirror Descent Algorithm

We are ready to state the mirror descent algorithm (Algorithm 3) in its general form. For it to be well defined, we need to make sure that w^{t+1} always exists. Formally, we assume that the regularizer $R \colon \Omega \to \mathbb{R}$ has a domain Ω, which contains K as a subset. Moreover, as in the case of the entropy function, we assume that the map $\nabla R \colon \Omega \to \mathbb{R}^n$ is a bijection – this is perhaps more than what we really need, but such an assumption makes the picture much more clear. In fact, R is sometimes referred to as the **mirror map.**

By the theory of conjugate functions developed in Chapter 5, we know that if R is convex and closed, then the inverse of ∇R is ∇R^*, where R^* is the conjugate of R; see Lemma 5.10. To be more precise, for the above to hold we need that both R and R^* are differentiable. We can also modify the mirror descent method to work with subgradients; we omit the details. Further, as mentioned earlier, if we assume that as x tends to the boundary of the domain of R, the norm of the gradient of R tends to infinity, then, along with the strict convexity of the map $x \mapsto D_R(x, y)$ and the compactness of the domain, we can be sure about the existence and uniqueness of the projection x^{t+1} above.

Algorithm 3: Mirror descent

Input:
- First-order oracle access to a convex function $f : K \to \mathbb{R}$
- Oracle access to the ∇R mapping and its inverse
- Projection operator with respect to $D_R(\cdot, \cdot)$
- An initial point $x^0 \in K$
- A parameter $\eta > 0$
- An integer $T > 0$

Output: A point $\bar{x} \in K$
Algorithm:
1: **for** $t = 0, 1, \ldots, T - 1$ **do**
2:     Obtain $g^t := \nabla f(p^t)$
3:     Let w^{t+1} be such that $\nabla R(w^{t+1}) = \nabla R(x^t) - \eta \nabla f(x^t)$
4:     $x^{t+1} = \operatorname{argmin}_{x \in K} D_R(x, w^{t+1})$
5: **end for**
6: **return** $\bar{x} := \frac{1}{T} \sum_{t=0}^{T-1} x^t$

Note that in order for the algorithm to be useful, the mirror map ∇R (and its inverse) should be efficiently computable. Similarly, the projection step

$$\operatorname*{argmin}_{x \in K} D_R(x, w^{t+1})$$

should also be computationally easy to perform. The efficiency of these two operations determines the time required to perform one iteration of mirror descent.

7.4.3 Convergence Proof

We are now ready to state the iteration bound guarantee for the mirror descent algorithm presented in Algorithm 3.

Theorem 7.9 (Guarantees for mirror descent). *Let* $f : K \to \mathbb{R}$ *and* $R : \Omega \to \mathbb{R}$ *be convex functions with* $K \subseteq \Omega \subseteq \mathbb{R}^n$, *and suppose the following assumptions hold:*

(1) *The gradient map* $\nabla R : \Omega \to \mathbb{R}^n$ *is a bijection.*
(2) *The function* f *has bounded gradients with respect to norm* $\|\cdot\|$, *i.e.,*

$$\forall x \in K, \quad \|\nabla f(x)\| \leq G.$$

(3) *R is σ-strongly convex with respect to the dual norm $\|\cdot\|^*$, i.e.,*

$$\forall x \in \Omega, \quad D_R(x,y) \geq \frac{\sigma}{2} \|x - y\|^{*2}.$$

If we let $\eta := \Theta\left(\frac{\sqrt{\sigma D_R(x^*,x^0)}}{\sqrt{T}G}\right)$ *then, after* $T := \Theta\left(\frac{G^2 D_R(x^*,x^0)}{\sigma \varepsilon^2}\right)$ *iterations of the mirror descent algorithm, the point $\bar{x}$ satisfies*

$$f(\bar{x}) - f(x^*) \leq \varepsilon,$$

where x^* is any minimizer of $f(x)$.

Proof: The proof of the above theorem follows exactly as the one we gave for Theorem 7.5 by replacing the generalized negative entropy function H with a regularizer R and replacing KL-divergence terms D_H with D_R.

We now go step by step through the proof of Theorem 7.5 and emphasize which properties of R and D_R are being used.

In **Step 1,** the reasoning in (7.11) used to obtain

$$f(\bar{x}) - f(x^*) \leq \frac{1}{T} \sum_{t=0}^{T-1} \langle g^t, x^t - x^* \rangle$$

is general and relies only on the convexity of f.

In **Step 2,** the facts used in equations (7.12) and (7.13) to prove that

$$\langle g^t, x^t - x^* \rangle = \frac{1}{\eta} \left(D_R(x^*, x^t) + D_R(x^t, w^{t+1}) - D_R(x^*, w^{t+1}) \right)$$

are the definition of w^{t+1} and the law of cosines, which is valid for any Bregman divergence (see Lemma 7.6). Subsequently, in **Step 3,** to arrive at the conclusion of (7.14),

$$\eta \sum_{t=0}^{T-1} \langle g^t, x^t - x^* \rangle \leq D_R(x^*, x^0) + \sum_{t=0}^{T-1} \left[D_R(x^t, w^{t+1}) - D_R(x^{t+1}, w^{t+1}) \right],$$

only the generalized Pythagorean theorem (Theorem 7.7) is necessary.

Finally in **Step 4,** an analog of (7.17) that can be proved under our current assumptions is

$$D_R(x^t, w^{t+1}) - D_R(x^{t+1}, w^{t+1}) \leq \|g^t\| \|x^t - x^{t+1}\|^* - \frac{\sigma}{2} \|x^{t+1} - x^t\|^{*2}.$$

The above follows from the strong convexity assumption with respect to $\|\cdot\|$ (which is used in place of Pinsker's inequality) and the Cauchy-Schwarz inequality for dual norms:

$$\langle u, v \rangle \leq \|u\| \|v\|^*.$$

The rest of the proof is the same and does not rely on any specific properties of R or D_R. ∎

7.5 Multiplicative Weights Update

In the proof of Theorem 7.5, the only place we used the fact that the vectors g^t are gradients of the function f at points p^t (for $t = 0, 1, \ldots, T$) is the bound in (7.11). Subsequently, g^ts were treated as arbitrary vectors, and we proved a guarantee that in order to reach

$$\frac{1}{T} \sum_{t=0}^{T-1} \langle g^t, p^t \rangle - \min_{p \in \Delta_n} \frac{1}{T} \sum_{t=0}^{T-1} \langle g^t, p \rangle \le \varepsilon,$$

it is enough to take $T = O\left(\frac{G^2 \log n}{\varepsilon^2}\right)$. Let us now state this observation as a theorem. Before doing so, we first state this general meta-algorithm, known under the name **multiplicative weights update (MWU) method**; see Algorithm 4. In the exercises, we develop the more standard variant of the MWU method and prove guarantees about it.

Algorithm 4: Multiplicative weights update (MWU) algorithm

Input:
- An oracle providing vectors $g^t \in \mathbb{R}^n$ at every step $t = 0, 1, \ldots$
- A parameter $\eta > 0$
- An integer $T > 0$

Output: A sequence of probability distributions $p^0, p^1, \ldots, p^{T-1} \in \Delta_n$
Algorithm:
1: Initialize $p^0 := \frac{1}{n}\mathbf{1}$ (the uniform probability distribution)
2: **for** $t = 0, 1, \ldots, T-1$ **do**
3:   Obtain $g^t \in \mathbb{R}^n$ from the oracle
4:   Let $w^{t+1} \in \mathbb{R}^n$ and $p^{t+1} \in \Delta_n$ be defined as

$$w_i^{t+1} := p_i^t \exp(-\eta g_i^t)$$

and

$$p_i^{t+1} := \frac{w_i^{t+1}}{\sum_{j=1}^n w_j^{t+1}}$$

5: **end for**

By reasoning exactly as in the proof of Theorem 7.5, we obtain the following theorem.

Theorem 7.10 (Guarantees for MWU algorithm). *Consider the MWU algorithm presented in Algorithm 4. Assume that all of the vectors g^t provided by the oracle satisfy $\|g^t\|_\infty \leq G$. Then, taking $\eta = \Theta\left(\frac{\sqrt{\log n}}{\sqrt{TG}}\right)$, after $T = \Theta\left(\frac{G^2 \log n}{\varepsilon^2}\right)$ iterations we have*

$$\frac{1}{T} \sum_{t=0}^{T-1} \langle g^t, p^t \rangle - \min_{p \in \Delta_n} \frac{1}{T} \sum_{t=0}^{T-1} \langle g^t, p \rangle \leq \varepsilon.$$

At this point, it might not be clear what the purpose of stating such a theorem is. However, as we will shortly see (including in several exercises), this theorem allows us to come up with algorithms for numerous different problems based on the idea of maintaining weights and changing them multiplicatively. In the example we provide, we design an algorithm for checking if a bipartite graph has a perfect matching. This can be further extended to linear programming or even semidefinite programming.

7.6 Application: Perfect Matching in Bipartite Graphs

We formally define the problem of finding a perfect matching in a bipartite graph. The input to this problem consists of an undirected and unweighted bipartite graph $G = (V = A \cup B, E)$, where A, B are two disjoint sets of vertices with $A \cup B = V$, and all edges in E have one endpoint in A and another in B. The goal is to find a **perfect matching** in G: A subset of edges $M \subseteq E$ such that every vertex $v \in V$ is incident to exactly one of the edges in M. We assume that in the bipartition (A, B) we have $|A| = |B| = n$, so that the total number of vertices is $2n$ (note that if the cardinalities of A and B are not the same, then there is no perfect matching in G). Let $m := |E|$ as usual. Our approach to solving this problem is based on solving the following linear programming reformulation of the perfect matching problem:

$$\begin{aligned}
\text{Find} \quad & x \in \mathbb{R}^m \\
\text{such that} \quad & \sum_{e \in E} x_e = n, \\
\forall v \in V, \quad & \sum_{e : v \in e} x_e \leq 1, \\
\forall e \in E, \quad & x_e \geq 0.
\end{aligned} \tag{7.20}$$

A solution to the above linear feasibility program is called a **fractional perfect matching**. The question that arises very naturally is whether the "fractional" problem is equivalent to the original one. The following is a classical exercise in combinatorial optimization (see Exercise 2.27). It asserts that the "fractional" bipartite matching polytope (defined in the linear programming description above) has only integral vertices.

Theorem 7.11 (Integrality of the bipartite matching polytope). *If G is a bipartite graph, then G has a perfect matching if and only if G has a fractional perfect matching. Alternatively, the vertices of the bipartite matching polytope of G, defined as the convex hull of the indicator vectors of all perfect matchings in G, are exactly these indicator vectors.*

Note that one direction of this theorem is trivial: If there is a perfect matching $M \subseteq E$ in G, then its characteristic vector $x = 1_M$ is a fractional perfect matching. The other direction is harder and relies on the assumption that the graph is bipartite.

Algorithmically, one can also convert fractional matchings into matchings in $\widetilde{O}(|E|)$ time; we omit the details. Thus, solving (7.20) suffices to solve the perfect matching problem in its original form.

As our algorithm naturally produces approximate answers, for an $\varepsilon > 0$, we also define an ε-**approximate fractional perfect matching** to be an $x \in \mathbb{R}^m$ that satisfies

$$\sum_{e \in E} x_e = n,$$

$$\forall v \in V, \quad \sum_{e:v \in e} x_e \le 1 + \varepsilon,$$

$$\forall e \in E, \quad x_e \ge 0.$$

From such an approximate fractional matching, one can (given the ideas discussed above) construct a matching in G of cardinality at least $(1 - \varepsilon)n$ and, thus, also solve the perfect matching problem exactly by taking $\varepsilon < \frac{1}{n}$.

7.6.1 The Main Result

We construct an algorithm based on the MWU algorithm to construct ε-approximate fractional perfect matchings. Below, we formally state its running time guarantee.

Theorem 7.12 (Algorithm for the fractional bipartite matching problem). *Algorithm 5, given a bipartite graph G on $2n$ vertices and m edges that has a perfect matching, and an $\varepsilon > 0$, outputs an ε-approximate fractional perfect matching in G in time $\widetilde{O}(\varepsilon^{-2}n^2m)$.*

The running time of the above algorithm is certainly not comparable to the best-known algorithms for this problem, but its advantage is its overall simplicity.

7.6.2 The Algorithm

We construct an algorithm for finding fractional solutions to the perfect matching problem, i.e., to (7.20). In every step of the algorithm, we would like to construct a point $x^t \in \mathbb{R}_{\geq 0}^m$ that satisfies the constraint $\sum_{e \in E} x_e^t = n$ but is not necessarily a fractional matching (meaning that it does not have to satisfy $\sum_{e:v \in e} x_e^t \leq 1 + \varepsilon$ for every v). However, x^t should (in a certain sense) bring us closer to satisfying all the constraints.

More precisely, we maintain positive weights $w^t \in \mathbb{R}^{2n}$ over vertices V of the graph G. The value w_v^t corresponds to the importance of the inequality $\sum_{e:v \in e} x_e \leq 1$ at the current state of the algorithm. Intuitively, the importance is large whenever our "current solution" (which one should think of as the average of all x^t produced so far) violates this inequality, and more generally, the larger the violation of the vth constraints, the larger w_v^t is.

Given such weights, we then compute a new point x^t to be any point that satisfies $\sum_{e \in E} x_e^t = n$ and satisfies the **weighted average** (with respect to w^t) of all the inequalities $\sum_{e:v \in e} x_e^t \leq 1$. Next, we update our weights based on the violations of the inequalities by the new point x^t.

Algorithm 5 is not completely specified, as we have not yet provided a method for finding x^t. In the analysis, we specify one particular method for finding x^t and show that it gives an algorithm with a running time as in Theorem 7.12.

7.6.3 Analysis

The analysis is divided into two steps: how to find x^t, and the correctness of the algorithm given in the previous section (assuming a method for finding x^t).

Step 1: An oracle to find x^t. In the lemma below, we prove that x^t can be always found efficiently such that the infinity norm of g^t is bounded by 1. As we see soon, the bound on $\|g^t\|_\infty$ is crucial for the efficiency of our algorithm.

Lemma 7.13 (Oracle). *If G has a perfect matching then*

(1) *x^t always exists and can be found in $O(m)$ time, and*
(2) *we can guarantee that $\|g^t\|_\infty \leq 1$.*

Algorithm 5: Approximate perfect matching in bipartite graphs

Input:
- A bipartite graph $G = (V, E)$
- An $\eta > 0$
- A positive integer $T > 0$

Output: An approximate fractional perfect matching $x \in [0,1]^m$
Algorithm:
1: Initialize $w^0 := (1, 1, \ldots, 1) \in \mathbb{R}^{2n}$
2: **for** $t = 0, 1, \ldots, T - 1$ **do**
3:    Find a point $x^t \in \mathbb{R}^m$ satisfying

$$\sum_{v \in V} w_v^t \left(\sum_{e:v \in e} x_e^t \right) \leq \sum_{v \in V} w_v^t$$

$$\sum_{e \in E} x_e^t = n$$

   and

$$x_e^t \geq 0 \quad \text{for all } e \in E$$

4:    Construct a vector $g^t \in \mathbb{R}^{2n}$

$$g_v^t := \frac{1 - \sum_{e:v \in e} x_e^t}{n}$$

5:    Update the weights:

$$w_v^{t+1} := w_v^t \cdot \exp(-\eta \cdot g_v^t) \quad \text{for all } v \in V$$

6: **end for**
7: **return** $x := \frac{1}{T} \sum_{t=0}^{T-1} x^t$

Proof: If M is a perfect matching, then $x^t = 1_M$ (the indicator vector of M) satisfies all conditions. However, we do not know M and cannot compute it easily, but still we would like to find such a point. Let us rewrite the condition

$$\sum_{v \in V} w_v^t \left(\sum_{e:v \in e} x_e \right) \leq \sum_{v \in V} w_v^t$$

in the form

$$\sum_{e \in E} \alpha_e x_e \leq \beta, \tag{7.21}$$

where all the coefficients α_e and β are nonnegative and as follows:

$$\alpha_e := \sum_{e \in N(v)} w_v^t \quad \text{and} \quad \beta := \sum_{v \in V} w_v^t.$$

If G has a perfect matching M, then there are edges $e^1, \ldots, e^n$ that do not share any vertex. Hence,

$$\sum_{i=1}^n \alpha_{e^i} = \beta.$$

Further, let $e^\star$ be the edge such that

$$e^\star := \arg\min_{e \in E} \alpha_e.$$

Then, we have that

$$n\alpha_{e^\star} \leq \sum_{i=1}^n \alpha_{e^i} = \beta.$$

Hence, setting

$$x_{e^\star}^t = n \quad \text{and} \quad x_{e'}^t = 0 \ \ \forall e' \neq e^\star$$

is also a valid solution to (7.21). Such a choice of x^t also guarantees that for every $v \in V$,

$$-1 \leq \sum_{e \in N(v)} x_e^t - 1 \leq n - 1,$$

which in particular implies that $\|g^t\|_\infty \leq 1$. ∎

Step 2: Proof of Theorem 7.10. We now invoke Theorem 7.10 to obtain the guarantee claimed in Theorem 7.12 on the output of Algorithm 5. We start by noticing that, if we set

$$p^t := \frac{w^t}{\sum_{v \in V} w_v^t},$$

Algorithm 5 is a special case of the MWU algorithm with g^t satisfying $\|g^t\|_\infty \leq 1$.

Further, we can plug in $p := e_v$ for any fixed $v \in V$ in Theorem 7.10 to conclude

$$-\frac{1}{T} \sum_{t=0}^{T-1} g_v^t \leq -\frac{1}{T} \sum_{t=0}^{T-1} \langle p^t, g^t \rangle + \delta \tag{7.22}$$

for $T = \Theta\left(\frac{\log n}{\delta^2}\right)$ (since $G = 1$). The fact that x^t satisfies

$$\sum_{v \in V} w_v^t \left(\sum_{e:v \in e} x_e\right) \leq \sum_{v \in V} w_v^t$$

implies that

$$\sum_{v \in V} w_v^t \left(1 - \left(\sum_{e:v \in e} x_e\right)\right) \geq 0.$$

Dividing by n and $\|w^t\|_1$, the above inequality can be seen to be the same as

$$\langle p^t, g^t\rangle \geq 0.$$

Therefore, from the guarantee (7.22), for any $v \in V$, we get

$$\frac{1}{T} \cdot \frac{1}{n}\left(\sum_{e:v \in e} x_e^t - 1\right) \leq \frac{1}{T} \cdot T \cdot 0 + \delta.$$

This implies that for all $v \in V$,

$$\sum_{e:v \in e} x_e \leq 1 + n\delta.$$

Thus, to make the right-hand side in the above inequality $1 + \varepsilon$, we pick $\delta := \frac{\varepsilon}{n}$ and, hence, T becomes $\Theta\left(\frac{n^2 \log n}{\varepsilon^2}\right)$. Further, since x is a convex combination of x^t for $t = 0, \ldots, T - 1$, it also satisfies $\sum_{e \in E} x_e = n$ and $x \geq 0$. Thus, if G contains a perfect matching, the oracle keeps outputting a point x^t for $t = 0, \ldots, T - 1$, and the final point x is an ε-approximate fractional perfect matching.

It remains to reason about the running time. The number of iterations is $O\left(\frac{n^2 \log n}{\varepsilon^2}\right)$ and the goal of each iteration is to find x^t and update the weights, which can be done in $O(m)$ time as it just requires to find the edge e with minimum $\sum_{e:v \in e} w_v^t$. This completes the proof of Theorem 7.12.

Remark 7.14. It can be easily seen that the reason for the n^2 factor in the running time is because of our bound $|\sum_{e:v \in e} x_e^t - 1| \leq n$. If one could always produce a point x^t with

$$\forall v \in V \quad \left|\sum_{e:v \in e} x_e^t - 1\right| \leq \rho,$$

then the running time would become $O(\varepsilon^{-2} m\rho^2 \log n)$. Note that intuitively, this should be possible to do, since $x^t = 1_M$ (for any perfect matching M)

gives $\rho = 1$. However, at the same time we would like our procedure for finding x^t to be efficient; preferably it should run in nearly linear time. It is an interesting exercise to design a nearly linear time algorithm for finding x^t with the guarantee $\rho = 2$, which yields a much better running time of only $O(\varepsilon^{-2} m \log^2 n)$.

7.7 Exercises

7.1 Prove that if $f : \mathbb{R}^n \to \mathbb{R}$ is a convex function that is G-Lipschitz continuous, then $\|\nabla f(x)\| \le G$ for all $x \in \mathbb{R}^n$. Extend this result to the case when $f : K \to \mathbb{R}$ for some convex set K.

7.2 Give an example of a function $f : \mathbb{R}^n \to \mathbb{R}$ such that $\|\nabla f(x)\|_2 \le 1$ for all $x \in \mathbb{R}^n$, but the Lipschitz constant of its gradient is unbounded.

7.3 **Smoothed absolute value.** Consider the function $f(x) := \frac{x^2}{|x|+1}$ (see Figure 7.1). As one can see, the function f is a "smooth" variant of $x \mapsto |x|$: It is differentiable everywhere, and $|f(x) - |x|| \to 0$ when x tends to either $+\infty$ or $-\infty$. Similarly, one can consider a multivariate extension $F : \mathbb{R}^n \to \mathbb{R}$ of f given by

$$F(x) := \sum_{i=1}^{n} \frac{x_i^2}{|x_i| + 1}.$$

This can be seen as a smoothening of the ℓ_1-norm $\|x\|_1$. Prove that

$$\|\nabla F(x)\|_\infty \le 1$$

for all $x \in \mathbb{R}^n$.

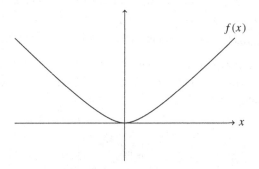

Figure 7.1 The plot of the function $f(x) = \frac{x^2}{|x|+1}$.

7.4   **Soft-max function.** Since the function $x \mapsto \max\{x_1, x_2, \ldots, x_n\}$ is not differentiable, one often considers the so-called soft-max function

$$s_\alpha(x) := \frac{1}{\alpha} \log \left(\sum_{i=1}^{n} e^{\alpha x_i} \right).$$

for some $\alpha > 0$, as a replacement for the maximum. Prove that

$$\max\{x_1, x_2, \ldots, x_n\} \le s_\alpha(x) \le \frac{\log n}{\alpha} + \max\{x_1, x_2, \ldots, x_n\},$$

thus, the larger α is, the better approximation we obtain. Further, prove that for every $x \in \mathbb{R}^n$,

$$\|\nabla s_\alpha(x)\|_\infty \le 1.$$

7.5   Prove the following properties of KL-divergence:

(a) D_{KL} is not symmetric: $D_{KL}(p, q) \ne D_{KL}(q, p)$ for all $p, q \in \Delta_n$.

(b) D_{KL} is indeed a Bregman divergence of a convex function on Δ_n and $D_{KL}(p, q) \ge 0$.

7.6   Let $F : \mathbb{R}^n \to \mathbb{R}$ be a convex function. Prove that the function mapping $x \mapsto D_F(x, y)$ for a fixed $y \in \mathbb{R}^n$ is strictly convex.

7.7   Prove Lemma 7.6.

7.8   Prove that for all $p \in \Delta_n$, $D_{KL}(p, p^0) \le \log n$. Here, p^0 is the uniform probability distribution with $p_i^0 = \frac{1}{n}$ for $1 \le i \le n$.

7.9   Prove that for $F(x) := \|x\|_2^2$ over $\mathbb{R}^n$,

$$D_F(x, y) = \|x - y\|_2^2.$$

7.10   **Gradient descent when the Euclidean norm of gradient is bounded.** Use Theorem 7.9 to prove that there is an algorithm that, given a convex and differentiable function $f : \mathbb{R}^n \to \mathbb{R}$ with a gradient bounded in the Euclidean norm by G, an $\varepsilon > 0$, and an initial point x^0 satisfying $\|x^0 - x^\star\|_2 \le D$, produces $x \in \mathbb{R}^n$ satisfying

$$f(x) - f(x^\star) \le \varepsilon$$

in T iterations using a step size η, where

$$T := \left(\frac{DG}{\varepsilon} \right)^2 \quad \text{and} \quad \eta := \frac{D}{G\sqrt{T}}.$$

7.11   **Stochastic gradient descent.** In this problem we study how well gradient descent does when we have a relatively weak access to the gradient. In the previous problem, we assumed that for a differentiable convex function $f : \mathbb{R}^n \to \mathbb{R}$, we have a first-order oracle: Given x, it outputs $\nabla f(x)$. Now assume that when we give a point x, we get a random vector $g(x) \in \mathbb{R}^n$ from some underlying distribution such that

$$\mathbb{E}[g(x)] = \nabla f(x).$$

(If x itself has been chosen from some random distribution, then $\mathbb{E}[g(x)|x] = \nabla f(x)$.) Assume that $\|\nabla f(x)\|_2 \leq G$ for all $x \in \mathbb{R}^n$. Subsequently, we do gradient descent in the following way. Pick some $\eta > 0$, and assume that the starting point x^0 is such that $\|x^0 - x^\star\|_2 \leq D$. Let

$$x^{t+1} := x^t - \eta g(x^t).$$

Now note that since g is a random variable, so is x^t for all $t \geq 1$. Let

$$x := \frac{1}{T} \sum_{t=0}^{T-1} x^i.$$

(a) Prove that if we set

$$T := \left(\frac{DG}{\varepsilon}\right)^2 \quad \text{and} \quad \eta := \frac{D}{G\sqrt{T}},$$

then

$$\mathbb{E}(f(x)) - f(x^\star) \leq \varepsilon.$$

(b) Suppose we have a number of labeled examples

$$(a_1, l_1), (a_2, l_2), \ldots, (a_m, l_m),$$

where each $a_i \in \mathbb{R}^n$ and $l_i \in \mathbb{R}$. The goal is to find an x that minimizes

$$f(x) := \frac{1}{m} \sum_{i=1}^{m} |\langle x, a_i \rangle - l_i|^2.$$

In this case, for a given x, pick a number i uniformly at random from $\{1, 2, \ldots, m\}$ and output

$$g(x) = 2a_i(\langle x, a_i \rangle - l_i).$$

(1) Prove that for this example, $\mathbb{E}[g(x)] = \nabla f(x)$.
(2) What does the result proved above imply for this example?

(c) What is the advantage of this method over the traditional gradient descent?

7.12 **$s - t$-minimum cut problem.** Recall the formulation of the $s - t$-minimum cut problem in an undirected graph $G = (V, E)$ with n vertices and m edges that was studied in Exercise 6.11, i.e.,

$$\text{MinCut}_{s,t}(G) := \min_{x \in \mathbb{R}^n, x_s - x_t = 1} \sum_{ij \in E} |x_i - x_j|.$$

Apply the mirror descent algorithm with the regularizer $R(x) = \|x\|_2^2$ along with Theorem 7.9 to find $\text{MinCut}_{s,t}(G)$ exactly (note that it is an integer of value at most m). Estimate all relevant parameters and provide a bound on the running time. Explain how to deal with the (simple) constraint $x_s - x_t = 1$.

7.13 **Min-max theorem for zero-sum games.** In this problem, we apply the MWU algorithm to approximately find equilibria in two-player zero-sum games.

Let $A \in \mathbb{R}^{n \times m}$ be a matrix with $A(i, j) \in [0, 1]$ for all $i \in [n]$ and $j \in [m]$. We consider a game between two players: a row player and a column player. The game consists of one round in which the row player picks one row $i \in \{1, 2, \ldots, n\}$ and the column player picks one column $j \in \{1, 2, \ldots, m\}$. The goal of the row player is to minimize the value $A(i, j)$ that she pays to the column player after such a round; the goal of the column player is of course the opposite (to maximize the value $A(i, j)$).

The min-max theorem asserts that

$$\max_{q \in \Delta_m} \min_{i \in \{1, \ldots, n\}} \mathbb{E}_{J \leftarrow q} A(i, J) = \min_{p \in \Delta_n} \max_{j \in \{1, \ldots, m\}} \mathbb{E}_{I \leftarrow p} A(I, j) \quad (7.23)$$

Here, $\mathbb{E}_{I \leftarrow p} A(I, j)$ is the expected loss of the row player when using the randomized strategy $p \in \Delta_n$ against a fixed strategy $j \in \{1, 2, \ldots, m\}$ of the column player. Similarly, define $\mathbb{E}_{J \leftarrow q} A(i, J)$. Formally,

$$\mathbb{E}_{I \leftarrow p} A(I, j) := \sum_{i=1}^{n} p_i A(i, j) \quad \text{and} \quad \mathbb{E}_{J \leftarrow q} A(i, J) := \sum_{j=1}^{m} q_j A(i, J).$$

Let opt be the common value of the two quantities in (7.23) corresponding to two optimal strategies $p^\star \in \Delta_n$ and $q^\star \in \Delta_m$, respectively. Our goal is to use the MWU method to construct, for any $\varepsilon > 0$, a pair of strategies $p \in \Delta_n$ and $q \in \Delta_m$ such that

$$\max_{j} \mathbb{E}_{I \leftarrow p} A(I, j) \leq \text{opt} + \varepsilon \quad \text{and} \quad \min_{i} \mathbb{E}_{J \leftarrow q} A(i, J) \geq \text{opt} - \varepsilon.$$

(a) Prove the following "easier" direction of von Neumann's theorem:

$$\max_{q \in \Delta_m} \min_{i \in \{1,...,n\}} \mathbb{E}_{J \leftarrow q} A(i, J) \le \min_{p \in \Delta_n} \max_{j \in \{1,...,m\}} \mathbb{E}_{I \leftarrow p} A(I, j).$$

(b) Give an algorithm that, given $p \in \Delta_n$, constructs a $j \in \{1, 2, \ldots, m\}$ that maximizes $\mathbb{E}_{I \leftarrow p} A(I, j)$. What is the running time of the algorithm? Show that for such a choice of j, we have $\mathbb{E}_{I \leftarrow p} A(I, j) \ge$ opt.

We follow the MWU scheme with $p^0, \ldots, p^{T-1} \in \Delta_n$ and the loss vector at step t being $g^t := Aq^t$, where $q^t := e_j$ with j chosen as to maximize $\mathbb{E}_{I \leftarrow p^t} A(I, j)$. (Recall that e_j is the vector with 1 at coordinate j and 0 otherwise.)

(c) Prove that $\|g^t\|_\infty \le 1$ and $\langle p^\star, g^t \rangle \le$ opt for every $t = 0, 1, \ldots, T - 1$.

(d) Use Theorem 7.10 to show that for T large enough,

$$\text{opt} \le \frac{1}{T} \sum_{t=0}^{T-1} \langle p^t, g^t \rangle \le \text{opt} + \varepsilon.$$

What is the smallest value of T that suffices for this to hold? Conclude that for some t, it holds that $\max_j \mathbb{E}_{I \leftarrow p^t} A(I, j) \le \text{opt} + \varepsilon.$

(e) Let

$$q := \frac{1}{T} \sum_{t=0}^{T-1} q^t.$$

Prove that for T as in part (d),

$$\min_i \mathbb{E}_{J \leftarrow q} A(i, J) \ge \text{opt} - \varepsilon.$$

(f) What is the total running time of the whole procedure to find an ε-approximate pair of strategies p and q that we set out to find at the beginning of this problem?

7.14 **Winnow algorithm for classification.** Suppose we are given m labeled examples, (a_1, l_1), (a_2, l_2), $\ldots$, (a_m, l_m), where $a_i \in \mathbb{R}^n$ are feature vectors and $l_i \in \{-1, +1\}$ are their labels. Our goal is to find a hyperplane separating the points labeled with a $+1$ from the points labeled -1. Assume that the dividing hyperplane contains 0 and its normal is nonnegative. Hence, formally, our goal is to find $p \in \mathbb{R}^n$ with $p \geq 0$ such that

$$\text{sign}\,\langle a_i, p \rangle = l_i$$

for every $i \in \{1, \ldots, m\}$. By scaling, we can assume that $\|a_i\|_\infty \leq 1$ for every $i \in \{1, \ldots, m\}$ and that $\langle 1, p \rangle = 1$ (recall 1 is the vector of all 1s). For notational convenience, we redefine a_i to be $l_i a_i$. The problem is thus reduced to finding a solution to the following linear programming problem: Find a p such that

$$\langle a_i, p \rangle > 0 \quad \text{for every } i \in \{1, \ldots, m\} \text{ where } p \in \Delta_n.$$

Prove the following theorem.

Theorem 7.15. *Given $a_1, \ldots, a_m \in \mathbb{R}^n$ and $\varepsilon > 0$, if there exists $p^\star \in \Delta_n$ such that $\langle a_i, p^\star \rangle \geq \varepsilon$ for every $i \in \{1, \ldots, m\}$, the Winnow algorithm (Algorithm 6) produces a point $p \in \Delta_n$ such that $\langle a_i, p \rangle > 0$ for every $i \in \{1, \ldots, m\}$ in $T = \Theta\left(\frac{\ln n}{\varepsilon^2}\right)$ iterations.*

What is the running time of the entire algorithm?

7.15 **Feasibility of linear inequalities.** Consider a general linear feasibility problem that asks for a point x satisfying a system of inequalities

$$\langle a_i, x \rangle \geq b_i$$

for $i = 1, 2, \ldots, m$, where $a_1, a_2, \ldots, a_m \in \mathbb{R}^n$ and $b_1, b_2, \ldots, b_m \in \mathbb{R}$. The goal of this problem is to give an algorithm that, given an error parameter $\varepsilon > 0$, outputs a point x such that

$$\langle a_i, x \rangle \geq b_i - \varepsilon \qquad (7.24)$$

for all i whenever there is a solution to the above system of inequalities. We also assume the existence of an *oracle* that, given vector $p \in \Delta_m$, solves the following relaxed problem: Does there exist an x such that

$$\sum_{i=1}^{m} \sum_{j=1}^{n} p_i a_{ij} x_j \geq \sum_{i=1}^{m} p_i b_i? \qquad (7.25)$$

Assume that when the oracle returns a feasible solution for a p, the solution x that it returns is not arbitrary but has the following property:

$$\max_i |\langle a_i, x \rangle - b_i| \leq 1.$$

Algorithm 6: The Winnow algorithm

Input:
- A set of m points $a_1, \ldots, a_m$ where $a_i \in \mathbb{R}^n$ for every i
- An $\varepsilon > 0$

Output: A point $p \in \Delta_n$ satisfying Theorem 7.15

Algorithm:

1: Let $T := \Theta\left(\frac{\ln n}{\varepsilon^2}\right)$
2: Let $w_i^0 := 1$ for every $i \in \{1, \ldots, n\}$
3: **for** $t = 0, 1, \ldots, T - 1$ **do**
4:     Let $p_j^t := \frac{w_j^t}{\|w^t\|_1}$ for every j
5:     Check for all $1 \leq i \leq m$ whether $\langle a_i, p^t \rangle \leq 0$
6:     If no such i exists then stop and return p^t
7:     If there exists an i such that $\langle a_i, p^t \rangle \leq 0$:

    (a) Let $g^t := -a_i$
    (b) Update $w_j^{t+1} := w_j^t \exp(-\varepsilon g_j^t)$ for every j

8: **end for**
9: **return** $\frac{1}{T} \sum_{t=0}^{T-1} p^t$

Prove the following theorem:

Theorem 7.16. *There is an algorithm that, if there exists an x such that $\langle a_i, x \rangle \geq b_i$ for all i, outputs an $\bar{x}$ that satisfies (7.24). The algorithm makes at most $O\left(\frac{\ln m}{\varepsilon^2}\right)$ calls to the oracle for the problem mentioned in (7.25).*

7.16 **Online convex optimization.** Given a sequence of convex and differentiable functions $f^0, f^1, \ldots : K \to \mathbb{R}$ and a sequence of points $x^0, x^1, \ldots \in K$, define the **regret** up to time T to be

$$\text{Regret}_T := \sum_{t=0}^{T-1} f^t(x^t) - \min_{x \in K} \sum_{t=0}^{T-1} f^t(x).$$

Consider the following strategy inspired by the mirror descent algorithm in this chapter (called **follow the regularized leader**):

$$x^t := \underset{x \in K}{\text{argmin}} \sum_{i=0}^{t-1} f^i(x) + R(x)$$

for a convex regularizer $R\colon K \to \mathbb{R}$ and $x^0 := \mathrm{argmin}_{x \in K}\, R(x)$. Assume that each the gradient of each f^i is bounded everywhere by G and that the diameter of K is bounded by D.

Prove the following:

(a)

$$\mathrm{Regret}_T \leq \sum_{t=0}^{T-1} (f^t(x^t) - f^t(x^{t+1})) - R(x^0) + R(x^\star)$$

for every $T = 0, 1, \ldots$, where

$$x^\star := \mathop{\mathrm{argmin}}_{x \in K} \sum_{t=0}^{T-1} f^t(x).$$

(b) Given an $\varepsilon > 0$, use this method for

$$R(x) := \frac{1}{\eta} \|x\|_2^2$$

for an appropriate choice of η and T to get

$$\frac{1}{T}\mathrm{Regret}_T \leq \varepsilon.$$

7.17 **Bandit optimization.** The notation in this exercise is the same as that in the MWU method. We consider a variant of the MWU setting called the **bandit** setting. Unlike the MWU setting, in each iteration of the bandit setting, the vector g^t is not revealed entirely. Instead, in iteration t, the algorithm has a probability distribution p^t over the set of n **experts**, it samples an expert (say i) from p^t, and only the ith coordinate of g^t is revealed to the algorithm as feedback. Define

$$\hat{g}_i^t := \begin{cases} \frac{g_i^t}{p_i^t} & \text{if expert } i \text{ was chosen at time } t, \text{ and} \\ 0 & \text{otherwise.} \end{cases} \tag{7.26}$$

The goal of this exercise is to show that Algorithm 7 can give a guarantee on the regret as in Theorem 7.10.

Theorem 7.17 (Guarantees for EXP3 algorithm). *Consider the EXP3 algorithm presented in Algorithm 7. Assume that all of the vectors g^t provided by the oracle satisfy $\|g^t\|_\infty \leq 1$. Let $0 < \varepsilon \leq \frac{1}{n}$. Then, the probability distributions $p^0, \ldots, p^{T-1}$ satisfy*

$$\frac{1}{T} \sum_{t=0}^{T-1} \langle p^t, g^t \rangle - \frac{1}{T} \inf_{p \in \Delta_n} \sum_{t=0}^{T-1} \langle p, g^t \rangle \leq \frac{\ln n}{T\varepsilon} + 2n\varepsilon. \tag{7.27}$$

Algorithm 7: EXP3 algorithm

Input:
- A stochastic access to vectors $g^t \in \mathbb{R}^n$ at every step $t = 0, 1, \ldots$
- A parameter $\varepsilon > 0$
- An integer $T > 0$

Output: A sequence of probability distributions $p^0, p^1, \ldots, p^{T-1} \in \Delta_n$
Algorithm:
1: Initialize $w^0 := 1$ (the all-ones vector)
2: **for** $t = 0, 1, \ldots, T - 1$ **do**
3:    Let $\phi^t := \sum_{j=1}^n w_j^t$
4:    Sample i with probability

$$p_i^t := (1 - n\varepsilon) \cdot \frac{w_i^t}{\phi^t} + \varepsilon$$

5:    Obtain $g_i^t \in \mathbb{R}$ from the oracle
6:    Let $\hat{g}_i^t := \frac{g_i^t}{p_i^t}$
7:    Update the weight of expert i as such

$$w_i^{t+1} := w_i^t \exp(-\varepsilon \hat{g}_i^t)$$

8: **end for**

Thus, by choosing $\varepsilon := \min\left\{\frac{1}{n}, \sqrt{\frac{\ln n}{2nT}}\right\}$, we can bound the regret (left-hand side of Equation (7.27)) by $2\sqrt{\frac{2n \ln n}{T}}$.

(a) Prove that for all t, the following always holds:

$$\sum_{j=1}^n p_j^t (\hat{g}_j^t)^2 \leq \sum_{j=1}^n \hat{g}_j^t.$$

(b) Let $\phi^t := \sum_{j=1}^n w_j^t$. Prove that for all $T \geq 1$ and any fixed i, the following always holds:

$$\ln \frac{\phi^T}{\phi^0} \geq -\varepsilon \sum_{t=0}^{T-1} \hat{g}_i^t - \ln n.$$

(c) Use part (a) along with the equality that

$$\ln \frac{\phi^{T-1}}{\phi^0} = \sum_{t=0}^{T-1} \ln \frac{\phi^{t+1}}{\phi^t}$$

and the inequality that

$$e^x \le 1 + x + x^2,$$

which holds for every $x \le 1$, to prove that for all $T \ge 1$ the following always holds:

$$\ln \frac{\phi^T}{\phi^0} \le -\frac{\varepsilon}{1-n\varepsilon} \sum_{t=0}^{T-1} \langle p^t, \hat{g}^t \rangle + \frac{2\varepsilon^2}{1-n\varepsilon} \sum_{t=0}^{T-1} \sum_{j=1}^{n} \hat{g}_j^t.$$

(d) Use parts (b) and (c) along with our assumption $\|g^t\|_\infty \le 1$ for all t to prove that the following always holds:

$$-\varepsilon \sum_{t=0}^{T-1} \hat{g}_i^t - \ln n \le -\frac{\varepsilon}{1-n\varepsilon} \sum_{t=0}^{T-1} \langle p^t, \hat{g}^t \rangle + \frac{2\varepsilon^2}{1-n\varepsilon} nT.$$

(e) Complete the proof of Theorem 7.17.

Note: When compared to Theorem 7.10, Theorem 7.17 has an additional factor n. The intuition behind the slowdown of the performance of this algorithm is the fact that we only have access to the loss of one expert, and so it seems that to catch up with the knowledge developed by MWU, we have to explore almost all n experts through n iterations. This means the knowledge gathered by MWU takes a linear time more to gather by EXP3.

Notes

Mirror descent was introduced by Nemirovski and Yudin (1983). Beck and Teboulle (2003) presented an alternative derivation and analysis of mirror descent. In particular, they showed that mirror descent can be viewed as a nonlinear, projected-gradient type method, derived using a general distance-like function instead of the ℓ_2^2-distance. This chapter covers both viewpoints.

The MWU method appeared at least as early as the 1950s and has been rediscovered in many fields since then. It has applications to optimization (e.g., Exercise 7.15), game theory (e.g., Exercise 7.13), machine learning (e.g., Exercise 7.14), and theoretical computer science (Plotkin et al. (1995);

Garg and Könemann (2007); Barak et al. (2009)). We refer the reader to the comprehensive survey by Arora et al. (2012). We note that the variant of the MWU method we present is often called the "hedge" (see Arora et al. (2012)). The algorithm for the $s - t$-maximum flow problem by Christiano et al. (2011) (mentioned in Chapter 1) relies on MWU; see Vishnoi (2013) for a presentation.

Matrix variants of the MWU method are studied in papers by Arora and Kale (2016), Arora et al. (2005), Orecchia et al. (2008), and Orecchia et al. (2012). This variant of the MWU method is used to design fast algorithms for solving semidefinite programs that, in turn, are used to come up with approximation algorithms for problems such as maximum cut and sparsest cut.

The MWU method is one method in the area of online convex optimization (introduced in Exercise 7.16). See the monographs by Hazan (2016) and Shalev-Shwartz (2012) for in-depth treatment of online convex optimization, including bandit optimization introduced in Exercise 7.17.

The perfect matching problem on bipartite graphs has been extensively studied in the combinatorial optimization literature; see the book by Schrijver (2002a). It can be reduced to the $s - t$-maximum flow problem and, thus, solved in $O(nm)$ time using an algorithm that needs to compute at most n augmenting paths, where each such iteration takes $O(m)$ time (as it runs depth-first search). A more refined variant of the above algorithm, which runs in $O(m\sqrt{n})$ time, was presented in the papers by Dinic (1970), Karzanov (1973), and Hopcroft and Karp (1973). Forty years after these results, a partial improvement (for the sparse regime, i.e., when $m = O(n)$) was obtained in a paper by Madry (2013). His algorithm runs in $\widetilde{O}(m^{10/7})$ time and, in fact, works for the $s - t$-maximum flow problem on directed graphs with unit capacity. Very recently, a paper by van den Brand et al. (2020) presents an $\widetilde{O}(m+n^{1.5})$ time-randomized algorithm for the maximum cardinality bipartite matching and related problems. While we do not present these algorithms, we remark that both algorithms rely on novel interior point methods (introduced in Chapters 10 and 11).

8

Accelerated Gradient Descent

We present Nesterov's accelerated gradient descent algorithm. This algorithm can be viewed as a hybrid of the previously introduced gradient descent and mirror descent methods. We also present an application of the accelerated gradient method to solving a linear system of equations.

8.1 The Setup

In this chapter, we revisit the unconstrained optimization problem studied in Chapter 6:

$$\min_{x \in \mathbb{R}^n} f(x),$$

where f is convex and its gradient is L-Lipschitz continuous. While most of the results in Chapter 6 were stated for the Euclidean norm, here we work with a general pair of dual norms $\| \cdot \|$ and $\| \cdot \|^*$. We first extend the notion of L-Lipschitz continuous gradient to all norms.

Definition 8.1 (L-Lipschitz continuous gradient with respect to an arbitrary norm). A function $f : \mathbb{R}^n \to \mathbb{R}$ is said to be L-Lipschitz gradient with respect to a norm $\| \cdot \|$ if for all $x, y \in \mathbb{R}^n$,

$$\|\nabla f(x) - \nabla f(y)\|^* \leq L\|x - y\|.$$

For a convex function, this condition is the same as L-smoothness:

$$\forall x, y \in \mathbb{R}^n, \quad f(y) \leq f(x) + \langle y - x, \nabla f(x) \rangle + \frac{L}{2} \|x - y\|^2. \quad (8.1)$$

We saw this before (see Exercise 6.2), when $\| \cdot \|$ is the Euclidean norm. The general norm case can be established in a similar manner; see Exercise 8.1.

As in Chapter 7, we let $R : \mathbb{R}^n \to \mathbb{R}$ be an σ-strongly convex regularizer with respect to a norm $\|\cdot\|$, i.e.,

$$D_R(x, y) := R(x) - R(y) - \langle \nabla R(y), x - y \rangle \geq \frac{\sigma}{2} \|x - y\|^2. \qquad (8.2)$$

Recall that $D_R(x, y)$ is called the Bregman divergence of R at x with respect to y. In this chapter, we consider only regularizers for which the map $\nabla R :$ $\mathbb{R}^n \to \mathbb{R}^n$ is bijective. When reading this chapter, it might be instructive to keep in mind the special case of

$$R(x) := \frac{1}{2} \|x\|_2^2.$$

Then, $D_R(x, y) = \frac{1}{2} \|x - y\|_2^2$ and ∇R is the identity map.

In Chapter 6, we saw that there is an algorithm for optimizing L-smooth functions in roughly $O(\varepsilon^{-1})$ iterations. The goal of this chapter is to give a new algorithm that combines ideas from gradient descent and mirror descent and achieves $O(\varepsilon^{-1/2})$. In Exercise 8.4, we prove that in the black box model, this is optimal.

8.2 Main Result on Accelerated Gradient Descent

The main result of this chapter is the following theorem. We present the crucial steps of the underlying algorithm at the end of the proof of this theorem as it requires setting several parameters whose choice becomes clear from the proof. We are also back to our usual notation of using subscripts (x_t) instead of superscripts (x^t) to denote the iterates in the algorithm.

Theorem 8.2 (Guarantees on accelerated gradient descent). *There is an algorithm (called accelerated gradient descent) that, given*

- *a first-order oracle access to a convex function $f : \mathbb{R}^n \to \mathbb{R}$,*
- *a number L such that the gradient of f is L-Lipschitz continuous with respect to a norm $\|\cdot\|$,*
- *an oracle access to the gradient map ∇R and its inverse $(\nabla R)^*$ or $(\nabla R)^{-1}$ for a convex regularizer $R : \mathbb{R}^n \to \mathbb{R}$,*
- *a bound on the strong convexity parameter $\sigma > 0$ of R with respect to $\|\cdot\|$,*
- *an initial point $x_0 \in \mathbb{R}^n$ such that $D_R(x^\star, x_0) \leq D^2$ (where $x^\star$ is an optimal solution to $\min_{x \in \mathbb{R}^n} f(x)$), and*
- *an $\varepsilon > 0$,*

outputs a point $x \in \mathbb{R}^n$ such that $f(x) \leq f(x^\star) + \varepsilon$. The algorithm makes $T :=$
$O\left(\sqrt{\frac{LD^2}{\sigma\varepsilon}}\right)$ *queries to the respective oracles and performs $O(nT)$ arithmetic*
operations.

Note that the algorithm in Theorem 6.2 required $O\left(\frac{LD^2}{\sigma\varepsilon}\right)$ iterations – exactly
the square of what the above theorem achieves.

8.3 Proof Strategy: Estimate Sequences

In our proof of Theorem 8.2, instead of first stating the algorithm and then
proving its properties, we instead proceed in the opposite order. We first
formulate an important theorem asserting the existence of a so-called estimate
sequence. In the process of proving this theorem we derive – step by step –
an accelerated gradient descent algorithm, which then turns out to imply
Theorem 8.2.

A crucial notion used in deriving the accelerated gradient descent algorithm
is that of an **estimate sequence.**

Definition 8.3 (Estimate sequence). A sequence $(\phi_t, \lambda_t, x_t)_{t\in\mathbb{N}}$, with function
$\phi_t : \mathbb{R}^n \to \mathbb{R}$, value $\lambda_t \in [0,1]$ and vector $x_t \in \mathbb{R}^n$ (for all $t \in \mathbb{N}$) is said to
be an estimate sequence for a function $f : \mathbb{R}^n \to \mathbb{R}$ if it satisfies the following
properties:

(1) **Lower bound.** For all $t \in \mathbb{N}$ and for all $x \in \mathbb{R}^n$,

$$\phi_t(x) \leq (1 - \lambda_t)f(x) + \lambda_t\phi_0(x).$$

(2) **Upper bound.** For all $x \in \mathbb{R}^n$,

$$f(x_t) \leq \phi_t(x).$$

Intuitively, we can think of the sequence $(x_t)_{t\in\mathbb{N}}$ as converging to a minimizer
of f. The functions $(\phi_t)_{t\in\mathbb{N}}$ serve as approximations to f, which provide
tighter and tighter (as t increases) bounds on the gap $f(x_t) - f(x^\star)$. More
precisely, condition (1) says that $\phi_t(x)$ is an approximate lower bound to $f(x)$
and condition (2) says that the minimum value of ϕ_t is above $f(x_t)$.

To illustrate this definition, suppose for a moment that $\lambda_t = 0$ for some
$t \in \mathbb{N}$ in the estimate sequence. Then, from conditions (2) and (1), we obtain

$$f(x_t) \leq \phi_t(x^\star) \leq f(x^\star).$$

This implies that x_t is an optimal solution. Thus, as $\lambda_t = 0$ may be too ambitious, $\lambda_t \to 0$ is what we aim for. In fact, the accelerated gradient method constructs a sequence λ_t that goes to zero as $\frac{1}{t^2}$, a quadratic speed-up over the standard gradient descent method. Formally, we prove the following theorem.

Theorem 8.4 (Existence of optimal estimate sequences). *For every convex, L-smooth (with respect to $\|\cdot\|$) function $f : \mathbb{R}^n \to \mathbb{R}$, for every σ-strongly convex regularizer R (with respect to the same norm $\|\cdot\|$), and for every $x_0 \in \mathbb{R}^n$, there exists an estimate sequence $(\phi_t, \lambda_t, x_t)_{t \in \mathbb{N}}$ with*

$$\phi_0(x) := f(x_0) + \frac{L}{2\sigma} D_R(x, x_0)$$

and

$$\lambda_t \le \frac{c}{t^2}$$

for some absolute constant $c > 0$.

Suppose now that $D_R(x^\star, x_0) \le D^2$. Then, what we obtain for such a sequence, using conditions (2) and (1) with $x = x^\star$, is

$$
\begin{aligned}
f(x_t) &\overset{\text{(Upper Bound)}}{\le} \phi_t(x^\star) && (8.3) \\
&\overset{\text{(Lower Bound)}}{\le} (1 - \lambda_t) f(x^\star) + \lambda_t \phi_0(x^\star) && (8.4) \\
&= (1 - \lambda_t) f(x^\star) + \lambda_t f(x_0) + \lambda_t \frac{L}{2\sigma} D_R(x^\star, x_0) && (8.5) \\
&= f(x^\star) + \lambda_t (f(x_0) - f(x^\star)) + \lambda_t \frac{L}{2\sigma} D_R(x^\star, x_0) && (8.6) \\
&\overset{\text{(L-smoothness)}}{\le} f(x^\star) + \lambda_t \left(\langle x_0 - x^\star, \nabla f(x^\star) \rangle + \frac{L}{2} \|x_0 - x^\star\|^2 \right) && (8.7) \\
&\quad + \lambda_t \frac{L}{2\sigma} D_R(x^\star, x_0) && (8.8) \\
&= f(x^\star) + \lambda_t L \left(\frac{1}{2} \|x_0 - x^\star\|^2 + \frac{1}{2\sigma} D_R(x^\star, x_0) \right) && (8.9) \\
&\overset{(\lambda_t \le \frac{c}{t^2})}{\le} f(x^\star) + \frac{cL}{t^2} \left(\frac{1}{2} \|x_0 - x^\star\|^2 + \frac{1}{2\sigma} D^2 \right) && (8.10) \\
&\overset{(8.2)}{\le} f(x^\star) + \frac{cLD^2}{\sigma t^2}. && (8.11)
\end{aligned}
$$

Thus, it is enough to take $t \approx \sqrt{\frac{LD^2}{\sigma \varepsilon}}$ to make sure that $f(x_t) - f(x^\star) \le \varepsilon$. We cannot yet deduce Theorem 8.2 from Theorem 8.4, as in the form as stated it is not algorithmic – we need to know that such a sequence can be efficiently computed using a first-order oracle to f and R only, while Theorem 8.4 only claims existence. However, as we will see, the proof of Theorem 8.4 provides an efficient algorithm to compute estimate sequences.

8.4 Construction of an Estimate Sequence

This section is devoted to proving Theorem 8.4. To start, we make a simplifying assumption that $L = 1$. This can be ensured by considering $\frac{f}{L}$ instead of f. Similarly, we assume that R is 1-strongly convex, scaling R by σ if necessary.

8.4.1 Step 1: Iterative Construction

The construction of the estimate sequence is iterative. Let $x_0 \in \mathbb{R}^n$ be an arbitrary point. We set

$$\phi_0(x) := D_R(x, x_0) + f(x_0) \quad \text{and} \quad \lambda_0 = 1.$$

Thus, the lower bound condition in Definition 8.3 is trivially satisfied. The upper bound condition follows from noting that

$$\phi_0^\star := \min_x \phi_0(x) = f(x_0).$$

Thus,

$$\phi_0(x) = \phi_0^\star + D_R(x, x_0), \tag{8.12}$$

and in the case when $R(x) := \frac{1}{2}\|x\|_2^2$, this is just a parabola centered at x_0.

The construction of subsequent elements of the estimate sequence is inductive. Suppose we are given $(\phi_{t-1}, x_{t-1}, \lambda_{t-1})$. Then ϕ_t will be a convex combination of ϕ_{t-1} and the linear lower bound L_{t-1} to f at a carefully chosen point $y_{t-1} \in \mathbb{R}^n$ (to be defined later). More precisely, we set

$$L_{t-1}(x) := f(y_{t-1}) + \langle x - y_{t-1}, \nabla f(y_{t-1}) \rangle. \tag{8.13}$$

Note that by the first-order convexity criterion,

$$L_{t-1}(x) \le f(x) \tag{8.14}$$

for all $x \in \mathbb{R}^n$. We set the new estimate to be

$$\phi_t(x) := (1 - \gamma_t)\phi_{t-1}(x) + \gamma_t L_{t-1}(x), \tag{8.15}$$

where $\gamma_t \in [0, 1]$ will be determined later.

We would like to now observe a nice property of Bregman divergences: If we shift a Bregman divergence term of the form $x \mapsto D_R(x, z)$ by a linear function $\langle l, x \rangle$, we again obtain a Bregman divergence, from a possibly different point z. This is easy to check for the case $R(x) := \frac{1}{2} \|x\|_2^2$.

Lemma 8.5 (Shifting Bregman divergence by a linear term). *Let $z \in \mathbb{R}^n$ be an arbitrary point and $R : \mathbb{R}^n \to \mathbb{R}$ be a convex regularizer for which $\nabla R : \mathbb{R}^n \to \mathbb{R}^n$ is a bijection. Then, for every $l \in \mathbb{R}^n$ there exists $z' \in \mathbb{R}^n$ such that*

$$\forall x \in \mathbb{R}^n, \quad \langle l, z - x \rangle = D_R(x, z) + D_R(z, z') - D_R(x, z').$$

Moreover, z' is uniquely determined by the following relation:

$$l = \nabla R(z) - \nabla R(z').$$

The proof of this lemma follows from the generalized Pythagorean theorem (Theorem 7.7).

It can now be seen by induction that, if we denote the minimum value of ϕ_t by $\phi_t^\star$ and denote by z_t the global minimum of ϕ_t, i.e.,

$$\phi_t^\star = \phi_t(z_t),$$

we have

$$\phi_t(x) = \phi_t^\star + \lambda_t D_R(x, z_t). \tag{8.16}$$

From (8.12), it follows that this is true for $t = 0$ if we let $z_0 := x_0$. Assume that this is true for $t - 1$. From the induction hypothesis, (8.15), (8.13), and $\lambda_t = (1 - \gamma_t)\lambda_{t-1}$ we know that

$$
\begin{aligned}
\phi_t(x) \;\overset{(8.15)}{=}\; & (1 - \gamma_t)(\phi_{t-1}^\star + \lambda_{t-1} D_R(x, z_{t-1})) \\
& + \gamma_t(f(y_{t-1}) + \langle x - y_{t-1}, \nabla f(y_{t-1}) \rangle) \\
\overset{(1-\gamma_t)\lambda_{t-1}=\lambda_t}{=}\; & (1 - \gamma_t)\phi_{t-1}^\star + \gamma_t(f(y_{t-1}) - \langle y_{t-1}, \nabla f(y_{t-1}) \rangle) \\
& + \gamma_t \langle x, \nabla f(y_{t-1}) \rangle + \lambda_t D_R(x, z_{t-1}) \\
=\; & (1 - \gamma_t)\phi_{t-1}^\star + \gamma_t(f(y_{t-1}) - \langle y_{t-1}, \nabla f(y_{t-1}) \rangle) \\
& + \lambda_t\left(D_R(x, z_{t-1}) + \frac{\gamma_t}{\lambda_t}\langle x, \nabla f(y_{t-1}) \rangle \right) \\
=\; & (1 - \gamma_t)\phi_{t-1}^\star + \gamma_t(f(y_{t-1}) - \langle y_{t-1}, \nabla f(y_{t-1}) \rangle) \\
& + \lambda_t\left(D_R(x, z_t) - D_R(z_{t-1}, z_t) + \frac{\gamma_t}{\lambda_t}\langle z_{t-1}, \nabla f(y_{t-1}) \rangle \right).
\end{aligned}
$$

Here, in the last equality we have used Lemma 8.5 (with $x = x$, $z = z_{t-1}$, $z' = z_t$ and $l = \frac{\gamma_t}{\lambda_t}\nabla f(y_{t-1})$). Now, it follows that the minimum of $\phi_t(x)$ is when $D_R(x, z_t) = 0$, which happens when $x = z_t$ (as no other term depends on x).

This establishes (8.16). Importantly, Lemma 8.5 also gives us the following recurrence on z_t for all $t \geq 1$:

$$\nabla R(z_t) = \nabla R(z_{t-1}) - \frac{\gamma_t}{\lambda_t} \nabla f(y_{t-1}).$$

In the next steps of the proof, we use the above scheme to prove conditions (1) and (2) of the estimate sequence. This is proved by induction, i.e., when proving the claim for $t \in \mathbb{N}$ we assume that it holds for $(t - 1)$. On the way, we state several constraints on x_t, y_t, γ_t, and λ_t, which are necessary for our proofs to work. At the final stage of the proof we collect all these constraints and show that they can be simultaneously satisfied and, thus, there is a way to set these parameters in order to obtain a valid estimate sequence.

8.4.2 Step 2: Ensuring the Lower Bound Condition

We would like to ensure that

$$\phi_t(x) \leq (1 - \lambda_t) f(x) + \lambda_t \phi_0(x).$$

From our inductive construction we have

$$\begin{aligned}
\phi_t(x) &= (1 - \gamma_t)\phi_{t-1}(x) + \gamma_t L_{t-1}(x) \\
&\quad \text{(by def. of } \phi_t \text{ in (8.15))} \\
&\leq (1 - \gamma_t)[(1 - \lambda_{t-1}) f(x) + \lambda_{t-1}\phi_0(x)] + \gamma_t L_{t-1}(x) \\
&\quad \text{(by the induction hypothesis for } t - 1) \\
&\leq (1 - \gamma_t)[(1 - \lambda_{t-1}) f(x) + \lambda_{t-1}\phi_0(x)] + \gamma_t f(x) \\
&\quad \text{(by } L_{t-1}(x) \leq f(x) \text{ in (8.14))} \\
&\leq ((1 - \gamma_t)(1 - \lambda_{t-1}) + \gamma_t) f(x) + (1 - \gamma_t)\lambda_{t-1}\phi_0(x). \\
&\quad \text{(rearranging)}
\end{aligned} \tag{8.17}$$

Recall that we set

$$\lambda_t := (1 - \gamma_t)\lambda_{t-1}, \tag{8.18}$$

hence

$$\phi_t(x) \leq (1 - \lambda_t) f(x) + \lambda_t \phi_0(x).$$

Thus, as long as (8.18) holds, we obtain the lower bound condition. Note also that a different way to state (8.18) is that

$$\lambda_t = \prod_{1 \leq i \leq t} (1 - \gamma_t).$$

8.4.3 Step 3: Ensuring the Upper Bound and the Dynamics of y_t

To satisfy the upper bound condition, our goal is to set x_t in such a way that

$$f(x_t) \leq \min_{x \in \mathbb{R}^n} \phi_t(x) = \phi_t^\star = \phi_t(z_t).$$

Note that this in particular requires us to specify y_{t-1}, as the right-hand side depends on y_{t-1}. Toward this, consider any $x \in \mathbb{R}^n$, then

$$\phi_t(x) = (1 - \gamma_t)\phi_{t-1}(x) + \gamma_t L_{t-1}(x)$$

(by def. of ϕ_t as in (8.15))

$$= (1 - \gamma_t)(\phi_{t-1}(z_{t-1}) + \lambda_{t-1} D_R(x, z_{t-1})) + \gamma_t L_{t-1}(x)$$

(by (8.16))

$$= (1 - \gamma_t)(\phi_{t-1}(z_{t-1}) + \lambda_{t-1} D_R(x, z_{t-1})) + \gamma_t(f(y_{t-1})$$
$$+ \langle x - y_{t-1}, \nabla f(y_{t-1}) \rangle)$$

(by def. of L_{t-1} as in (8.13))

$$\geq (1 - \gamma_t)f(x_{t-1}) + \lambda_t D_R(x, z_{t-1}) + \gamma_t(f(y_{t-1})$$
$$+ \langle x - y_{t-1}, \nabla f(y_{t-1}) \rangle)$$

(by the upper bound condition for ϕ_{t-1})

$$\geq (1 - \gamma_t)(f(y_{t-1}) + \langle x_{t-1} - y_{t-1}, \nabla f(y_{t-1}) \rangle$$
$$+ \gamma_t(f(y_{t-1}) + \langle x - y_{t-1}, \nabla f(y_{t-1}) \rangle) + \lambda_t D_R(x, z_{t-1})$$

(by convexity of f)

$$= f(y_{t-1}) + \langle (1 - \gamma_t)(x_{t-1} - y_{t-1}) + \gamma_t(x - y_{t-1}), \nabla f(y_{t-1}) \rangle$$
$$+ \lambda_t D_R(x, z_{t-1})$$

(rearranging)

$$= f(y_{t-1}) + \langle (1 - \gamma_t)x_{t-1} + \gamma_t z_{t-1} - y_{t-1}, \nabla f(y_{t-1}) \rangle$$
$$+ \gamma_t \langle x - z_{t-1}, \nabla f(y_{t-1}) \rangle + \lambda_t D_R(x, z_{t-1})$$

(by adding and subtracting $\gamma_t \langle x - z_{t-1}, \nabla f(y_{t-1}) \rangle$ and rearranging)

$$= f(y_{t-1}) + \gamma_t \langle x - z_{t-1}, \nabla f(y_{t-1}) \rangle + \lambda_t D_R(x, z_{t-1}).$$

Where the last equality follows by setting

$$y_{t-1} := (1 - \gamma_t)x_{t-1} + \gamma_t z_{t-1}.$$

To give some intuition as to why we make such a choice for y_{t-1}, consider for a moment the case when $R(x) = \|x\|_2^2$ and $D_R(x, y)$ is the squared Euclidean distance. In the above, we would like to obtain a term that looks like a second-order (quadratic) upper bound on $f(\widetilde{x})$ around $f(y_{t-1})$ (here $\widetilde{x}$ is variable), i.e.,

$$f(y_{t-1}) + \langle \widetilde{x} - y_{t-1}, \nabla f(y_{t-1}) \rangle + \frac{1}{2} \|\widetilde{x} - y_{t-1}\|^2. \tag{8.19}$$

Such a choice of y_{t-1} allows us to cancel out an undesired linear term. We do not quite succeed in getting the form as in (8.19) – our expression has z_{t-1} instead of y_{t-1} in several places and has additional constants in front of the linear and quadratic term. We deal with these issues in the next step and make our choice of x_t accordingly.

8.4.4 Step 4: Ensuring Condition (2) and the Dynamics of x_t

We continue the derivation from Step 3:

$$\phi_t(x) \geq f(y_{t-1}) + \gamma_t \langle x - z_{t-1}, \nabla f(y_{t-1}) \rangle + \lambda_t D_R(x, z_{t-1})$$

(as established in Step 3)

$$\geq f(y_{t-1}) + \gamma_t \langle x - z_{t-1}, \nabla f(y_{t-1}) \rangle + \frac{\lambda_t}{2} \|x - z_{t-1}\|^2$$

(by 1-strong convexity of R)

$$= f(y_{t-1}) + \langle \widetilde{x} - y_{t-1}, \nabla f(y_{t-1}) \rangle + \frac{\lambda_t}{2\gamma_t^2} \|\widetilde{x} - y_{t-1}\|^2$$

(by a change of variables: $\widetilde{x} - y_{t-1} := \gamma_t (x - z_{t-1})$)

$$\geq f(y_{t-1}) + \langle \widetilde{x} - y_{t-1}, \nabla f(y_{t-1}) \rangle + \frac{1}{2} \|\widetilde{x} - y_{t-1}\|^2$$

(assuming $\frac{\lambda_t}{\gamma_t^2} \geq 1$)

$$\geq f(x_t).$$

The last step follows by setting

$$x_t := \underset{\widetilde{x}}{\operatorname{argmin}} \ \langle \widetilde{x}, \nabla f(y_{t-1}) \rangle + \frac{1}{2} \|\widetilde{x} - y_{t-1}\|^2.$$

The reason for renaming of variables and introducing $\widetilde{x}$ follows the same intuition as the choice of y_{t-1} in Step 4. We would like to arrive at an expression that is a quadratic upper bound on f around y_{t-1}, evaluated at a point $\widetilde{x}$. Such a choice of $\widetilde{x}$ allows us to cancel the γ_t in front of the linear part of this upper bound and hence to obtain the desired expression assuming that $\frac{\lambda_t}{\gamma_t^2} \geq 1$. As we will see later, this constraint really determines the convergence rate of the resulting method. Finally, the choice of x_t follows straightforwardly: We simply pick a point that minimizes this quadratic upper bound on f over $\widetilde{x}$.

8.5 The Algorithm and Its Analysis

We now collect all the constraints and summarize the updates rules according to which new points are obtained. Initially, $x_0 \in \mathbb{R}^n$ is arbitrary,

$$z_0 = x_0,$$

$$\gamma_0 = 0 \text{ and } \lambda_0 = 1.$$

Further, for $t \geq 1$ we have

$$\lambda_t := \prod_{1 \leq i \leq t} (1 - \gamma_i)$$

and

$$y_{t-1} := (1 - \gamma_t)x_{t-1} + \gamma_t z_{t-1},$$

$$\nabla R(z_t) := \nabla R(z_{t-1}) - \frac{\gamma_t}{\lambda_t} \nabla f(y_{t-1}), \tag{8.20}$$

$$x_t := \operatorname*{argmin}_{\tilde{x}} \langle \tilde{x}, \nabla f(y_{t-1}) \rangle + \frac{1}{2} \|\tilde{x} - y_{t-1}\|^2.$$

For instance, when $\|\cdot\|$ is the ℓ_2-norm, then

$$x_t = y_{t-1} - \nabla f(y_{t-1}).$$

Note that y_t is just a "hybrid" of the sequences (x_t) and (z_t), which follow two different optimization primitives:

(1) The update rule to obtain x_t is simply to perform one step of gradient descent starting from y_{t-1}.
(2) The sequence z_t is just performing mirror descent with respect to R, taking gradients at y_{t-1}.

Thus, accelerated gradient descent is simply a result of combining gradient descent with mirror descent. Note that, in particular, if we choose $\gamma_t = 0$ for all t, then y_t is simply the gradient descent method from Chapter 6, and if we choose $\gamma_t = 1$ for all t, then y_t is mirror descent from Chapter 7.

Pictorially, in algorithm (8.20), the parameters are fixed in the following order:

$$
\begin{array}{ccccccccc}
x_0 & \searrow & & x_1 & \searrow & \nearrow & & \searrow & x_t \\
& \nearrow y_0 \searrow & & \nearrow y_1 \nwarrow & \cdots\cdots & \nearrow y_{t-1} \nwarrow & \\
z_0 & \nearrow & & z_1 & \nearrow & & \searrow & z_t
\end{array}
$$

The proof of Theorem 8.2 follows simply from the construction of the estimate sequence. The only remaining piece that we have not established yet is that one can take $\gamma_t \approx \frac{1}{t}$ and $\lambda_t \approx \frac{1}{t^2}$ – this follows from a straightforward calculation and is proved in the next section.

From the update rules in (8.20), one can see that one can keep track of x_t, y_t, z_t by using a constant number of oracle queries to ∇f, ∇R and $(\nabla R)^{-1}$. Furthermore, as already demonstrated in (8.3), we have

$$f(x_t) \leq f(x^\star) + O\left(\frac{LD^2}{\sigma t^2}\right).$$

Thus, to attain $f(x_t) \leq f(x^\star) + \varepsilon$, taking $t = O\left(\sqrt{\frac{LD^2}{\sigma \varepsilon}}\right)$ is sufficient. This completes the proof of Theorem 8.2.

Choice of γ_ts. When deriving the estimate sequence, we have made an assumption that

$$\lambda_t \geq \gamma_t^2,$$

which does not allow us to set γ_ts arbitrarily. The following lemma provides an example setting of γ_ts that satisfy this constraint.

Lemma 8.6 (Choice of γ_ts). Let $\gamma_0 = \gamma_1 = \gamma_2 = \gamma_3 = 0$ and $\gamma_i = \frac{2}{i}$ for all $i \geq 4$; then

$$\forall t \geq 0, \quad \prod_{i=1}^{t}(1 - \gamma_i) \geq \gamma_t^2.$$

Proof: For $t \leq 4$, one can verify the claim directly. Let $t > 4$. We have

$$\prod_{i=1}^{t}(1 - \gamma_i) = \frac{2}{4} \cdot \frac{3}{5} \cdot \frac{4}{6} \cdot \ldots \cdot \frac{t-2}{t} = \frac{2 \cdot 3}{(t-1)t}$$

by cancelling all but two terms in the numerator and denominator. It is now easy to verify that $\frac{6}{t(t-1)} \geq \frac{4}{t^2} = \gamma_t^2$. ∎

8.6 An Algorithm for Strongly Convex and Smooth Functions

From Theorem 8.2, one can derive numerous other algorithms. Here, for instance, we deduce a method for minimizing functions that are both L-smooth and β-strongly convex (with respect to the Euclidean norm) at the same time, i.e., for all $x, y \in \mathbb{R}^n$,

$$\frac{\beta}{2} \|x - y\|_2^2 \leq f(x) - f(y) - \langle x - y, \nabla f(y)\rangle \leq \frac{L}{2} \|x - y\|_2^2.$$

Theorem 8.7 (Accelerated gradient descent for strongly convex functions).
*There is an algorithm that for any function $f : \mathbb{R}^n \to \mathbb{R}$, which is both
β-strongly convex and L-smooth with respect to the Euclidean norm, given*

- *a first-order oracle access to a convex function f,*
- *numbers $L, \beta \in R$,*
- *an initial point $x_0 \in \mathbb{R}^n$ such that $\|x^\star - x_0\|_2^2 \leq D^2$ (where $x^\star$ is an optimal
  solution to $\min_{x \in \mathbb{R}^n} f(x)$),*
- *an $\varepsilon > 0$, and*

*outputs a point $x \in \mathbb{R}^n$ such that $f(x) \leq f(x^\star) + \varepsilon$. The algorithm makes
$T = O\left(\sqrt{\frac{L}{\beta}} \log \frac{LD^2}{\varepsilon}\right)$ queries to the respective oracles and performs $O(nT)$
arithmetic operations.*

Note that, importantly, the above method has **logarithmic** dependency on $\frac{1}{\varepsilon}$.

Proof: Consider $R(x) = \|x\|_2^2$ as our choice of regularizer in Theorem 8.2.
Note that R is 1-strongly convex with respect to the Euclidean norm. Thus, the
algorithm in Theorem 8.2 constructs a sequence of points $x_0, x_1, x_2, \ldots$ such
that

$$f(x_t) - f(x^\star) \leq O\left(\frac{LD^2}{t^2}\right).$$

Denote

$$E_t := f(x_t) - f(x^\star).$$

Initially, we have

$$E_0 \geq \frac{\beta}{2} \|x_0 - x^\star\|_2^2 = \frac{\beta}{2} D^2,$$

because of strong convexity of f. Thus, the convergence guarantee of the
algorithm can be rewritten as

$$E_t \leq O\left(\frac{LD^2}{t^2}\right) \leq O\left(\frac{LE_0}{\beta t^2}\right).$$

In particular, the number of steps required to bring the gap from E_0 to $\frac{E_0}{2}$ is
$O\left(\sqrt{\frac{L}{\beta}}\right)$. Thus, to go from E_0 to ε, we need

$$O\left(\sqrt{\frac{L}{\beta}} \cdot \log \frac{E_0}{\varepsilon}\right) = O\left(\sqrt{\frac{L}{\beta}} \cdot \log \frac{LD^2}{\varepsilon}\right)$$

steps. Here, we used the L-smoothness of f and the fact that $\nabla f(x^\star) = 0$ to obtain

$$E_0 = f(x_0) - f(x^\star) \le \frac{L}{2}\|x - x^\star\|_2^2 \le \frac{LD^2}{2}.$$

The map ∇R is the identity in this case, hence no additional computational cost is incurred because of R. ∎

8.7 Application: Linear System of Equations

Recall the problem of solving linear systems of equations

$$Ax = b,$$

where $A \in \mathbb{R}^{n \times n}$ and a vector $b \in \mathbb{R}^n$. For simplicity, we assume that A is non-singular and hence the system $Ax = b$ has a unique solution. Hence, $A^\top A$ is positive definite. Let $\lambda_1(A^\top A)$ and $\lambda_n(A^\top A)$ be the smallest and largest eigenvalue of $A^\top A$, respectively. We define the condition number of $A^\top A$ to be

$$\kappa(A^\top A) := \frac{\lambda_n(A^\top A)}{\lambda_1(A^\top A)}.$$

The following theorem on solving a system of linear equations now follows from Theorem 8.7.

Theorem 8.8 (Solving a system of linear equations in $\sqrt{\kappa(A^\top A)}$ iterations). *There is an algorithm, which given an invertible square matrix $A \in \mathbb{R}^{n \times n}$, a vector b, and a precision parameter $\varepsilon > 0$, outputs a point $y \in \mathbb{R}^n$ – an approximate solution to the linear system $Ax = b$, which satisfies*

$$\|Ay - b\|_2^2 \le \varepsilon.$$

The algorithm performs $T := O\left(\sqrt{\kappa(A^\top A)} \log\left(\frac{\lambda_n(A^\top A)\|x^\star\|_2}{\varepsilon}\right)\right)$ iterations (where $x^\star \in \mathbb{R}^n$ satisfies $Ax^\star = b$) each iteration requires computing a constant number of matrix-vector multiplications and inner products.

Proof: We apply Theorem 8.7 to solve the optimization problem

$$\min_{x \in \mathbb{R}^n} \|Ax - b\|_2^2.$$

We denote

$$f(x) := \|Ax - b\|_2^2.$$

Note that the optimal value of the above is 0, and is achieved for $x = x^\star$, where $x^\star$ is the solution to the linear systems considered.

We now derive all the relevant parameters of f that are required to apply Theorem 8.7. By computing the Hessian of f, we have

$$\nabla^2 f(x) = A^\top A.$$

Since $\lambda_1(A^\top A) \cdot I \preceq A^\top A$ and $A^\top A \preceq \lambda_n(A^\top A)$, we have that f is L-smooth for $L := \lambda_n(A^\top A)$ and β-strongly convex for $\beta := \lambda_1(A^\top A)$.

As a starting point x_0, we can choose

$$x_0 := 0,$$

which is at distance

$$D := \|x_0 - x^\star\|_2 = \|x^\star\|_2$$

from the optimal solution. Thus, from Theorem 8.7 we obtain the running time

$$O\left(\sqrt{\kappa(A^\top A)} \cdot \log\left(\frac{\lambda_n(A^\top A)\,\|x^\star\|}{\varepsilon}\right)\right).$$

Note that computing the gradient of $f(x)$ is

$$\nabla f(x) = A^\top(Ax - b),$$

hence it boils down to performing two matrix-vector multiplications.   ∎

8.8 Exercises

8.1   Prove that, for a convex function, the L-smoothness condition (8.1) is equivalent to the L-Lipschitz continuous gradient condition in any norm.

8.2   **Conjugate gradient.** Consider the following strategy for minimizing a convex function $f : \mathbb{R}^n \to \mathbb{R}$. Construct a sequence $(\phi_t, L_t, x_t)_{t \in \mathbb{N}}$, where for every $t \in \mathbb{N}$ there is a function $\phi_t : \mathbb{R}^n \to \mathbb{R}$, a linear subspace L_t of $\mathbb{R}^n$ such that $\{0\} = L_0 \subseteq L_1 \subseteq L_2 \subseteq \cdots$, and a point $x_t \in L_t$ such that, together, they satisfy the following conditions:

- **Lower bound.** $\forall t,\ \forall x \in L_t, \quad \phi_t(x) \leq f(x)$,
- **Common minimizer.** $\forall t,\ x_t = \operatorname{argmin}_{x \in \mathbb{R}^n} \phi_t(x) = \operatorname{argmin}_{x \in L_t} f(x)$.

Consider applying this to the function

$$f(x) = \left\| x - x^\star \right\|_A^2,$$

where A is an $n \times n$ PD matrix and $x^\star \in \mathbb{R}^n$ is the unique vector satisfying $Ax^\star = b$. Let

$$L_t := \operatorname{span}\{b, Ab, A^2b, \ldots, A^{t-1}b\}$$

and

$$\phi_t(x) := \left\| x - x_t \right\|_A^2 + \left\| x_t - x^\star \right\|_A^2,$$

where $x_t \in \mathbb{R}^n$ is the unique choice that makes the common minimizer property satisfied.

(a) Show that by choosing $(\phi_t, L_t, x_t)_{t \in \mathbb{N}}$ as above, the lower bound property is satisfied.

(b) Show that given A and b, there is an algorithm to compute $x_1, \ldots, x_t$ in total time $O(t \cdot (T_A + n))$, where T_A is the time required to multiply the matrix A by a vector.

(c) Show that if A has only k pairwise distinct eigenvalues, then $x_{k+1} = x^\star$.

8.3 **Heavy ball method.** Given an $n \times n$ PD matrix A and a $b \in \mathbb{R}^n$, consider the following optimization problem:

$$\min_{x \in \mathbb{R}^n} \frac{1}{2} x^\top A x - \langle b, x \rangle.$$

Let $x^\star := A^{-1}b$, and notice that it is the same as solving the following problem:

$$f(x) := \min_{x \in \mathbb{R}^n} \frac{1}{2} (x - x^\star)^\top A (x - x^\star).$$

Consider the following method to solve this problem:

$$x_{t+1} := x_t - \eta \nabla f(x_t) + \theta(x_t - x_{t-1}).$$

The term $x_t - x_{t-1}$ can be viewed as the **momentum** of the particle.

(a) Prove that

$$\begin{bmatrix} x_{t+1} - x^\star \\ x_t - x^\star \end{bmatrix} = \begin{bmatrix} (1+\theta)I - \eta A & -\theta I \\ I & 0 \end{bmatrix} \begin{bmatrix} x_t - x^\star \\ x_{t-1} - x^\star \end{bmatrix}.$$

(b) Let λ_1 be the smallest eigenvalue of A and λ_n be the largest eigenvalue of A. For $\eta := \frac{4}{(\sqrt{\lambda_n}+\sqrt{\lambda_1})^2}$ and $\theta := \max\{|1 - \sqrt{\eta\lambda_1}|, |1 - \sqrt{\eta\lambda_n}|\}$, prove that

$$\|x_{t+1} - x^\star\| \le \left(\frac{\sqrt{\kappa(A)} - 1}{\sqrt{\kappa(A)} + 1}\right)^t \|x_0 - x^\star\|_2.$$

Here $\kappa(A) := \frac{\lambda_n}{\lambda_1}$.

(c) Generalize this result to an L-smooth and σ-strongly convex function.

8.4 **Lower bound.** In this problem, we prove Theorem 6.4. Consider a general model for first-order black box minimization that includes gradient descent, mirror descent, and accelerated gradient descent. The algorithm is given access to a gradient oracle for a convex function $f : \mathbb{R}^n \to \mathbb{R}$ and $x_0 := 0$. It produces a sequence of points $x_0, x_1, x_2, \ldots$ such that

$$x_t \in x_0 + \text{span}\{\nabla f(x_0), \ldots, \nabla f(x_{t-1})\}, \qquad (8.21)$$

i.e., the algorithm might move only in the subspace spanned by the gradients at previous iterations. We do not restrict the running time of one iteration of such an algorithm; in fact, we allow it to do an arbitrarily long calculation to compute x_t from $x_0, \ldots, x_{t-1}$ and the corresponding gradients and are interested only in the number of iterations.

Consider the quadratic function $f : \mathbb{R}^n \to \mathbb{R}$ (for $n > 2t$) defined as

$$f(y_1, \ldots, y_n) := \frac{L}{4}\left(\frac{1}{2}y_1^2 + \frac{1}{2}\sum_{i=1}^{2t}(y_i - y_{i+1})^2 + \frac{1}{2}y_{2t+1}^2 - y_1\right).$$

Here, y_i denotes the ith coordinate of y.

(a) Prove that F is L-smooth with respect to the Euclidean norm.

(b) Prove that the minimum of f is $\frac{L}{8}\left(\frac{1}{2t+2} - 1\right)$ and is attained for a point $x^\star$ whose ith coordinate is $1 - \frac{i}{2t+2}$.

(c) Prove that the span of the gradients at the first t points is just the span of $\{e_1, \ldots, e_t\}$.

(d) Deduce that

$$\frac{f(x_t) - f(x^\star)}{\|x_0 - x^\star\|_2^2} \ge \frac{3L}{32(t+1)^2}.$$

Thus, the accelerated gradient method is tight up to constants.

8.5 **Acceleration for the $s-t$-maximum flow problem.** Use the accelerated gradient method developed in this chapter to improve the running time in Theorem 6.6 for the $s-t$-maximum flow to $\tilde{O}\left(\frac{m^{1.75}}{\sqrt{\varepsilon F^*}}\right)$.

8.6 **Acceleration for the $s-t$-minimum cut problem .** Recall the formulation of the $s-t$-minimum problem in an undirected graph $G=(V,E)$ with n vertices and m edges that was studied in Exercise 6.11:

$$\text{MinCut}_{s,t}(G) := \min_{x \in \mathbb{R}^n, x_s - x_t = 1} \sum_{ij \in E} |x_i - x_j|.$$

Apply Theorem 8.7 with the regularizer $R(x) = \|x\|_2^2$ to find $\text{MinCut}_{s,t}$ (G) exactly. Obtain a method with running time $O(m^{3/2}n^{1/2}\Delta^{1/2})$, where Δ is the maximum degree of a vertex in G. In other words,

$$\Delta := \max_{v \in V} |N(v)|.$$

Hint: To make the objective L-smooth, use the following approximation of the ℓ_1-norm of a vector $y \in \mathbb{R}^m$: $\|y\|_1 \approx \sum_{j=1}^m \sqrt{y_i^2 + \delta^2}$ for an appropriately chosen $\delta > 0$.

Notes

The accelerated gradient descent method was discovered by Nesterov (1983) (see also Nesterov (2004)). This idea of acceleration was then extended to variants of gradient descent and led to the introduction of algorithms such as FISTA by Beck and Teboulle (2009). Allen-Zhu and Orecchia (2017) present the accelerated gradient method as a coupling between the gradient descent method and the mirror descent method. The lower bound (Theorem 6.4) was first established in a paper by Nemirovski and Yudin (1983). The heavy ball method (Exercise 8.3) is due to Polyak (1964). Exercises 8.5 and 8.6 are adapted from the paper by Lee et al. (2013).

Algorithms for solving a linear system of equations have a rich history. It is well known that Gaussian elimination has a worst-case time complexity of $O(n^3)$. This can be improved upon by using fast matrix multiplication to $O(n^\omega) \approx O(n^{2.373})$; see the books by Trefethen and Bau (1997), Saad (2003), and Golub and Van Loan (1996). The bound presented in Theorem 8.8 is comparable to the conjugate gradient method (introduced in Exercise 8.2) and is due to Hestenes and Stiefel (1952); see also the monograph by Sachdeva and Vishnoi (2014). For references on linear solvers for Laplacian solvers, refer to the notes in Chapter 6.

9

Newton's Method

We begin our journey towards designing algorithms for convex optimization whose number of iterations scale polylogarithmically with the error. As a first step, we derive and analyze the classic Newton's method, which is an example of a second-order method. We argue that Newton's method can be seen as steepest descent on a Riemannian manifold, which then motivates an affinely invariant analysis of its convergence.

9.1 Finding a Root of a Univariate Function

Newton's method, also known as the Newton-Raphson method, is a method for finding successively better approximations to the roots, or zeroes, of a real-valued function. Formally, given a sufficiently differentiable function $g : \mathbb{R} \to \mathbb{R}$, the goal is to find its root (or one of its roots): a point r such that $g(r) = 0$. The method assumes a zeroth- and first-order access to g and a point x_0 that is sufficiently close to some root of g. It does not assume that g is convex. We use the notation g' and g'' in this chapter to denote the first and the second derivative of g.

9.1.1 Derivation of the Update Rule

Like all the methods studied in this book, Newton's method is also iterative and generates a sequence of points $x_0, x_1, \dots$. To explain Newton's method visually, consider the graph of g as a subset of $\mathbb{R} \times \mathbb{R}$ and the point $(x_0, g(x_0))$. Draw a line through this point, which is tangent to the graph of g. Let x_1 be the intersection of the line with the x-axis (see Figure 9.1). The hope is, at least if one were to believe the figure, that by moving from x_0 to x_1 we have made

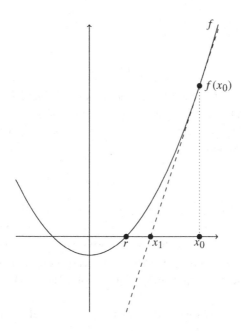

Figure 9.1 One step of Newton's method.

progress in reaching a zero of g. By a simple calculation, one can see that x_1 arises from x_0 as follows:

$$x_1 := x_0 - \frac{g(x_0)}{g'(x_0)}$$

Thus, the following iterative algorithm for computing a root of g naturally follows: Start with an $x_0 \in \mathbb{R}$ and use the inductive definition below to compute $x_1, x_2, x_3, \ldots$:

$$x_{t+1} := x_t - \frac{g(x_t)}{g'(x_t)} \qquad \text{for all } t \geq 0. \tag{9.1}$$

It is evident that the method requires the differentiability of g. In fact, the analysis assumes even more – that g is twice continuously differentiable.

We now present a simple optimization problem, and see how we can attempt to use Newton's method to solve it. This example also illustrates that the convergence of Newton's method may heavily depend on the starting point.

An example. Suppose that for some $a > 0$ we would like to minimize the function

$$f(x) := ax - \log x$$

over all positive $x > 0$. To solve this optimization problem, one can first take the derivative $g(x) := f'(x)$ and try to find a root of g. As f is convex, we know by first-order optimality conditions that the root of g (if it exists) is an optimizer for f. We have

$$g(x) := f'(x) = a - \frac{1}{x}.$$

While it is trivial to see that this equation can be solved exactly and the solution is $\frac{1}{a}$, we would still like to apply Newton's method to solve it. One reason is that we would like to illustrate the method on a particularly simple example. Another reason is historical – early computers used Newton's method to compute the reciprocal, as it only involved addition, subtraction, and multiplication.

We initialize Newton's method at any point $x_0 > 0$ and iterate as follows:

$$x_{t+1} = x_t - \frac{g(x_t)}{g'(x_t)} = 2x_t - ax_t^2.$$

Note that computing x_{t+1} from x_t indeed does not use division.

We now try to analyze the sequence $\{x_t\}_{t\in\mathbb{N}}$ and see when it converges to $\frac{1}{a}$. By denoting

$$e_t := 1 - ax_t,$$

we obtain the following recurrence relation for e_t:

$$e_{t+1} = e_t^2.$$

Thus, it is now easy to see that whenever $|e_0| < 1$, then $e_t \to 0$. Further, if $|e_0| = 1$ then $e_t = 1$ for all $t \geq 1$ and if $|e_0| > 1$, then $e_t \to \infty$.

In terms of x_0 this means that whenever $0 < x_0 < \frac{2}{a}$ then $x_t \to \frac{1}{a}$. However, if we initialize at $x_0 = \frac{2}{a}$, or x_0, then the algorithm gets stuck at 0. And even worse, if we initialize at $x_0 > \frac{2}{a}$ then $x_t \to -\infty$. This example shows that choosing the right starting point has a crucial impact on whether Newton's method succeeds or fails.

It is interesting to note that by modifying the function g, for example by taking $g(x) = x - \frac{1}{a}$, one obtains different algorithms to compute $\frac{1}{a}$. Some of these algorithms might not make sense (for instance, the iteration $x_{t+1} = \frac{1}{a}$ is not how we would like to compute $\frac{1}{a}$), or might not be efficient.

9.1.2 Quadratic Convergence

We now formally analyze Newton's method. Notice that, for the example in the previous section, we encountered a phenomenon that the "distance" to the root was being squared at every iteration – this ends up holding in full generality and is sometimes referred to as **quadratic convergence.**

Theorem 9.1 (Quadratic convergence of Newton's method for finding roots). *Suppose* $g \colon \mathbb{R} \to \mathbb{R}$ *is twice differentiable and its second derivative is continuous,* $r \in \mathbb{R}$ *is a root of* g, $x_0 \in \mathbb{R}$ *is a starting point, and*

$$x_1 = x_0 - \frac{g(x_0)}{g'(x_0)};$$

then

$$|r - x_1| \leq M |r - x_0|^2,$$

where $M := \sup_{\xi \in (r, x_0)} \left| \frac{g''(\xi)}{2g'(x_0)} \right|.$

The proof of this theorem requires the mean value theorem.

Theorem 9.2 (Mean value theorem). *If* $h \colon \mathbb{R} \to \mathbb{R}$ *is a continuous function on the closed interval* $[a, b]$ *and differentiable on the open interval* (a, b), *then there exists a point* $c \in (a, b)$ *such that*

$$h'(c) = \frac{h(b) - h(a)}{b - a}.$$

Proof of Theorem 9.1: We start by a quadratic, or second-order, approximation of g around the point x_0 and using the mean value theorem (Theorem 9.2) for g'' to obtain

$$g(r) = g(x_0) + (r - x_0)g'(x_0) + \frac{1}{2}(r - x_0)^2 g''(\xi)$$

for some ξ in the interval (r, x_0). Here, we have used the fact that g'' is continuous. From the definition of x_1, we know that

$$g(x_0) = g'(x_0)(x_0 - x_1).$$

We also know that $g(r) = 0$. Hence, we obtain

$$0 = g'(x_0)(x_0 - x_1) + (r - x_0)g'(x_0) + \frac{1}{2}(r - x_0)^2 g''(\xi),$$

which implies that

$$g'(x_0)(x_1 - r) = \frac{1}{2}(r - x_0)^2 g''(\xi).$$

This gives us the bound on the distance from x_1 to r in terms of the distance from x_0 to r,

$$|r - x_1| = \left| \frac{g''(\xi)}{2g'(x_0)} \right| |r - x_0|^2 \le M|r - x_0|^2,$$

where M is as in the statement of the theorem.   ∎

Assuming that M is a small constant, say $M \le 1$ (and remains so throughout the execution of this method) and that $|x_0 - r| < \frac{1}{2}$, we obtain **quadratically** fast convergence of x_t to r. Indeed, after t steps we have

$$|x_t - r| \le |x_0 - r|^{2^t} \le 2^{-2^t}$$

and hence, for the error $|x_t - r|$ to become smaller than ε, it is enough to take

$$t \approx \log \log \frac{1}{\varepsilon}.$$

As one can imagine, for this reason Newton's method is very efficient. In addition, in practice it turns out to be very robust and sometimes converges rapidly even when no bounds on M or $|x_0 - r|$ are available.

9.2 Newton's Method for Multivariate Functions

We now extend Newton's method to the multivariate setting where we would like to find a "root" of a function $g : \mathbb{R}^n \to \mathbb{R}^n$:

$$g_1(r) = 0,$$
$$g_2(r) = 0,$$
$$\vdots$$
$$g_n(r) = 0.$$

In other words, $g : \mathbb{R}^n \to \mathbb{R}^n$ is of the form $g(x) = (g_1(x), g_2(x), \ldots, g_n(x))^\top$, and we would like to find $x \in \mathbb{R}^n$ such that $g(x) = 0$.

To find an analog of Newton's method in this setting, we mimic the update rule (9.1) for the univariate setting, i.e.,

$$x_1 = x_0 - \frac{g(x_0)}{g'(x_0)}.$$

Previously, $g(x_0)$ and $g'(x_0)$ were numbers, but if we go from $n = 1$ to $n > 1$, then $g(x_0)$ becomes a vector, and it is not immediately clear what $g'(x_0)$ should be. It turns out that the right analog of $g'(x_0)$ in the multivariate setting is the **Jacobian** matrix of g at x_0, i.e., $J_g(x_0)$ is the matrix of partial derivatives

$$\left[\frac{\partial g_i}{\partial x_j}(x_0) \right]_{1 \le i, j \le n}.$$

Hence, we can now consider the following extension of (9.1) to the multivariate setting:

$$x_{t+1} := x_t - J_g(x_t)^{-1} g(x_t) \qquad \text{for all } t \ge 0. \tag{9.2}$$

By extending the proof of Theorem 9.1, we can recover an analogous local quadratic convergence rate of Newton's method in the multivariate setting. We do not state a precise theorem for this variant, but as one might expect, the corresponding value M involves the following two quantities: an upper bound on the "magnitude" of the second derivative of g (or in other words a bound on the Lipschitz constant of $x \mapsto J_g(x)$) and a lower bound on the "magnitude" of $J_g(x)$ of the form

$$\frac{1}{\left\| J_g(x)^{-1} \right\|_2},$$

where $\|\cdot\|_2$ denotes the spectral norm of a matrix (see Definition 2.13). For more details, we refer to Section 9.4, where we present a closely related convergence result that can be adapted to this setting.

9.3 Newton's Method for Unconstrained Optimization

How could Newton's method be used to solve convex programs? The key lies in the observation from Chapter 3 that the task of minimizing a differentiable convex function in the unconstrained setting is equivalent to finding a root of its derivative. In this section, we abstract out the method from the previous section and present Newton's method for unconstrained optimization.

9.3.1 From Optimization to Root Finding

Recall that in the unconstrained case, the problem is to find

$$x^\star := \operatorname*{argmin}_{x \in \mathbb{R}^n} f(x),$$

where f is a convex function. We assume that f is sufficiently differentiable in this chapter. The gradient ∇f of f can be thought as a function from $\mathbb{R}^n$ to $\mathbb{R}^n$, and its Jacobian $J_{\nabla f}$ is the Hessian $\nabla^2 f$. Hence, the update rule (9.2) for finding a root of a multivariate function g, adjusted to this setting, is

$$x_{t+1} := x_t - (\nabla^2 f(x_t))^{-1} \nabla f(x_t) \qquad \text{for all } t \geq 0. \qquad (9.3)$$

For notational convenience, we define the **Newton step** at point x to be

$$n(x) := -(\nabla^2 f(x))^{-1} \nabla f(x).$$

Then (9.3) can be compactly written as

$$x_{t+1} := x_t + n(x_t).$$

9.3.2 Newton's Method as a Second-Order Method

We now derive Newton's method from an optimization perspective. Suppose we would like to find a global minimum of f and x_0 is our current approximate solution. Let $\tilde{f}(x)$ denote the quadratic, or second-order, approximation of $f(x)$ around x_0, i.e.,

$$\tilde{f}(x) := f(x_0) + \langle x - x_0, \nabla f(x_0) \rangle + \frac{1}{2}(x - x_0)^\top \nabla^2 f(x_0)(x - x_0).$$

A natural idea to compute the new approximation x_1 (to a minimizer $x^\star$ of f) is then to minimize $\tilde{f}(x)$ over $x \in \mathbb{R}^n$. Since we hope that $\tilde{f}$ approximates f, at least locally, this new point should be an even better approximation to $x^\star$.

To find x_1, we need to solve

$$x_1 := \operatorname*{argmin}_{x \in \mathbb{R}^n} \tilde{f}(x).$$

Assuming that f is strictly convex, or rather that the Hessian of f at x_0 is PD, such an x_1 is equivalent to finding an x such that $\nabla \tilde{f}(x) = 0$, i.e.,

$$\nabla f(x_0) + \nabla^2 f(x_0)(x - x_0) = 0.$$

This, assuming $\nabla^2 f(x_0)$ is invertible, translates to

$$x - x_0 = -\left(\nabla^2 f(x_0)\right)^{-1} \nabla f(x_0).$$

Hence

$$x_1 = x_0 - \left(\nabla^2 f(x_0)\right)^{-1} \nabla f(x_0),$$

and we recover Newton's method. Thus, at every step, Newton's method minimizes the second-order approximation around the current point and takes the minimizer as the next point. This has the following consequence: Whenever we apply Newton's method to a strictly convex quadratic function, i.e., of the form $h(x) = \frac{1}{2}x^\top M x + b^\top x$ for $M \in \mathbb{R}^{n \times n}$ PD and $b \in \mathbb{R}^n$, no matter which point we start at, after one iteration we land in the unique minimizer.

It is instructive to compare Newton's method to the algorithms we studied in previous chapters. They were all first-order methods and required multiple iterations to reach a point close to the optimizer. Does it mean that Newton's method is a better algorithm? On the one hand, the fact that Newton's method also uses the Hessian to perform the iteration makes it more powerful than first-order methods. On the other hand, this power comes at a cost: Computationally one iteration is now more costly, as we need a second-order oracle to the function. More precisely, at every step t, to compute x_{t+1} we need to solve a system of n linear equations in n variables of the form

$$\left(\nabla^2 f(x_t)\right) x = \nabla f(x_t).$$

In the worst case, this takes $O(n^3)$ time using Gaussian elimination (or $O(n^\omega)$ using fast matrix multiplication). However, if the Hessian matrix has a special form, e.g., it is a Laplacian corresponding to some graph, Newton's method can lead to fast algorithms due to the availability of nearly linear time Laplacian solvers.

9.4 First Take on the Analysis

In this section, we take a first shot at analyzing Newton's method for optimization. The theorem we state is analogous to Theorem 9.1 (for univariate root finding) – it says that one step of Newton's method yields a quadratic improvement of the distance to the optimal solution whenever a condition that we call **NE** (for Newton-Euclidean) is satisfied.

Definition 9.3 (NE condition). Let $f : \mathbb{R}^n \to \mathbb{R}$ be a function, $x^\star$ be one of its minimizers, and x_0 be an arbitrary point. Denote by $H(x)$ the Hessian of f at the point $x \in \mathbb{R}^n$. We say that the **NE(M)** condition is satisfied for some $M > 0$ if there exists a Euclidean ball $B(x^\star, R)$ of radius R around $x^\star$, containing x_0, two constants $h, L > 0$ such that $M \geq \frac{L}{2h}$, and

- for every $x \in B(x^\star, R)$, $\left\| H(x)^{-1} \right\| \leq \frac{1}{h}$,
- for every $x, y \in B(x^\star, R)$, $\| H(x) - H(y) \| \leq L \, \| x - y \|_2$.

Here the norm of a matrix is the $2 \to 2$ or spectral norm.

Theorem 9.4 (Quadratic convergence with respect to the Euclidean norm). *Let $f : \mathbb{R}^n \to \mathbb{R}$ and $x^\star$ be one of its minimizers. Let x_0 be an arbitrary starting point and define*

$$x_1 := x_0 + n(x_0).$$

If the **NE**(M) *condition is satisfied, then*

$$\|x_1 - x^\star\|_2 \le M \|x_0 - x^\star\|_2^2.$$

One can observe a rough analogy between Theorem 9.4 and Theorem 9.1. In the latter, for the method to have quadratic convergence, $|g'(x)|$ should be large (relatively to $|g''(x)|$). Here, the role of g is played by the gradient ∇f of f. The first condition on $H(x)$ in Definition 9.3 basically says that the "magnitude" of the second derivative of f is "big." The second condition may be a bit more tricky to decipher: It says that $\nabla^2 f(x)$ is Lipschitz-continuous and upper-bounds the Lipschitz constant. Assuming f is thrice continuously differentiable, this roughly gives an upper bound on the magnitude of $D^{(3)} f$. This intuitive explanation is not quite formal; however, we only wanted to emphasize that the spirit of Theorem 9.4 is the same as Theorem 9.1.

The proof of Theorem 9.4 is similar to the proof of Theorem 9.1 and, thus, is moved to the end of this chapter for the interested reader; see Section 9.7.

9.4.1 The Problem with the Convergence in Euclidean Norm

While the statement (and the proof) of Theorem 9.4 might seem to be natural extensions of Theorem 9.1, the fact that it is stated with respect to quantities based on the Euclidean norm $\|\cdot\|_2$ makes it hard to apply in many cases. We see in a later section that there is a more natural choice of a norm within the context of Newton's method – the **local norm**. However, before we introduce the local norm, we first show that there is indeed a problem with the use of the Euclidean norm through a particular example in which Theorem 9.4 fails to give reasonable bounds.

For $K_1, K_2 > 0$ (to be thought of as large constants), consider the function

$$f(x_1, x_2) := -\log(K_1 - x_1) - \log(K_1 + x_1)$$
$$- \log\left(\frac{1}{K_2} - x_2\right) - \log\left(\frac{1}{K_2} + x_2\right).$$

f is defined whenever $(x_1, x_2) \in (-K_1, K_1) \times \left(-\frac{1}{K_2}, \frac{1}{K_2}\right) \subseteq \mathbb{R}^2$. It is convex and its Hessian is

$$H(x_1, x_2) = \begin{pmatrix} \frac{1}{(K_1 - x_1)^2} + \frac{1}{(K_1 + x_1)^2} & 0 \\ 0 & \frac{1}{\left(\frac{1}{K_2} - x_2\right)^2} + \frac{1}{\left(\frac{1}{K_2} + x_2\right)^2} \end{pmatrix}.$$

We would like to find estimates on the parameters h and L (and, hence, M) for the $\mathbf{NE}(M)$ condition to hold in a close neighborhood of the optimal point $(x_1^\star, x_2^\star) = (0,0)$. As we show, the M parameter is always prohibitively large, so that Theorem 9.4 cannot be applied to reason about the convergence of Newton's method in this case. Nevertheless, as we argue in a later section, Newton's method works very well when applied to f, no matter how large K_1 and K_2 might be.

We start by observing that the first point in the $\mathbf{NE}(M)$ condition requires an $h > 0$ such that

$$hI \preceq H(x_1, x_2)$$

in the neighborhood of $x^\star$. Even at $x^\star$, we already have

$$h \leq \frac{2}{K_1^2},$$

i.e., we can make h arbitrarily small by just changing K_1. This is because

$$H(x^\star) = H((0,0)) = \begin{pmatrix} \frac{2}{K_1^2} & 0 \\ 0 & 2K_2^2 \end{pmatrix}.$$

The second condition requires a bound on the Lipschitz constant of the Hessian of $H(x)$. To see that L is large, consider the point $\widetilde{x} := \left(0, \frac{1}{K_2^2} \right)$. Note that

$$\|H(\widetilde{x}) - H(x^\star)\| = \left\| \begin{pmatrix} 0 & 0 \\ 0 & \frac{1}{\left(\frac{1}{K_2} - \frac{1}{K_2^2}\right)^2} + \frac{1}{\left(\frac{1}{K_2} - \frac{1}{K_2^2}\right)^2} - 2K_2^2 \end{pmatrix} \right\|$$

$$= \left\| \begin{pmatrix} 0 & 0 \\ 0 & \Theta(1) \end{pmatrix} \right\|$$

$$= \Theta(1).$$

This establishes a lower bound of

$$\frac{\|H(\widetilde{x}) - H(x^\star)\|}{\|\widetilde{x} - x^\star\|} = \Theta(K_2^2)$$

on the Lipschitz constant L.

Thus, $M := \frac{L}{2h}$, which determines the quadratic convergence of Newton's method, is at least $\Omega(K_1^2 K_2^2)$ and, in particular, even when we initialize it at $\widetilde{x}$, which is relatively close to the analytic center $x^\star$, the guarantee in Theorem 9.4 is too weak to imply that in one step the distance to the analytic center drops. In fact, we get that if we set $x_0 = \widetilde{x}$, then the next point x_1 satisfies

$$\|x_1\| \leq M \|x_0\|^2 \leq M \frac{1}{K_2^4} = \Omega \left(\frac{K_1^2}{K_2^2} \right).$$

Thus, whenever K_1 is at least a constant, Theorem 9.4 does not imply that the distance drops. However, Newton's method does in fact converge rapidly to $x^\star$ when initialized at $\widetilde{x}$ (this can be checked by hand for this simple 2-dimensional example).

9.4.2 Affine Invariance of Newton's Method

One of the important features of Newton's method is its **affine invariance**: If we consider an affine change of coordinates

$$y := \phi(x) = Ax + b,$$

where $A \in \mathbb{R}^{n \times n}$ is an invertible matrix and $b \in \mathbb{R}^n$, then Newton's method will proceed over the same sequence of points in the x- and y-coordinates.

Formally, consider the function $f : \mathbb{R}^n \to \mathbb{R}$ written in the y-coordinates and $\widetilde{f} : \mathbb{R}^n \to \mathbb{R}$ written in x-coordinates, i.e.,

$$\widetilde{f}(x) = f(Ax + b).$$

Then, if $x_0 \in \mathbb{R}^n$ moves to $x_1 \in \mathbb{R}^n$ by applying one step of Newton's method with respect to $\widetilde{f}$, then $y_0 = \phi(x_0)$ moves to $y_1 = \phi(x_1)$ by applying one step of Newton's method with respect to f. This property does not hold for gradient descent or mirror descent, or any of the first-order methods that we have studied so far. Hence, it is sometimes possible to improve the convergence rate of gradient descent by **preconditioning,** i.e., changing coordinates, which is not the case for Newton's method.

This gives another reason why the bound obtained in Theorem 9.4 is not satisfactory: It depends on quantities (such as matrix norms) that are not affinely invariant. Thus, even though Newton's method still takes the same trajectory after we change the coordinates in which the function f is expressed, the parameters L and h in the **NE(M)** condition change and, thus, the final bound in Theorem 9.4 also changes.

To overcome these issues, in the next section, we present a different interpretation of Newton's method – as a discretization of a gradient flow with respect to a Riemannian metric – which allows us to analyze Newton's method based only on affinely invariant quantities in the previous section.

9.5 Newton's Method as Steepest Descent

Suppose we would like to minimize the convex and quadratic function $f : \mathbb{R}^2 \to \mathbb{R}$, given by

$$f(x_1, x_2) := x_1^2 + K x_2^2,$$

where $K > 0$ is a large constant. One can see by inspection that the minimum is $x^\star = (0,0)$. Nevertheless, we would like to compare the gradient descent method and Newton's method for this function.

The gradient descent method takes a starting point, say $\tilde{x} := (1,1)$, and goes to

$$x' := \tilde{x} - \eta \nabla f(\tilde{x})$$

for some step size $\eta > 0$. In this case,

$$\nabla f(\tilde{x}) = (2, 2K)^\top.$$

Thus, if we take η of constant size, the new point x' is at distance roughly $\Omega(K)$ from the optimum; hence, instead of getting closer to $x^\star$, we move farther away. The reason is that our step size η is too large. Indeed, to make the distance to $x^\star$ drop when going from $\tilde{x}$ to x', we must take a step size of roughly $\eta \approx \frac{1}{K}$. This makes the convergence slow.

The Newton step at $\tilde{x}$, on the other hand, is

$$-(\nabla^2 f(\tilde{x}))^{-1} \nabla f(\tilde{x}) = -(1,1). \tag{9.4}$$

This direction points directly towards the minimum $x^\star = (0,0)$ of f and, thus, we are no longer forced to take small steps (see Figure 9.2). How can we reconcile this difference between the predictions of the gradient descent method and Newton's method?

Recall that in the gradient descent method, we chose to follow the negative gradient direction because it was the direction of steepest descent with respect to Euclidean distance (see Section 6.2.1). However, since the role of coordinates x_1 and x_2 is not symmetric in f, the Euclidean norm is no longer appropriate and it makes sense to select a different norm to measure the length of such vectors. Consider the norm

$$\|(u_1, u_2)\|_\circ := \sqrt{u_1^2 + K u_2^2}.$$

(Check that this is indeed a norm when $K > 0$.) Let us now redo the derivation of gradient descent as steepest descent from Chapter 6 with respect to this new norm. This gives rise to the following optimization problem (analogous to (6.1)):

$$\underset{\|u\|_\circ = 1}{\operatorname{argmax}} \, (-Df(x)[u]). \tag{9.5}$$

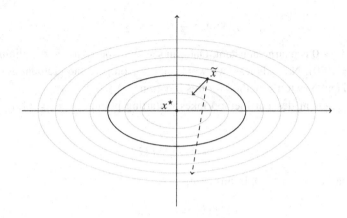

Figure 9.2 Illustration of the difference in directions suggested by gradient descent and Newton's method for the function $x_1^2 + 4x_2^2$. $\tilde{x} = (1,1)$ and $x^* = (0,0)$. The solid arrow is a step of length $1/2$ in the direction $(-1, -1)$ (Newton step) and the dashed arrow is a step of length $1/2$ in the direction $(-1, -4)$ (gradient step).

Since $Df(x)[u] = 2(x_1u_1 + Kx_2u_2)$, (9.5) is the same as

$$\max_{u_1^2 + Ku_2^2 = 1} -2(x_1u_1 + Kx_2u_2).$$

By the Cauchy-Schwarz inequality, we obtain that

$$-(x_1u_1 + Kx_2u_2) \le \sqrt{x_1^2 + Kx_2^2}\sqrt{u_1^2 + Ku_2^2} = \|x\|_\circ \|u\|_\circ.$$

Moreover, the inequality above is tight when u points in the opposite direction as x. Thus, the optimal solution to (9.5) at x points in the direction $-x$. For $\tilde{x} = (1,1)$, up to scaling, this direction is $(-1, -1)$ – the Newton step (9.5).

This example extends immediately to a convex quadratic function of the form

$$h(x) := x^\top A x$$

for PD A. Instead of using the gradient direction $\nabla h(x) = 2Ax$, we determine a new search direction by solving the following optimization problem with respect to $\| \cdot \|_A$:

$$\underset{\|u\|_A = 1}{\operatorname{argmax}} (-Dh(x)[u]) = \underset{u^\top Au = 1}{\operatorname{argmax}} (- \langle \nabla h(x), u \rangle).$$

Here, the rationale behind using the A-norm is again (as in the 2-dimensional example) to counter the effect of stretching caused by the quadratic term $x^\top A x$ in the objective. This turns out to be norm that gives us the right direction as the optimal vector u (up to scaling) is equal to $-x$ (Exercise 9.6). Hence, again, pointing towards the optimum $x^* = 0$. Moreover,

$$-x = -(2A)^{-1}(2Ax) = -(\nabla^2 h(x))^{-1}\nabla h(x),$$

which is the Newton step for h at x.

9.5.1 Steepest Descent with Respect to a Local Norm

In this section, we present a new norm for a general convex function $f : \mathbb{R}^n \to \mathbb{R}$ so that the Newton step coincides with the direction of steepest descent with respect to this norm. Unlike the quadratic case where the norm was $\|\cdot\|_A$, this new norm will vary with x. However, as in the quadratic case, it will related to the Hessian of f.

Let $f : \mathbb{R}^n \to \mathbb{R}$ be a strictly convex function, i.e., the Hessian $\nabla^2 f(x)$ is PD at every point $x \in \mathbb{R}^n$. For brevity, we denote the Hessian $\nabla^2 f(x)$ by $H(x)$. Such a strictly convex function f induces an inner product on $\mathbb{R}^n$. Indeed, at every point $x \in \mathbb{R}^n$, an inner product $\langle \cdot, \cdot \rangle_x$ can be defined as

$$\forall u, v \in \mathbb{R}^n, \quad \langle u, v \rangle_x := u^\top H(x)v.$$

The corresponding norm is

$$\forall u \in \mathbb{R}^n, \quad \|u\|_x := \sqrt{u^\top H(x)u}.$$

The above are sometimes called **local inner product** and **local norm** with respect to the Hessian $\nabla^2 f(\cdot)$, respectively, as they vary with x. Sometimes we say local norm when the underlying function f is clear from the context. They can be used to measure angles or distances between vectors u, v at each x and give rise to a new geometry on $\mathbb{R}^n$. We now revisit the derivation of the gradient descent method as steepest descent, which relied on the use of Euclidean norm $\|\cdot\|_2$, and see what this new geometry yields.

Recall that when deriving the gradient descent algorithm, we decided to pick the direction of steepest descent which is a solution to the following optimization problem:

$$\underset{\|u\|=1}{\operatorname{argmax}} \left(-Df(x)[u] \right) = \underset{\|u\|=1}{\operatorname{argmax}} \left(-\langle \nabla f(x), u \rangle \right). \tag{9.6}$$

By taking the optimal direction u^* with respect to the Euclidean norm, i.e., $\|\cdot\| = \|\cdot\|_2$, we obtained that u^* is in the direction of $-\nabla f(x)$ and arrived at the gradient flow:

$$\frac{dx}{dt} = -\nabla f(x).$$

What if we instead maximize over all u of local norm 1? Then, Equation (9.6) becomes

$$\max_{\|u\|_x=1} (-\langle \nabla f(x), u \rangle) = \max_{u^\top H(x)u=1} (-\langle \nabla f(x), u \rangle). \tag{9.7}$$

The rationale behind the above is clear given our discussion on the quadratic case – we would like to capture the "shape" of the function f around a point x with our choice of the norm, and now, our best guess for that is the quadratic term of f around x, which is given by the Hessian. Again, using the Cauchy-Schwarz inequality, we see that the optimal solution to (9.7) is in the direction

$$-H(x)^{-1} \nabla f(x), \tag{9.8}$$

which is exactly the Newton step. Indeed, let $v := H(x)^{-1} \nabla f(x)$ and observe that

$$-\langle \nabla f(x), u \rangle = -\left\langle H(x)^{1/2} v, H(x)^{1/2} u \right\rangle$$
$$\leq \sqrt{v^\top H(x) v} \sqrt{u^\top H(x) u}$$
$$= \|v\|_x \|u\|_x, \tag{9.9}$$

and equality if and only if $H(x)^{1/2} u = -H(x)^{1/2} v$. This is the same as

$$u = -v = -H(x)^{-1} \nabla f(x)$$

as claimed. The associated continuous-time dynamical system is

$$\frac{dx}{dt} = -H(x)^{-1} \nabla f(x) = -\left(\nabla^2 f(x)\right)^{-1} \nabla f(x).$$

9.5.2 Local Norms Are Riemannian Metrics

The local norm $H(x)$ introduced in the previous section is an example of a **Riemannian metric.**[1] Roughly speaking, a Riemannian metric on $\mathbb{R}^n$ is a mapping g from $\mathbb{R}^n$ to the space of $n \times n$ PD matrices. For an $x \in \mathbb{R}^n$, $g(x)$ determines the local inner product between any $u, v \in \mathbb{R}^n$ as

$$\langle u, v \rangle_x := u^\top g(x) v.$$

This inner product $g(x)$ should be a "smooth" function of x. The Riemannian metric induces the norm $\|u\|_x := \sqrt{\langle u, u \rangle_x}$. The space $\mathbb{R}^n$ along with a Riemannian metric g is an example of a **Riemannian manifold.** It will take us too far to define a Riemannian manifold formally, but let us just mention that a manifold Ω is a topological space that locally resembles Euclidean space near each point. More precisely, an n-dimensional manifold is a topological

---

[1] Note that the use of the word metric here should not be confused with a distance metric.

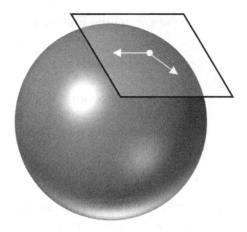

Figure 9.3 The tangent space of a point on the 2-dimensional sphere S^2.

space with the property that each point has a neighborhood that topologically resembles the Euclidean space of dimension n. It is important to note that, in general, at a point x on a manifold Ω, one may not be able to move in all possible directions while still being in Ω (see Figure 9.3). The set of all directions that one can move in at a point x is referred to as the **tangent space** at x and is denoted by $T_x\Omega$. In fact, it can be shown to be a vector space. The inner product at $x \in \Omega$ gives us a way to measure inner products on $T_x\Omega$:

$$g(x) \colon T_x\Omega \times T_x\Omega \to \mathbb{R}.$$

Thus, we can rephrase our result from the previous section as: Newton's method is a steepest descent with respect to a Riemannian metric. In fact, the term $H(x)^{-1}\nabla f(x)$ is the **Riemannian gradient** of f at x with respect to the metric $H(\cdot)$. Note that this type of Riemannian metric is very special: The inner product at every point is given by a Hessian of a strictly convex function. Such Riemannian metrics are referred to as **Hessian metrics.**

9.6 Analysis Based on a Local Norm

The bound on M provided in Theorem 9.4 was stated with respect to the Euclidean distance from the current iterate x_t to the optimal solution $x^\star$. In this section, we use the local norm introduced in the previous sections to present an affinely invariant analysis of Newton's method for optimization, which gets around issues with restricting ourselves to the use of the Euclidean norm, as in Theorem 9.4.

9.6.1 A New Potential Function

Since we deal with convex functions, a natural quantity that can tell us how close or how far are we from the optimum is the norm of the gradient $\|\nabla f(x)\|$. However, as observed in the previous section, Newton's method is really a gradient descent with respect to the Hessian metric $H(x)$. Since the gradient of f at x with respect to this metric is $H(x)^{-1}\nabla f(x)$, we should use the local norm of this gradient. Consequently, we arrive at the following potential function:

$$\|n(x)\|_x := \left\|H(x)^{-1}\nabla f(x)\right\|_x = \sqrt{(\nabla f(x))^\top H(x)^{-1}\nabla f(x)}.$$

It can be verified that $\|n(x)\|_x$ is indeed affinely invariant (Exercise 9.4).

We note that $\|n(x)\|_x$ also has a different interpretation: $\frac{1}{2}\|n(x)\|_x^2$ is the gap between the current value of f and the minimum value of the second-order quadratic approximation of f at x. To see this, we take an arbitrary point x_0 and set

$$x_1 := x_0 + n(x_0).$$

We consider the quadratic approximation $\widetilde{f}$ of f at x_0:

$$\widetilde{f}(x) := f(x_0) + \langle \nabla f(x_0), x - x_0 \rangle + \frac{1}{2}(x - x_0)^\top \nabla^2 f(x)(x - x_0).$$

From our discussion in the previous sections, we know that x_1 minimizes $\widetilde{f}$; hence, using the fact that $n(x_0) = -(\nabla^2 f(x_0))^{-1}\nabla f(x_0)$, we obtain

$$\begin{aligned}
f(x_0) - \widetilde{f}(x_1) &= -\langle \nabla f(x_0), n(x_0)\rangle - \frac{1}{2}n(x_0)^\top \nabla^2 f(x_0)n(x_0)\\
&= \langle \nabla^2 f(x_0)n(x_0), n(x_0)\rangle - \frac{1}{2}n(x_0)^\top \nabla^2 f(x_0)n(x_0)\\
&= \frac{1}{2}\|n(x_0)\|_{x_0}^2.
\end{aligned}$$

At this point, it is instructive to revisit the example studied in Section 9.4.1. First, observe that the new potential $\|n(\widetilde{x})\|_{\widetilde{x}}$ is small at the point $\widetilde{x} = \left(0, \frac{1}{K_2^2}\right)$. Indeed, thinking of K_2 as large and suppressing lower-order terms, we obtain

$$n(\widetilde{x}) = -H(\widetilde{x})^{-1}\nabla F(\widetilde{x}) \approx -\begin{pmatrix}0 & 0\\ 0 & K_2^{-2}\end{pmatrix}\cdot\begin{pmatrix}0\\ 2\end{pmatrix} = -\begin{pmatrix}0\\ 2K_2^{-2}\end{pmatrix}.$$

Further,

$$\|n(\widetilde{x})\|_{\widetilde{x}} \approx \Theta\left(\frac{1}{K_2}\right).$$

More generally, $\|n(x)\|_x$ corresponds to the (Euclidean) distance from x to 0 when the polytope P is scaled (along with point x) to become the square $[-1, 1] \times [-1, 1]$. As our next theorem says, the error measured as $\|n(x)\|_x$ decays quadratically fast in Newton's method.

9.6.2 Statement of the Bound in the Local Norm

We first define a more convenient and natural **NL** condition (for Newton-Local) instead of the **NE** condition used in Theorem 9.4.

Definition 9.5 (NL condition). Let $f: \mathbb{R}^n \to \mathbb{R}$. We say that f satisfies the **NL** condition for $\delta_0 < 1$ if for all $0 < \delta \leq \delta_0 < 1$, and for all x, y such that

$$\|y - x\|_x \leq \delta,$$

we have

$$(1 - 3\delta)H(x) \preceq H(y) \preceq (1 + 3\delta)H(x).$$

Roughly, a function satisfies this condition if for any two points close enough in the local norm, their Hessians are close enough. It is worth noting that the **NL** condition is indeed affinely invariant (Exercise 9.4). This means that $x \mapsto f(x)$ satisfies this condition if and only if $x \mapsto f(\phi(x))$ satisfies it, for any affine change of variables ϕ. We now state the main theorem of this chapter.

Theorem 9.6 (Quadratic convergence with respect to the local norm). *Let* $f: \mathbb{R}^n \to \mathbb{R}$ *be a strictly convex function satisfying the* **NL** *condition for* $\delta_0 = \frac{1}{6}$, $x_0 \in \mathbb{R}^n$ *be any point, and*

$$x_1 := x_0 + n(x_0).$$

If $\|n(x_0)\|_{x_0} \leq \frac{1}{6}$, *then*

$$\|n(x_1)\|_{x_1} \leq 3 \|n(x_0)\|_{x_0}^2.$$

We now inspect the **NL** condition in more detail. To this end, assume for simplicity that $f(x)$ is a univariate function. Then, the **NL** condition says, roughly, that

$$|H(x) - H(y)| \leq 3 \|x - y\|_x |H(x)|$$

whenever $\|x - y\|_x$ is small enough. In other words,

$$\frac{|f''(x) - f''(y)|}{\|x - y\|_x} \cdot \frac{1}{|f''(x)|} \leq 3.$$

Note that the first term in the left-hand side above, roughly, corresponds to bounding the third derivative of f in the local norm. Thus, the above says something very similar to "$M \leq 3$," where M is the quantity from Theorem 9.1 (recall that $g(x)$ corresponds to $f'(x)$ here). The difference is that the quantities we consider here are computed with respect to the local norm as opposed to the Euclidean norm, as in Theorem 9.1 or Theorem 9.4. The constant "3" is by no means crucial to the definition of the **NL** condition; it is only chosen for the convenience of our future calculations.

9.6.3 Proof of Convergence in the Local Norm

Before proving Theorem 9.6, we need to establish one simple yet important lemma first. It says that if the **NL** condition is satisfied, then the local norms of nearby points are also close or, more formally, they have low "distortion" with respect to each other. If we go from x to y and their local distance is a (small) constant, then the local norms at x and y differ just by a factor of 2.

Lemma 9.7 (Low distortion of close-by norms). *Let $f : \mathbb{R}^n \to \mathbb{R}$ be a strictly convex function that satisfies the **NL** condition for $\delta_0 = 1/6$. Then, whenever $x, y \in \mathbb{R}^n$ are such that $\|y - x\|_x \leq \frac{1}{6}$, for every $u \in \mathbb{R}^n$ we have*

(1) $\frac{1}{2} \|u\|_x \leq \|u\|_y \leq 2 \|u\|_x$ *and*

(2) $\frac{1}{2} \|u\|_{H(x)^{-1}} \leq \|u\|_{H(y)^{-1}} \leq 2 \|u\|_{H(x)^{-1}}$.

We remark that in the above, $\|\cdot\|_{H(x)^{-1}}$ is dual to the local norm $\|\cdot\|_x = \|\cdot\|_{H(x)}$, i.e., $\|\cdot\|_{H(x)^{-1}} = \|\cdot\|_x^*$.

Proof: From the **NL** condition, we have

$$\frac{1}{2} H(y) \preceq H(x) \preceq 2H(y),$$

and, hence,

$$\frac{1}{2} H(y)^{-1} \preceq H(x)^{-1} \preceq 2H(y)^{-1}.$$

Here we used the fact that for two PD matrices A and B, $A \preceq B$ if and only if $B^{-1} \preceq A^{-1}$. The lemma follows now by the definition of the PSD ordering. ∎

Before we proceed to the proof of Theorem 9.6, we state a simple lemma on the relationship between the PSD ordering and spectral norms of symmetric matrices, which will be helpful to us in the proof. The proof of this is left as an exercise (Exercise 9.13).

Lemma 9.8. *Suppose $A \in \mathbb{R}^{n \times n}$ is a symmetric positive definite matrix and $B \in \mathbb{R}^{n \times n}$ is symmetric such that*

$$-\alpha A \preceq B \preceq \alpha A$$

for some $\alpha \geq 0$; then

$$\left\| A^{-1/2} B A^{-1/2} \right\| \leq \alpha.$$

We now proceed to prove Theorem 9.6.

Proof of Theorem 9.6: Recall that our goal is to prove that

$$\|n(x_1)\|_{x_1} \leq 3 \|n(x_0)\|_{x_0}^2 .$$

Note that $\|n(x_1)\|_{x_1}$ can also be written as $\|\nabla f(x_1)\|_{H(x_1)^{-1}}$ and, similarly, $\|n(x_0)\|_{x_0} = \|\nabla f(x_0)\|_{H(x_0)^{-1}}$. Therefore, using the fact that the local norms at x_1 and x_0 are the same up to a factor of 2 (see Lemma 9.7), it is enough to prove that

$$\|\nabla f(x_1)\|_{H(x_0)^{-1}} \leq \frac{3}{2} \|\nabla f(x_0)\|_{H(x_0)^{-1}}^2 . \tag{9.10}$$

To see this, we use the second part of Lemma 9.7 with

$$x := x_1 \quad \text{and} \quad y := x_0 \quad \text{and} \quad u := \nabla f(x_1)$$

to obtain

$$\frac{1}{2}\|\nabla f(x_1)\|_{H^{-1}(x_1)} \leq \|\nabla f(x_1)\|_{H^{-1}(x_0)}.$$

Towards proving (9.10), we first write the gradient $\nabla f(x_1)$ in the form $A(x_0)\nabla f(x_0)$, where $A(x_0)$ is a certain explicit matrix. Subsequently, we show that the norm of $A(x_0)$ is (in a certain sense) small, which in turn allows us to establish Equation (9.10).

$$\nabla f(x_1) = \nabla f(x_0) + \int_0^1 H(x_0 + t(x_1 - x_0))(x_1 - x_0)dt$$

(by the fundamental theorem of calculus applied to ∇f)

$$= \nabla f(x_0) - \int_0^1 H(x_0 + t(x_1 - x_0))H(x_0)^{-1}\nabla f(x_0)dt$$

(by rewriting $(x_1 - x_0)$ as $-H(x_0)^{-1}\nabla f(x_0)$)

$$= \nabla f(x_0) - \left[\int_0^1 H(x_0 + t(x_1 - x_0)) dt \right] H(x_0)^{-1} \nabla f(x_0)$$

(by linearity of integral)

$$= \left[H(x_0) - \int_0^1 H(x_0 + t(x_1 - x_0)) dt \right] H(x_0)^{-1} \nabla f(x_0)$$

(by writing $\nabla f(x_0)$ as $H(x_0) H(x_0)^{-1} \nabla f(x_0)$)

$$= M(x_0) H(x_0)^{-1} \nabla f(x_0).$$

In the last equation we used the notation

$$M(x_0) := H(x_0) - \int_0^1 H(x_0 + t(x_1 - x_0)) dt.$$

By taking $\|\cdot\|_{H(x_0)^{-1}}$ on both sides of the above derived equality, we obtain

$$\|\nabla f(x_1)\|_{H(x_0)^{-1}} = \left\| M(x_0) H(x_0)^{-1} \nabla f(x_0) \right\|_{H(x_0)^{-1}}$$

$$= \left\| H(x_0)^{-1/2} M(x_0) H(x_0)^{-1} \nabla f(x_0) \right\|_2$$

(by the fact that $\|u\|_A = \left\| A^{-1/2} u \right\|_2$)

$$\leq \left\| H(x_0)^{-1/2} M(x_0) H(x_0)^{-1/2} \right\| \cdot \left\| H(x_0)^{-1/2} \nabla f(x_0) \right\|_2$$

(since $\|Au\|_2 \leq \|A\| \|u\|_2$)

$$= \left\| H(x_0)^{-1/2} M(x_0) H(x_0)^{-1/2} \right\| \cdot \|\nabla f(x_0)\|_{H(x_0)^{-1}}.$$

(by the fact that $\|u\|_A = \left\| A^{-1/2} u \right\|_2$)

Thus, to conclude the proof, it remains to show that the matrix $M(x_0)$ is "small" in the following sense:

$$\left\| H(x_0)^{-1/2} M(x_0) H(x_0)^{-1/2} \right\| \leq \frac{3}{2} \|\nabla f(x_0)\|_{H(x_0)^{-1}}.$$

For this, by Lemma 9.8, it is enough to show that

$$-\frac{3}{2} \delta H(x_0) \preceq M(x_0) \preceq \frac{3}{2} \delta H(x_0), \tag{9.11}$$

where, for brevity, $\delta := \|\nabla f(x_0)\|_{H(x_0)^{-1}} \leq \frac{1}{6}$ by the hypothesis of the theorem. This in turn follows from the **NL** condition. Indeed, since

$$\delta = \|\nabla f(x_0)\|_{H(x_0)^{-1}} = \|x_1 - x_0\|_{x_0},$$

if we define

$$z := x_0 + t(x_1 - x_0)$$

for $t \in [0, 1]$, we have that

$$\|z - x_0\|_{x_0} = t \|x_1 - x_0\|_{x_0} = t\delta \leq \delta.$$

Hence, from the **NL** condition, for every $t \in [0, 1]$, we obtain

$$-3t\delta H(x_0) \preceq H(x_0) - H(z) = H(x_0) - H(x_0 + t(x_1 - x_0)) \preceq 3t\delta H(x_0).$$

By integrating this inequality with respect to dt from $t = 0$ to $t = 1$, Equation (9.11) follows. This completes the proof of Theorem 9.6. ∎

9.7 Analysis Based on the Euclidean Norm

Proof of Theorem 9.4: The basic idea of the proof is the same as in the proof of Theorem 9.1. We consider the function $\phi \colon [0, 1] \to \mathbb{R}^n$ given by $\phi(t) := \nabla f(x + t(y - x))$. Applying the fundamental theorem of calculus to ϕ (to each coordinate separately) yields

$$\phi(1) - \phi(0) = \int_0^1 \nabla \phi(t) dt$$

$$\nabla f(y) - \nabla f(x) = \int_0^1 H(x + t(y - x))(y - x) dt. \qquad (9.12)$$

We start by writing $x_1 - x^\star$ in a convenient form:

$$\begin{aligned}
x_1 - x^\star &= x_0 - x^\star + n(x_0) \\
&= x_0 - x^\star - H(x_0)^{-1} \nabla f(x_0) \\
&= x_0 - x^\star + H(x_0)^{-1} (\nabla f(x^\star) - \nabla f(x_0)) \\
&= x_0 - x^\star + H(x_0)^{-1} \int_0^1 H(x_0 + t(x^\star - x_0))(x^\star - x_0) dt \\
&= H(x_0)^{-1} \int_0^1 (H(x_0 + t(x^\star - x_0)) - H(x_0))(x^\star - x_0) dt.
\end{aligned}$$

Now, take Euclidean norms on both sides to obtain

$$\left\| x_1 - x^\star \right\|_2 \leq \left\| H(x_0)^{-1} \right\| \int_0^1 \left\| (H(x_0 + t(x^\star - x_0)) - H(x_0))(x^\star - x_0) \right\|_2 dt$$

$$\leq \left\| H(x_0)^{-1} \right\| \left\| x^\star - x_0 \right\|_2 \int_0^1 \left\| (H(x_0 + t(x^\star - x_0)) - H(x_0)) \right\| dt.$$

$$(9.13)$$

We can then use the Lipschitz condition on H to bound the integral as follows:

$$\int_0^1 \left\| (H(x_0 + t(x^\star - x_0)) - H(x_0)) \right\| dt \leq \int_0^1 L \left\| t(x^\star - x_0) \right\|_2 dt$$

$$\leq L \left\| x^\star - x_0 \right\|_2 \int_0^1 t \, dt$$

$$= \frac{L}{2} \left\| x^\star - x_0 \right\|_2 .$$

Together with (9.13), this implies

$$\left\| x_1 - x^\star \right\|_2 \leq \frac{L \left\| H(x_0)^{-1} \right\|}{2} \left\| x^\star - x_0 \right\|_2^2 . \tag{9.14}$$

We can then take $M = \frac{L \| H(x_0)^{-1} \|}{2} \leq \frac{L}{2h}$, which completes the proof. ∎

9.8 Exercises

9.1 Consider the problem of minimizing the function $f(x) = x \log x$ over $x \in \mathbb{R}_{\geq 0}$. Perform the full convergence analysis of Newton's method applied to minimizing f – consider all starting points $x_0 \in \mathbb{R}_{\geq 0}$ and determine where the method converges for each of them.

9.2 **Newton's method to find roots of polynomials.** Consider a real-rooted polynomial $p \in \mathbb{R}[x]$. Prove that if Newton's method is applied to finding roots of p and is initialized at a point $x_0 > \lambda_{\max}(p)$ (where $\lambda_{\max}(p)$ is the largest root of p), then it converges to the largest root of p. For a given $\varepsilon > 0$, derive a bound on the number of iterations required to reach a point ε additively close to $\lambda_{\max}$.

9.3 Verify that for a twice-differentiable function $f : \mathbb{R}^n \to \mathbb{R}$,

$$J_{\nabla f}(x) = \nabla^2 f(x).$$

9.4 Let $f : \mathbb{R}^n \to \mathbb{R}$ and let $n(x)$ be the Newton step at x with respect to f.

(a) Prove that Newton's method is affinely invariant.
(b) Prove that the quantity $\|n(x)\|_x$ is affinely invariant while $\|\nabla f(x)\|_2$ is not.
(c) Prove that the **NL** condition is affinely invariant.

9.5 Consider the following functions $f : K \to \mathbb{R}$. Check if they satisfy the **NL** condition for some constant $0 < \delta_0 < 1$.

(a) $f(x) := -\log \cos(x)$ on $K = (-\frac{\pi}{2}, \frac{\pi}{2})$

(b) $f(x) := x \log x + (1 - x) \log(1 - x)$ on $K = (0, 1)$

(c) $f(x) := -\sum_{i=1}^{n} \log x_i$ on $K = \mathbb{R}_{>0}^{n}$

9.6 Consider the function

$$h(x) := x^{\top} A x - \langle b, x \rangle$$

for PD A. Prove that

$$\operatorname*{argmax}_{\|u\|_A = 1} (-Dh(x)[u]) = -\frac{x}{\|x\|_A}.$$

9.7 For an $n \times m$ real matrix A and a vector $b \in \mathbb{R}^n$, consider the set

$$\Omega := \{x : Ax = b\}.$$

Prove that for any $x \in \Omega$,

$$T_x \Omega = \{y : Ay = 0\}.$$

9.8 Prove that the Riemannian metric $x \mapsto \operatorname{Diag}(x)^{-1}$ defined for $x \in \mathbb{R}_{>0}^{n}$ is a Hessian metric. *Hint:* Consider the function $f(x) := \sum_{i=1}^{n} x_i \log x_i$.

9.9 Let Ω be a subset of $\mathbb{R}^{n \times n}$ consisting of all positive definite matrices. Prove that the tangent space at any point of Ω is the set of all $n \times n$ real symmetric matrices. Further, prove that for any PD matrix X, the inner product

$$\langle U, V \rangle_X := \operatorname{Tr}(X^{-1} U X^{-1} V)$$

for $n \times n$ symmetric matrices U, V is a Hessian metric. *Hint:* Consider the function $f(X) := -\log \det X$.

9.10 Verify Equation (9.9).

9.11 **Directed Physarum dynamics.** For an $n \times m$ full-rank real matrix A and a vector $b \in \mathbb{R}^n$, consider the set

$$\Omega := \{x : Ax = b, x > 0\}$$

endowed with the Riemannian metric

$$\langle u, v \rangle_x := u^{\top} X^{-1} v$$

at every $x \in \Omega$. Here $X := \operatorname{Diag}(x)$. Prove that the vector

$$P(x) := X \left(A^{\top} \left(A X A^{\top} \right)^{-1} b - 1 \right)$$

is the direction of steepest descent for the function $\sum_{i=1}^{m} x_i$ with respect to the Riemannian metric.

9.12   Consider a matrix $A \in \mathbb{R}^{n \times n}$ with strictly positive entries. Prove that the function $f : \mathbb{R}^{2n} \to \mathbb{R}$ given by

$$f(x, y) = \sum_{1 \leq i, j \leq n} A_{i,j} e^{x_i - y_j} - \sum_{i=1}^{n} x_i + \sum_{j=1}^{n} y_j$$

satisfies the following condition similar to the **NL** condition but with the local norm replaced by ℓ_∞:

$\forall w, v \in \mathbb{R}^{2n}$ such that $\|w - v\|_\infty \leq 1$,

$$\frac{1}{10} \nabla^2 f(w) \preceq \nabla^2 f(v) \preceq 10 \nabla^2 f(w).$$

9.13   Prove Lemma 9.8.

Notes

For a thorough discussion of Newton's method, we refer to the books by Galántai (2000) and Renegar (2001). Exercise 9.2 is adapted from the paper by Louis and Vempala (2016). Exercise 9.11 is from the paper by Straszak and Vishnoi (2016b). Exercise 9.12 is extracted from the papers by Cohen et al. (2017) and Zhu et al. (2017). For a formal introduction to Riemannian manifolds, including Riemannian gradients and Hessian metrics, the reader is referred to the survey by Vishnoi (2018).

10

An Interior Point Method for Linear Programming

We build upon Newton's method and its convergence to derive a polynomial time algorithm for linear programming. Key to this algorithm is a reduction from constrained to unconstrained optimization using the notion of a barrier function and the corresponding central path.

10.1 Linear Programming

Linear programming is the problem of finding a point that minimizes a linear function over a polyhedron. Formally, it is the following optimization problem.

Definition 10.1 (Linear program – canonical form). The input consists of a matrix $A \in \mathbb{Q}^{m \times n}$ and a vector $b \in \mathbb{Q}^m$ that together specify a polyhedron,

$$P := \{x \in \mathbb{R}^n : Ax \preceq b\},$$

and a cost vector $c \in \mathbb{Q}^n$. The goal is to find an

$$x^\star \in \operatorname*{argmin}_{x \in P} \langle c, x \rangle$$

if $P \neq \emptyset$ or, say **infeasible** if $P = \emptyset$. The bit complexity of the input is the total number of bits required to encode (A, b, c) and is sometimes denoted by L.

Note that, in general, $x^\star$ may not be unique. Moreover, there may be ways to specify a polyhedron other than as a collection of linear inequalities. We refer to this version of linear programming as **canonical.** We study some other variants of linear programming in subsequent chapters. A word of caution is that when we transform one form of linear programming into another, we should carefully account for the running time, including the cost of transformation.

185

Linear programming is a central problem in optimization and has made its appearance, implicitly or explicitly, in some of the previous chapters. We also developed various approximate algorithms for some special cases of linear programming using methods such as gradient descent, mirror descent, and MWU. These algorithms require an additional parameter $\varepsilon > 0$ and guarantee to find an $\hat{x}$ such that

$$\langle c, \hat{x} \rangle \leq \langle c, x^\star \rangle + \varepsilon$$

in time that depends inverse polynomially on the error parameter ε. For instance, the method based on the MWU scheme that we introduced for the bipartite matching problem in Chapter 7 can be applied to general linear programs and yields an algorithm that, given $\varepsilon > 0$, computes a solution $\hat{x}$, which has value at most $\langle c, x^\star \rangle + \varepsilon$ (for an optimal solution $x^\star$) and violates all of the constraints by at most ε (additively), in time proportional to $\frac{1}{\varepsilon^2}$. Not only is the dependency on ε unsatisfactory, but when no additional assumptions on A, b, or c are made, these methods run in time exponential in the bit complexity of the input. As discussed in Chapter 4, for a method to be regarded as polynomial time, we require the dependency on the error parameter $\varepsilon > 0$ in the running time to be polynomial in $\log \frac{1}{\varepsilon}$; moreover, the dependency on the bit complexity L should be also polynomial. In this chapter, we derive a method that satisfies both these requirements for linear programming.

Theorem 10.2 (Polynomial time algorithm for solving LPs). *There is an algorithm that, given a description of a linear program (A, b, c) with n variables, m constraints and bit complexity L as in Definition 10.1, an $\varepsilon > 0$, and assuming that P is full-dimensional and nonempty, outputs a feasible solution $\hat{x}$ with*

$$\langle c, \hat{x} \rangle \leq \langle c, x^\star \rangle + \varepsilon$$

or terminates stating that the polyhedron is infeasible.[1] The algorithm runs in $\text{poly}\left(L, \log \frac{1}{\varepsilon}\right)$ *time.*

Here, we do not discuss how to get rid of the full-dimensionality and nonemptiness assumptions. Given the proof of this theorem, it is not too difficult, but tedious, and we omit it. Also, note that the above theorem does not solve the linear programming problem mentioned in Definition 10.1 as it does not output $x^\star$ but only an approximation for it. However, with a bit more work, one can transform the above algorithm into one that outputs $x^\star$.

---

[1] If the solutions of $Ax \leq b$ do not lie in a proper affine subspace of $\mathbb{R}^n$, then the polytope is full-dimensional.

Roughly, this is achieved by picking $\varepsilon > 0$ small enough (about $2^{-\text{poly}(L)}$) and rounding the output $\hat{x}$ to $x^\star$ (which is guaranteed to be rational and have bit complexity bounded by $O(L)$). This is why the poly-logarithmic dependency on $\frac{1}{\varepsilon}$ is crucial.

10.2 Constrained Optimization via Barrier Functions

What makes linear programming hard is the set of constraints encoded as a polyhedron P. However, thus far we have largely discussed methods for unconstrained optimization problems. Projection-based variants of these optimization methods (such as projected gradient descent presented in Chapter 6) can be shown to reduce back to linear programming via an equivalence between separation and optimization discussed in Chapters 12 and 13. In short, we need an entirely new method for constrained optimization. The main goal of this section is to present a different and general methodology to reduce constrained optimization problems to unconstrained optimization problems – via **barrier functions.**

We consider constrained convex optimization problems of the form

$$\min_{x \in K} f(x), \tag{10.1}$$

where f is a convex, real-valued function and $K \subseteq \mathbb{R}^n$ is a convex set. To simplify our discussion, we assume that the objective function is linear, i.e., $f(x) = \langle c, x \rangle$ and the convex body K is bounded and full-dimensional.

Suppose we have a point $x_0 \in K$ and we want to perform an improvement step with respect to the objective $\langle c, x \rangle$ while maintaining the condition of being inside K. Perhaps the simplest idea is to keep moving in the direction $-c$ to decrease the objective value as much as possible. This will end up on the boundary of K. The second and subsequent iterates would then lie on to the boundary, which could force our steps to be short and potentially make this method inefficient. Indeed, such a method (when applied to polytopes) is equivalent to a variant of the **simplex method** that is known to have an exponential worst-case running time, and we do not pursue this any further.

Instead, we study the possibility of moving the constraints defining K to the objective function and consider the optimization problem

$$\min_{x \in \mathbb{R}^n} \langle c, x \rangle + F(x), \tag{10.2}$$

where $F(x)$ can be regarded as a penalty for violating constraints. Thus, $F(x)$ should become big when x is close to the boundary (∂K) of the convex set K.

One seemingly perfect choice of F would be a function that is 0 on an inside K and $+\infty$ on the complement of K. However, this objective may no longer be continuous.

If one would like the methods for unconstrained optimization that we developed in the previous chapters to be applicable here, then F should satisfy certain properties and, at the very least, convexity. Instead of giving a precise definition of a **barrier function** F for K, we list some properties that are expected:

(1) F is defined in the interior of K, i.e., the domain of F is int(K),
(2) for every point $q \in \partial K$ it holds that: $\lim_{x \in K \to q} F(x) = +\infty$, and
(3) F is strictly convex.

Suppose F is such a barrier function. Then, note that solving (10.2) might give us some idea of what $\min_{x \in K} \langle c, x \rangle$ is, but it does not give us the right answer, since the addition of $F(x)$ to the objective alters the location of the point we are looking for. For this reason, one typically considers a family of perturbed objective functions f_η parameterized by $\eta > 0$ as follows:

$$f_\eta(x) := \eta \langle c, x \rangle + F(x). \tag{10.3}$$

For mathematical convenience, we can imagine that f_η is defined on all of $\mathbb{R}^n$ but attains finite values only on int(K). Intuitively, making η bigger and bigger reduces the influence of $F(x)$ on the optimal value of $f_\eta(x)$. We now focus on the concrete problem at hand – linear programming.

10.3 The Logarithmic Barrier Function

Recall that the linear programming introduced earlier is the problem of minimizing a linear function $\langle c, x \rangle$ over the following polyhedron:

$$P := \{x \in \mathbb{R}^n : \langle a_i, x \rangle \le b_i, \text{ for } i = 1, 2, \ldots, m\}, \tag{10.4}$$

where $a_1, a_2, \ldots, a_m$ are the rows of A (treated as column vectors). To implement the high-level idea sketched in the previous section, we use the following barrier function:

Definition 10.3 (Logarithmic barrier function). For a matrix $A \in \mathbb{R}^{m \times n}$ (with rows $a_1, a_2, \ldots, a_m \in \mathbb{R}^n$) and a vector $b \in \mathbb{R}^m$, we define the logarithmic barrier function $F : \text{int}(P) \to \mathbb{R}$ as

$$F(x) := -\sum_{i=1}^{m} \log(b_i - \langle a_i, x \rangle).$$

The domain of this function is the **interior** of P defined as

$$\text{int}(P) := \{x \in P : \langle a_i, x \rangle < b_i, \text{ for } i = 1, 2, \dots, m\}.$$

For the definition to make sense, we assume that P is bounded (a polytope) and full-dimensional in $\mathbb{R}^n$.[2] Note that $F(x)$ is strictly convex on $\text{int}(P)$ and tends to infinity when approaching the boundary of P (Exercise 10.1). Intuitively, one can think of each term $-\log(b_i - \langle a_i, x \rangle)$ as exerting a force at the constraint $\langle a_i, x \rangle \leq b_i$, which becomes larger the closer the point x comes to the hyperplane $\{y : \langle a_i, y \rangle = b_i\}$ and is $+\infty$ if the point x lies on or on the wrong side of this hyperplane.

10.4 The Central Path

Given the logarithmic barrier function, we go back to the parameterized family of perturbed objectives $\{f_\eta\}_{\eta \geq 0}$ introduced in Equation (10.3). Observe that since $\langle c, x \rangle$ is a linear function, the second-order behavior of f_η is completely determined by F as

$$\nabla^2 f_\eta = \nabla^2 F.$$

In particular, f_η is also strictly convex and has a unique minimizer. This motivates the following notion:

Definition 10.4 (Central path). For $\eta \geq 0$, denote by $x_\eta^\star$ the unique minimizer of $f_\eta(x)$ over $x \in \text{int}(P)$. We call $x_0^\star$ the **analytic center** of P. The set of all these minimizers is called the central path (with respect to the cost vector c) and is denoted by

$$\Gamma_c := \{x_\eta^\star : \eta \geq 0\}.$$

While it is not used here, the central path Γ_c can be shown to be continuous. It originates at the analytic center $x_0^\star$ of P and approaches $x^\star$, as $\eta \to \infty$ (Figure 10.1). In other words,

$$\lim_{\eta \to \infty} x_\eta^\star = x^\star.$$

---

[2] Of course, this is not always the case for general linear programs. However, if the polyhedron is feasible, then we can perturb coefficients of each of the constraints by an exponentially small value to force the feasible set to be full-dimensional.

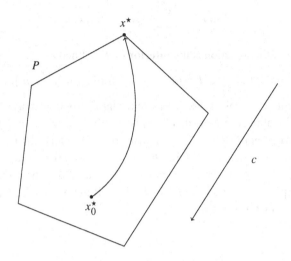

Figure 10.1 Example of a central path for the cost vector c.

The idea now is to start at some point, say x_1^* (i.e., for $\eta = 1$) on the central path, and progress along the path by gradually taking η to infinity. A method that follows this general approach is referred to as a **path-following interior point method (IPM).** The key questions from the algorithmic point of view are as follows:

(1) **Initialization:** How to find the analytic center of P?
(2) **Following the central path:** How to follow the central path using discrete steps?
(3) **Termination:** How to decide when to stop following the central path (our goal is to reach a close enough neighborhood of x^*)?

We make this method precise in the next section and answer all of these questions in our analysis of the path-following IPM in Section 10.6.

10.5 A Path-Following Algorithm for Linear Programming

While the initialization and termination questions stated as 1 and 3 in the list at the end of the previous section are certainly important, we first focus on 2 and explain how to progress along the path. This is where the power of Newton's method developed in the previous chapter is leveraged.

Suppose for a moment that we are given a point $x_0 \in P$ that is close to the central path, i.e., to $x_{\eta_0}^\star$ for some $\eta_0 > 0$. Further assume that the function f_{η_0} satisfies the **NL** condition from Chapter 9 (we show this later). Then, we know that by performing a Newton step

$$x_1 := x_0 + n_{\eta_0}(x_0),$$

where for any x and $\eta > 0$, we define

$$n_\eta(x) := -\left(\nabla^2 f_\eta(x)\right)^{-1} \nabla f_\eta(x) = -\left(\nabla^2 F(x)\right)^{-1} \nabla f_\eta(x),$$

we make significant progress towards $x_{\eta_0}^\star$. Note that since F is strictly convex; $\left(\nabla^2 F(x)\right)^{-1}$ exists for all $x \in \text{int}(P)$. The main idea is to use this progress, and the opportunity it presents, to increase the value of η_0 to

$$\eta_1 := \eta_0 \cdot (1 + \gamma)$$

for some $\gamma > 0$ so that x_1 is close enough to $x_{\eta_1}^\star$ and again satisfies the **NL** condition, enabling us to repeat this procedure and continue.

The key question becomes, how large a γ can we pick in order to make this scheme work and produce a sequence of pairs $(x_0, \eta_0), (x_1, \eta_1), \ldots$ such that η_t increases at a rate $(1 + \gamma)$ and that x_t is in the quadratic convergence region of f_{η_t}. We show in Section 10.6 that the right value for γ is roughly $\frac{1}{\sqrt{m}}$. A more precise description of this algorithm is presented in Algorithm 8. This algorithm description is not complete and we explain how to set η_0, why $\eta_T > m/\varepsilon$ suffices, how to compute the Newton step, and how to terminate in upcoming sections.

The notion of closeness of a point x_t to the central path, i.e., to $x_{\eta_t}^\star$, which we employ here is

$$\left\| n_{\eta_t}(x_t) \right\|_{x_t} \leq \frac{1}{6}.$$

This is directly motivated by the guarantee obtained in Chapter 9 for Newton's method – this condition means precisely that x_t belongs to the quadratic convergence region for f_{η_t}.

10.5.1 Structure of the Proof of Theorem 10.2

In this section, we present an outline of the proof of Theorem 10.2. We show that an appropriate implementation of the path-following IPM presented in Algorithm 8 yields a polynomial time algorithm for linear programming. This requires making the scheme a little bit more precise (explaining how to perform

---

Algorithm 8: Path-following IPM for linear programming

Input:
- $A \in \mathbb{Q}^{m \times n}, b \in \mathbb{Q}^m, c \in \mathbb{Q}$
- An $\varepsilon > 0$

Output: A point $\hat{x}$ such that $A\hat{x} \leq b$ and $\langle c, \hat{x} \rangle - \langle c, x^* \rangle \leq \varepsilon$

Algorithm:

1: **Initialization:** Find an initial $\eta_0 > 0$ and x_0 with $\left\| n_{\eta_0}(x_0) \right\|_{x_0} < \frac{1}{6}$

2: Let T be such that $\eta_T := \eta_0 \left(1 + \frac{1}{20 \sqrt{m}} \right)^T > \frac{m}{\varepsilon}$

3: **for** $t = 0, 1, \ldots, T$ **do**

4:     **Newton step:** $x_{t+1} := x_t + n_{\eta_t}(x_t)$

5:     **Changing η:** $\eta_{t+1} := \eta_t \left(1 + \frac{1}{20 \sqrt{m}} \right)$

6: **end for**

7: **Termination:** Calculate $\hat{x}$ by performing two Newton steps with respect to f_{η_T} starting at x_T

8: **return** $\hat{x}$

Step 1). However, the crucial part of the analysis is showing that Steps 4 and 5 indeed guarantee to track the central path closely. To this end, we prove that the following closeness invariant holds:

Lemma 10.5 (Closeness invariant). *For every $t = 0, 1, 2, \ldots, T$ it holds that*

$$\left\| n_{\eta_t}(x_t) \right\|_{x_t} \leq \frac{1}{6}.$$

To prove that this invariant holds, we consider one iteration and show that, if the invariant holds for t, then it also holds for $t + 1$. Needless to say, we have to ensure the closeness invariant holds for $t = 0$. Every iteration consists of two steps: the Newton step with respect to f_{η_t} and the increase of η_t to η_{t+1}. We formulate two more lemmas that capture what happens when performing each these steps. The first lemma uses Theorem 9.6.

Lemma 10.6 (Effect of a Newton step on centrality). *The logarithmic barrier function F satisfies the **NL** condition for $\delta_0 = \frac{1}{6}$. Therefore, for every $x \in \text{int}(P)$ and every $\eta > 0$, such that $\left\| n_\eta(x) \right\|_x \leq \frac{1}{6}$, it holds that*

$$\left\| n_\eta(x') \right\|_{x'} \leq 3 \left\| n_\eta(x) \right\|_x^2,$$

where $x' := x + n_\eta(x)$.

This implies that one Newton step brings us closer to the central path. The lemma below tells us that if we are very close to the central path, then it is safe to increase η_t by a factor of roughly $\left(1 + \frac{1}{\sqrt{m}}\right)$ so that the centrality is still preserved.

Lemma 10.7 (Effect of recentering on centrality). *For every point* $x \in$ int(P) *and every two positive* $\eta, \eta' > 0$, *we have*

$$\left\| n_{\eta'}(x) \right\|_x \leq \frac{\eta'}{\eta} \left\| n_\eta(x) \right\|_x + \sqrt{m} \left| \frac{\eta'}{\eta} - 1 \right|.$$

Thus, if we initialize the algorithm at η_0 and terminate it at η_T then, after $O\left(\sqrt{m} \log \frac{\eta_T}{\eta_0}\right)$ iterations, each of which is just solving one $m \times m$ linear system (corresponding to $\nabla^2 F(x) y = z$, for two given vectors $x \in P$ and v) we recover an ε-approximate optimal solution. This concludes the part of the analysis concerning the loop in Step 3 in the algorithm and the issue of centrality. We now move to the part concerning initialization.

We would like an algorithm to find a good starting point, i.e., one for which η_0 is not too small and for which the corresponding Newton step is short.

Lemma 10.8 (Efficient initialization). *Step 1 of Algorithm 8 can be implemented in polynomial time to yield*

$$\eta_0 = 2^{-\tilde{O}(nL)}$$

and $x_0 \in$ int(P) *such that*

$$\left\| n_{\eta_0}(x_0) \right\|_{x_0} \leq \frac{1}{6}.$$

Here n is the dimension of P and L is the bit complexity of (A, b, c).

Note that it is crucial that the above lemma provides a lower bound on η_0. This allows us to deduce that the number of iterations T in Algorithm 8 is polynomially bounded and, hence, leading to a polynomial time algorithm for linear programming. It is also worth noting here that for well-structured linear programs one can sometimes find starting points with a larger value of η_0, such as $\eta_0 = \frac{1}{m}$, which can have an impact on the number of iterations; see Chapter 11.

Finally, we consider Step 7 of the algorithm – termination. This says that by adjusting the point x_T just a little bit we can reach a point $\hat{x}$ very close to $x^\star$ in the objective value. More precisely, we prove the following.

Lemma 10.9 (Efficient termination). *By performing two Newton steps initialized at x_T, where T is such that $\eta_T \geq m/\varepsilon$, we obtain a point $\hat{x}$ that satisfies*

$$\langle c, \hat{x} \rangle \leq \langle c, x^\star \rangle + 2\varepsilon.$$

We are now ready to state the main theorem characterizing the performance of Algorithm 8.

Theorem 10.10 (Convergence of the path-following IPM). *Algorithm 8, after $T = O\left(\sqrt{m}\log\frac{m}{\varepsilon\eta_0}\right)$ iterations, outputs a point $\hat{x} \in P$ that satisfies*

$$\langle c, \hat{x} \rangle \leq \langle c, x^\star \rangle + 2\varepsilon.$$

Moreover, every iteration (Step 4) requires solving one linear system of the form $\nabla^2 F(x)y = z$, where $x \in \text{int}(P)$, $z \in \mathbb{R}^n$ is determined by x, and we solve for y. Thus, it can be implemented in polynomial time.

Note now that by combining Theorem 10.10 with Lemma 10.8, the proof of Theorem 10.2 follows easily.

10.6 Analysis of the Path-Following Algorithm

The purpose of this section is to prove Lemma 10.5, i.e., that the invariant

$$\left\| n_{\eta_t}(x_t) \right\|_{x_t} \leq \frac{1}{6}$$

holds for all $t = 1, 2, \ldots, T$. As explained in the previous section, this just follows from Lemmas 10.6 and 10.7 – we now proceed with their proofs.

Effect of Newton step on centrality. We recall the **NL** condition introduced in Chapter 9.

Definition 10.11 (Condition NL). Let $f : \mathbb{R}^n \to \mathbb{R}$. We say that f satisfies the **NL** condition for $\delta_0 < 1$ if for all $0 < \delta \leq \delta_0 < 1$, and for all x, y such that

$$\|y - x\|_x \leq \delta,$$

we have

$$(1 - 3\delta)H(x) \preceq H(y) \preceq (1 + 3\delta)H(x).$$

Proof of Lemma 10.6: We need to prove that f_η (or equivalently F) satisfies the **NL** condition for $\delta = \frac{1}{6}$. In fact, we prove that F satisfies the NL condition for any $\delta < 1$. To this end, check that the Hessian

$$H(x) = \nabla^2 f_\eta(x) = \nabla^2 F(x)$$

is given by

$$H(x) = \sum_{i=1}^m \frac{a_i a_i^\top}{s_i(x)^2},$$

where

$$s_i(x) := b_i - \langle a_i, x \rangle;$$

see Exercise 10.1(b). Consider any two points x, y with $\|y - x\|_x = \delta < 1$. We have

$$\delta^2 = (y - x)^\top H(x)(y - x) = \sum_{i=1}^m \left| \frac{\langle a_i, y - x \rangle}{s_i(x)} \right|^2.$$

Thus, in particular, every term in this sum is upper bounded by δ^2. Hence, for every $i = 1, 2, \ldots, m$ we have

$$\left| \frac{s_i(x) - s_i(y)}{s_i(x)} \right| = \left| \frac{\langle a_i, y - x \rangle}{s_i(x)} \right| \le \delta.$$

Consequently, for every $i = 1, 2, \ldots, m$ we have

$$(1 - \delta)s_i(x) \le s_i(y) \le (1 + \delta)s_i(x)$$

and, thus,

$$\frac{(1 + \delta)^{-2}}{s_i(x)^2} \le \frac{1}{s_i(y)^2} \le \frac{(1 - \delta)^{-2}}{s_i(x)^2}.$$

It now follows that

$$\frac{(1 + \delta)^{-2} a_i a_i^\top}{s_i(x)^2} \preceq \frac{a_i a_i^\top}{s_i(y)^2} \preceq \frac{(1 - \delta)^{-2} a_i a_i^\top}{s_i(x)^2}$$

and, thus, by summing the above for all i, we obtain

$$(1 + \delta)^{-2} H(x) \preceq H(y) \preceq (1 - \delta)^{-2} H(x).$$

To arrive at the **NL** condition, it remains to observe that for every $\delta \in (0, 0.23)$ it holds that

$$1 - 3\delta \le (1 + \delta)^{-2} \quad \text{and} \quad (1 - \delta)^{-2} \le 1 + 3\delta. \qquad \blacksquare$$

Effect of changing η on centrality. We proceed to the proof of Lemma 10.7, which asserts that changing η slightly does not increase $\|n_\eta(x)\|_x$ by much for a fixed point x. Let

$$g(x) := \nabla F(x).$$

Proof of Lemma 10.7: We have

$$
\begin{aligned}
n_{\eta'}(x) &= H(x)^{-1}\nabla f_{\eta'}(x)\\
&= H(x)^{-1}(\eta'c + g(x))\\
&= \frac{\eta'}{\eta}H(x)^{-1}(\eta c + g(x)) + \left(1 - \frac{\eta'}{\eta}\right)H(x)^{-1}g(x)\\
&= \frac{\eta'}{\eta}H(x)^{-1}\nabla f_\eta(x) + \left(1 - \frac{\eta'}{\eta}\right)H(x)^{-1}g(x).
\end{aligned}
$$

After taking norms and applying triangle inequality with respect to $\|\cdot\|_x$, we obtain

$$\left\|H(x)^{-1}\nabla f_{\eta'}(x)\right\|_x \le \frac{\eta'}{\eta}\left\|H(x)^{-1}\nabla f_\eta(x)\right\|_x + \left|1 - \frac{\eta'}{\eta}\right|\left\|H(x)^{-1}g(x)\right\|_x.$$

We take a pause for a moment and try to understand the significance of the specific terms in the right-hand side of the inequality above. By the closeness invariant, the term $\|H(x)^{-1}\nabla f_\eta(x)\|_x$ is a small constant. The goal is to show that the whole right-hand side is also bounded by a small constant. We should think of η' as $\eta(1 + \gamma)$ for some small $\gamma > 0$. Thus, $\frac{\eta'}{\eta}\|H(x)^{-1}(x)\nabla f_\eta(x)\|_x$ is still a small constant, and what prevents us from choosing a large γ is the second term $\left|1 - \frac{\eta'}{\eta}\right|\|H(x)^{-1}g(x)\|_x$. Thus, what remains to do is to derive an upper bound on $\|H(x)^{-1}g(x)\|_x$. To this end, we show something stronger:

$$\sup_{y\in\text{int}(P)}\|H(y)^{-1}g(y)\|_y \le \sqrt{m}.$$

To see this, we pick any $y \in \text{int}(P)$ and denote $z := H^{-1}(y)g(y)$. From the Cauchy-Schwarz inequality, we obtain

$$\|z\|_y^2 = g(y)^\top H(y)^{-1}g(y) = \langle z, g(y)\rangle = \sum_{i=1}^m \frac{\langle z, a_i\rangle}{s_i(y)} \le \sqrt{m}\sqrt{\sum_{i=1}^m \frac{\langle z, a_i\rangle^2}{s_i(y)^2}}.$$

$$(10.5)$$

By inspecting the rightmost expression in the inequality above, we obtain

$$\sum_{i=1}^{m} \frac{\langle z, a_i \rangle^2}{s_i(y)^2} = z^\top \left(\sum_{i=1}^{m} \frac{a_i a_i^\top}{s_i(y)^2} \right) z = z^\top H(y) z = \|z\|_y^2. \qquad (10.6)$$

Putting (10.5) and (10.6) together, we obtain

$$\|z\|_y^2 \le \sqrt{m} \|z\|_y.$$

Hence,

$$\|z\|_y \le \sqrt{m}. \qquad \blacksquare$$

Concluding that the invariant holds.

Proof of Lemma 10.5: Suppose that

$$\left\| n_{\eta_t}(x_t) \right\|_{x_t} \le \frac{1}{6}$$

for $t \ge 0$. Then, by the quadratic convergence of Newton's method – Lemma 10.6 – we obtain that x_{t+1} satisfies

$$\left\| n_{\eta_t}(x_{t+1}) \right\|_{x_{t+1}} \le 3 \left\| n_{\eta_t}(x_t) \right\|_{x_t}^2 \le \frac{1}{12}.$$

Further, by Lemma 10.7 it follows that

$$\left\| n_{\eta_{t+1}}(x_{t+1}) \right\|_{x_{t+1}} \le \frac{\eta_{t+1}}{\eta_t} \left\| n_{\eta_t}(x_{t+1}) \right\|_{x_{t+1}} + \sqrt{m} \left| \frac{\eta_{t+1}}{\eta_t} - 1 \right|$$
$$< (1 + o(1)) \cdot \frac{1}{12} + \frac{1}{20}$$
$$\le \frac{1}{6}. \qquad \blacksquare$$

10.6.1 Termination Condition

First, we give a proof of Lemma 10.9 under the "ideal assumption" that in the termination step of Algorithm 8, we actually reach $x_{\eta_T}^\star$ (and not only a point close to it). Subsequently, we strengthen this result and show that an approximate minimum of f_{η_T} (which we get as a result of our algorithm) also gives a suitable approximation guarantee.

Termination under the "ideal assumption." Assume that the point output by Algorithm 8 is really

$$\hat{x} := x_{\eta_T}^\star.$$

Then, the lemma below explains our choice of $\eta_T \approx \frac{m}{\varepsilon}$.

Lemma 10.12 (Dependence of the approximation on the choice of η). *For every $\eta > 0$, we have*

$$\langle c, x_\eta^\star \rangle - \langle c, x^\star \rangle < \frac{m}{\eta}.$$

Proof: Recall that

$$\nabla f_\eta(x) = \nabla(\eta\langle c, x\rangle + F(x)) = \eta c + \nabla F(x) = \eta c + g(x).$$

The point $x_\eta^\star$ is the minimum of f_η; hence, by the first-order optimality condition, we know

$$\nabla f_\eta(x_\eta^\star) = 0$$

and, thus,

$$g(x_\eta^\star) = -\eta c. \tag{10.7}$$

Using this observation, we obtain that

$$\langle c, x_\eta^\star \rangle - \langle c, x^\star \rangle = -\left\langle c, x^\star - x_\eta^\star \right\rangle = \frac{1}{\eta}\left\langle g(x_\eta^\star), x^\star - x_\eta^\star \right\rangle.$$

To complete the proof, it remains to argue that $\left\langle g(x_\eta^\star), x^\star - x_\eta^\star \right\rangle < m$. We show even more: For every two points x, y in the interior of P, we have

$$\langle g(x), y - x \rangle < m.$$

This follows from the simple calculation

$$\langle g(x), y - x \rangle = \sum_{i=1}^{m} \frac{\langle a_i, y - x \rangle}{s_i(x)}$$

$$= \sum_{i=1}^{m} \frac{s_i(x) - s_i(y)}{s_i(x)}$$

$$= m - \sum_{i=1}^{m} \frac{s_i(y)}{s_i(x)}$$

$$< m,$$

where in the last inequality we make use of the fact that our points x, y are strictly feasible, i.e., $s_i(x), s_i(y) > 0$ for all i. ∎

Dropping the "ideal assumption." We now show that even after dropping the ideal assumption, we still get an error, which is $O(\varepsilon)$. For this, we perform a constant number of Newton iterations starting from x_T, so that the local norm of the output $\hat{x}$, $\left\| n_{\eta_T}(\hat{x}) \right\|_{\hat{x}}$, becomes small.

We derive a relation between the length of the Newton step at a point x (with respect to the function f_η) and the distance to the optimum $x_\eta^\star$. We show that whenever $\|n(x)\|_x$ is sufficiently small, $\|x - x_\eta^\star\|_x$ is small as well. This fact, together with a certain strengthening of Lemma 10.12, implies that in the last step of Algorithm 8, only two additional Newton steps bring us 2ε-close to the optimum.

We start with an extension of Lemma 10.12 that shows that to get a decent approximation of the optimum, we do not necessarily need to be on the central path, but only close enough to it.

Lemma 10.13 (Approximation guarantee for points close to central path). *For every point $x \in \operatorname{int}(P)$ and every $\eta > 0$, if $\|x - x_\eta^\star\|_x < 1$, then*

$$\langle c, x \rangle - \langle c, x^\star \rangle \leq \frac{m}{\eta} \left(1 - \|x - x_\eta^\star\|_x \right)^{-1}.$$

Proof: For every $y \in \operatorname{int}(P)$, we have

$$
\begin{aligned}
\langle c, x - y \rangle &= \langle H(x)^{-1/2} c, H^{1/2}(x)(x - y) \rangle \\
&\leq \left\| H(x)^{-1/2} c \right\|_2 \left\| H^{1/2}(x)(x - y) \right\|_2 \\
&= \|H(x)^{-1} c\|_x \|x - y\|_x,
\end{aligned}
$$

where the inequality above follows from the Cauchy-Schwarz inequality. Let

$$c_x := H(x)^{-1} c.$$

This term is also the Riemannian gradient of the objective function $\langle c, x \rangle$ at x with respect to the Hessian metric. Now, we bound $\|c_x\|_x$. Imagine we are at point x and we move in the direction of $-c_x$ until we hit the boundary of the unit ball (in the local norm) around x. We will land at the point $x - \frac{c_x}{\|c_x\|_x}$, which is still inside P (as proved in Exercise 10.4). Therefore,

$$\left\langle c, x - \frac{c_x}{\|c_x\|_x} \right\rangle \geq \langle c, x^\star \rangle.$$

Since $\langle c, c_x \rangle = \|c_x\|_x^2$, by substituting and rearranging in the inequality above, we obtain

$$\|c_x\|_x \leq \langle c, x \rangle - \langle c, x^\star \rangle.$$

Thus,

$$\langle c, x - y \rangle \le \|x - y\|_x (\langle c, x \rangle - \langle c, x^* \rangle). \tag{10.8}$$

Now, we express

$$\langle c, x \rangle - \langle c, x^* \rangle = \langle c, x \rangle - \langle c, x_\eta^* \rangle + \langle c, x_\eta^* \rangle - \langle c, x^* \rangle$$

and use (10.8) with $y = x_\eta^*$. We obtain

$$\langle c, x \rangle - \langle c, x^* \rangle \le (\langle c, x \rangle - \langle c, x^* \rangle) \|x - x_\eta^*\|_x + (\langle c, x_\eta^* \rangle - \langle c, x^* \rangle).$$

Thus,

$$(\langle c, x \rangle - \langle c, x^* \rangle)(1 - \|x - x_\eta^*\|_x) \le \langle c, x_\eta^* \rangle - \langle c, x^* \rangle.$$

By applying Lemma 10.12, the result follows. ■

Note that in Algorithm 8, we never mention the condition that $\|x - x_\eta^*\|_x$ is small. However, we show that it follows from $\|n_\eta(x)\|_x$ being small. In fact, we prove the following more general lemma, which holds for any function f satisfying the **NL** condition.

Lemma 10.14 (Distance to the optimum and the Newton step). *Let $f : \mathbb{R}^n \to \mathbb{R}$ be any strictly convex function satisfying the **NL** condition for $\delta_0 = \frac{1}{6}$. Let x be any point in the domain of f. Consider the Newton step $n(x)$ at a point x. If*

$$\|n(x)\|_x < \frac{1}{24},$$

then

$$\|x - z\|_x \le 4\|n(x)\|_x,$$

where z is the minimizer of f.

Proof: Pick any h such that $\|h\|_x \le \frac{1}{6}$. Expand $f(x + h)$ into a Taylor series around x and use the mean value theorem (Theorem 9.2) to write

$$f(x + h) = f(x) + \langle h, \nabla f(x) \rangle + \frac{1}{2} h^\top \nabla^2 f(\theta) h \tag{10.9}$$

for some point θ lying in the interval $(x, x + h)$. We proceed by lower bounding the linear term. Note that

$$|\langle h, \nabla f(x) \rangle| = |\langle h, n(x) \rangle_x| \le \|h\|_x \|n(x)\|_x \tag{10.10}$$

by the Cauchy-Schwarz inequality. Subsequently, note that

$$h^\top \nabla^2 f(\theta) h = h^\top H(\theta) h \ge \frac{1}{2} h^\top H(x) h = \frac{1}{2} \|h\|_x^2, \tag{10.11}$$

where we used the **NL** condition with $y := \theta$ for $\delta = \frac{1}{6}$ for which $1 - 3\delta = \frac{1}{2}$. Applying bounds (10.10) and (10.11) to the expansion (10.9) results in

$$f(x + h) \geq f(x) - \|h\|_x \|n(x)\|_x + \frac{1}{4}\|h\|_x^2. \tag{10.12}$$

Set $r := 4\|n(x)\|_x$ and consider points y satisfying

$$\|y\|_x = r,$$

i.e., points on the boundary of the local norm ball of radius r centered at x. For such a point y,

$$\|y\|_x = 4\|n(x)\|_x \leq \frac{4}{24} = \frac{1}{6}.$$

Hence, (10.12) applies. Moreover, (10.12) simplifies to

$$\begin{aligned} f(x + y) &\geq f(x) - \|y\|_x \|n(x)\|_x + \frac{1}{4}\|y\|_x^2 \\ &= f(x) - 4\|n(x)\|_x^2 + 4\|n(x)\|_x^2 \\ &\geq f(x). \end{aligned}$$

Since f is strictly convex and its value at the center x of the ball is no more than its value at the boundary, z, the unique minimizer of f, must belong to the above-mentioned ball, completing the proof of the lemma. ∎

Proof of Lemma 10.9: Let $\hat{x}$ be the point obtained by doing two additional Newton steps with a fixed η_T and starting at x_T. Then, since

$$\|n_{\eta_T}(x_T)\|_{x_T} \leq \frac{1}{6},$$

we know that

$$\|n_{\eta_T}(\hat{x})\|_{\hat{x}} \leq \frac{1}{48}.$$

Applying Lemma 10.13 and Lemma 10.14 for such an $\hat{x}$, we obtain that if $\eta \geq \frac{m}{\varepsilon}$, then

$$\langle c, \hat{x} \rangle - \langle c, x^\star \rangle \leq \varepsilon \frac{1}{1 - 4\|n_{\eta_T}(\hat{x})\|_{\hat{x}}} < 2\varepsilon. \qquad ∎$$

10.6.2 Initialization

In this section, we present a method for finding an appropriate starting point. More precisely, we show how to find efficiently some $\eta_0 > 0$ and x_0 such that $\|n_{\eta_0}(x_0)\|_{x_0} \leq \frac{1}{6}$. Before we start, we remark that we provide a very small η_0 – of order $2^{-\text{poly}(L)}$. While this enables us to prove that Algorithm 8 can solve linear programming in polynomial time, it does not seem promising when trying to apply IPM to devise fast algorithms for combinatorial problems. Indeed, there is a factor of $\log \eta_0^{-1}$ in the bound on the number of iterations, which translates to L. To make an algorithm fast, we need to have ideally $\eta_0 = \Omega(1/\text{poly}(m))$. It turns out that for specific problems (such as maximum flow), we can devise some specialized methods to find such an η_0 and x_0; see Chapter 11.

Finding (η_0, x_0) given a point in the interior of P. First we show that assuming we are given a point $x' \in \text{int}(P)$, we can find a starting pair (η_0, x_0) with the desired property. In fact, we assume something stronger: that each constraint is satisfied with slack at least $2^{-\tilde{O}(nL)}$ at x', i.e.,

$$b_i - \langle a_i, x' \rangle \geq 2^{-\tilde{O}(nL)}.$$

Our procedure for finding a point in P provides such an x', assuming that P is full-dimensional and nonempty. Here, we do not discuss how to get rid of the full-dimensionality assumption. It is possible to deal with, but tedious.

Recall that we want to find a point x_0 close to the central path

$$\Gamma_c := \{x_\eta^\star : \eta \geq 0\},$$

which corresponds to the objective function $\langle c, x \rangle$. Note that as $\eta \to 0$, $x_\eta^\star \to x_0^\star$, the analytic center of P. Hence, finding a point x_0 close to the analytic center and choosing η_0 to be some small number should be a good strategy. But how do we find a point close to $x_0^\star$?

While it is the path Γ_c that is of interest, in general, one can define other central paths. If $d \in \mathbb{R}^n$ is any vector, define

$$\Gamma_d := \left\{ \underset{x \in \text{int}(P)}{\text{argmin}} \left(\eta \langle d, x \rangle + F(x) \right) : \eta \geq 0 \right\}.$$

As one varies d, what do the paths Γ_d have in common? The origin. They all start at the same point: the analytic center of P; see Figure 10.2. The idea now is to pick one such path on which the initial point x' lies and traverse it in **reverse** to reach a point close to the analytic center of this path, giving us x_0.

Recall that g is used to denote the gradient of the logarithmic barrier F. If we define

$$d := -g(x'),$$

then $x' \in \Gamma_d$ for $\eta = 1$. To see this, denote

$$f_\eta'(x) := \eta \langle d, x \rangle + F(x)$$

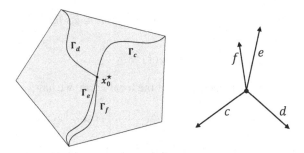

Figure 10.2 Illustration of central paths Γ_c, Γ_d, Γ_e, and Γ_f for four different objective vectors c, d, e, and f. All the paths originate at the analytic center $x_0^\star$ and converge to some boundary point of P. Note that because we minimize the linear objective, the cost vectors point in the "opposite" direction to the direction traversed by the corresponding central path.

and let $x_\eta'^\star$ be the minimizer of f_η'. Then, $x_1'^\star = x'$ since $\nabla f_1'(x') = 0$. If we use $n_\eta'(x)$ to denote the Newton step at x with respect to f_η', then note that

$$n_1'(x') = 0.$$

As mentioned above, our strategy is to move along the Γ_d path in the direction of decreasing η. We use an analogous method as in the Algorithm 8. In each iteration, we perform one Newton step with respect to current η and then, in the centering step, decrease η by a factor of $\left(1 - \frac{1}{20\sqrt{m}}\right)$. At each step, it holds that $\|n_\eta'(x)\|_x \leq \frac{1}{6}$ by an argument identical to the proof of Lemma 10.5. It remains to be seen how small an η is required (this determines the number of iterations we need to perform) to allow us to "jump" from Γ_d to Γ_c.

For this we first prove that, by taking η small enough, we reach a point x very close to the analytic center, i.e., for which $\left\|H(x)^{-1}g(x)\right\|_x$ is small. Next we show that having such a point x with an appropriate η_0 satisfies

$$\left\|n_{\eta_0}(x)\right\|_x \leq \frac{1}{6}.$$

The first part is formalized in the lemma below.

Lemma 10.15 (Following the central path in reverse). *Suppose that x' is a point such that for all $i = 1, 2, \ldots, m$,*

$$s_i(x') \geq \beta \cdot \max_{x \in P} s_i(x).$$

For any $\eta > 0$ denote by $n_\eta'(x)$ the Newton step

$$n_\eta'(x) := -H(x)^{-1}(-\eta g(x') + g(x)).$$

Then, whenever $\eta \le \frac{\beta}{24\sqrt{m}}$ and $\left\| n'_\eta(x) \right\|_x \le \frac{1}{24}$, it holds that

$$\left\| H(x)^{-1}g(x) \right\|_x \le \frac{1}{12}.$$

Proof: From the triangle inequality of the local norm, we have

$$\left\| H(x)^{-1}g(x) \right\|_x \le \left\| n'_\eta(x) \right\|_x + \eta \left\| H(x)^{-1}g(x') \right\|_x.$$

Thus, it remains to show a suitable upper bound on $\left\| H(x)^{-1}g(x') \right\|_x$. Denote by S_x and $S_{x'}$ the diagonal matrices with $s(x)$ and $s(x')$ (the slack vectors at x and x', respectively) on the diagonals. Then, one can compactly write

$$H(x) = A^\top S_x^{-2} A, \qquad g(x) = A^\top S_x^{-1} 1, \quad \text{and} \quad g(x') = A^\top S_{x'}^{-1} 1,$$

where $1 \in \mathbb{R}^m$ is the all-ones vector. Thus,

$$\left\| H(x)^{-1}g(x') \right\|_x^2 = g(x')^\top H(x)^{-1}g(x') = 1^\top S_{x'}^{-1} A(A^\top S_x^{-2}A)^{-1} A^\top S_{x'}^{-1} 1.$$

This can also be rewritten as

$$\left\| H(x)^{-1}g(x') \right\|_x^2 = v^\top \Pi v, \qquad (10.13)$$

where $\Pi := S_x^{-1} A(A^\top S_x^{-2}A)^{-1} A^\top S_x^{-1}$ and $v := S_x S_{x'}^{-1} 1$. One can note now that Π is an orthogonal projection matrix: Indeed, Π is symmetric and $\Pi^2 = \Pi$. Therefore,

$$v^\top \Pi v = \|\Pi v\|_2^2 \le \|v\|_2^2. \qquad (10.14)$$

Further,

$$\|v\|_2^2 = \sum_{i=1}^m \frac{s_i(x)^2}{s_i(x')^2} \le \frac{m}{\beta^2}. \qquad (10.15)$$

Thus, combining (10.13), (10.14), and (10.15), we obtain

$$\left\| H(x)^{-1}g(x') \right\|_x \le \frac{\sqrt{m}}{\beta},$$

and the lemma follows. ∎

The next lemma shows that given a point close to the analytic center, we can use it to initialize our algorithm, assuming that η_0 is small enough.

Lemma 10.16 (Switching the central path). *Suppose that $x \in \text{int}(P)$ is a point such that $\left\| H(x)^{-1}g(x) \right\|_x \le \frac{1}{12}$ and η_0 is such that*

$$\eta_0 \le \frac{1}{12} \cdot \frac{1}{\langle c, x - x^\star \rangle},$$

where $x^\star$ is an optimal solution to the linear program. Then $\left\| n_{\eta_0}(x) \right\|_x \le \frac{1}{6}$.

Proof: We have

$$\left\| n_{\eta_0}(x) \right\|_x = \left\| H(x)^{-1}(\eta_0 c + g(x)) \right\|_x \le \eta_0 \left\| H(x)^{-1} c \right\|_x + \left\| H(x)^{-1} g(x) \right\|_x.$$

Since $\left\| H(x)^{-1} g(x) \right\|_x \le \frac{1}{12}$, to arrive at the conclusion, it suffices to prove that

$$\left\| H(x)^{-1} c \right\|_x \le \langle c, x - x^\star \rangle.$$

To see this, denote

$$c_x := H(x)^{-1} c.$$

The following is an exercise (we used this fact before in Lemma 10.13):

$$E_x := \{ y : (y - x)^\top H(x)(y - x) \le 1 \} \subseteq P.$$

Thus,

$$x - \frac{c_x}{\|c_x\|_x} \in P$$

because this point belongs to E_x. Therefore,

$$\left\langle c, x - \frac{c_x}{\|c_x\|_x} \right\rangle \ge \langle c, x^\star \rangle,$$

since $x^\star$ minimizes this linear objective over P. The above, after rewriting, gives

$$\left\langle c, \frac{c_x}{\|c_x\|_x} \right\rangle \le \langle c, x \rangle - \langle c, x^\star \rangle.$$

By observing that

$$\left\langle c, \frac{c_x}{\|c_x\|_x} \right\rangle = \left\| H(x)^{-1} c \right\|_x,$$

the lemma follows.   ∎

Given Lemmas 10.15 and 10.16, we are now ready to prove that a good starting point can be found in polynomial time.

Lemma 10.17 (Finding a starting point given an interior point). *There is an algorithm that, given a point $x' \in \text{int}(P)$ such that for all $i = 1, 2, \ldots, m$,*

$$s_i(x') \geq \beta \cdot \max_{x \in P} s_i(x)$$

outputs a point $x_0 \in \text{int}(P)$ and an $\eta_0 > 0$ such that

$$\left\| n_{\eta_0}(x_0) \right\|_{x_0} \leq \frac{1}{6}$$

and

$$\eta_0 \geq \frac{1}{\|c\|_2 \cdot \text{diam}(P)} \geq 2^{-\tilde{O}(nL)}.$$

The running time of this algorithm is a polynomial in n, m, L, and $\log \frac{1}{\beta}$. Here, $\text{diam}(P)$ is the diameter of the smallest ball that contains P.

Proof: The lemma follows from a combination of Lemmas 10.15 and 10.16.

(1) Start by running the path-following IPM in reverse for the cost function $d := -g(x')$, starting point as x', and the starting value of η as 1. Since, by choice, x' is optimal for the central path Γ_d, we know that $\|n_1(x')\|_{x'} = 0$.

(2) Thus, we keep running it until η becomes less than

$$\eta_0 := \min \left\{ \frac{\beta}{24\sqrt{m}}, \frac{1}{\|c\|_2 \cdot \text{diam}(P)} \right\}.$$

At this point x, we know that $\|n_{\eta_0}(x)\|_x \leq \frac{1}{6}$.

(3) We now do a couple of iterations of the Newton method (with fixed η_0) to come to a point y such that

$$\left\| n_{\eta_0}(y) \right\|_y \leq \frac{1}{24}.$$

(4) Since all the conditions of Lemma 10.15 are satisfied, we can use it to ensure that

$$\left\| H(y)^{-1} g(y) \right\|_y \leq \frac{1}{12}.$$

(5) Finally, we use Lemma 10.16 to switch and note that y and η_0 satisfy the initial conditions required to start the path-following IPM in the forward direction for the cost vector c. Here, we use the fact that for $x \in P$, using the Cauchy-Schwarz inequality, we have

$$\langle c, x - x^\star \rangle \leq \|c\|_2 \cdot \|x - x^\star\|_2 \leq \|c\|_2 \cdot \text{diam}(P).$$

Thus,

$$\eta_0 \leq \frac{1}{\|c\|_2 \cdot \text{diam}(P)} \leq \frac{1}{\langle c, y - x^\star \rangle}.$$

To conclude, we use Exercise 10.2, which shows that $\text{diam}(P) \leq 2^{\widetilde{O}(nL)}$. ∎

Finding a point in the interior of P. To complete our proof, we show how to find a suitable $x' \in \text{int}(P)$. Towards this, we consider an auxiliary linear program,

$$\min_{(t,x) \in \mathbb{R}^{n+1}} \ t$$

$$\text{such that } a_i^\top x \leq b_i + t, \ \forall 1 \leq i \leq m, \tag{10.16}$$

$$-C \leq t \leq C,$$

for some large integer $C := 2 + \sum_i |b_i|$. Taking $x = 0$ and t big enough ($t := 1 + \sum_i |b_i|$), we obtain a strictly feasible solution with at least $O(1)$ slack at every constraint. Thus, we can use the Algorithm 8 in conjunction with Lemma 10.17 to solve it up to precision $2^{-\widetilde{\Theta}(nL)}$ in polynomial time; see Exercise 10.5. If P is full-dimensional and nonempty, then the optimal solution $t^\star$ to (10.16) is negative and in fact $t^\star \leq -2^{-\widetilde{\Theta}(nL)}$; see Exercise 10.2. Thus, by solving Equation (10.16) up to $2^{-\widetilde{\Theta}(nL)}$ precision, we obtain a feasible point x' whose slacks are all at least $2^{-\widetilde{\Theta}(nL)}$, hence, β in Lemma 10.17 is $2^{-\widetilde{\Theta}(nL)}$.

10.6.3 Proof of Theorem 10.10

Theorem 10.10 can be now concluded from Lemmas 10.12 and 10.5. Indeed, Lemma 10.12 says that $\hat{x}$ is an ε-approximate solution whenever $\eta \geq \frac{m}{\varepsilon}$. Since $\eta_T = \eta_0 \left(1 + \frac{1}{20\sqrt{m}}\right)^T$, it is enough to take $T = \Omega\left(\sqrt{m} \log \frac{m}{\varepsilon \eta_0}\right)$ for $\eta_T \geq \frac{m}{\varepsilon}$ to hold.

Since the invariant $\left\|n_{\eta_t}(x_t)\right\|_{x_t} \leq \frac{1}{6}$ is satisfied at every step t (by Lemma 10.5), including for $t = T$, x_T lies in the region of quadratic convergence of Newton's method for f_{η_T}. Hence, $x_{\eta_T}^\star$ can be computed from x_T. Note that we are not entirely precise here: We made a simplifying assumption that once we arrive at the region of quadratic convergence around $x_{\eta_T}^\star$ then we can actually reach this point – but we showed how to get around this issue in Section 10.6.1 at the expense of doubling the error from ε to 2ε.

It remains to observe that in every iteration, the only nontrivial operation is computing the Newton step $n_{\eta_t}(x_t)$, which in turn boils down to solving the following linear system:

$$H(x_t)y = \nabla f_{\eta_t}(x_t).$$

Note in particular that computing the inverse of $H(x_t)$ is not necessary. Sometimes, just solving the above linear system might be much faster than inverting a matrix.

10.7 Exercises

10.1   Consider a bounded polyhedron,

$$P := \{x \in \mathbb{R}^n : \langle a_i, x \rangle \le b_i, \text{for } i = 1, 2, \dots, m\},$$

and let $F(x)$ be the logarithmic barrier function on the interior of P, i.e.,

$$F(x) := -\sum_{i=1}^m \log(b_i - \langle a_i, x \rangle).$$

(a)   Prove that F is strictly convex.
(b)   Write the gradient and Hessian of F. What is the running time of evaluating the gradient and multiplying the Hessian with a vector?

Further, define the following function G on the interior of P:

$$G(x) := \log \det \left(\nabla^2 F(x) \right).$$

(a)   Prove that G is strictly convex.
(b)   Write the gradient and Hessian of G. What is the running time of evaluating the gradient and multiplying the Hessian with a vector?

10.2   This exercise is a continuation of Exercise 4.9. The goal is to bound bit complexities of certain additional quantities that show up in the analysis of the interior point method for linear programming. Let $A \in \mathbb{Q}^{m \times n}$ be a matrix and $b \in \mathbb{Q}^m$ be a vector, and let L be the bit complexity of (A, b). In particular, $L \ge m$ and $L \ge n$. We assume that $P = \{x \in \mathbb{R}^n : Ax \le b\}$ is a bounded and full-dimensional polytope in $\mathbb{R}^n$.

(a)   Prove that $\lambda_{\min}(A^\top A) \ge 2^{-\tilde{O}(nL)}$ and $\lambda_{\max}(A^\top A) \le 2^{\tilde{O}(L)}$. Here $\lambda_{\min}$ denotes the smallest eigenvalue and $\lambda_{\max}$ is the largest eigenvalue.
(b)   Assuming that P is a polytope, prove that the diameter of P (in the Euclidean metric) is bounded by $2^{\tilde{O}(nL)}$.
(c)   Prove that there exists a point x_0 in the interior of P such that

$$b_i - \langle a_i, x_0 \rangle \ge 2^{-\tilde{O}(nL)}$$

for every $i = 1, 2, \dots, m$.

(d) Prove that if $x_0^\star$ is the analytic center of P, then

$$2^{-\tilde{O}(mnL)} I \preceq H(x_0^\star) \preceq 2^{\tilde{O}(mnL)} I,$$

where $H(x_0^\star)$ is the Hessian of the logarithmic barrier at $x_0^\star$.

10.3 In this problem we would like to show the following intuitive fact: If the gradient of the logarithmic barrier at a given point x is short, then the point x is far away from the boundary of the polytope. In particular, the analytic center lies well inside the polytope. Let $A \in \mathbb{R}^{m \times n}$, $b \in \mathbb{R}^m$ and $P = \{x \in \mathbb{R}^n : Ax \le b\}$ be a polytope. Suppose that $x_0 \in P$ is a point such that

$$b_i - \langle a_i, x_0 \rangle \ge \delta$$

for every $i = 1, 2, \ldots, m$ and some $\delta > 0$. Prove that if D is the diameter of P (in the Euclidean norm), then for every $x \in P$ we have

$$\forall\ i = 1, 2, \ldots, m, \qquad b_i - \langle a_i, x \rangle \ge \delta \cdot (m + \|g(x)\| \cdot D)^{-1},$$

where $g(x)$ is the gradient of the logarithmic barrier function at x.

10.4 **Dikin ellipsoid.** Let $A \in \mathbb{R}^{m \times n}$, $b \in \mathbb{R}^m$ and $P = \{x \in \mathbb{R}^n : Ax \le b\}$ be a full-dimensional polytope. For $x \in P$, let $H(x)$ be the Hessian of the logarithmic barrier function for P. We define the Dikin ellipsoid at a point $x \in P$ as

$$E_x := \{y \in \mathbb{R}^n : (y - x)^\top H(x)(y - x) \le 1\}.$$

Let $x_0^\star$ be the analytic center, i.e., the minimizer of the logarithmic barrier over the polytope.

(a) Prove that for all $x \in \text{int}(P)$,

$$E_x \subseteq P.$$

(b) Assume without loss of generality (by shifting the polytope) that $x_0^\star = 0$. Prove that

$$P \subseteq m E_{x_0^\star}.$$

(c) Prove that if the set of constraints is symmetric, i.e., for every constraint of the form $\langle a', x \rangle \le b'$ there is a corresponding constraint $\langle a', x \rangle \ge -b'$, then

$$x_0^\star = 0 \text{ and } P \subseteq \sqrt{m} E_{x_0^\star}.$$

10.5 Assume $C > 0$ is some large constant (say, $C := 2 + \sum_i |b_i|$).

(a) Verify that the constraint region in the auxiliary linear program of Equation (10.16) is full-dimensional and bounded (assume that P is full-dimensional and bounded).

(b) Verify that the starting point $x := 0$ and $t := 1 + \sum_i |b_i|$ for the auxiliary linear program of Equation (10.16) satisfy the condition in Lemma 10.17 with

$$\beta = \min \left(\Omega(C^{-1}), 2^{-\tilde{O}(n(L+nL_C))} \right),$$

where L is the bit complexity of P and L_C is the bit complexity of C.

10.6 **Primal-dual path-following IPM for linear programming.** In this problem, we derive a different interior point algorithm to solve linear programs.

The formulation. Consider the following linear program and its dual:

$$\begin{align} \min \quad & \langle c, x \rangle \\ \text{such that} \quad & Ax = b, \\ & x \geq 0. \end{align} \tag{10.17}$$

$$\begin{align} \max \quad & \langle b, y \rangle \\ \text{such that} \quad & A^\top y + s = c, \\ & s \geq 0. \end{align} \tag{10.18}$$

Here, $A \in \mathbb{R}^{n \times m}$, $b \in \mathbb{R}^n$, and $c \in \mathbb{R}^m$. Further, $x \in \mathbb{R}^m$, $y \in \mathbb{R}^n$, and $s \in \mathbb{R}^m$, are variables. For simplicity, A is assumed to have rank n (i.e., A is full rank). Every triple (x, y, s) such that x satisfies the constraints of (10.17) and (y, s) satisfies the constraints of (10.18) we call a feasible primal-dual solution. The set of all such feasible triples we denote by $\mathcal{F}$. The *strictly* feasible set, where in addition $x > 0$ and $s > 0$, we denote by $\mathcal{F}_+$.

(a) Prove that the linear programs (10.17) and (10.18) are dual to each other.

(b) Prove that if $(x, y, s) \in \mathcal{F}$ is a feasible primal-dual solution, then the duality gap $\langle c, x \rangle - \langle b, y \rangle = \sum_{i=1}^m x_i s_i$.

(c) Prove, using the above, that if $x_i s_i = 0$ for every $i = 1, 2, \ldots, m$, then x is optimal for (10.17) and (y, s) is optimal for (10.18).

Thus, finding a solution $(x, y, s) \in \mathcal{F}$ with $x_i s_i = 0$ for all i is equivalent to solving the linear program.

The high-level idea. The main idea of this IPM is to approach this goal by maintaining a solution to the following equations:

$$x_i s_i = \mu, \quad \forall\, i = 1, 2, \ldots, m \;\; (x, y, s) \in \mathcal{F}_+, \tag{10.19}$$

for a positive parameter $\mu > 0$. As it turns out, the above defines a unique pair $(x(\mu), s(\mu))$ and, hence, the set of all solutions (over $\mu > 0$) forms a continuous path in $\mathcal{F}$. The strategy is to approximately follow this path: We initialize the algorithm at a (perhaps large) value μ^0 and reduce it multiplicatively. More precisely, we start with a triple (x^0, y^0, s^0) that approximately satisfies condition (10.19) (with $\mu := \mu^0$) and, subsequently, produce a sequence (x^t, y^t, s^t, μ^t) of solutions, with $t = 1, 2, 3, \ldots$ such that (x^t, y^t, s^t) also approximately satisfies (10.19), with $\mu := \mu^t$. We will show that the value of μ can be reduced by a factor of $(1 - \gamma)$ with $\gamma := \Theta(m^{-1/2})$ in every step.

Description of the update. We describe how to construct the new point $(x^{t+1}, y^{t+1}, s^{t+1})$ given (x^t, y^t, s^t). For brevity, we drop the superscript t for now. Given a point $(x, y, s) \in \mathcal{F}$ and a value μ, we use the following procedure to obtain a new point: We compute vectors Δx and Δy and Δs such that

$$\begin{cases} A\Delta x & = 0, \\ A^\top \Delta y + \Delta s & = 0, \\ x_i s_i + (\Delta x_i) s_i + x_i (\Delta s_i) & = \mu, \quad \forall\, i = 1, 2, \ldots, m, \end{cases} \tag{10.20}$$

and the new point is $(x + \Delta x, y + \Delta y, s + \Delta s)$.

(d) Prove that the above coincides with one step of the Newton method for root finding applied to the following system of equations. *Hint:* Use the fact that $(x, y, s) \in \mathcal{F}$.

$$\begin{cases} Ax & = b, \\ A^\top y + s & = c, \\ x_i s_i & = \mu, \quad \forall\, i = 1, 2, \ldots, m. \end{cases}$$

Potential function and stopping criteria. We will not be able to find solutions that satisfy Equation (10.19) exactly, but only approximately.

To measure how accurate our approximation is, we use the following potential function

$$v(x,s,\mu) := \sqrt{\sum_{i=1}^{m} \left(\frac{x_i s_i}{\mu} - 1\right)^2}.$$

Note in particular that $v(x,s,\mu) = 0$ if and only if Equation (10.19) holds. Moreover, an approximate variant of this observation is also true.

(e) Prove that if $v(x,s,\mu) \le \frac{1}{2}$, then

$$\sum_{i=1}^{m} x_i s_i \le 2\mu m.$$

Thus, it suffices to take $\mu := \frac{\varepsilon}{2m}$ in order to bring the duality gap down to ε. To obtain a complete algorithm, it remains to prove that the following invariant is satisfied in every step t:

$$(x^t, y^t, s^t) \in \mathcal{F}_+,$$
$$v(x^t, s^t, \mu^t) \le \frac{1}{2}. \tag{10.21}$$

Given the above, we will be able to deduce that after $t = O\left(\sqrt{m} \log \frac{\mu^0}{\varepsilon}\right)$ steps, the duality gap drops below ε. We analyze the behavior of the potential in two steps. We first study what happens when going from (x,y,s) to $(x + \Delta x, y + \Delta y, s + \Delta s)$ while keeping the value of μ unchanged, and later we analyze the effect of changing μ to $\mu(1 - \gamma)$.

Analysis of the potential: Newton step. As one can show, the linear system (10.20) has always a solution. We need to show now that after one such Newton step, the new point is still strictly feasible and the value of the potential is reduced.

(f) Prove that if Δx and Δs satisfy Equation (10.20) and $v(x + \Delta x, s + \Delta s, \mu) < 1$, then $x + \Delta x > 0$ and $s + \Delta s > 0$.

(g) Prove that if Δx and Δs satisfy Equation (10.20), then

$$\sum_{i=1}^{m} (\Delta x_i)(\Delta s_i) = 0. \tag{10.22}$$

(h) Prove that if Δx and Δs satisfy Equation (10.20) and $v(x, s, \mu) < 1$, then

$$v(x + \Delta x, s + \Delta s, \mu) \leq \frac{1}{2} \cdot \frac{v(x, s, \mu)^2}{1 - v(x, s, \mu)}.$$

Analysis of the potential: changing μ. We have shown that $v(x, s, \mu)$ drops when μ is kept intact, it remains to see what happens when we reduce its value from μ to $(1 - \gamma)\mu$ for some $\gamma > 0$.

(i) Prove that if Δx and Δs satisfy Equation (10.20), then

$$v(x + \Delta x, s + \Delta s, (1 - \gamma)\mu)$$
$$\leq \frac{1}{1 - \gamma} \cdot \sqrt{v(x + \Delta x, s + \Delta s, \mu)^2 + \gamma^2 m}.$$

The above guarantee allows us to conclude that we can maintain the invariant (10.21) by taking $\gamma = \frac{1}{3\sqrt{m}}$. For this, in every step we perform one step of Newton's method and then reduce the value of μ by $(1 - \gamma)$ and still satisfy $v(x, s, \mu) \leq \frac{1}{2}$. We obtain the following theorem.

Theorem 10.18. *There is an algorithm for linear programming that, given an initial solution (x^0, y^0, s^0, μ^0) satisfying (10.21) and an $\varepsilon > 0$, performs $O(\sqrt{m} \log \frac{\mu^0}{\varepsilon})$ iterations (in every iteration an $m \times m$ linear system is being solved) and outputs an ε-approximate solution $\hat{x}$ to the primal problem (10.17) and $(\hat{y}, \hat{s})$ to the dual problem (10.18).*

Notes

Interior point methods (IPMs) in the form of affine scaling first appeared in the Ph.D. thesis of I. I. Dikin in the 1960s; see Vanderbei (2001). Karmarkar (1984) gave a polynomial-time algorithm to solve linear programs using an IPM based on projective scaling. By then, there was a known polynomial time algorithm for solving LPs, namely the ellipsoid algorithm by Khachiyan (1979, 1980) (see Chapter 12). However, the method of choice in practice was the simplex method due to Dantzig (1990), despite it being known to be inefficient in the worst case (see Klee and Minty (1972)).[3] Karmarkar, in his paper, also presented empirical evidence demonstrating that his algorithm was

---

[3] Spielman and Teng (2009) showed that, under certain assumptions on the data (A, b, c), a variant of the simplex method is provably efficient.

consistently faster than the simplex method. For a comprehensive historical perspective on IPMs, we refer to the survey by Wright (2005).

Karmarkar's algorithm needs roughly $O(mL)$ iterations to find a solution; here L is the bit complexity of the input linear program and m is the number of constraints. Renegar (1988) combined Karmarkar's approach with Newton's method to design a path-following interior point method that took $O(\sqrt{m}L)$ iterations to solve a linear program, and each iteration just had to solve a linear system of equations of size $m \times m$. A similar result was independently proven by Gonzaga (1989). This is the result presented in this chapter. For more on the existence and continuity of central path, see the monograph by Renegar (2001).

There is also a class of primal-dual interior point methods for solving linear programs (see Exercise 10.6), and the reader is referred to the book by Wright (1997) for a discussion. It is possible, though nontrivial, to remove the full-dimensionality Theorem 10.2; we refer the reader to the book by Grötschel et al. (1988) for a thorough treatment on this.

11

Variants of Interior Point Method and Self-Concordance

We present various generalizations and extensions of the path-following IPM for the case of linear programming. As an application, we derive a fast algorithm for the $s - t$-minimum cost flow problem. Subsequently, we introduce the notion of self-concordance and give an overview of barrier functions for polytopes and more general convex sets.

11.1 The Minimum Cost Flow Problem

We start by investigating if the interior point method for linear programming developed in Chapter 10 is applicable for an important generalization of the $s - t$-maximum flow in a directed graph called the $s - t$-minimum cost flow problem. In this problem, we are given a directed graph $G - (V, E)$ with $n := |V|$ and $m := |E|$, two special vertices $s \neq t \in V$, where s is the source and t is the sink, capacities $\rho \in \mathbb{Q}_{\geq 0}^m$, a target flow value $F \in \mathbb{Z}_{\geq 0}$, and a cost vector $c \in \mathbb{Q}_{\geq 0}^m$. The goal is to find a flow in G that sends F units of flow from s to t that respects the capacities and is of minimum cost. The cost of a flow is defined to be the sum of costs over all edges, and the cost of transporting x_i units through edge $i \in E$ incurs a cost of $c_i x_i$. See Figure 11.1 for an illustration.

We can capture this problem using linear programming as follows:

$$
\begin{aligned}
\min \ & \langle c, x \rangle \\
\text{such that} \ & Bx = F \chi_{st}, \\
& 0 \leq x_i \leq \rho_i, \quad \forall i \in E,
\end{aligned}
\tag{11.1}
$$

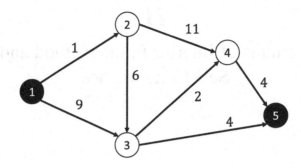

Figure 11.1 An $s - t$-minimum cost flow problem instance. The vertices 1 and 5 correspond to s and t respectively. We assume that all capacities are 1 and the costs of edges are as given in the picture. The minimum cost flow of value $F = 1$ has cost 11, for $F = 2$ it is $11 + 15 = 26$ and there are no feasible flows for $F > 2$.

where B is the vertex-edge incidence matrix (introduced in Section 2.9.2) of G and $\chi_{st} := e_s - e_t \in \mathbb{R}^n$.

One can immediately see that the analogous problem for undirected graphs is a special case of the one we defined here, since one can simply put two directed edges (w, v) and (v, w) in place of every undirected edge $\{w, v\}$. Moreover, this problem is more general than the $s - t$-maximum flow problem and the bipartite matching problem introduced in Chapters 6 and 7, respectively.

11.1.1 Linear Programming–Based Fast Algorithm?

Most of the (long and rich) research history on the $s - t$-minimum cost flow problem revolved around combinatorial algorithms – based on augmenting paths, push-relabel, and cycle cancelling; see the notes for references. The best known algorithm obtained using methods from this family has running time roughly $\widetilde{O}(mn)$. Since the $s - t$-minimum cost problem (11.1) can be naturally stated as a linear program, one can ask whether it is possible to derive a competitive, or even faster, algorithm for the minimum cost flow problem using linear programming methods. The main result from Chapter 10 suggests that obtaining an algorithm that performs roughly $\sqrt{m}$ iterations might be possible. Further, while the worst case running time of one such iteration could be as high as $O(m^3)$, in this case, we can hope to do much better: The matrix

B captures a graph, and hence one might hope that each iteration boils down to solving a Laplacian system for which we have $\tilde{O}(m)$ time algorithms. If the number and complexity of the iterations can be bounded as we hope, this would yield an algorithm that runs in $\tilde{O}(m^{3/2})$ time. This would beat the best known combinatorial algorithm whenever $m = o(n^2)$.

However, to derive such an algorithm we need to resolve several issues – the first being that the method we developed in Chapter 10 was for linear programming in the **canonical form** (Definition 10.1), which does not seem to capture the linear programming formulation the minimum cost flow problem in (11.1). Moreover, we need to show that one iteration of an appropriate variant of the path-following method can be reduced to solving a Laplacian system. Finally, the issue of finding a suitable point to initialize the interior point method becomes crucial and we develop a fast algorithm for finding such a point.

11.1.2 The Issue with the Path-Following IPM

Recall that the primal path-following IPM developed in Chapter 10 was geared towards linear programs of the following form:

$$\min_{x \in \mathbb{R}^m} \ \langle c, x \rangle \tag{11.2}$$
$$\text{such that} \quad Ax \leq b.$$

By inspecting the form of the linear program (11.2), it is evident that it has a different form than that of (11.1). However, this linear programming framework is very expressive and one can easily translate the program (11.1) to the form (11.2). This follows simply by turning equalities $Bx = F\chi_{st}$ into pairs of inequalities

$$Bx \leq F\chi_{st} \quad \text{and} \quad -Bx \leq -F\chi_{st}$$

and expressing $0 \leq x_i \leq \rho_i$ as

$$-x_i \leq 0 \quad \text{and} \quad x_i \leq \rho_i.$$

However, one of the issues is that the resulting polytope,

$$P := \{x \in \mathbb{R}^m : Ax \leq b\},$$

is not full-dimensional, which was a crucial assumption for the path-following IPM from Chapter 10. Indeed, the running time of this algorithm depends on $\frac{1}{\beta}$, where β is the distance from the boundary of P of an initial point $x' \in P$;

see Lemma 10.17. Since P is not full-dimensional, it is not possible to pick a point x' with positive β.

One can try to fix this problem by modifying the feasible set and considering

$$P_\varepsilon := \{x \in \mathbb{R}^m : Ax \leq b + 1\varepsilon\}$$

for some tiny $\varepsilon > 0$, where 1 is the all-ones vector. P_ε is a slightly "inflated" version of P and, in particular, is full-dimensional. One can then minimize $\langle c, x \rangle$ over P_ε, hoping that this gives a decent approximation of (11.2). However, there is at least one issue that arises when doing so. The $\varepsilon > 0$ needs to be exponentially small – roughly $\approx 2^{-L}$ (where L is the bit complexity of the linear program) in order to guarantee that we get a decent approximation of the original program. However, for such a small $\varepsilon > 0$, the polytope P_ε is very "thin" and, thus, we cannot provide a starting point x' that is far away from the boundary of P_ε. This adds at least an $\Omega(L) = \Omega(m)$ term in the number of iterations of the method and also forces us to use extended precision arithmetic (of roughly L bits) in order to execute the algorithm.

11.1.3 Beyond Full-Dimensional Linear Programs

There are several different ways one can try to resolve these issues and obtain fast linear programming–based algorithms for the minimum cost flow problem. One idea is based on the primal-dual path interior point method, which is a method to solve the primal and the dual problems simultaneously using Newton's method; see Exercise 10.6 in Chapter 10.

Another idea, which we are going to implement in this chapter, is to abandon the full-dimensional requirement on the polytope and develop a method that directly solves linear programs with equality constraints. Towards this, the first step is to formulate the minimum cost flow problem (11.1) in a form that involves only equality constraints and nonnegativity of variables. We introduce a new set of m variables $\{y_i\}_{i \in E}$ – the "edge slacks" – and add equality constraints of the form

$$\forall i \in E, \quad y_i = \rho_i - x_i.$$

Thus, by denoting $b := F\chi_{st}$, our linear program becomes

$$\min_{x \in \mathbb{R}^m} \ \langle c, x \rangle$$

$$\text{such that} \quad \begin{pmatrix} B & 0 \\ I & I \end{pmatrix} \begin{pmatrix} x \\ y \end{pmatrix} = \begin{pmatrix} b \\ u \end{pmatrix}, \tag{11.3}$$

$$x, y \geq 0.$$

The number of variables in this new program is $2m$ and the number of linear constraints is $n + m$.

By developing a Newton's method for equality-constrained problems and then deriving a new, corresponding path-following interior point method for linear problems in the form as (11.3), we prove the following theorem.

Theorem 11.1 ($s - t$-minimum cost flow using IPM). *There is an algorithm to solve the minimum cost flow problem* (11.3) *up to an additive error of $\varepsilon > 0$ in $\tilde{O}\left(\sqrt{m}\log\frac{CU}{\varepsilon}\right)$ iterations, where $U := \max_{i \in E} |\rho_i|$ and $C := \max_{i \in E} |c_i|$. Each iteration involves solving one Laplacian linear system, i.e., of the form*

$$(BWB^\top)h = d,$$

where W is a positive diagonal matrix, $d \in \mathbb{R}^n$, and $h \in \mathbb{R}^n$ is the variable vector.

As solving one such Laplacian system takes time $\tilde{O}(m)$, we obtain an algorithm solving the minimum cost flow problem in time, roughly, $\tilde{O}(m^{3/2})$. To be precise, employing fast Laplacian solvers requires one to show that their approximate nature does not introduce any problems in the path-following scheme.

Our proof of Theorem 11.1 is divided into three parts. First, we derive a new variant of the path-following method for linear programs of the form (11.3) (see Section 11.2) and show that it takes roughly $\sqrt{m}$ iterations to solve it. Subsequently, in Section 11.2 we show that each iteration of this new method applied to (11.3) can be reduced (in $O(m)$ time) to solving one Laplacian system. Finally, in Section 11.3 we show how one can efficiently find a good starting point to initialize the interior point method.

11.2 An IPM for Linear Programming in Standard Form

The goal of this section is to derive a path-following interior point method for linear programs of the form (11.3) (the reformulation of the $s-t$-minimum cost flow problem). More generally, the method derived works for linear programs that have the following form:

$$\begin{aligned} \min_{x \in \mathbb{R}^m} \quad & \langle c, x \rangle \\ \text{such that} \quad & Ax = b, \\ & x \geq 0, \end{aligned} \tag{11.4}$$

where $A \in \mathbb{R}^{n \times m}$, $b \in \mathbb{R}^n$, and $c \in \mathbb{R}^m$. This is often referred to as a linear program in standard form. It is easy to check that the canonical form studied in Chapter 10 is the dual of the standard form (up to renaming vectors and switching min to max). Note that in this section we denote the number of variables by m and the number of (linear) constraints by n, i.e., the roles of n and m are swapped when compared to Chapter 10. Also, note that we are overloading m and n that meant the number of edges and number of vertices in the context of the $s - t$-minimum cost problem; the distinction should be clear from the context. This is done intentionally and is actually consistent with the previous Chapter 10 since, via duality, the constraints become variables and vice versa. For the sake of brevity, in this section we use the notation

$$E_b := \{x \in \mathbb{R}^m : Ax = b\} \quad \text{and} \quad E := \{x \in \mathbb{R}^m : Ax = 0\},$$

where the matrix A and the vector b are fixed throughout.

The idea of the algorithm for solving (11.4) is similar to the path-following IPM introduced in Chapter 10: We use the logarithmic barrier function to define a central path in the relative interior of the feasible set and then use Newton's method to progress along the path. To implement this idea, the first step is to derive a Newton's method for minimizing a function restricted to an affine subspace of $\mathbb{R}^m$.

11.2.1 Equality Constrained Newton's Method

Consider a constrained optimization problem of the form

$$\min_{x \in \mathbb{R}^m} \quad f(x) \tag{11.5}$$
$$\text{such that} \quad Ax = b,$$

where $f : \mathbb{R}^m \to \mathbb{R}$ is a convex function, $A \in \mathbb{R}^{n \times m}$, and $b \in \mathbb{R}^n$. We assume without loss of generality that A has full rank n, i.e., the rows of A are linearly independent (otherwise there are redundant rows in A, that can be removed). We denote the function f restricted to the domain E_b by $\tilde{f} : E_b \to \mathbb{R}$, i.e., $\tilde{f}(x) = f(x)$.

In the absence of equality constraints $Ax = b$, we saw that the Newton step at a point x is defined as

$$n(x) := -H(x)^{-1} g(x),$$

where $H(x) \in \mathbb{R}^{m \times m}$ is the Hessian of f at x and $g(x)$ is the gradient of f at x, and the next iterate is computed as

$$x' := x + n(x).$$

When started at $x \in E_b$, the point $x + n(x)$ may no longer belong to E_b and, hence, we need to adjust the Newton's method to move only in directions tangent to E_b. To this end, in the next section, we define the notions of a gradient $\tilde{g}(x)$ and a Hessian $\tilde{H}(x)$ so that the Newton step, defined by the formula

$$\tilde{n}(x) := \tilde{H}(x)^{-1}\tilde{g}(x),$$

gives a well-defined method for minimizing $\tilde{f}$. Moreover, by defining an appropriate variant of the **NL** condition for $\tilde{f}$, we obtain the following theorem.

Theorem 11.2 (Quadratic convergence of equality-constrained Newton's method). *Let $\tilde{f} \colon E_b \to \mathbb{R}$ be a strictly convex function satisfying the* **NL** *condition for $\delta_0 = \frac{1}{6}$, $x_0 \in E_b$ be any point, and*

$$x_1 := x_0 + \tilde{n}(x_0).$$

If $\|\tilde{n}(x_0)\|_{x_0} \leq \frac{1}{6}$ then

$$\|\tilde{n}(x_1)\|_{x_1} \leq 3 \|\tilde{n}(x_0)\|_{x_0}^2.$$

We note that the above is completely analogous to Theorem 9.6 in Chapter 9, where we dealt with the unconstrained setting – indeed, the above theorem ends up being a straightforward extension of this theorem.

11.2.2 Defining the Hessian and Gradient on a Subspace

The crucial difference between working in $\mathbb{R}^m$ and working in E_b is that, given $x \in E_b$, we cannot move in every possible direction from x but only in tangent directions, i.e., to $x + h$ for some $h \in E$. In fact, E is the tangent space (as introduced in Chapter 9) corresponding to E_b. Let $\{v_1, \ldots, v_k\}$ be an orthonormal basis for E where $v_i \in \mathbb{R}^m$. Let Π_E denote the orthogonal projection operator onto E. We can see that

$$\Pi_E := \sum_{i=1}^{k} v_i v_i^{\top}.$$

The gradient $\tilde{g}(x)$ should be a vector in E such that for $h \in E$, the linear function

$$h \mapsto \langle h, \tilde{g}(x) \rangle$$

provides a good approximation of $f(x + h) - f(x)$ whenever $\|h\|$ is small. Thus, for $x \in E_b$, we can define

$$\tilde{g}(x) := \sum_{i=1}^{k} v_i Df(x)[v_i]$$

$$= \sum_{i=1}^{k} v_i \langle \nabla f(x), v_i \rangle$$

$$= \sum_{i=1}^{k} v_i v_i^\top \nabla f(x)$$

$$= \Pi_E \nabla f(x).$$

Similarly, we can obtain a formula for the Hessian

$$\tilde{H}(x)_{ij} := D^2 f(x)[v_i, v_j]$$

$$= v_i^\top H(x) v_j$$

$$= \left(\Pi_E^\top H(x) \Pi_E \right)_{ij}.$$

These definitions might look abstract, but in fact, the only way they differ from their unconstrained variants is the fact that we consider E to be the tangent space instead of $\mathbb{R}^m$. As an example, consider the function

$$f(x_1, x_2) := 2x_1^2 + x_2^2.$$

When constrained to a "vertical" line

$$E_b := \{(x_1, x_2)^\top : x_1 = b, x_2 \in \mathbb{R}\},$$

we obtain that the gradient is

$$\tilde{g}(x_1, x_2) = \begin{pmatrix} 0 \\ 2x_2 \end{pmatrix}$$

and the Hessian $\tilde{H}(x_1, x_2)$ is a linear operator $E \to E$ (where $E = \left\{ \begin{pmatrix} 0 \\ h \end{pmatrix} : h \in \mathbb{R} \right\}$ such that

$$\tilde{H}(x_1, x_2) \begin{pmatrix} 0 \\ h \end{pmatrix} = \begin{pmatrix} 0 \\ 2h \end{pmatrix}.$$

Indeed, this is consistent with the intuition that by restricting the function to a vertical line, only the variable x_2 matters.

To summarize, we have the lemma below.

Lemma 11.3 (Gradient and Hessian in a subspace). *Let* $f : \mathbb{R}^m \to \mathbb{R}$ *be strictly convex and let* $\widetilde{f} : E_b \to \mathbb{R}$ *be its restriction to* E_b. *Then we have*

$$\widetilde{g}(x) = \Pi_E \nabla f(x),$$
$$\widetilde{H}(x) = \Pi_E^\top H(x) \Pi_E,$$

where $\Pi_E : \mathbb{R}^m \to E$ *is the orthogonal projection operator onto* E. *Note that*

$$\Pi_E = I - A^\top (AA^\top)^{-1} A.$$

11.2.3 Defining the Newton Step and the NL Condition on a Subspace

We would like to define the Newton step to be

$$\widetilde{n}(x) := -\widetilde{H}(x)^{-1} \widetilde{g}(x).$$

Note that in the above, $\widetilde{H}(x)$ is an invertible operator $E \to E$, and hence $\widetilde{n}(x)$ is well defined. The following lemma states the form of the Newton step restricted to the subspace E in terms of the Hessian and gradient in the ambient space $\mathbb{R}^m$.

Lemma 11.4 (Newton step in a subspace). *Let* $f : \mathbb{R}^m \to \mathbb{R}$ *be a strictly convex function and let* $\widetilde{f} : E_b \to \mathbb{R}$ *be its restriction to* E_b. *Then, for every* $x \in E_b$, *we have*

$$\widetilde{n}(x) = -H(x)^{-1} g(x) + H(x)^{-1} A^\top (AH(x)^{-1} A^\top)^{-1} AH(x)^{-1} g(x).$$

Proof: The Newton step $\widetilde{n}(x)$ is defined as $-H(x)^{-1} \widetilde{g}(x)$ and, hence, can be obtained as the unique solution h to the following linear system:

$$\begin{cases} \widetilde{H}(x)h = -\widetilde{g}(x), \\ Ah = 0. \end{cases} \tag{11.6}$$

Since Π_E is symmetric and $h \in E$, the first equation gives that

$$\Pi_E H(x)h = -\Pi_E g(x).$$

Hence,

$$\Pi_E(H(x)h + g(x)) = 0.$$

In other words, this means that $H(x)h + g(x)$ belongs to the space orthogonal to E (denoted by $E^\perp$), i.e.,

$$H(x)h + g(x) \in E^\perp = \{A^\top \lambda : \lambda \in \mathbb{R}^n\}.$$

Consequently, (11.6) can be equivalently rewritten as a linear system of the form

$$\begin{pmatrix} H(x) & A^\top \\ A & 0 \end{pmatrix} \cdot \begin{pmatrix} h \\ \lambda \end{pmatrix} = \begin{pmatrix} -g(x) \\ 0 \end{pmatrix}$$

with unknowns $h \in \mathbb{R}^m$ and $\lambda \in \mathbb{R}^n$. From the above, λ can be eliminated to yield

$$\tilde{n}(x) = H(x)^{-1}(A^\top (AH(x)^{-1}A^\top)^{-1}AH(x)^{-1} - I)g(x),$$

as stated in the lemma. ∎

The Newton's method for minimizing f over E_b then simply starts at any $x_0 \in E_b$ and iterates according to

$$x_{t+1} := x_t + \tilde{n}(x_t), \qquad \text{for } t = 0, 1, 2, \ldots. \tag{11.7}$$

As in the unconstrained setting, we consider the local norm $\|\cdot\|_x$ defined on the tangent space at x by

$$\forall h \in E, \qquad \|h\|_x^2 := \langle h, \tilde{H}(x)h \rangle = h^\top \tilde{H}(x)h$$

and define the **NL** condition as follows.

Definition 11.5 (Condition NL on a subspace). Let $\tilde{f} \colon E_b \to \mathbb{R}$. We say that $\tilde{f}$ satisfies the **NL** condition for $\delta_0 < 1$ if, for all $0 < \delta \le \delta_0 < 1$ and $x, y \in E_b$ such that

$$\|y - x\|_x \le \delta,$$

we have

$$(1 - 3\delta)\tilde{H}(x) \preceq \tilde{H}(y) \preceq (1 + 3\delta)\tilde{H}(x).$$

In the above, the PSD ordering $\preceq$ is understood in the usual sense, yet restricted to the space E. To make this precise, we need to define a notion similar to a symmetric matrix for linear operators. A linear operator $H \colon E \to E$ is said to be self-adjoint if $\langle Hh_1, h_2 \rangle = \langle h_1, Hh_2 \rangle$ for all $h_1, h_2 \in E$.

Definition 11.6. For two self-adjoint operators $H_1, H_2 \colon E \to E$, we say that $H_1 \preceq H_2$ if $\langle h, H_1h \rangle \le \langle h, H_2h \rangle$ for every $h \in E$.

At this point, all components present in Theorem 11.2 have been formally defined. The proof of Theorem 11.2 is identical to the proof of Theorem 9.6 in Chapter 9; in fact, one just has to replace f, g, and H with $\tilde{f}$, $\tilde{g}$ and $\tilde{H}$ for the proof to go through.

11.2.4 The IPM for Linear Programs in Standard Form

To develop an interior point method for solving linear programs in the standard form (11.4), we work in the affine subspace E_b and apply a similar path-following scheme as in Chapter 10. More precisely, we define the point $x_\eta^\star$ as

$$x_\eta^\star := \underset{x \in E_b}{\operatorname{argmin}} \left(\eta \langle c, x \rangle + F(x) \right),$$

where F is the logarithmic barrier function for $\mathbb{R}_{>0}^m$, i.e.,

$$F(x) := - \sum_{i=1}^{m} \log x_i.$$

The idea is to use Newton's method to progress along the central path, i.e., the set $\Gamma_c := \{x_\eta^\star \colon \eta \geq 0\}$.

For completeness, we now adjust the notation to this new setting. We define the function

$$f_\eta(x) := \eta \langle c, x \rangle + F(x)$$

and let $\widetilde{f}_\eta$ denote its restriction to E_b. We let $\widetilde{n}_\eta(x)$ be the Newton step with respect to $\widetilde{f}_\eta$, i.e., (using Lemma 11.4)

$$\widetilde{n}_\eta(x) := H(x)^{-1} (A^\top (AH(x)^{-1} A^\top)^{-1} AH(x)^{-1} - I)(\eta c + g(x)),$$

where $H(x)$ and $g(x)$ are the Hessian and gradient of $F(x)$ in $\mathbb{R}^m$. Note that, in this case, the Hessian and the gradient of $F(x)$ have particularly simple forms:

$$H(x) = X^{-2}, \qquad\qquad g(x) = X^{-1}1,$$

where $X := \operatorname{Diag}(x)$ is the diagonal matrix with the entries of x on the diagonal and 1 is the all-ones vector. Thus,

$$\widetilde{n}_\eta(x) := X^2 (A^\top (AX^{-2} A^\top)^{-1} AX^2 - I)(\eta c + X^{-1}1). \tag{11.8}$$

The algorithm for this setting is analogous to Algorithm 8 that was presented in Chapter 10; the only difference is the use of the equality-constrained Newton step $\widetilde{n}_\eta(x)$ instead of the unconstrained one $n_\eta(x)$. The theorem that one can formulate in this setting is as follows.

Theorem 11.7 (Convergence of the equality-constrained path-following IPM). *The equality-constrained version of Algorithm 8, after*

$$T := O\left(\sqrt{m} \log \frac{m}{\varepsilon \eta_0} \right)$$

iterations, outputs a point $\hat{x} \in E_b \cap \mathbb{R}^m_{>0}$ *that satisfies*

$$\langle c, \hat{x} \rangle \leq \langle c, x^* \rangle + \varepsilon.$$

Moreover, every Newton step requires $O(m)$ *time, plus the time required to solve one linear system of equations of the form* $(AWA^\top)y = d$, *where* $W \succ 0$ *is a diagonal matrix,* $d \in \mathbb{R}^n$ *is a given vector and* y *is the vector of variables.*

For the application to the $s-t$-minimum cost flow problem, it is also important to show that finding the initial point on the central path is not a bottleneck. From arguments presented in Section 10.6.2, one can derive the following lemma that is an analog of Lemma 10.17.

Lemma 11.8 (Starting point). *There is an algorithm that, given a point* $x' \in E_b \cap \mathbb{R}^m_{>0}$ *such that* $x'_i > \beta$ *for every* $i = 1, 2, \ldots, m$, *finds a pair* (η_0, x_0) *such that*

- $x_0 \in E_b \cap \mathbb{R}^m_{>0}$,
- $\left\| \tilde{n}_{\eta_0}(x_0) \right\|_{x_0} \leq \frac{1}{6}$,
- $\eta_0 \geq \Omega \left(\frac{1}{D} \cdot \frac{1}{\|c\|_2} \right)$, *where* D *is the (Euclidean) diameter of the feasible set* $E_b \cap \mathbb{R}^m_{\geq 0}$.

The algorithm performs $\tilde{O}\left(\sqrt{m} \log \frac{D}{\beta} \right)$ *iterations of the interior point method.*

In particular, whenever we can show that the diameter of the feasible set is bounded by a polynomial in the dimension and we can find a point that is at least an inverse polynomial distance away from the boundary, then the total number of iterations of the equality-constrained path-following IPM (to find the starting point and then find a point ε-close to optimum) is roughly $\tilde{O}\left(\sqrt{m} \log \frac{\|c\|_2}{\varepsilon} \right)$.

11.3 Application: The Minimum Cost Flow Problem

We show how to conclude Theorem 11.1 using the equality-constrained path-following method IPM mentioned in the previous section.

Number of iterations. We first note that by Theorem 11.7 the linear program (11.3) can be solved in $O\left(\sqrt{m} \log \frac{m}{\varepsilon \eta_0} \right)$ iterations of the path-following method. In order to match the number of iterations claimed in Theorem 11.1

we need to show that we can initialize the path-following method at η_0 such that $\eta_0^{-1} = \text{poly}(m, C, U)$. We show this in Section 11.3.1.

Time per iteration.

Lemma 11.9 (Computing a Newton step by solving a Laplacian system).
One iteration of the equality-constrained path-following IPM applied to the linear program (11.3) *can be implemented in time* $O(m + T_{Lap})$, *where* T_{Lap} *is the time required to solve a linear system of the form* $(BWB^\top)h = d$, *where* W *is a positive diagonal matrix,* $d \in \mathbb{R}^n$, *and* $h \in \mathbb{R}^n$ *is an unknown vector.*

One can use the formula (11.8) as a starting point for proving the above. However, one still needs to determine how the task of solving a certain $2m \times 2m$ linear system reduces to a Laplacian system. We leave this as an exercise (Exercise 11.3).

11.3.1 Finding a Starting Point Efficiently

It remains to show how one can find a point close enough to the central path so that we can initialize the path-following IPM. To this end, we apply Lemma 11.8. It says that we just need to provide a strictly feasible solution (x, y) to (11.3), i.e., one that satisfies the equality constraints and such that $x_i, y_i > \delta > 0$ for some not too small δ (inverse-polynomial in m, C, and U suffices).

We start by showing how to find a positive flow of any value and then argue that by a certain **preconditioning** of the graph G, we can also find a flow of a prescribed value F using this method

Lemma 11.10 (Finding a strictly positive flow). *There is an algorithm that, given a directed graph* $G = (V, E)$ *and two vertices* $s, t \in G$, *outputs a vector* $x \in [0, 1]^E$ *such that*

(1) $Bx = \frac{1}{2}\chi_{st}$,
(2) *if an edge* $i \in E$ *does not belong to any directed path from* s *to* t, *then* $x_i = 0$,
(3) *if an edge* $i \in E$ *belongs to some directed path from* s *to* t, *then*

$$\frac{1}{2m} \le x_i \le \frac{1}{2}.$$

The algorithm runs in $O(m)$ *time.*

Note that the edges that do not belong to any path from s to t can be removed from the graph, as they cannot be part of any feasible flow. Below, we prove that one can find such a flow in roughly $O(nm)$ time – the question of how to make this algorithm more efficient is left as an exercise (Exercise 11.4).

Proof sketch: We initialize $x \in \mathbb{R}^m$ to 0. We fix an edge $i = (v, w) \in E$. We start by checking whether i belongs to *any* path connecting s and t in G. This can be done by checking (using depth-first search) whether v is reachable from s and whether t is reachable from w.

If there is no such path, then we ignore i. Otherwise, let $P_i \subseteq E$ be such a path. We send $\frac{1}{2m}$ units of flow through this path, i.e., update

$$x := x + \frac{1}{2m} \cdot \chi_{P_i},$$

where χ_{P_i} is the indicator vector of the set P_i.

At the end of this procedure, every edge that lies on a path from s to t has

$$x_i \geq \frac{1}{2m} \quad \text{and} \quad x_i \leq m \cdot \frac{1}{2m} \leq \frac{1}{2}.$$

The remaining edges i have $x_i = 0$. In every step we need to update x at $O(n)$ positions (the length of P_i), hence the total running time is $O(nm)$. ∎

Flows constructed in the lemma above are strictly positive, yet they fail to satisfy the constraint $Bx = F\chi_{st}$, i.e., not enough flow is pushed from s to t. To get around this problem we need the final idea of preconditioning. We add one directed edge $\hat{i} := (s, t)$ to the graph with large enough capacity

$$u_{\hat{i}} := 2F$$

and very large cost

$$c_{\hat{i}} := 2 \sum_{i \in E} |c_i|.$$

We denote the new graph $(V, E \cup \{\hat{i}\})$ by $\hat{G}$ and call it the preconditioned graph.

By Lemma 11.10, we can construct a flow of value $f = \min\left\{\frac{1}{2}, \frac{F}{2}\right\}$ in G that strictly satisfies all capacity constraints since the capacities are integral. We can then make it have value exactly F by sending the remaining

$$F - f \geq \frac{F}{2}$$

units directly from s to t through $\hat{i}$. This allows us to construct a strictly positive feasible solution on the preconditioned graph.

Note, importantly, that this preconditioning does not change the optimal solution to the original instance of the problem, since sending even one unit of flow through $\hat{i}$ incurs a large cost – larger than taking any path from s to t in the original graph G. Therefore, solving the $s - t$-minimum cost flow problem on $\hat{G}$ is equivalent to solving it on G. Given this observation, it is enough to run the path-following algorithm on the preconditioned graph. Below we show how to find a suitable starting point for the path-following method in this case.

Lemma 11.11 (Finding a point on the central path). *There is an algorithm that, given a preconditioned instance of $s - t$-minimum cost flow problem (11.3), outputs a feasible starting point $z_0 = (x_0, y_0)^\top \in \mathbb{R}_{>0}^{2m}$ and $\eta_0 := \Omega\left(\frac{1}{m^3 CU}\right)$ with $U := \max_{i \in E} |u_i|$ and $C := \max_{i \in E} |c_i|$ such that*

$$\left\|\tilde{n}_{\eta_0}(z_0)\right\|_{z_0} \leq \frac{1}{6}.$$

This algorithm performs $\tilde{O}\left(\sqrt{m} \log \frac{U}{\min\{1, F\}}\right)$ iterations of the equality-constrained path-following IPM.

Proof: First, note that we may assume without loss of generality that all edges belong to some directed path from s to t in G. Next, we apply Lemma 11.10 to find a flow satisfying

$$x > 1 \cdot \min\left\{\frac{1}{2m}, \frac{F}{2m}\right\}$$

in G of value $f = \min\left\{\frac{1}{2}, \frac{F}{2}\right\}$ and set

$$x_{\hat{i}} = F - f.$$

This implies that

$$Bx = \Gamma\chi_{st}$$

and, moreover, for every edge $i \in E$, we have

$$\min\left\{\frac{1}{2m}, \frac{F}{2m}\right\} \leq x_i \leq \rho_i - \frac{1}{2},$$

as $\rho_i \in \mathbb{Z}_{\geq 0}$ for every edge $i \in E$. For $x_{\hat{i}}$, we have

$$\frac{F}{2} \leq x_{\hat{i}} \leq F = u_{\hat{i}} - F.$$

Therefore, by setting the slack variables y_i to

$$y_i := \rho_i - x_i,$$

we obtain that

$$\min\left\{\frac{1}{2}, \frac{F}{2}\right\} \leq y_i.$$

We now apply Lemma 11.8 with

$$\beta := \min \left\{ \frac{1}{2m}, \frac{F}{2m}, \frac{1}{2}, \frac{F}{2}, F \right\} \geq \frac{\min\{1, F\}}{2m}.$$

It remains to find an appropriate bound on the diameter of the feasible set. Note that we have, for every $i \in E \cup \{\hat{i}\}$,

$$0 \leq x_i, y_i \leq \rho_i.$$

This implies that the Euclidean diameter of the feasible set is bounded by

$$\sqrt{2 \sum_{i=1}^{m} \rho_i^2} \leq \sqrt{2m}U.$$

Thus, by plugging these parameters into Lemma 11.8, the bound on η_0 and the bound on the number of iterations follow.   ∎

11.4 Self-Concordant Barriers

In this section, by abstracting out the key properties of the logarithmic barrier and the convergence proof of the path-following IPM from Chapter 10, we arrive at the central notion of self-concordance. Not only allows does the notion of self-concordance help us to develop path-following algorithms for more general convex bodies (beyond polytopes), it also allows us search for better barrier functions and leads to some of the fastest-known algorithms for linear programming.

11.4.1 Revisiting the Properties of the Logarithmic Barrier

Recall Lemma 10.5 in Chapter 10, which asserts that the invariant

$$\left\| n_{\eta_t}(x_t) \right\|_{x_t} \leq \frac{1}{6}$$

is preserved at every step of the path-following IPM. The proof of this lemma relies on two important properties of the logarithmic barrier function.

Lemma 11.12 (Properties of the logarithmic barrier function). *Let*

$$F(x) := - \sum_{i=1}^{m} \log s_i(x)$$

be the logarithmic barrier function for a polytope, let $g(x)$ be its gradient, and let $H(x)$ be its Hessian. Then, we have

(1) *for every $x \in \text{int}(P)$,*

$$\left\| H(x)^{-1} g(x) \right\|_x^2 \leq m,$$

and

(2) *for every $x \in \text{int}(P)$ and every $h \in \mathbb{R}^n$,*

$$\left| \nabla^3 F(x)[h, h, h] \right| \leq 2 \left(h^\top H(x) h \right)^{3/2}.$$

Recall that the first property was used to show that one can progress along the central path by changing η multiplicatively by $\left(1 + \frac{1}{20\sqrt{m}}\right)$ (see Lemma 10.7 in Chapter 10). The second property was not explicitly mentioned in the proof, however, it results in the logarithmic barrier F satisfying the **NL** condition. Thus, it allows the repeated recentering of the point (bringing it closer to the central path) using Newton's method (see Lemma 10.6 in Chapter 10).

Proof: Part 1 was proved in Chapter 10. We provide a slightly different proof here. Let $x \in \text{int}(P)$ and let $S_x \in \mathbb{R}^{m \times m}$ be the diagonal matrix with slacks $s_i(x)$ on the diagonal. Thus, we know that

$$H(x) = A^\top S_x^{-2} A \qquad \text{and} \qquad g(x) = A^\top S_x^{-1} 1,$$

where $1 \in \mathbb{R}^m$ is the all-ones vector. We have

$$\begin{aligned}
\left\| H(x)^{-1} g(x) \right\|_x &= g(x)^\top H(x)^{-1} g(x) \\
&= 1^\top S_x^{-1} A (A^\top S_x^{-2} A)^{-1} A^\top S_x^{-1} 1 \\
&= 1^\top \Pi 1,
\end{aligned}$$

where $\Pi := S_x^{-1} A (A^\top S_x^{-2} A)^{-1} A^\top S_x^{-1}$. Note that Π is an orthogonal projection matrix: Indeed, Π is symmetric and $\Pi^2 = \Pi$ (by a direct calculation). Hence,

$$\left\| H(x)^{-1} g(x) \right\|_x = 1^\top \Pi 1 = \|\Pi 1\|_2^2 \leq \|1\|_2^2 = m.$$

To prove Part 2, first note that

$$\nabla^3 F(x)[h, h, h] = 2 \sum_{i=1}^m \frac{\langle a_i, h \rangle^3}{s_i(x)^3} \qquad \text{and} \qquad h^\top H(x) h = \sum_{i=1}^m \frac{\langle a_i, h \rangle^2}{s_i(x)^2}.$$

Therefore, the claim follows from the inequality

$$\|z\|_3 \leq \|z\|_2$$

applied to the vector $z \in \mathbb{R}^m$ defined by $z_i := \frac{\langle a_i, h \rangle}{s_i(x)}$ for all $i = 1, 2, \ldots, m$. ∎

11.4.2 Self-Concordant Barrier Functions

The two conditions stated in Lemma 11.12 are useful to understand path-following IPMs more generally. Any convex function that satisfies these two properties and is a barrier for the polytope P (i.e., tends to infinity when approaching the boundary) is called a **self-concordant barrier function**.

Definition 11.13 (Self-concordant barrier function). Let $K \subseteq \mathbb{R}^d$ be a convex set and let $F : \text{int}(K) \to \mathbb{R}$ be a thrice differentiable function. We say that F is a self-concordant barrier function with parameter v if it satisfies the following properties:

(1) **(Barrier)** $F(x) \to \infty$ as $x \to \partial K$.
(2) **(Convexity)** F is strictly convex.
(3) **(Complexity parameter v)** For all $x \in \text{int}(K)$,

$$\nabla F(x)^\top \left(\nabla^2 F(x)\right)^{-1} \nabla F(x) \leq v.$$

(4) **(Self-concordance)** For all $x \in \text{int}(K)$ and for all allowed vectors h (in the tangent space of the domain of F),

$$\left|\nabla^3 F(x)[h, h, h]\right| \leq 2 \left(h^\top \nabla^2 F(x) h\right)^{3/2}.$$

Note that the logarithmic barrier on P satisfies the above conditions with the complexity parameter equal to $v = m$. Indeed, the third condition above coincides with the first property in Lemma 11.12 and fourth condition is the same as the second property in Lemma 11.12.

11.5 Linear Programming Using Self-Concordant Barriers

Given any self-concordant barrier function $F(x)$ for a polytope P, one can consider the following objective

$$f_\eta(x) := \eta \langle c, x \rangle + F(x)$$

and define the central path to consist of minimizers x_η^* of the above parametric family of convex functions. Algorithm 8 presented in Chapter 10 for linear programming can be adapted straightforwardly for this self-concordant barrier function F. The only difference is that m is replaced by v, the complexity parameter of the barrier F; i.e., the value η is updated according to the rule

$$\eta_{t+1} := \eta_t \left(1 + \frac{1}{20\sqrt{v}}\right),$$

and the iteration terminates once $\eta_T > \frac{v}{\varepsilon}$.

By following the proof of Theorem 10.10 from Chapter 10 for such an F, one obtains the following result.

Theorem 11.14 (Convergence of the path-following IPM for general barrier functions). *Let $F(x)$ be a self-concordant barrier function for $P = \{x \in \mathbb{R}^n : Ax \leq b\}$ with complexity parameter v. The corresponding path-following IPM, after $T := O\left(\sqrt{v}\log\frac{v}{\varepsilon\eta_0}\right)$ iterations, outputs $\hat{x} \in P$ that satisfies*

$$\langle c, \hat{x}\rangle \leq \langle c, x^*\rangle + \varepsilon.$$

Moreover, every iteration of the algorithm requires computing the gradient and Hessian $(H(\cdot))$ of F at given point $x \in \text{int}(P)$ and solving one linear system of the form $H(x)y = z$, where $z \in \mathbb{R}^n$ is determined by x and we solve for y.

A lower bound on the complexity parameter of self-concordance. Theorem 11.14 implies that if we could come up with an efficient second-order oracle to a self-concordant barrier function with parameter $v < m$, we could obtain an algorithm that performs roughly $\sqrt{v}$ iterations (instead of $\sqrt{m}$ as for the logarithmic barrier). Thus, a natural question arises: Can we get arbitrarily good barriers? In particular, can we bring the complexity parameter down to, say, $O(1)$? Unfortunately, the self-concordance complexity parameter cannot go below the dimension of the convex set as established by the following theorem.

Theorem 11.15 (Lower bound on the complexity parameter for hypercube). *Every self-concordant barrier function for the hypercube $K := [0,1]^d$ has complexity parameter at least d.*

We give some intuition for this fact by proving it for $d = 1$.

Proof of Theorem 11.14 for the special case of $d = 1$: Let $F : [0,1] \to \mathbb{R}$ be a self-concordant barrier function for $K = [0,1]$. Self-concordance in the univariate setting translates to: For every $t \in (0,1)$,

$$F'(t)^2 \leq v \cdot F''(t),$$
$$|F'''(t)| \leq 2F''(t)^{3/2}.$$

We prove that if F is a strictly convex barrier, then the above imply that $v \geq 1$. For the sake of contradiction, assume $v < 1$. Let

$$g(t) := \frac{F'(t)^2}{F''(t)}$$

and consider the derivative of g:

$$g'(t) = 2F'(t) - \left(\frac{F'(t)}{F''(t)}\right)^2 F'''(t) = F'(t)\left(2 - \frac{F'(t)F'''(t)}{F''(t)^2}\right). \quad (11.9)$$

Now, using the self-concordance of F, we obtain

$$\frac{F'(t)F'''(t)}{F''(t)^2} \leq 2\sqrt{\nu}. \quad (11.10)$$

Moreover, since F is a strictly convex function, it holds that $F'(t) > 0$ for $t \in (\alpha, 1]$ for some $\alpha \in (0, 1)$. Hence, for $t > \alpha$, by combining (11.9) and (11.10), we have

$$g'(t) \geq 2F'(t)(1 - \sqrt{\nu}).$$

Hence,

$$g(t) \geq g(\alpha) + 2(1 - \sqrt{\nu})(F(t) - F(\alpha)),$$

which gives us a contradiction as, on the one hand, $g(t) \leq \nu$ (from the self-concordance of F), and on the other hand, $g(t)$ is unbounded (as $\lim_{t \to 1} F(t) = +\infty$). ∎

Interestingly, it has also been shown that every full-dimensional convex subset of $\mathbb{R}^d$ admits a self-concordant barrier – called the **universal barrier** – with parameter $O(d)$. Note, however, that just the existence of an $O(d)$-self-concordant barrier does not imply that we can construct efficient algorithms for optimizing over P in $O(\sqrt{d})$ iterations. Indeed, the universal and related barriers are largely mathematical results that are rather hard to make practical with from the computational viewpoint – computing gradients and Hessians of these barriers is nontrivial. We now give an overview of two important examples of barrier function for linear programming that have good computational properties.

11.5.1 The Volumetric Barrier

Definition 11.16 (The volumetric barrier). Let $P = \{x \in \mathbb{R}^n : Ax \leq b\}$, where A is an $m \times n$ matrix, and let $F : \text{int}(P) \to \mathbb{R}$ be the logarithmic barrier for P. The volumetric barrier function on P is defined as,

$$V(x) := \frac{1}{2} \log \det \nabla^2 F(x).$$

Moreover, the **hybrid barrier** on P is defined as

$$G(x) := V(x) + \frac{n}{m} F(x).$$

Discussion. The barrier functions $V(x)$ and $G(x)$ improve upon the $\sqrt{m}$ iterations bound obtained for linear programming using the logarithmic barrier. To understand what the volumetric barrier represents, consider the Dikin ellipsoid centered at x,

$$E_x := \{u \in \mathbb{R}^n : (u - x)^\top H(x)(u - x) \leq 1\},$$

where $H(x)$ is the Hessian of $F(x)$. Define a function that at a point x measures the volume (under the Lebesgue measure) of the Dikin ellipsoid E_x (denoted by $\mathrm{vol}(E_x)$). Then, the volumetric barrier, up to an additive constant, is the logarithm of this volume:

$$V(x) = -\log \mathrm{vol}(E_x) + \mathrm{const}.$$

To see why this is a barrier function, note that, since for every $x \in \mathrm{int}(P)$, the Dikin ellipsoid E_x is contained in P (see Exercise 10.4), whenever x comes close to the boundary of P, E_x becomes very flat and, thus, $V(x)$ tends to $+\infty$.

$V(x)$ can also be thought of as a weighted logarithmic barrier function. Indeed, one can prove that the Hessian of $\nabla^2 V(x)$ is multiplicatively close[1] to the following matrix $Q(x)$:

$$Q(x) := \sum_{i=1}^{m} \sigma_i(x) \frac{a_i a_i^\top}{s_i(x)^2},$$

where $\sigma(x) \in \mathbb{R}^m$ is the vector of **leverage scores** at x, i.e., for $i = 1, 2, \ldots, m$,

$$\sigma_i(x) := \frac{a_i^\top H(x)^{-1} a_i}{s_i(x)^2}.$$

The vector $\sigma(x)$ estimates the relative importance of each of the constraints. In fact, it holds that

$$\sum_{i=1}^{m} \sigma_i(x) = n \qquad \text{and} \qquad \forall i, \ 0 \leq \sigma_i(x) \leq 1.$$

Note that, unlike the logarithmic barrier, if some constraint is repeated multiple times, its importance in the volumetric barrier does not scale with the number of repetitions.

If for a moment we assumed that the leverage scores $\sigma(x)$ do not vary with x, i.e.,

$$\sigma(x) \equiv \sigma,$$

---

[1] By that, we mean that there is a constant $\gamma > 0$ such that $\gamma Q(x) \preceq \nabla^2 V(x) \preceq \gamma^{-1} Q(x)$.

then $Q(x)$ would correspond to the Hessian $\nabla^2 F_\sigma(x)$ of the following weighted logarithmic barrier:

$$F_\sigma(x) = \sum_{i=1}^{m} \sigma_i \log s_i(x).$$

Recall that, in the case of the logarithmic barrier, each $\sigma_i = 1$ and, hence, the total importance of constraints is m, while here $\sum_{i=1}^{m} \sigma_i = n$. This idea is further generalized in Section 11.5.2.

Complexity parameter. The above interpretation of the volumetric barrier $V(x)$ as a weighted logarithmic barrier can be then used to prove that its complexity parameter is $\nu = O(n)$. However, it does not satisfy the self-concordance condition. Instead, one can show the following weaker condition:

$$\frac{1}{2}\nabla^2 V(x) \preceq \nabla^2 V(y) \preceq 2\nabla^2 V(x) \quad \text{whenever } \|x - y\|_x \leq O\left(m^{-1/2}\right).$$

To make the above hold not only for x and y with $\|x - y\|_x \leq O\left(m^{-1/2}\right)$ but also when $\|x - y\|_x \leq O(1)$, one can consider an adjustment of the volumetric barrier: The hybrid barrier $G(x) := V(x) + \frac{n}{m}F(x)$.

Theorem 11.17 (Self-concordance of the hybrid barrier). *The barrier function $G(x)$ is self-concordant with complexity parameter $\nu = O(\sqrt{nm})$.*

Note that this gives an improvement over the logarithmic barrier whenever $n = o(m)$, but does not achieve the optimal bound of $O(n)$.

Computational complexity. While the hybrid barrier is not optimal as far as the complexity parameter is concerned, the cost of using it to do a Newton step can be shown to be reasonable.

Theorem 11.18 (Computational complexity of the hybrid barrier). *A Newton step in the path-following IPM with respect to the hybrid barrier $G(x)$ can be performed in the time it takes to multiply two $m \times m$ matrices ($O(m^\omega)$ where ω is the matrix multiplication exponent and is about 2.373).*

Recall that one iteration using the logarithmic barrier reduces to solving one linear system. Thus, the above matches the cost per iteration for the logarithmic barrier in the worst case scenario. However, for certain special cases (as for the $s - t$-minimum cost flow problem) the cost per iteration using the logarithmic barrier might be significantly smaller, even $\widetilde{O}(m)$ instead of $O(m^\omega)$.

11.5.2 The Lee-Sidford Barrier

While the volumetric barrier considered the log-volume of the Dikin ellipsoid, roughly, the Lee-Sidford barrier considers the log-volume of an object that is a "smoothening" of the John ellipsoid.

Definition 11.19 (John ellipsoid). Given a polytope $P := \{x \in \mathbb{R}^n : a_i^\top x \leq b_i$ for $i = 1, \ldots, m\}$ and a point $x \in \text{int}(P)$, the John ellipsoid of P at x is defined to be the ellipsoid of maximum volume that is centered at x and contained in P. For an ellipsoid described by a PD matrix B, its log volume is $-\frac{1}{2} \log \det B$.

It is an exercise (Exercise 11.15) to show that the following convex optimization formulation captures the John ellipsoid:

$$\log \text{vol}(J(x)) := \max_{w \geq 0, \ \sum_{i=1}^m w_i = n} \left[\log \det \left(\sum_{i=1}^m w_i \frac{a_i a_i^\top}{s_i(x)^2} \right) \right]. \quad (11.11)$$

Such a barrier $J(x)$ indeed has complexity parameter n, however, the optimal weight vector $w(x) \in \mathbb{R}^m$ turns out to be nonsmooth, which makes it impossible to use $J(x)$ as a barrier for optimization.

The problem with defining $J(x)$ as a barrier function is that the optimal weight vector $w(x) \in \mathbb{R}^m$ turns out to be nonsmooth. To counter this issue, one can consider smoothenings of $J(x)$. One possible smoothening is the barrier $LS(x)$ as defined as follows.

Definition 11.20 (The Lee-Sidford barrier). Let $P := \{x \in \mathbb{R}^n : Ax \leq b\}$, where A is an $m \times n$ matrix, be a full-dimensional polytope and let $F : \text{int}(P) \to \mathbb{R}$ be the logarithmic barrier for P. Consider the following barrier function defined at a point $x \in \text{int}(P)$ as a solution to the following optimization problem:

$$LS(x) := \max_{w \geq 0} \left[\log \det \left(\sum_{i=1}^m w_i \frac{a_i a_i^\top}{s_i(x)^2} \right) - \frac{n}{m} \sum_{i=1}^m w_i \log w_i \right] + \frac{n}{m} F(x).$$

$$(11.12)$$

The entropy term in $LS(x)$ makes the dependency of w on x smoother, and as in the hybrid barrier, this one has also the logarithmic barrier added with coefficient $\frac{n}{m}$.

Discussion. Remarkably, the Lee-Sidford barrier has led to an IPM algorithm for linear programming with $O(\sqrt{n} \log^{O(1)} m)$ iterations, each of which solves a small number of linear systems. Thus, it not only improves upon the hybrid barrier in terms of the number of iterations, but it also has better computability properties.

Complexity parameter. A property of the Dikin ellipsoid, which intuitively is the reason for the $\sqrt{m}$ iteration bound, is that whenever P is symmetric (i.e., $x \in P$ if and only if $-x \in P$),

$$E_0 \subseteq P \subseteq \sqrt{m}E_0.$$

That is, E_0 is a subset of P, and by inflating it by a factor of $\sqrt{m}$, it contains the polytope P. Here, E_0 is the Dikin ellipsoid centered at 0. See Figure 11.2 for an illustration. Thus, if we take one step towards the negative cost $-c$ to the boundary of E_0, a multiplicative progress of $\left(1 + \frac{1}{\sqrt{m}}\right)$ in the objective is made. This intuition is not completely accurate as it holds only if we start at the analytic center of P, however, one may think of intersecting P with a constraint $\langle c, x \rangle \leq C$ for some guess C that shifts the analytic center of P to the new iterate, and proceeding in this manner. This provides us with the intuition that the Dikin ellipsoid is a $\sqrt{m}$-rounding of the polytope P is responsible for the $\sqrt{m}$ iterations bound. One can prove that in a similar setting as considered above for the Dikin ellipsoid, it holds that

$$J_0 \subseteq P \subseteq \sqrt{n}J_0,$$

where J_0 is the John ellipsoid centered at 0. This looks promising as, indeed, m turned into n when compared to the bound for Dikin ellipsoid and is, roughly, the reason for the improvement the Lee-Sidford barrier provides. This can be formalized in the form of the following theorem.

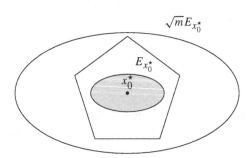

Figure 11.2 A polytope P and the Dikin ellipsoid center at $x_0^\star$ – the analytic center of P. While the Dikin ellipsoid is fully contained in P, its $\sqrt{m}$-scaling contains P.

Theorem 11.21 (Self-concordance of the Lee-Sidford barrier). *The barrier function $LS(x)$ is self-concordant with complexity parameter $O(n \cdot \mathrm{polylog}(m))$.*

Note in particular that this matches (up to logarithmic factors) the lower bound of n on the complexity parameter of a barrier of an n-dimensional polytope.

Computational complexity. While the complexity parameter of the barrier $LS(x)$ is close to optimal, it is far from clear how one can maintain the Hessian of such a barrier and be able to perform every iteration of Newton's method in time comparable to one iteration for the logarithmic barrier (solving one linear system). The way this algorithm is implemented is by keeping track of the current iterate x_t and the current vector of weights w_t. At every iteration, both the point x_t and the weights w_t are updated so as to advance on the central path (determined by the current w_t) towards the optimum solution. For the sake of computational efficiency, the weights w_t never really correspond to optimizers of (11.12) with respect to x_t but are obtained as another Newton step with respect to the old weights w_{t-1}. This finally leads to the following result.

Theorem 11.22 (Informal, Lee-Sidford algorithm for LP). *There is an algorithm for the linear programming problem based on the path-following scheme using the Lee-Sidford barrier $LS(x)$ that performs $\widetilde{O}\left(\sqrt{n}\log\frac{1}{\varepsilon}\right)$ iterations to compute an ε-approximate solution. Every iteration of this algorithm requires solving a poly-logarithmic number of $m \times m$ linear systems.*

11.6 Semidefinite Programming Using Self-Concordant Barriers

Recall that in Section 11.1, we used the logarithmic barrier for the positive orthant to come up with a linear programming algorithm for linear programs in the standard form:

$$\min_{x \in \mathbb{R}^m} \ \langle c, x \rangle$$

$$\text{such that} \quad Ax = b,$$

$$x \geq 0.$$

A generalization of the above to matrices is the following convex optimization problem over PSD matrices, called **semidefinite programming** (SDP):

$$\min_{X} \ \langle C, X \rangle$$

such that $\langle A_i, X \rangle = b_i, \quad$ for $i = 1, 2, \dots, m,$ \hfill (11.13)

$$X \succeq 0.$$

Above, X is a variable that is a symmetric $n \times n$ matrix, C and $A_1, \dots, A_m$ are symmetric $n \times n$ matrices, and $b_i \in \mathbb{R}$. The inner product on the space of symmetric matrices we use above is

$$\langle M, N \rangle := \mathrm{Tr}\,(MN).$$

One can extend path-following IPMs to the world of SDPs. All one needs is an efficiently computable self-concordant barrier function for the set of PD matrices:

$$C_n := \{ X \in \mathbb{R}^{n \times n} : X \text{ is PD} \}.$$

11.6.1 A Barrier for PD Matrices

Definition 11.23 (Logarithmic barrier for PD matrices). The logarithmic barrier function $F : C_n \to \mathbb{R}$ on C_n is defined to be

$$F(X) := -\log \det X.$$

Discussion. The logarithmic barrier for C_n is a generalization of the logarithmic barrier for the positive orthant. Indeed, if we restrict to C_n to the set of diagonal, positive definite matrices, we obtain

$$F(X) = -\sum_{i=1}^{n} \log X_{i,i}.$$

More generally, it is not hard to see that

$$F(x) = -\sum_{i=1}^{n} \log \lambda_i(X),$$

where $\lambda_1(X), \dots, \lambda_n(X)$ are the eigenvalues of X.

Complexity parameter. Note that the logarithmic barrier for the positive orthant is self-concordant with parameter n. We show that this also holds when we move to C_n.

Theorem 11.24 (Complexity parameter of the log barrier function for PD matrices). *The logarithmic barrier function F on the set of positive definite matrices C_n is self-concordant with parameter n.*

Proof: To start, note that to verify the conditions in Definition 11.13, we need to understand first what vectors h to consider. As we are moving in the set C_n, we would like to consider any H of the form $X_1 - X_2$ for $X_1, X_2 \in C_n$, which coincides with the set of all symmetric matrices. Let $X \in C_n$ and $H \in \mathbb{R}^{n \times n}$ be a symmetric matrix. We have

$$\nabla F(X)[H] = -\operatorname{Tr}\left(X^{-1}H\right),$$
$$\nabla^2 F(X)[H, H] = \operatorname{Tr}\left(X^{-1}HX^{-1}H\right), \qquad (11.14)$$
$$\nabla^3 F(X)[H, H, H] = -2\operatorname{Tr}\left(X^{-1}HX^{-1}HX^{-1}H)\right).$$

We are now ready to verify the self-concordance of $F(X)$. The fact that X is a barrier follows simply from the fact that if X tends to ∂C_n then $\det(X) \to 0$. The convexity of F also follows as

$$\nabla^2 F(X)[H, H] = \operatorname{Tr}\left(X^{-1}HX^{-1}H\right) = \operatorname{Tr}\left(H_X^2\right) \geq 0,$$

where $H_X := X^{-1/2}HX^{-1/2}$. To prove the last condition, note that

$$\nabla^3 F(X)[H, H, H] = -2\operatorname{Tr}\left(H_X^3\right)$$

and

$$2\left|\operatorname{Tr}\left(H_X^3\right)\right| \leq \operatorname{Tr}\left(H_X^2\right)^{3/2} = \nabla^2 F(X)[H, H]^{3/2}.$$

We are left with the task of determining the complexity parameter of F. This follows simply from the Cauchy-Schwarz inequality, as

$$\nabla F(X)[H] = -\operatorname{Tr}(H_X) \leq \sqrt{n} \cdot \operatorname{Tr}\left(H_X^2\right)^{1/2} = \sqrt{n}\nabla^2 F(X)[H, H]^{1/2}.$$

This completes the proof.   ∎

Computational complexity. To apply the logarithmic barrier for optimization over the set C_n, we also need to show that $F(X)$ is efficient, as the next theorem (whose proof follows from the calculations above) demonstrates.

Theorem 11.25 (Gradient and Hessian of logdet). *The Hessian and the gradient of the logarithmic barrier F at a point $X \in C_n$ can be computed in time required to invert the matrix X.*

11.7 Convex Optimization Using Self-Concordant Barriers

Finally, we note that when defining the notion of self-concordance, we did not assume that the underlying set K is a polytope. We only required that K is a full-dimensional convex subset of $\mathbb{R}^n$. Consequently, we can use the path-following IPM to optimize over arbitrary convex sets, provided we have access to a good starting point and a computationally efficient self-concordant barrier function. In fact, this allows us to solve the problem of minimizing a linear function $\langle c, x \rangle$ over a convex set K and the corresponding convergence guarantee is analogous to Theorem 11.14.

Theorem 11.26 (Path-following IPM for arbitrary convex sets). *Let $F(x)$ be a self-concordant barrier function on a convex set $K \subseteq \mathbb{R}^n$ with complexity parameter v. An analog of the Algorithm 8, after $T := O\left(\sqrt{v} \log \frac{1}{\varepsilon \eta_0}\right)$ iterations, outputs $\hat{x} \in K$ that satisfies*

$$\langle c, \hat{x} \rangle \le \langle c, x^\star \rangle + \varepsilon.$$

Moreover, every iteration requires computing the gradient and Hessian $(H(\cdot))$ of F at given point $x \in \text{int}(K)$ and solving one linear system of the form $H(x)y = z$, where $z \in \mathbb{R}^n$ is a given vector and y is a vector of variables.

We remark that one can also use the above framework to optimize general convex functions over K. This follows from the fact that every convex program $\min_{x \in K} f(x)$ can be transformed into one that minimizes a linear function over a convex set. Indeed, the above is equivalent to

$$\min_{(x,t) \in K'} t,$$

where

$$K' := \{(x,t) \colon x \in K, f(x) \le t\}.$$

This means that we just need to construct a self-concordant function F on the set K' to solve $\min_{x \in K} f(x)$.[2]

11.8 Exercises

11.1   Prove Theorem 11.2.

11.2   Prove Lemma 11.3.

11.3   Prove Lemma 11.9.

11.4   Prove that one can indeed find the required starting point promised in Lemma 11.10 in $O(m)$ time.

---

[2] Note that this reduction makes the convex set K' rather complicated, as the function f is built in to its definition. Nevertheless, this reduction is still useful in many interesting cases.

11.5   Prove that for every $1 \leq p_1 \leq p_2 \leq \infty$,

$$\|z\|_{p_2} \leq \|z\|_{p_1} .$$

11.6   The goal of this problem is to develop a method for solving the $s - t$-minimum cost flow problem exactly. We assume here that there exists an algorithm solving the $s - t$-minimum cost flow problem up to additive error $\varepsilon > 0$ (in value) in $\tilde{O}\left(m^{3/2} \log \frac{CU}{\varepsilon}\right)$, where C is the maximum magnitude of a cost of an edge and U is the maximum capacity of an edge.

(a) Prove that if an instance of the $s - t$-minimum cost flow problem has a unique optimal solution $x^\star$, then $x^\star$ can be found in $\tilde{O}\left(m^{3/2} \log CU\right)$ time.

(b) **Isolation Lemma.** Prove the following lemma. Let $\mathcal{F} \subseteq 2^{[m]}$ be a family of subsets of $[m] := \{1, 2, \ldots, m\}$ and let $w : [m] \to [N]$ be a weight function chosen at random (i.e., $w(i)$ is a random number in $\{1, 2, \ldots, N\}$ for every $i \in [m]$). Then the probability that there is a **unique** $S^\star \in \mathcal{F}$ maximizing $w(S) := \sum_{i \in S} w(i)$ over all $S \in \mathcal{F}$ is at least $1 - \frac{m}{N}$.

(c) Conclude that there exists a randomized algorithm that with probability at least $1 - \frac{1}{m^{10}}$ finds an optimal solution to the $s - t$-minimum cost flow problem in $\tilde{O}\left(m^{3/2} \log CU\right)$ time. *Hint:* All feasible flows for a graph with integral capacities and integral flow value form a convex polytope with integral vertices.

11.7   **Optimal assignment problem.** There are n workers and n tasks; the profit for assigning task j to worker i is $w_{ij} \in \mathbb{Z}$. The goal is to assign exactly one task to each worker so that no task is assigned twice and the total profit is maximized.

(a) Prove that the optimal assignment problem is captured by the following linear program:

$$\max_{x \in \mathbb{R}^{n \times n}} \sum_{i=1}^{n} \sum_{j=1}^{n} w_{ij} x_{ij},$$

$$\text{such that } \sum_{i=1}^{n} x_{ij} = 1, \quad \forall j = 1, 2, \ldots, n, \tag{11.15}$$

$$\sum_{j=1}^{n} x_{ij} = 1, \quad \forall i = 1, 2, \ldots, n,$$

$$x \geq 0.$$

(b) Develop an algorithm based on the path-following framework for solving this problem.

(i) The method should perform $\widetilde{O}(n)$ iterations.
(ii) Analyze the time per iteration (time to compute the equality-constrained Newton's step).
(iii) Give an efficient algorithm to find a strictly positive initial solution along with a bound on η_0.
(iv) Give a bound on the total running time.

Note: While the optimal assignment problem can be combinatorially reduced to the $s - t$-minimum cost flow problem, this problem asks to solve it directly using a path-following IPM and not via a reduction to the $s - t$-minimum cost flow problem.

11.8 **Directed Physarum dynamics.** In this problem, we develop a different interior point method for solving linear programs in the standard form

$$\min_{x \in \mathbb{R}^m} \quad \langle c, x \rangle$$

$$\text{such that} \quad Ax = b, \tag{11.16}$$

$$x \geq 0.$$

We assume here that the program is strictly feasible, i.e., $S := \{x > 0 : Ax = b\} \neq \emptyset$.

The idea is to use a barrier function $F(x) := \sum_{i=1}^{m} x_i \log x_i$ to endow the positive orthant $\mathbb{R}^m_{>0}$ with the local inner product coming from the Hessian of $F(x)$. That is, for $x \in \mathbb{R}^m_{>0}$, we define

$$\forall u, v \in \mathbb{R}^m, \quad \langle u, v \rangle_x := u^\top \nabla^2 F(x) v.$$

We now specify the update rule of a new algorithm. Let $x \in S$; we define

$$x' := x - g(x),$$

where $g(x)$ is defined as the gradient of the linear function $x \mapsto \langle c, x \rangle$ with respect to the inner product $\langle \cdot, \cdot \rangle_x$ and restricted to the affine subspace $\{x : Ax = b\}$. Derive a closed form expression for $g(x)$ in terms of A, b, c and x.

11.9 Prove that the logarithmic barrier for the positive orthant $\mathbb{R}^n_{>0}$ is self-concordant with parameter n.

11.10 Prove that for a strictly convex function F defined on a convex set K, the self-concordance condition

$$\forall x \in K, \quad \forall h \in \mathbb{R}^n, \quad \left| \nabla^3 F(x)[h,h,h] \right| \le 2 \, \|h\|_x^3$$

implies the **NL** condition for some $\delta_0 < 1$. *Hint:* It is useful to first show that self-concordance implies that for all $x \in K$ and for all $h_1, h_2, h_3 \in \mathbb{R}^n$, it holds that

$$\left| \nabla^3 F(x)[h_1, h_2, h_3] \right| \le 2 \, \|h_1\|_x \, \|h_2\|_x \, \|h_3\|_x .$$

11.11 Let $K \subseteq \mathbb{R}^n$ be a convex set and let $F : \mathrm{int}(K) \to \mathbb{R}$. Prove that, for every $\nu \ge 0$, the Condition (11.17) holds if and only if Condition (11.18) does.

$$\text{For all } x \in \mathrm{int}(K), \quad \nabla F(x)^\top \left(\nabla^2 F(x) \right)^{-1} \nabla F(x) \le \nu.$$

$$(11.17)$$

$$\text{For all } x \in \mathrm{int}(K),\ h \in \mathbb{R}^n, \quad (DF(x)[h])^2 \le \nu \cdot D^2 F(x)[h,h].$$

$$(11.18)$$

11.12 Prove the following properties of self-concordant barrier functions defined over convex sets:

(a) If F_1 is a self-concordant barrier for $K_1 \subseteq \mathbb{R}^n$ and F_2 is a self-concordant barrier for $K_2 \subseteq \mathbb{R}^n$ with parameters ν_1 and ν_2, respectively, then $F_1 + F_2$ is a self-concordant barrier for $K_1 \cap K_2$ with parameter $\nu_1 + \nu_2$.

(b) If F is a self-concordant barrier for $K \subseteq \mathbb{R}^n$ with parameter ν and $A \in \mathbb{R}^{m \times n}$ is a matrix, then $x \mapsto F(Ax)$ is a self-concordant barrier for $\{ y \in \mathbb{R}^m : A^\top y \in K \}$ with the same parameter.

11.13 Consider an ellipsoid defined by an $n \times n$ PD matrix B:

$$E_B := \{x : x^\top B x \le 1\}.$$

Define its volume to be

$$\mathrm{vol}(E_B) := \int_{x \in E_B} d\lambda_n(x),$$

where λ_n is the Lebesgue measure in $\mathbb{R}^n$. Prove that

$$\log \mathrm{vol}(E_B) = -\frac{1}{2} \log \det B + \beta$$

for some constant β.

11.14 **Volumetric barrier.** Let $P = \{x \in \mathbb{R}^n : Ax \le b\}$, where A is an $m \times n$ matrix, be a full-dimensional polytope and let $V(x)$ denote the volumetric barrier.

(a) Prove that $V(x)$ is a barrier function.

(b) Recall the definition of the leverage score vector $\sigma(x) \in \mathbb{R}^m$ for $x \in P$ from this chapter:

$$\sigma_i(x) := \frac{a_i^\top H(x)^{-1} a_i}{s_i(x)^2},$$

where $H(x)$ is the Hessian of the logarithmic barrier function on P.

(1) Prove that $\sum_{i=1}^m \sigma_i(x) = n$ for every $x \in P$.

(2) Prove that $0 \le \sigma_i(x) \le 1$ for every $x \in P$ and every $i = 1, 2, \ldots, m$.

(c) For $x \in P$, let

$$A_x := S(x)^{-1} A,$$

where $S(x)$ is the diagonal matrix corresponding to the slacks $s_i(x)$. Let

$$P_x := A_x (A_x^\top A_x)^{-1} A_x^\top$$

and let $P_x^{(2)}$ denote the matrix whose each entry is the square of the corresponding entry of P_x. Let Σ_x denote the diagonal matrix corresponding to $\sigma(x)$. Prove that for all $x \in P$,

(1) $\nabla^2 V(x) = A_x^\top (3\Sigma_x - 2P_x^{(2)}) A_x$.

(2) Let $Q(x) := \sum_{i=1}^m \sigma_i(x) \frac{a_i a_i^\top}{s_i(x)^2}$. Prove that for all $x \in P$,

$$Q(x) \preceq \nabla^2 V(x) \preceq 5Q(x).$$

(d) Prove that for all $x \in P$,

$$\frac{1}{4m} H(x) \preceq Q(x) \preceq H(x).$$

(e) Conclude the complexity parameter of $V(x)$ is n.

(f) Prove that for all $x, y \in \text{int}(P)$ such that $\|x - y\|_x \le \frac{1}{8m^{1/2}}$,

$$\frac{1}{\beta} \nabla^2 V(x) \preceq \nabla^2 V(y) \preceq \beta \nabla^2 V(x)$$

for some $\beta = O(1)$.

11.15 **John ellipsoid.** Let $P = \{x \in \mathbb{R}^n : Ax \le b\}$ be a bounded, full-dimensional polytope and $x_0 \in P$ be a fixed point in its interior. For an $n \times n$ matrix $X \succ 0$, define an ellipsoid E_X centered at x_0 by

$$E_X := \{y \in \mathbb{R}^n : (y - x_0)^\top X (y - x_0) \le 1\}.$$

Consider the problem of finding the ellipsoid of largest volume centered at a point x_0 in the interior of P that is fully contained in P.

(a) State the problem as convex program over positive definite matrices X.

(b) Prove that the dual of the above convex program is

$$\min_{w \geq 0: \sum_i w_i = n} - \log \det \left(\sum_{i=1}^{m} w_i \frac{a_i a_i^\top}{s_i(x)^2} \right).$$

(c) Assume that P is symmetric around the origin, i.e., $P = -P$, $0 \in \text{int}(P)$, and let E_0 be the John ellipsoid of P at 0. Then the ellipsoid $\sqrt{n} E_0$ contains P.

(d) Write the Lagrangian dual of the SDP mentioned in (11.13).

Notes

The book by Cormen et al. (2001) contains a comprehensive discussion on the $s - t$-minimum cost flow problem. The main theorem presented in this chapter (Theorem 11.1) was first proved by Daitch and Spielman (2008). The proof presented here is slightly different from the one by Daitch and Spielman (2008) (which was based on the primal-dual framework). Their algorithm improved over the previously fastest algorithm by Goldberg and Tarjan (1987) by a factor of about $\widetilde{O}(n/m^{1/2})$. Using ideas mentioned towards the end of this chapter, Lee and Sidford (2014) improved this bound further to $\widetilde{O}(m \sqrt{n} \log^{O(1)} U)$.

As discussed in this chapter, the $s - t$-maximum flow problem is a special case of the $s - t$-minimum cost flow problem. Hence, the result of Lee and Sidford (2014) also implies an $\widetilde{O}(m \sqrt{n} \log^{O(1)} U)$ time algorithm for the $s - t$-maximum flow problem; the first improvement since Goldberg and Rao (1998).

Self-concordant functions are presented in the book by Nesterov and Nemirovskii (1994). The lower bound in Theorem 11.14 can also be found in their book. An alternative proof of the existence of a barrier function with $O(n)$-self-concordance can be found in the paper by Bubeck and Eldan (2015). Coming up with efficient $O(n)$-self-concordant barriers for various convex sets K is still an important open problem. The volumetric barrier was introduced by Vaidya (1987, 1989a,b), and the Lee-Sidford barrier was introduced by Lee and Sidford (2014).

The Physarum dynamics-based algorithm for linear programming (Exercise 11.8) was analyzed by Straszak and Vishnoi (2016b). For more on the isolation lemma (introduced in Exercise 11.6), see the papers by Mulmuley et al. (1987) and Gurjar et al. (2018).

12

Ellipsoid Method for Linear Programming

We introduce a class of cutting plane methods for convex optimization and present an analysis of a special case, namely, the ellipsoid method. We then show how to use this ellipsoid method to solve linear programs over 0-1-polytopes when we only have access to a separation oracle for the polytope.

12.1 0-1-Polytopes with Exponentially Many Constraints

In combinatorial optimization one often deals with problems of the following type: Given a set family $\mathcal{F} \subseteq 2^{[m]}$, i.e., a collection of subsets of $[m] := \{1, 2, \ldots, m\}$, and a cost vector $c \in \mathbb{Z}^m$, find a minimum cost set $S \in \mathcal{F}$:

$$S^{\star} := \operatorname*{argmin}_{S \in \mathcal{F}} \sum_{i \in S} c_i.$$

Many familiar problems on graphs can be formulated as above. For instance, by taking $\mathcal{F} \subseteq 2^E$ to be the set of all matchings in a graph $G = (V, E)$ and letting $c = -1$ (the negative of the all-ones vector of length $|E|$), we obtain the maximum cardinality matching problem. Similarly, one can obtain the minimum spanning tree problem, the $s - t$-maximum flow problem (for unit capacity graphs), or the $s - t$-minimum cut problem.

When tackling these problems using continuous methods, such as the ones introduced in this book, an idea we have used on several occasions is to first associate a convex set to the domain. In the particular setting of combinatorial optimization, given a family $\mathcal{F} \subseteq 2^{[m]}$, a natural object is the polytope

$$P_{\mathcal{F}} := \operatorname{conv}\{1_S : S \in \mathcal{F}\},$$

where $1_S \in \{0, 1\}^m$ is the indicator vector of the set $S \subseteq [m]$. Such polytopes are called **0-1-polytopes** as all their vertices belong to the set $\{0, 1\}^m$.

Below are some important examples of 0-1-polytopes involving graphs; many of them have already made their appearance in this book.

Definition 12.1 (Examples of combinatorial polytopes associated to graphs). For an undirected graph $G = (V, E)$ with n vertices and m edges we define:

(1) The matching polytope $P_M(G) \subseteq [0, 1]^m$ to be

$$P_M(G) := \mathrm{conv}\{1_S : S \subseteq E \text{ is a matching in } G\}.$$

(2) The perfect matching polytope $P_{PM}(G) \subseteq [0, 1]^m$ to be

$$P_{PM}(G) := \mathrm{conv}\{1_S : S \subseteq E \text{ is a perfect matching in } G\}.$$

(3) The spanning tree polytope $P_{PM}(G) \subseteq [0, 1]^m$ to be

$$P_{ST}(G) := \mathrm{conv}\{1_S : S \subseteq E \text{ is a spanning tree in } G\}.$$

Solving the maximum matching problem in G reduces to the problem of minimizing a linear function over $P_M(G)$. More generally, one can consider the following linear optimization problem over such polytopes: Given a 0-1-polytope $P \subseteq [0, 1]^m$ and a cost vector $c \in \mathbb{Z}^m$, find a vector $x^\star \in P$ such that

$$x^\star := \underset{x \in P}{\mathrm{argmin}} \ \langle c, x \rangle.$$

Note that by solving this linear optimization problem over $P_{\mathcal{F}}$ for the cost vector c, we can solve the corresponding combinatorial optimization problem over $\mathcal{F}$. Indeed, as the optimal solution is always attained at a vertex, say $x^\star = 1_{S^\star}$, then $S^\star$ is the optimal solution to the discrete problem and vice versa.[1] As this is a type of linear program, a natural question is: Can we solve such linear programs using the interior point method?

12.1.1 The Problem with IPMs: The Case of Matching Polytope

The matching polytope of a graph $G = (V, E)$ was defined as a convex hull of its vertices. While it is a valid description, this is not a particularly useful notion from a computational point of view; especially when it comes to applying IPMs that require polyhedral description of the polytope. Remarkably, it turns out that there is a complete description of all the inequalities defining this polytope.

---

[1] Here we assume for simplicity that the optimal solution is unique.

Theorem 12.2 (Polyhedral description of the matching polytope). *Let* $G = (V, E)$ *be an undirected graph with* n *vertices and* m *edges; then*

$$P_M(G) = \left\{ x \in [0,1]^m : \sum_{i \in S} x_i \leq \frac{|S| - 1}{2}, \ S \subseteq [m] \ and \ |S| \ is \ odd \right\}.$$

While this does give us all the inequalities describing $P_M(G)$, there are 2^{m-1} of them, one for each odd subset of $[m]$. Thus, plugging these inequalities into the logarithmic barrier would result in $2^{O(m)}$ terms, exponential in the size of the input: $O(n+m)$. Similarly, computing either the volumetric barrier or the Lee-Sidford barrier would require exponential time. In this much time, we might as well just enumerate all possible subsets of $[m]$ and output the best matching. One may ask if there are more compact representations of this polytope and the answer (see notes) turns out to be no: Any representation (even with more variables) of $P_M(G)$ requires exponentially many inequalities. Thus, applying an algorithm based on the path-following method to minimize over $P_M(G)$ does not seem to lead to an efficient algorithm.

In fact, the situation is even worse, this description does not even seem useful in checking if a point is in $P_M(G)$. Interestingly, the proof of Theorem 12.2 leads to a polynomial time algorithm to solve the separation problem over $P_M(G)$ exactly. There are also (related) combinatorial algorithms to find the maximum matching in a graph. In the next chapter, we see that efficient separation oracles can also be constructed for a large class of combinatorial polytopes using the machinery of convex optimization (including techniques presented in this chapter). Meanwhile, the question is: Can we do linear optimization over a polytope if we just have access to a separation oracle for it? The answer to this leads us to the ellipsoid method that, historically, predates IPMs.

While we have abandoned the goal of developing IPMs for optimizing linear functions over 0-1-polytopes with exponentially many constraints in this book, it is an interesting question if self-concordant barrier functions for polytopes such as $P_M(G)$ that are also computationally tractable exist. More specifically, is there a self-concordant barrier function $F : P_M(G) \rightarrow \mathbb{R}$ with complexity parameter polynomial in m such that the gradient $\nabla F(x)$ and the Hessian $\nabla^2 F(x)$ are efficiently computable? By efficiently computable we not only mean polynomial time in m, but also that computing the gradient and Hessian should be simpler than solving the underlying linear program itself.

12.1.2 Efficient Separation Oracles

The following separation problem was introduced in Chapter 4.

Definition 12.3 (Separation problem for polytopes). Given a polytope $P \subseteq \mathbb{R}^m$ and a vector $x \in \mathbb{Q}^m$, the goal is to output one of the following:

- if $x \in P$ output YES, and
- if $x \notin P$ output NO and provide a vector $h \in \mathbb{Q}^m \setminus \{0\}$ such that

$$\forall y \in P, \quad \langle h, y \rangle < \langle h, x \rangle.$$

Recall that in the NO case, the vector h defines a hyperplane separating x from the polytope P. An important class of results in combinatorial optimization is that for many graph-based combinatorial 0-1-polytopes, such as those introduced in Definition 12.1, the separation problem can be solved in polynomial time. Here, we measure the running time of a separation oracle as a function of the size of the graph ($O(n + m)$) and the bit complexity of the input vector x.

Theorem 12.4 (Separation oracles for combinatorial polytopes). *There are polynomial time separation oracles for the polytopes $P_M(G)$, $P_{PM}(G)$ and $P_{ST}(G)$.*

We leave the proof of this theorem as an exercise (Exercise 12.2). The question that arises is: Given a separation oracle for $P_M(G)$, does it allow us to optimize linear functions over this polytope? The main result of this chapter is the following theorem that says that this is indeed the case, not only for the matching polytope but for all 0-1-polytopes.

Theorem 12.5 (Linear optimization over 0-1-polytopes using a separation oracle). *There is an algorithm that given a separation oracle for a 0-1-polytope $P \subseteq [0, 1]^m$ and a vector $c \in \mathbb{Z}^m$ outputs,*

$$x^\star \in \underset{x \in P}{\operatorname{argmin}} \langle c, x \rangle.$$

The algorithm runs in polynomial time in m and $L(c)$, and makes a polynomial number of queries to the separation oracle of P.

Combining the above with the existence of an efficient separation oracle for $P_M(G)$ (Theorem 12.4), we conclude, in particular, that the problem of computing the maximum cardinality matching in a graph is polynomial time solvable. Similarly, using the above, one can compute a matching (or a perfect matching, or a spanning tree) of maximum or minimum weight in polynomial time. The remainder of this chapter is devoted to the proof of Theorem 12.5. We start by sketching a general algorithm scheme in the subsequent section and recover the ellipsoid method as a special case of it. We then prove that the ellipsoid method indeed takes just a polynomial number of simple iterations to converge.

12.2 Cutting Plane Methods

We develop a generic approach for optimizing linear functions over polytopes, called cutting plane methods. We arc interested in solving the following problem:

$$\min \quad \langle c, x \rangle \\ \text{such that } x \in P, \tag{12.1}$$

where $P \subseteq \mathbb{R}^m$ is a polytope and we have access to a separation oracle for P. Throughout this section, we assume that P is full-dimensional. Later we comment on how to get around this assumption.

12.2.1 Reducing Optimization to Feasibility Using Binary Search

Before we proceed with the description of the algorithm, we introduce the first idea that allows us to reduce the optimization problem (12.1) to a series of simpler problems of the following form.

Definition 12.6 (Feasibility problem for polytopes). Given (in some form) a polytope $P \subseteq \mathbb{R}^m$ and a vector $x \in \mathbb{Q}^m$, the goal is to output one of the following:

- if $P \neq \emptyset$, output YES and provide a point $x \in P$, and
- if $P = \emptyset$, output NO.

The idea is quite simple: Suppose we have a rough estimate that the optimal value of (12.1) belongs to the interval $[l_0, u_0]$. We can then perform binary search, along with an algorithm for solving the feasibility problem to find an estimate on the optimal value $y^\star$ of (12.1) up to an arbitrary precision. Later, in the proof of Theorem 12.5, we show how one can implement this idea in the setting of 0-1-polytopes.

Algorithm 9: Reducing optimization to feasibility

Input:
- A separation oracle to a polytope P
- A cost function $c \in \mathbb{Q}^m$
- Estimates $l_0 \leq u_0 \in \mathbb{Q}$ such that $l_0 \leq y^* \leq u_0$
- An $\varepsilon > 0$

Output: A number u such that $u \leq y^* + \varepsilon$

Algorithm:

1: Set $l := l_0$ and $u := u_0$
2: **while** $u - l > \varepsilon$ **do**
3:     Set $g := \frac{l+u}{2}$
4:     **if** $P' := P \cap \{x \in \mathbb{R}^m : \langle c, x \rangle \leq g\} \neq \emptyset$ **then**
5:         Set $u := g$
6:     **else**
7:         Set $l := g$
8:     **end if**
9: **end while**
10: **return** u

To implement this idea, Algorithm 9 maintains an interval $[l, u]$ that contains the optimal value y^* to (12.1) and uses an algorithm to check nonemptiness of a polytope in step 4 to halve it in every step until its length is at most $\varepsilon > 0$. The number of iterations of Algorithm 9 is upper bounded by $O\left(\log \frac{u_0 - l_0}{\varepsilon}\right)$.

Thus, essentially, given an algorithm to check feasibility we are able to perform optimization. Several remarks are in order.

(1) Note that, given a separation oracle for P, the separation oracle for P' is easy to construct.

(2) Assuming that the optimal value y^* lies in the initial interval $[l_0, u_0]$, this algorithm allows us to learn an additive ε-approximate optimal value in roughly $\log \frac{u_0 - l_0}{\varepsilon}$ calls to the feasibility oracle. However, it is not clear how to recover the exact optimum y^*. We show that for certain classes of polytopes, such as 0-1-polytopes, one can compute y^* **exactly,** given a good enough estimate of y^*.

(3) Algorithm 9 only computes an approximate optimal value of (12.1) and not the optimal point x^*. One way to deal with this issue is to simply use the feasibility oracle to find a point $\hat{x}$ in $P' := P \cap \{x \in \mathbb{R}^m : \langle c, x \rangle \leq u\}$

for the final value of u. The polytope P' is guaranteed to be nonempty and the point $\hat{x}$ has value at most $y^{\star} + \varepsilon$. Again, in the proof of Theorem 12.5 we show how to round $\hat{x}$ to an exact optimal solution.

(4) To convert Algorithm 9 into a polynomial time reduction, one needs to make sure that the polytopes P' constructed in step 4 do not become difficult for the feasibility oracle. The running time of the algorithm we present for this task depends on the volume of P' and it becomes slower as the volume of P' gets smaller. Thus, in general, one has to carefully bound how complex the polytope P' becomes as we progress with the algorithm.

Thus, up to the details mentioned above, it is enough to construct an algorithm for checking nonemptiness of polytopes.

12.2.2 Checking Feasibility Using Cutting Planes

Suppose we are given a large enough convex set E_0 that contains the polytope P. To check whether P is empty or not, we construct a descending sequence of convex subsets

$$E_0 \supseteq E_1 \supseteq E_2 \supseteq \cdots ,$$

such that all of them contain P and their volume reduces significantly at every step. Eventually, the set E_t approximates P so well that a point $x \in E_t$ is likely to be in P as well. Note that we use the Lebesgue measure in $\mathbb{R}^m$ to measure volumes. We denote by $\mathrm{vol}(K)$ the m-dimensional Lebesgue measure of a set $K \subseteq \mathbb{R}^m$. Formally, we consider Algorithm 10; see Figure 12.1 for an illustration.

The following theorem characterizes the performance of the above scheme.

Theorem 12.7 (Number of iterations of the cutting plane method). *Suppose that the following conditions on P and the nested sequence of sets $E_0, E_1, E_2, \ldots$ are satisfied:*

(1) **(Bounding ball)** *the initial set E_0 is contained in an Euclidean ball of radius $R > 0$,*
(2) **(Inner ball)** *the polytope P contains an Euclidean ball of radius $r > 0$, and*
(3) **(Volume drop)** *for every step $t = 0, 1, \ldots ,$ we have*

$$\mathrm{vol}(E_{t+1}) \leq \alpha \cdot \mathrm{vol}(E_t),$$

where $0 < \alpha < 1$ is a quantity possibly depending on m.

Algorithm 10: Cutting plane method

Input:
- A separation oracle for a polytope P
- A convex set E_0 that is promised to contain P

Output: If $P \neq \emptyset$ then return YES and an $\hat{x} \in P$, else return NO

Algorithm:

1: **while** $\text{vol}(E_t) \geq \text{vol}(P)$ **do**
2:     Select a point $x_t \in E_t$
3:     Query the separation oracle for P on x_t
4:     **if** $x_t \in P$ **then**
5:         **return** YES and $\hat{x} := x_t$
6:     **else**
7:         Let $h_t \in \mathbb{Q}^m$ be the separating hyperplane output by the oracle
8:         Construct a new set E_{t+1} so that

$$E_t \cap \{x : \langle x, h_t \rangle \leq \langle x_t, h_t \rangle\} \subseteq E_{t+1}$$

9:     **end if**
10: **end while**
11: **return** NO

Then, the cutting plane method described in Algorithm 10 outputs a point $\hat{x} \in P$ after $O\left(m\left(\log\frac{1}{\alpha}\right)^{-1}\log\frac{R}{r}\right)$ iterations.

Proof: The algorithm maintains the invariant that $P \subseteq E_t$ at every step t. Hence, it never terminates with the verdict NO, as

$$\text{vol}(P) \leq \text{vol}(E_t)$$

for every t. However, since the volume of E_t is strictly decreasing at a fixed rate, for some t, the point x_t must be P.

We now estimate the smallest t for which $x_t \in P$. Note that, from the volume drop condition, we have

$$\text{vol}(E_t) \leq \alpha^t \cdot \text{vol}(E_0).$$

Moreover, since P contains some ball $B(x', r)$ and E_0 is contained in some ball $B(x'', R)$, we have

$$\text{vol}(B(x', r)) \leq \text{vol}(E_t) \leq \alpha^t \cdot \text{vol}(E_0) \leq \alpha^t \cdot \text{vol}(B(x'', R)).$$

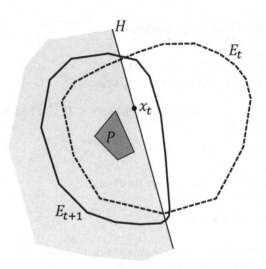

Figure 12.1 An illustration of one iteration of the cutting plane method. One starts
with a set E_t guaranteed to contain the polytope P and queries a point $x_t \in E_t$. If
x_t is not in P, then the separation oracle for P provides a separating hyperplane
H. Hence, one can reduce the region to which P belongs by picking a set E_{t+1}
containing the intersection of E_t with shaded halfspace.

Thus,

$$\frac{\text{vol}(B(x',r))}{\text{vol}(B(x'',R))} \leq \alpha^t. \tag{12.2}$$

However, both $B(x',r)$ and $B(x'',R)$ are scalings (and translations) of the unit
Euclidean ball $B(0,1)$ and, hence,

$$\text{vol}(B(x',r)) = r^m \cdot \text{vol}(B(0,1)) \quad \text{and} \quad \text{vol}(B(x'',R)) = R^m \cdot \text{vol}(B(0,1)).$$

By plugging the above into (12.2), we obtain

$$t \leq m \left(\log \frac{1}{\alpha} \right)^{-1} \log \frac{R}{r}.$$ ∎

Note that if we could find an instantiation of the cutting plane method (a way
of choosing E_t and x_t at every step t) such that the corresponding parameter
α is a constant less than 1, then it yields an algorithm for linear programming
that performs a polynomial number of iterations – indeed using the results in
one of the exercises, it follows that we can always enclose P in a ball of radius
roughly $R = 2^{O(Ln)}$ and find a ball inside of P of radius $r = 2^{-O(Ln)}$. Thus,
$\log \frac{R}{r} = O(Ln)$.

The method developed we present in this chapter does not quite achieve a constant drop in volume but rather

$$\alpha \approx 1 - \frac{1}{m}.$$

However, this still implies a method for linear programming that performs a polynomial number of iterations, and (as we see later) each iteration is just a simple matrix operation that can be implemented in polynomial time.

12.2.3 Possible Choices for E_t and x_t

Let us discuss two feasible and simple strategies of picking the set E_t (and the point x_t).

Approximation using Euclidean balls. One of the simplest ideas to implement the cutting plane method is to use Euclidean balls and let E_t and x_t be defined as

$$E_t := B(x_t, r_t)$$

for some radius r_t.

The problem with this method is that we cannot force the volume drop when Euclidean balls are used. Indeed, consider a simple an example in $\mathbb{R}^2$. Let $E_0 := B(0, 1)$ be the starting ball and suppose that the separation oracle provides the separating hyperplane $h = (1, 0)^\top$, meaning that

$$P \subseteq K := E_0 \cap \{x \in \mathbb{R}^2 : x_1 \le 0\}.$$

What is the smallest ball containing K? (See Figure 12.2 for an illustration.) It turns out that it is $B(0, 1)$ and we cannot find a ball with smaller radius containing K. This simply follows from the fact that the diameter of K is 2 (the distance between $(0, -1)^\top$ and $(0, 1)^\top$ is 2). Thus, we need to look for a larger family of sets that allows us to achieve a suitable volume drop in every step.

Approximation using polytopes. The second idea one can try is to use polytopes as E_ts. We start with $E_0 := [-R, R]^m$ – a polytope containing P. Whenever a new hyperplane is obtained from the separation oracle, we update

$$E_{t+1} := E_t \cap \{x : \langle x, h_t \rangle \le \langle x_t, h_t \rangle\},$$

a polytope again. This is certainly the most aggressive strategy one can imagine, as we always cut out as much a possible from E_t to obtain E_{t+1}.

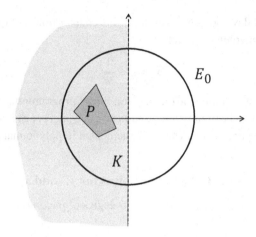

Figure 12.2 An illustration of the use of Euclidean balls in the cutting plane method. Note that the smallest ball containing the intersection of E with the shaded halfplane is E itself.

We also need to give a strategy for picking a point $x_t \in E_t$ at every iteration. For this, it is crucial that the point x_t is well in the interior of E_t, as otherwise we might end up cutting only a small piece out of E_t and, thus, not reducing the volume enough. Therefore, to make it work, at every step we need to find an approximate center of the polytope E_t and use it as the query point x_t. As the polytope gets more and more complex, finding a center also becomes more and more time-consuming. In fact, we are reducing a problem of finding a point in P to a problem of finding a point in another polytope, seemingly a cyclic process.

In one of the exercises we show that this scheme can be made to work by maintaining a suitable center of the polytope and using a recentering step whenever a new constraint is added. This is a significantly nontrivial approach and based on the hope that the new center will be close to the old one, when the polytope does not change too drastically and hence can be found rather efficiently using, for instance, Newton's method.

12.3 Ellipsoid Method

The discussion in the previous section indicates that using Euclidean balls is too restrictive, as we may not be able make any progress in subsequent steps. On the other hand, maintaining a polytope does not sound any easier that solving the original problem, as it is not easy to find a suitable point $x_t \in E_t$ to query, at every step t.

In Chapter 11, we saw another set of interesting convex sets associated to polytopes: ellipsoids. We saw that one can approximate polytopes using the so-called Dikin or John ellipsoid. It turns out that choosing E_ts ellipsoids is sufficient: They approximate polytopes well enough and their center is a part of their description. Since ellipsoids are central to this chapter, we recall their definition and introduce the notation we use to denote them in this chapter.

Definition 12.8 (Ellipsoid). An ellipsoid in $\mathbb{R}^m$ is any set of the form

$$E(x_0, M) := \left\{ x \in \mathbb{R}^m : (x - x_0)^\top M^{-1}(x - x_0) \leq 1 \right\},$$

such that $x_0 \in \mathbb{R}^m$ and M is an $m \times m$, positive definite matrix.

By definition, $E(x_0, M)$ is symmetric around its center x_0. Suppose that $E_t := E(x_t, M_t)$ and the separation oracle for P provides us with the information that the polytope P is contained in the set

$$\{x \in E_t : \langle x, h_t \rangle \leq \langle x_t, h_t \rangle\}.$$

Then, a natural strategy is to take E_{t+1} so as to contain this set and have the smallest volume among all such.

Definition 12.9 (Minimum volume enclosing ellipsoid). Given an ellipsoid $E(x_0, M) \subseteq \mathbb{R}^m$ and a halfspace

$$H := \{x \in \mathbb{R}^m : \langle x, h \rangle \leq \langle x_0, h \rangle\}$$

through its center, for some $h \in \mathbb{R}^m \setminus \{0\}$ we define the minimum enclosing ellipsoid of $E(x_0, M) \cap H$ to be the ellipsoid $E(x^\star, M^\star)$ being the optimal solution to

$$\min_{x \in \mathbb{R}^m, M' > 0} \quad \mathrm{vol}(E(x, M'))$$
$$\text{such that} \quad E(x_0, M) \cap H \subseteq E(x, M').$$

One can show that such a minimum enclosing ellipsoid always exists and is unique, as the above can be formulated as a convex program; see Exercise 12.5. For our application, we give an exact formula for the minimum volume ellipsoid containing the intersection of an ellipsoid with a halfspace.

12.3.1 The Algorithm

The ellipsoid method is an instantiation of the cutting plane method (Algorithm 10) where we just use an ellipsoid as the set E_t and its center as x_t. Moreover, for every step t we take the minimum enclosing ellipsoid as E_{t+1}. The ellipsoid

---

Algorithm 11: Ellipsoid method

Input:
- A separation oracle for a polytope P
- A radius $R \in \mathbb{Z}_{>0}$ so that $B(0, R)$ is promised to contain P

Output: If $P \neq \emptyset$ then return YES and an $\hat{x} \in P$, else return NO

Algorithm:

1: Let $E_0 := E(0, R \cdot I)$ where I is the $m \times m$ identity matrix
2: **while** $\text{vol}(E_t) \geq \text{vol}(P)$ **do**
3:     Let x_t be the center of E_t
4:     Query the separation oracle for P on x_t
5:     **if** $x_t \in P$ **then**
6:         **return** YES and $\hat{x} := x_t$
7:     **else**
8:         Let $h_t \in \mathbb{Q}^m$ be the separating hyperplane output by the oracle
9:         Let $E_{t+1} := E(x_{t+1}, M_{t+1})$ be the minimum volume ellipsoid such that

$$E_t \cap \{x \colon \langle x, h_t \rangle \leq \langle x_t, h_t \rangle\} \subseteq E_{t+1}$$

10:     **end if**
11: **end while**
12: **return** NO

---

method appears in Algorithm 11. Again, we assume that $P \subseteq \mathbb{R}^m$ is a full-dimensional polytope and a separation oracle is available for P.

Note that the description of Algorithm 11 is not yet complete as we have not provided a way to compute minimum enclosing ellipsoids (required in step 9). We discuss this question in Section 12.4.

12.3.2 Analysis of the Algorithm

We are now ready to state a theorem on the computation efficiency of the ellipsoid method. The main part of the proof is provided in Section 12.4.

Theorem 12.10 (Efficiency of the ellipsoid method). *Suppose that $P \subseteq \mathbb{R}^m$ is a full-dimensional polytope that is contained in an n-dimensional Euclidean ball of radius $R > 0$ and contains an n-dimensional Euclidean ball of radius $r > 0$. Then, the ellipsoid method (Algorithm 11) outputs a point $\hat{x} \in P$ after $O\left(m^2 \log \frac{R}{r}\right)$ iterations. Moreover, every iteration can be implemented* *in $O(m^2 + T_{SO})$ time, where T_{SO} is the time required to answer one query by the separation oracle.*

Given what has been already proved in Theorem 12.7, we are only missing the following two components (stated in a form of a lemma) to deduce Theorem 12.10.

Lemma 12.11 (Informal; see Lemma 12.12). *Consider the ellipsoid method defined in Algorithm 11. Then,*

(1) *the volume of the ellipsoids $E_0, E_1, E_2, \ldots$ constructed in the algorithm drops at a rate $\alpha \approx \left(1 - \frac{1}{2m}\right)$, and*

(2) *every iteration of the ellipsoid method can be implemented in polynomial time.*

Given the above lemma (stated formally as Lemma 12.12) we can deduce Theorem 12.10.

Proof of Theorem 12.10: By combining Theorem 12.7 with Lemma 12.11 we obtain the bound on the number of iterations:

$$O\left(m\left(\log\frac{1}{\alpha}\right)^{-1} \cdot \log\frac{R}{r}\right) = O\left(m^2 \log\frac{R}{r}\right).$$

Moreover, according to Lemma 12.11, every iteration can be performed efficiently. Hence, the second part of Theorem 12.10 also follows. ∎

12.4 Analysis of Volume Drop and Efficiency for Ellipsoids

In this section, we show that given an ellipsoid $E(x_0, M)$ and a vector $h \in \mathbb{R}^m$ we can efficiently construct a new ellipsoid $E(x', M')$ that has significantly smaller volume and

$$E(x_0, M) \cap \{x \in \mathbb{R}^m : \langle x, h \rangle \leq \langle x_0, h \rangle\} \subseteq E(x', M').$$

We leave it as an exercise (Exercise 12.5) to prove that the construction presented in this section is the minimum volume ellipsoid containing the intersection of $E(x_0, M)$ and the halfspace above. Nevertheless, the lemma below is enough to complete the description and analysis of the ellipsoid method.

Lemma 12.12 (Volume drop). *Let $E(x_0, M) \subseteq \mathbb{R}^m$ be any ellipsoid in $\mathbb{R}^m$ and let $h \in \mathbb{R}^m$ be a nonzero vector. There exists an ellipsoid $E(x', M') \subseteq \mathbb{R}^m$ such that*

$$E(x_0, M) \cap \{x \in \mathbb{R}^m : \langle x, h \rangle \leq \langle x_0, h \rangle\} \subseteq E(x', M')$$

and

$$\text{vol}(E(x', M')) \leq e^{-\frac{1}{2(m+1)}} \cdot \text{vol}(E(x_0, M)).$$

Moreover, x' and M' are as follows:

$$x' := x_0 - \frac{1}{m+1} M g, \tag{12.3}$$

$$M' := \frac{m^2}{m^2 - 1} \left(M - \frac{2}{m+1} M g (M g)^\top \right), \tag{12.4}$$

where $g := \left(h^\top M h \right)^{-1/2} h$.

The above lemma states that using ellipsoids we can implement the cutting plane method with volume drop:

$$\alpha = e^{-\frac{1}{2(m+1)}} \approx \left(1 - \frac{1}{2(m+1)} \right) < 1.$$

The proof of Lemma 12.12 is has two parts. In the first part, we prove Lemma 12.12 for a very simple and symmetric case. In the second part, we reduce the general case to the symmetric case studied in the first part using an affine transformation of $\mathbb{R}^m$.

12.4.1 Volumes and Ellipsoids under Affine Transformations

In this section, we review basic facts about affine transformations and ellipsoids. We start by proving how the volume of a set changes when an affine transformation is applied to it.

Lemma 12.13 (Change of volume under affine map). *Consider an affine map $\phi(x) := Tx + b$, where $T : \mathbb{R}^m \to \mathbb{R}^m$ is an invertible linear map and $b \in \mathbb{R}^m$ is any vector. Let $K \subseteq \mathbb{R}^m$ be a Lebesgue measurable set. Then*

$$\text{vol}(\phi(K)) = |\det(T)| \cdot \text{vol}(K).$$

Proof: This is a simple consequence of integrating by substitution. We have

$$\text{vol}(\phi(K)) = \int_{\phi(K)} d\lambda_m(x),$$

where λ_m is the m-dimensional Lebesgue measure. We apply the change of variables $x := \phi(y)$ and obtain

$$\int_{\phi(K)} d\lambda_m(x) = \int_K |\det(T)|\, d\lambda_m(y) = |\det(T)| \cdot \mathrm{vol}(K),$$

as T is the Jacobian of the mapping ϕ. ∎

The next fact analyzes the effect of applying an affine transformation on an ellipsoid.

Lemma 12.14 (Affine transformations of ellipsoids). *Consider an affine map $\phi(x) := Tx + b$, where $T : \mathbb{R}^m \to \mathbb{R}^m$ is an invertible linear map and $b \in \mathbb{R}^m$ is any vector. Let $E(x_0, M)$ be any ellipsoid in $\mathbb{R}^m$, then*

$$\phi(E(x_0, M)) = E(Tx_0 + b, T M T^\top).$$

Proof:

$$
\begin{aligned}
\phi(E(x_0, M)) &= \{\phi(x) : (x_0 - x)^\top M^{-1}(x_0 - x) \le 1\} \\
&= \{y : (x_0 - \phi^{-1}(y))^\top M^{-1}(x_0 - \phi^{-1}(y)) \le 1\} \\
&= \{y : (x_0 - T^{-1}(y - b))^\top M^{-1}(x_0 - T^{-1}(y - b)) \le 1\} \\
&= \{y : T^{-1}(Tx_0 - (y - b))^\top M^{-1} T^{-1}(Tx_0 - (y - b)) \le 1\} \\
&= \{y : (Tx_0 - (y - b))^\top (T^{-1})^\top M^{-1} T^{-1}(Tx_0 - (y - b)) \le 1\} \\
&= E(Tx_0 + b, T M T^\top).
\end{aligned}
$$

■

From the two previous facts one can easily derive the following corollary regarding the volume of an ellipsoid (Figure 12.3).

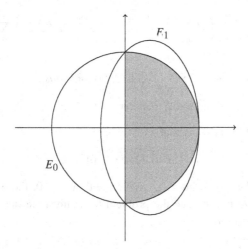

Figure 12.3 Illustration of the symmetric case of the argument. E_0 is the unit Euclidean ball in $\mathbb{R}^2$ and E_1 is the ellipse of smallest area that contains the right half (depicted in shaded) of E_0. The area of E_1 is $\frac{4\sqrt{3}}{9} < 1$.

Corollary 12.15 (Volume of an ellipsoid). *Let $x_0 \in \mathbb{R}^m$ and $M \in \mathbb{R}^{m \times m}$ be a PD matrix. Then*

$$\operatorname{vol}(E(x_0, M)) = \det(M)^{1/2} \cdot V_m,$$

where V_m denotes the volume of the unit Euclidean ball in $\mathbb{R}^m$.

Proof: We first observe (using Lemma 12.14) that

$$E(x_0, M) = \phi(E(0, I)), \tag{12.5}$$

where $\phi(x) = M^{1/2}x + x_0$. Lemma 12.13 implies that

$$\operatorname{vol}(E(x_0, M)) = \det(M)^{1/2}\operatorname{vol}(E(0, I)) = \det(M)^{1/2} \cdot V_m. \qquad \blacksquare$$

12.4.2 The Symmetric Case

In the symmetric case we assume that the ellipsoid is the unit ball $E(0, I)$ and we intersect it with the halfspace

$$H = \{x \in \mathbb{R}^m : x_1 \geq 0\}.$$

Then, one can obtain an ellipsoid of a relatively small volume that contains $E(0, I) \cap H$ via an explicit formula as in the lemma below.

Lemma 12.16 (Volume drop for the symmetric case). *Consider the Euclidean ball $E(0, I)$. Then the ellipsoid $E' \subseteq \mathbb{R}^m$ given by*

$$E' := \left\{ x \in \mathbb{R}^m : \left(\frac{m+1}{m}\right)^2 \left(x_1 - \frac{1}{m+1}\right)^2 + \frac{m^2 - 1}{m^2} \sum_{j=2}^{m} x_j^2 \leq 1 \right\}$$

has volume $\operatorname{vol}(E') \leq e^{-\frac{1}{2(m+1)}} \cdot \operatorname{vol}(E(0, I))$ and satisfies

$$\{x \in E(0, I) : x_1 \geq 0\} \subseteq E'.$$

Proof: We start by showing that

$$\{x \in E(0, I) : x_1 \geq 0\} \subseteq E'.$$

To this end, take any point $x \in E(0, I)$ with $x_1 \geq 0$, the goal is to show that $x \in E'$. We first reduce the problem to a univariate question using the following observation:

$$\sum_{j=2}^{m} x_j^2 \leq 1 - x_1^2,$$

which follows from the fact that x belongs to the unit ball. Thus, to conclude that $x \in E'$, we just need to show that

$$\left(\frac{m+1}{m}\right)^2 \left(x_1 - \frac{1}{m+1}\right)^2 + \frac{m^2-1}{m^2}(1 - x_1^2) \le 1. \qquad (12.6)$$

Note that the left-hand side of (12.6) is convex (show that the second derivative is positive) and nonnegative (in $[0,1]$) function in one variable. We would like to show that it is bounded by 1 for every $x_1 \in [0,1]$. To this end, it suffices to verify this for both end points $x_1 = 0, 1$. By directly plugging in $x_1 = 0$ and $x_1 = 1$ we obtain that the left-hand side of (12.6) equals 1 and thus the inequality is satisfied.

We now proceed to bounding the volume of E'. To this end, note that $E' = E(z, S)$ with

$$z := \left(\frac{1}{m+1}, 0, 0, \ldots, 0\right)^\top,$$

$$S := \text{Diag}\left(\left(\frac{m}{m+1}\right)^2, \frac{m^2}{m^2-1}, \ldots, \frac{m^2}{m^2-1}\right).$$

Here Diag (x) is a diagonal matrix with diagonal entries as in the vector x. To compute the volume of E' we simply apply Corollary 12.15:

$$\text{vol}(E') = \det(S)^{1/2} \cdot \text{vol}(E(0, I)).$$

We have

$$\det(S) = \left(\frac{m}{m+1}\right)^2 \cdot \left(\frac{m^2}{m^2-1}\right)^{m-1} = \left(1 - \frac{1}{m+1}\right)^2 \left(1 + \frac{1}{m^2-1}\right)^{m-1}.$$

Using the inequality $1 + x \le e^x$, which is valid for every $x \in \mathbb{R}$, we arrive at the upper bound,

$$\det(S) \le \left(e^{-\frac{1}{m+1}}\right)^2 \cdot \left(e^{\frac{1}{m^2-1}}\right)^{m-1} = e^{-\frac{1}{m+1}}.$$

Finally, we obtain

$$\text{vol}(E') = \det(S)^{1/2} \cdot \text{vol}(E(0, I)) \le e^{-\frac{1}{2(m+1)}} \cdot \text{vol}(E(0, I)). \qquad \blacksquare$$

12.4.3 The General Case

We now prove Lemma 12.12 in full generality by reducing it to the symmetric case.

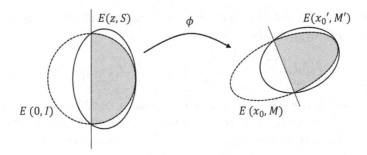

Figure 12.4 The nonsymmetric case follows by using an affine transformation ϕ to map the symmetric case to the general one. The unit ball $E(0, I)$ is mapped by ϕ to the ellipsoid $E(x_0, M)$ so that the shaded region $\{x \in E(0, I): x_1 \geq 0\}$ on the left-hand side is also mapped to the shaded region $\{x \in E(x_0, M): \langle x, h \rangle \leq \langle x_0, h \rangle\}$ on the right-hand side.

Proof of Lemma 12.12: First note that the ellipsoid $E' := E(z, S)$ defined for the symmetric case (Lemma 12.16) is given by

$$z = \frac{1}{m+1} e_1,$$

$$S = \frac{m^2}{m^2 - 1} \left(I - \frac{2}{m+1} e_1 e_1^\top \right).$$

Thus, indeed, this gives a proof of Lemma 12.12 in the case when $E(x_0, M)$ is the unit ball and $h = -e_1$.

The idea now is to find an affine transformation ϕ so that

(1) $E(x_0, M) = \phi(E(0, I))$,
(2) $\{x: \langle x, h \rangle \leq \langle x_0, h \rangle\} = \phi(\{x: x_1 \geq 0\})$.

We refer to Figure 12.4 for an illustration of this idea. We claim that when these conditions hold, the ellipsoid $E(x', M') := \phi(E')$ satisfies the conclusion of Lemma 12.12. Indeed, using Lemma 12.13 and Lemma 12.16, we have

$$\frac{\text{vol}(E(x', M'))}{\text{vol}(E(x_0, M))} = \frac{\text{vol}(\phi(E(x', M')))}{\text{vol}(\phi(E(x_0, M)))} = \frac{\text{vol}(E')}{\text{vol}(E(0, I))} \leq e^{-\frac{1}{2(m+1)}}.$$

Moreover, by applying ϕ to the inclusion

$$\{x \in E: x_1 \geq 0\} \subseteq E',$$

we obtain

$$\{x \in E(x_0, M): \langle x, h \rangle \leq \langle x_0, h \rangle\} \subseteq E(x', M').$$

It remains now to derive a formula for ϕ so that we can obtain an explicit expression for $E(x', M')$. We claim that the following affine transformation ϕ satisfies the above stated properties:

$$\phi(x) := x_0 + M^{1/2}Ux,$$

where U is any orthonormal matrix, i.e., $U \in \mathbb{R}^{m \times m}$ and satisfies $UU^\top = U^\top U = I$, such that $Ue_1 = v$ where

$$v = -\frac{M^{1/2}h}{\left\| M^{1/2}h \right\|_2}.$$

We have

$$\phi(E(0, I)) = E(x_0, M^{1/2}U^\top U M^{1/2}) = E(x_0, M).$$

This proves the first condition. Further,

$$\begin{aligned}
\phi(\{x: x_1 \geq 0\}) &= \{\phi(x): x_1 \geq 0\} \\
&= \{\phi(x): \langle -e_1, x \rangle \leq 0\} \\
&= \{y: \left\langle -e_1, \phi^{-1}(y) \right\rangle \leq 0\} \\
&= \{y: \left\langle -e_1, U^\top M^{-1/2}(y - x_0) \right\rangle \leq 0\} \\
&= \{y: \left\langle -M^{-1/2}Ue_1, y - x_0 \right\rangle \leq 0\} \\
&= \{y: \langle h, y - x_0 \rangle \leq 0\}.
\end{aligned}$$

Hence, the second condition follows.

It remains to derive a formula for $E(x', M')$. By Lemma 12.14, we obtain

$$E(x', M') = \phi(E(z, S)) = E(x_0 + M^{1/2}Uz, M^{1/2}USU^\top M^{1/2}).$$

Thus,

$$x' = x_0 + \frac{1}{m+1}M^{1/2}Ue_1 = x_0 - \frac{1}{m+1}\frac{Mh}{\left\| M^{1/2}h \right\|_2}.$$

and

$$M' = M^{1/2}U^{\top}\frac{m^2}{m^2-1}\left(I - \frac{2}{m+1}e_1e_1^{\top}\right)UM^{1/2}$$

$$= \frac{m^2}{m^2-1}\left(M - \frac{2}{m+1}\left(M^{1/2}Ue_1\right)\left(M^{1/2}Ue_1\right)^{\top}\right)$$

$$= \frac{m^2}{m^2-1}\left(M - \frac{2}{m+1}\frac{(Mh)(Mh)^{\top}}{h^{\top}Mh}\right).$$

By plugging in $g := \frac{h}{\|M^{1/2}h\|_2}$, the lemma follows.   ∎

12.4.4 Discussion on Bit Precision Issues

In all of the above discussion, we have assumed that the ellipsoids $E_0, E_1, \ldots$ can be computed exactly and no error is introduced at any step. In reality, this is not the case, as computing E_{t+1} from E_t involves taking a square root, an operation that cannot be performed exactly. Moreover, one needs to be careful about the bit complexities of the intermediate computations, as there is no simple reason why would they stay polynomially bounded over the course of the algorithm.

To address this issue one can use the following idea: Pick a polynomially bounded integer p and perform all calculations in the ellipsoid method using numbers with at most p bits of precision. In other words, we work with rational numbers with common denominators 2^p and round to such numbers whenever intermediate calculations yield more than p (binary) digits after the decimal point. Such a perturbation might have an undesired effect of slightly shifting (and reshaping) the ellipsoid E_{t+1} so that it is not guaranteed to contain P anymore. One can fix this by increasing it by a small factor such that

- it is guaranteed to contain $E_t \cap \{x : \langle x, h_t \rangle \le \langle x_t, h_t \rangle\}$ and
- the volume drop is still relatively large $\approx e^{-\frac{1}{5n}}$.

Further, one can reason that if $E_t = E(x_t, M_t)$, then the norm $\|x_t\|_2$ and the spectral norms $\|M_t\|$ and $\left\|M_t^{-1}\right\|$ grow by at most a factor of 2 in every iteration. This is enough to guarantee that the algorithm is still correct and converges in the same number of steps (up to a constant factor), assuming that p is large enough.

12.5 Application: Linear Optimization over 0-1-Polytopes

In this section, we are set to present a proof of Theorem 12.5 in the case when the polytope P is full-dimensional (at the end of this section, we discuss how to get rid of this assumption). For this, we use binary search to reduce the optimization problem to feasibility and then use the ellipsoid method to solve the feasibility question in every step. A sketch of the algorithm appears in Algorithm 12.

Note that in contrast to the scheme presented in Section 12.2.1, in Algorithm 12, the binary search runs over integers. We can do that since the cost function is integral and the optimum is guaranteed to be a vertex and, thus, the optimum value is also integral. Note that if $y^\star \in \mathbb{Z}$ is the optimal value then the polytope $P' = P \cap \{x \colon \langle c, x \rangle \leq y^\star\}$ is lower dimensional and, hence, has volume zero.

Algorithm 12: Linear optimization for 0-1-polytopes

Input:
- A separation oracle to a full-dimensional 0-1-polytope $P \subseteq [0,1]^m$
- A cost vector $c \in \mathbb{Z}^m$

Output: An optimal solution to $\min_{x \in P} \langle c, x \rangle$

Algorithm:

1: **Perturb** the cost function c to guarantee uniqueness of the optimal solution
2: Let $l := -\|c\|_1$ and $u := \|c\|_1 + 1$
3: **while** $u - l > 1$ **do**
4:    Set $g := \lfloor \frac{l+u}{2} \rfloor$
5:    Define $P' := P \cap \left\{ x \in \mathbb{R}^m \colon \langle c, x \rangle \leq g + \frac{1}{4} \right\}$
6:    **if** $P' \neq \emptyset$ (use ellipsoid method on P') **then**
7:       Set $u := g$
8:    **else**
9:       Set $l := g$
10:   **end if**
11: **end while**
12: Use the ellipsoid method to find a point

$$\hat{x} \in P \cap \left\{ x \in \mathbb{R}^m \colon \langle c, x \rangle \leq u + \frac{1}{4} \right\}$$

13: **Round** every coordinate of $\hat{x}$ to the nearest integer
14: **return** $\hat{x}$

For this reason, in Algorithm 12, we introduce a small slack and always ask for objective at most $g + \frac{1}{4}$ instead of at most g, for $g \in \mathbb{Z}$. This guarantees that P' is always full-dimensional and we can provide a lower bound on its volume (necessary for the ellipsoid method to run in polynomial time).

12.5.1 Guaranteeing Uniqueness of the Optimal Solution

We now describe the **Perturb** step of Algorithm 12, which ensures that there is only one optimal solution. This is done to be able to round a close to optimal solution to a vertex easily. To this end, one can simply define a new cost function $c' \in \mathbb{Z}^m$ such that

$$c'_i := 2^m c_i + 2^{i-1}.$$

The total contribution of the perturbation for any vertex solution is strictly less than 2^m and, hence, it does not create any new optimal vertex. Moreover, it is now easy to see that every vertex has a different cost and, thus, the optimal cost (and vertex) is unique.

Finally, note that by doing this perturbation, the bit complexity of c only grows by $O(m)$.

12.5.2 Lower Bounding the Volume of Polytopes

We now prove formally that the volume of the polytopes P' queried in the algorithm is never too small for the ellipsoid method to work in polynomial time.

Lemma 12.17 (Inner ball). *Suppose that $P \subseteq [0,1]^m$ is a full-dimensional 0-1-polytope and $c \in \mathbb{Z}^m$ is any cost vector and $C \in \mathbb{Z}$ is any integer. Consider the following polytope:*

$$P' := \left\{ x \in P : \langle c, x \rangle \leq C + \frac{1}{4} \right\}.$$

Then, either P' is empty or P' contains a Euclidean ball of radius at least $2^{-\mathrm{poly}(m, L)}$, where L is the bit complexity of c.

Proof: Assume without loss of generality that $0 \in P$ and that 0 is the unique optimal solution. It is then enough to consider $C = 0$, as for $C < 0$, the polytope P' is empty and, for $C \geq 1$, the optimal cost is larger than that for $C = 0$.

We start by noting that P contains a ball B of radius $2^{-\text{poly}(m)}$. To see this, we first pick $m+1$ affinely independent vertices of P and show that the simplex spanned by them contains a ball of such a radius.

Next, we show that by scaling this ball down, roughly by a factor of 2^L with respect to the origin, it is contained in

$$P' := \left\{ x \in P : \langle c, x \rangle \leq \frac{1}{4} \right\}.$$

To see this, note that for every point $x \in P$ we have

$$\langle c, x \rangle \leq \sum_i |c_i| \leq 2^L.$$

Thus, we have, for every $x \in P$,

$$\left\langle \frac{x}{2^{L+3}}, c \right\rangle \leq 2^{-3} = \frac{1}{8}.$$

In particular,

$$2^{-L-3} B \subseteq P',$$

but

$$\text{vol}\left(2^{-L-3} B \right) = 2^{-m(L+3)} \text{vol}(B) = 2^{-m(L+3) - \text{poly}(m)} = 2^{-\text{poly}(m, L)}. \quad\blacksquare$$

12.5.3 Rounding the Fractional Solution

Lemma 12.18 (Rounding the fractional solution). *Suppose that $P \subseteq [0, 1]^m$ is a full-dimensional 0-1-polytope and $c \in \mathbb{Z}^m$ is any cost vector such that there is a unique point $x^\star$ in P that minimizes $x \mapsto \langle c, x \rangle$ over $x \in P$. Then, if $x \in P$ satisfies*

$$\langle c, x \rangle \leq \langle c, x^\star \rangle + \frac{1}{3},$$

by rounding each coordinate of x to the nearest integer, we obtain $x^\star$.

Proof: Let us write x as

$$x := \alpha x^\star + (1 - \alpha) z,$$

where $\alpha \in [0, 1]$ and $z \in P$ is a convex combination of suboptimal vertices (not including $x^\star$). Then, we have

$$\langle c, x^\star \rangle + \frac{1}{3} \geq \langle c, x \rangle$$
$$= \langle c, \alpha x^\star + (1 - \alpha)z \rangle$$
$$= \alpha \langle c, x^\star \rangle + (1 - \alpha) \langle c, z \rangle$$
$$\geq \alpha \langle c, x^\star \rangle + (1 - \alpha)(\langle c, x^\star \rangle + 1)$$
$$\geq \langle c, x^\star \rangle + (1 - \alpha).$$

Here, we have used the fact that z is a suboptimal 0-1-vertex of cost strictly less than that of $x^\star$, hence, because c is integral, we get

$$\langle c, z \rangle \geq \langle c, x^\star \rangle + 1.$$

Thus,

$$1 - \alpha \leq \frac{1}{3}.$$

Hence, for every $i = 1, 2, \ldots, m$,

$$|x_i - x_i^\star| = (1 - \alpha)|x_i^\star - z_i| \leq 1 - \alpha \leq \frac{1}{3}.$$

Here, we use the fact that each $x_i^\star, z_i \in \{0, 1\}$, hence, their difference is bounded in absolute value by 1. It follows that rounding each coordinate of x to the nearest integer yields $x^\star$. ∎

12.5.4 The Proof

We are now ready to conclude the proof of Theorem 12.5.

Proof of Theorem 12.5: We show that Algorithm 12 is correct and runs in polynomial time. The correctness is a straightforward consequence of the definition of the algorithm. The only step that requires justification is why does the rounding produce the optimal solution $x^\star$. This follows from Lemma 12.18.

To bound the running time of the algorithm, observe that it performs

$$O(\log \|c\|_1) = O(L)$$

iterations and, in every iteration, it applies the ellipsoid method to check the (non)-emptiness of P'. Using Theorem 12.10, and the lower bound on the size of a ball that can be fit in P' provided in Lemma 12.17, we conclude that the running time of one such application is poly(m, L). ∎

12.5.5 The Full-Dimensionality Assumption

For the proof of Theorem 12.5, we have crucially used the fact that the polytope P is full-dimensional. Indeed, we used it to give a lower bound on the volume of P and its restrictions. When P is lower dimensional, no such bound holds and the analysis needs to be adjusted.

In principle, there are two ways to deal with this issue. The first is to assume that one is given an affine subspace $F = \{x \in \mathbb{R}^d : Ax = b\}$ such that the polytope P is full-dimensional when restricted to F. In such a case, one can simply apply the ellipsoid method restricted to F and obtain the same running time bound as in the full-dimensional case; we omit the details.

In the case when the description of a subspace in which P is full-dimensional is not available, the situation becomes much more complicated, but still manageable The idea is to apply the ellipsoid method to the low dimensional polytope P in order to first find the subspace F. To this end, after enough iterations of the ellipsoid method, the ellipsoid becomes flat and one can read off the directions along which this happens (the ones corresponding to tiny eigenvalues of the PD matrix generating the ellipsoid). Then, one can use the idea of simultaneous Diophantine approximations to round these vectors to a low bit complexity representation of the subspace F.

12.6 Exercises

12.1 Consider the undirected graph on three vertices $\{1, 2, 3\}$ with edges 12, 23, and 13. Prove that the following polytope does not capture the matching polytope of this graph.

$$x \geq 0, \quad x_1 + x_2 \leq 1, \quad x_2 + x_3 \leq 1, \quad x_1 + x_3 \leq 1.$$

12.2 Construct a polynomial time separation oracle for the perfect matching polytope using the following steps:

(a) Prove that separating over $P_{PM}(G)$ for a graph $G = (V, E)$ reduces to the following **odd minimum cut problem:** Given $x \in \mathbb{Q}^E$, find

$$\min_{S : |S| \text{ is odd}} \sum_{i \in S, j \in \bar{S}, ij \in E} x_{ij}.$$

(b) Prove that the odd minimum cut problem is polynomial time solvable.

12.3   Recall that for a polytope $P \subseteq \mathbb{R}^m$, the linear optimization problem
is: Given a cost vector $c \in \mathbb{Q}^n$, find a vertex $x^\star \in P$ minimizing $\langle c, x \rangle$
over $x \in P$.

Let $\mathcal{P}$ be a class of full-dimensional 0-1-polytopes for which the linear optimization problem is polynomial time solvable (i.e., polynomial
in m and the bit complexity of c). Prove that the separation problem for
the class $\mathcal{P}$ is also polynomial time solvable using the following steps:

(a) Prove that, if $P \in \mathcal{P}$, then the separation problem over P° (the
polar of P) is polynomial time solvable. In this problem it may be
convenient to define the polar of P with respect to a point x_0 that
is deep inside (i.e., its distance to the boundary of P is at least
$2^{-O(m^2)}$) P, i.e.,

$$P^\circ := \{y \in \mathbb{R}^n : \forall x \in P \, \langle y, x - x_0 \rangle \leq 1\}.$$

(b) Prove that a polynomial time linear optimization oracle for the
polar P° of P is enough to implement a polynomial time
separation oracle for P.

(c) Prove that every $P \in \mathcal{P}$ has a polynomial time linear optimization
oracle using the ellipsoid method. *Note:* One can assume that
polynomial time rounding to a vertex solution is possible, given a
method to find an ε-optimal solution in $\text{poly}(n, L(c), \log \frac{1}{\varepsilon})$ time.

12.4   Prove that there is a polynomial time algorithm (based on the ellipsoid
method) for linear programming in the explicit form, i.e., given a matrix
$A \in \mathbb{Q}^{m \times n}$, $b \in \mathbb{Q}^m$, and $c \in \mathbb{Q}^n$, find an optimal solution $x^\star \in \mathbb{Q}^n$ to
$\min_{x \in \mathbb{R}^n} \{\langle c, x \rangle : Ax \leq b\}$. The following hints may be helpful:

- Reduce the problem of finding an **optimal solution** to the problem
of finding a good enough approximation to the **optimal value.** For
this, think of dropping constraints $\langle a_i, x \rangle \leq b_i$ one by one and
solving the program again to see if this changes the optimal value.
In the end, only n constraints remain and allow us to determine the
optimal solution by solving one linear system.
- To deal with the problem of low dimensionality of the feasible
region, perturb the constraints by an exponentially small number
while making sure that this does not alter the optimal value by too
much.

12.5   Prove that the ellipsoid $E(x', M') \subseteq \mathbb{R}^m$ defined in Lemma 12.12
coincides with the minimum volume ellipsoid containing

$$E(x_0, M) \cap \{x \in \mathbb{R}^m : \langle x, h \rangle \leq \langle x_0, h \rangle\}.$$

12.6 In this problem, we derive a variant of the cutting plane method for solving the feasibility problem. In the feasibility problem, the goal is to find a point $\hat{x}$ in a convex set K. This algorithm (in contrast to the ellipsoid method) maintains a polytope as an approximation of K instead of an ellipsoid.

Description of the problem. The input to the problem is a convex set K such that

- $K \subseteq [0,1]^m$ (any bounded set K can be scaled down to satisfy this condition),
- K contains a Euclidean ball of radius r, for some parameter $r > 0$ (r is given as input), and
- a separation oracle for K is provided.

The goal is to find a point $\hat{x} \in K$.

Description of the algorithm. The algorithm maintains a sequence of polytopes $P_0, P_1, P_2, \ldots$, all containing K. The polytope P_t is defined by $2m + t$ constraints: $2m$ box constraints $0 \leq x_j \leq 1$ and t constraints of the form $\langle a_i, x \rangle \leq b_i$ (with $\|a_i\|_2 = 1$), added in the course of the algorithm. At every step t, the algorithm computes the analytic center x_t of the polytope P_t, i.e., the minimum of the logarithmic barrier $F_t(x)$ for the polytope P_t. More formally,

$$F_t(x) := -\sum_{j=1}^{m}(\log x_j + \log(1 - x_j)) - \sum_{i=1}^{t}\log(b_i - \langle a_i, x \rangle),$$

$$x_t := \underset{x \in P_t}{\operatorname{argmin}} F_t(x).$$

The algorithm is as follows.

- Let P_0 be $[0,1]^m$
- For $t = 0, 1, 2, \ldots$

  - Find x_t, the analytic center of P_t.
  - If $x_t \in K$ then return $\hat{x} := x_t$ and terminate.
  - Otherwise, use the separation oracle for K to cut the polytope by a hyperplane through x_t, i.e., add a new constraint of the form

$$\langle a_{t+1}, x \rangle \leq b_{t+1} := \langle a_{t+1}, x_t \rangle \qquad \text{with } \|a_{t+1}\|_2 = 1.$$

The new polytope is $P_{t+1} := P_t \cap \{x \in \mathbb{R}^n : \langle a_{t+1}, x \rangle \leq b_{t+1}\}$.

Upper bound on the potential. We analyze the above scheme, assuming that the analytic center x_t can be found efficiently. While we do not discuss the algorithmic task of computing x_t, we use its mathematical properties to give a bound on the number of iterations. We use the minimum value of the logarithmic barrier at iteration t as a potential, i.e.,

$$\phi_t := \min_{x \in P_t} F_t(x) = F_t(x_t).$$

We start by establishing an upper bound for this potential.

(a) Prove that at every step t of the algorithm (except possibly the last step)

$$\phi_t \leq (2m + t) \log \frac{1}{r}.$$

Lower bound on the potential. The next step is to show a lower bound on ϕ_t; intuitively, we would like to show that when t becomes large enough, then (on average) $\phi_{t+1} - \phi_t > 2 \log \frac{1}{r}$ and hence eventually ϕ_t becomes larger than the lower bound derived above – this gives us a bound on when does the algorithm terminate.

Let us denote by $H_t := \nabla^2 F_t(x_t)$ the Hessian of the logarithmic barrier at the analytic center.

(b) Prove that for every step t of the algorithm,

$$\phi_{t+1} \geq \phi_t - \frac{1}{2} \log(a_{t+1}^\top H_t^{-1} a_{t+1}), \tag{12.7}$$

and conclude that

$$\phi_t \geq \phi_0 - \frac{t}{2} \log \left(\frac{1}{t} \sum_{i=1}^{t} a_i^\top H_{i-1}^{-1} a_i \right).$$

The next step is to analyze (prove an upper bound on) the sum $\sum_{i=1}^{t} a_i^\top H_{i-1}^{-1} a_i$. Towards this, we establish the following sequence of steps.

(c) Prove that for every step t of the algorithm,

$$L_t := I + \frac{1}{m} \sum_{i=1}^{t} a_i a_i^\top \preceq H_t.$$

(d) Prove that, if $M \in \mathbb{R}^{m \times m}$ is an invertible matrix and $u, v \in \mathbb{R}^m$ are vectors, then

$$\det(M + uv^\top) = \det(M)(1 + v^\top M^{-1} u).$$

(e) Prove that for every step t of the algorithm,

$$\frac{1}{2m} \sum_{i=1}^{t} a_i^\top H_{i-1}^{-1} a_i \le \frac{1}{2m} \sum_{i=1}^{t} a_i^\top L_{i-1}^{-1} a_i \le \log \det(L_t).$$

(f) Prove that for every step t of the algorithm,

$$\log \det(L_t) \le m \log \left(1 + \frac{t}{m^2} \right).$$

From the above, it follows that

$$\phi_t \ge -\frac{t}{2} \log \left(\frac{2m^2}{t} \log \left(1 + \frac{t}{m^2} \right) \right),$$

and consequently, by combining it with the upper bound on ϕ_t, the algorithm does not make more than $t := \tilde{O}\left(\frac{m^2}{r^4}\right)$ steps until it finds a point $\hat{x} \in K$. We can thus deduce the following result.

Theorem 12.19. *There is an algorithm that, given access to a separation oracle for a set $K \subseteq [0,1]^m$ containing a ball of radius r, finds a point $\hat{x} \in K$ in $\tilde{O}\left(\frac{m^2}{r^4}\right)$ iterations where, in iteration t, the algorithm computes an analytic center of a polytope given by $O(m+t)$ constraints.*

Notes

We refer the reader to the book by Schrijver (2002a) for numerous examples of 0-1-polytopes related to various combinatorial objects. Theorem 12.2 was proved in a seminal paper by Edmonds (1965a). We note that a result similar to Theorem 12.2 also holds for the spanning tree polytope. However, while there are results showing that there is a way to encode the spanning tree polytope using polynomially many variables and inequalities, for the matching polytope, Rothvoss (2017) proved that any linear representation of $P_M(G)$ requires exponentially many constraints.

The ellipsoid method was first developed for linear programs by Khachiyan (1979, 1980), who built upon the ellipsoid method given by Shor (1972) and Yudin and Nemirovskii (1976). It was further generalized to the case of polytopes (when we only have access to a separation oracle for the polytope) by Grötschel et al. (1981), Padberg and Rao (1981), and Karp and Papadimitriou (1982). For details on how to deal with the bit precision issues mentioned in Section 12.4.4, see the book by Grötschel et al. (1988). For details on how to avoid the full-dimensionality assumption by "jumping" to a lower dimensional subspace, the reader is also referred to Grötschel et al. (1988). Exercise 12.6 is based on the paper by Vaidya (1989a).

13

Ellipsoid Method for Convex Optimization

We show how to adapt the ellipsoid method to solve general convex programs. As applications, we present a polynomial time algorithm for submodular function minimization and a polynomial time algorithm to compute maximum entropy distributions over combinatorial polytopes.

13.1 Convex Optimization Using the Ellipsoid Method?

The ellipsoid method for linear programming presented in Chapter 12 has several desirable features:

(1) it only requires a separation oracle to work,
(2) its running time depends poly-logarithmically on $\frac{u_0 - l_0}{\varepsilon}$ (where $\varepsilon > 0$ is the error and the optimal value lies between l_0 and u_0), and
(3) its running time depends poly-logarithmically on $\frac{R}{r}$, where $R > 0$ is the radius of the outer ball and r is the radius of the inner ball.

Property (1) shows that the ellipsoid method is applicable more generally than interior point methods, which in contrast require strong access to the convex set via a self-concordant barrier function. Properties (2) and (3) say that, at least asymptotically, the ellipsoid method outperforms first-order methods. However, so far we have only developed the ellipsoid method for linear programming, i.e., when K is a polytope and f is a linear function.

In this chapter, we extend the framework of the ellipsoid method to general convex sets and convex functions assuming an appropriate (oracle) access to f and a separation oracle for K. We also switch back from m to n to denote the ambient space of the optimization problem. More precisely, in Section 13.4 we prove the following theorem.

Theorem 13.1 (Ellipsoid method for convex optimization). *There is an algorithm that, given*

(1) *a first-order oracle for a convex function* $f : \mathbb{R}^n \to \mathbb{R}$,
(2) *a separation oracle for a convex set* $K \subseteq \mathbb{R}^n$,
(3) *numbers* $r > 0$ *and* $R > 0$ *such that* $K \subseteq B(0, R)$ *and* K *contains a Euclidean ball of radius* r,
(4) *bounds* l_0 *and* u_0 *such that for all* $x \in K$, $l_0 \leq f(x) \leq u_0$, *and*
(5) *an* $\varepsilon > 0$,

outputs a point $\hat{x} \in K$ *such that*

$$f(\hat{x}) \leq f(x^\star) + \varepsilon,$$

where $x^\star$ *is any minimizer of* f *over* K. *The running time of the algorithm is*

$$O\left(\left(n^2 + T_K + T_f\right) \cdot n^2 \cdot \log\left(\frac{R}{r} \cdot \frac{u_0 - l_0}{\varepsilon}\right)^2\right).$$

Here, T_K *and* T_f *are the running times for the separation oracle for* K *and the first-order oracle for* f, *respectively.*

A detailed discussion of the assumptions of Theorem 13.1 is provided in Section 13.4. Here, we mention a few things. A first-order oracle for a function f is understood to be a primitive that, given x, outputs the value $f(x)$ and any subgradient $h(x) \in \partial f(x)$. Thus, this theorem requires no smoothness or differentiability assumptions beyond convexity. In some applications, it is useful to get a **multiplicative** approximation (instead of an additive approximation): Given a $\delta > 0$, find a point $\hat{x}$ such that

$$f(\hat{x}) \leq f(x^\star)(1 + \delta).$$

It can be seen that Theorem 13.1 applies to this setting by letting $\varepsilon := \delta l_0$. If $\hat{x}$ is such that

$$f(\hat{x}) \leq f(x^\star) + \varepsilon,$$

then

$$f(\hat{x}) \leq f(x^\star) + \varepsilon \leq f(x^\star) + \delta l_0 \leq f(x^\star)(1 + \delta).$$

The running time remains polynomial in all parameters, including $\log \frac{1}{\delta}$.

13.1.1 Is Convex Optimization in P?

Given the algorithm in Theorem 13.1, we revisit the question of polynomial time solvability of general convex programs that have been mentioned (and answered negatively in Exercise 4.10) Chapter 4. Indeed, even though the result proved in this chapter seem to imply that convex optimization is in **P**, it does not follow, as it relies on a few subtle, yet important assumptions. To construct a polynomial time algorithm for a specific convex program one has to first find suitable bounds R and r on the magnitude of the optimal solution and bounds u_0 and l_0 on the magnitude of the optimal value. For the ellipsoid method, such a bound has to be provided as input to even run the algorithm (see Section 13.4). Moreover, the algorithm requires a separation oracle for K and an oracle to compute gradients of f – both these computational tasks might turn out to be provably computationally intractable (**NP**-hard) in certain cases.

We provide two important and interesting examples of convex optimization: **submodular function minimization** and **computing maximum entropy distributions**. Both these problems can, in the end, be reduced to optimizing convex functions over convex domains. However, the problem of computing subgradients for the submodular function minimization problem turns out to be nontrivial. And, for the problem of computing maximum entropy distributions, both – giving an estimate on the location of the optimizer and the computability of the gradient – turn out to be nontrivial. Thus, even if a problem can be formulated as a convex program, significant additional work may be required to conclude polynomial time computability, even in the light of Theorem 13.1.

13.2 Application: Submodular Function Minimization

In some of the earlier chapters, we have already encountered submodular functions and the problem of submodular function minimization, although it has never been mentioned explicitly. Below, we show how it arises rather naturally when trying to construct separation oracles for combinatorial polytopes.

13.2.1 Separation Oracles for 0-1-Polytopes

In Chapter 12, we proved that one can efficiently optimize linear functions over 0-1-polytopes,

$$P_{\mathcal{F}} := \text{conv}\{1_S : S \in \mathcal{F}\} \subseteq [0, 1]^n,$$

where $\mathcal{F} \subseteq 2^{[n]}$ is a family of subsets of $[n]$, whenever one can provide an efficient separation oracle for $P_{\mathcal{F}}$. Below we show how to construct separation oracles for a large family of polytopes called **matroid polytopes.**

Matroids and rank function. For a family $\mathcal{F}$, we start by defining a **rank function** $r_{\mathcal{F}} \colon 2^{[n]} \to \mathbb{N}$ as

$$r_{\mathcal{F}}(S) := \max\{|T| \colon T \in \mathcal{F}, T \subseteq S\},$$

i.e., the maximum cardinality of a set in $T \in \mathcal{F}$ contained in S. Note that $r_{\mathcal{F}}(S)$ may not be well defined in general. However, for **downward closed** families, i.e., families $\mathcal{F}$ such that for every $S \subseteq T \subseteq [n]$, if $T \in \mathcal{F}$ then $S \in \mathcal{F}$. Of special interest in this section are set families that are **matroids.**

Definition 13.2 (**Matroid**). A nonempty family of subsets $\mathcal{F}$ of a ground set $[n]$ is called a matroid if it satisfies the following conditions:

(1) (**Downward closure**) $\mathcal{F}$ is downward closed, and
(2) (**Exchange property**) if A and B are in $\mathcal{F}$ and $|B| > |A|$, then there exists $x \in B \setminus A$ such that $A \cup \{x\} \in \mathcal{F}$.

The motivation to define matroids comes from an attempt to generalize the notion of independence from the world of vectors in linear algebra. Recall that a set of vectors $\{v_1, \ldots, v_k\}$ in $\mathbb{R}^n$ is said to be linearly independent over $\mathbb{R}$ if no nontrivial linear combination of these vectors with coefficients from $\mathbb{R}$ is 0. Linear independence is a downward closed property, as removing a vector from a set of vectors that are linearly independent maintains the linear independence property. Moreover, if A and B are two sets of linearly independent vectors with $|A| < |B|$, then there is some vector in B that is linearly independent from all vectors in A and, hence, can be added to A while maintaining the linear independence property.

Other simple examples of matroids are the **uniform matroid,** i.e., the set of all subsets of $[n]$ of cardinality at most k for an integer k, and the **graphic matroid** (i.e., for an undirected graph G, the set of all acyclic subsets of edges of G.

The simplest computational question associated to a matroid is the **membership problem:** Given S, efficiently decide whether $S \in \mathcal{F}$ or not. This is usually a corollary of the description of the matroid at hand and we assume this problem can be solved efficiently. E.g., checking whether a set of vectors is linearly independent, or a set is of size at most k, or a subset of edges in a graph contains a cycle or not are all computationally easy. Using this, and the definition of a matroid, it is not too difficult to find an efficient greedy algorithm for the following problem: Given $S \subseteq [n]$, find the maximum cardinality $T \in \mathcal{F}$ such that $T \subseteq S$. As a consequence, one has the following theorem that states that one can evaluate the rank function of a matroid.

Theorem 13.3 (Evaluating the rank function of a matroid). *For a matroid $\mathcal{F}$ on a ground set $[n]$ that has a membership oracle, given an $S \subseteq [n]$, one can evaluate $r_\mathcal{F}(S)$ with a polynomial (in n) number of queries to the membership oracle.*

Polyhedral description of matroid polytopes. The following theorem provides a convenient description of the polytope $P_\mathcal{F}$ when $\mathcal{F}$ is a matroid.

Theorem 13.4 (Matroid polytopes). *Suppose that $\mathcal{F} \subseteq 2^{[n]}$ is a matroid, then*

$$P_\mathcal{F} = \left\{ x \geq 0 \colon \forall S \subseteq [n] \ \sum_{i \in S} x_i \leq r_\mathcal{F}(S) \right\}.$$

Note that the inclusion from left to right ($\subseteq$) is true for all families $\mathcal{F}$, the opposite direction relies on the matroid assumption, and is nontrivial.

For the matroid $\mathcal{F}$ consisting of all sets of size at most k, that rank function is particularly simple:

$$r_\mathcal{F}(S) = \min\{|S|, k\}.$$

Hence, the corresponding matroid polytope is

$$P_\mathcal{F} = \left\{ x \geq 0 \colon \forall S \subseteq [n] \ \sum_{i \in S} x_i \leq \min\{|S|, k\} \right\}.$$

Note that, as the rank of a singleton set can be at most 1, the right-hand side has constraints of the form $0 \leq x_i \leq 1$ for all $1 \leq i \leq n$. Hence, they trivially imply the rank constraint for any set S whose cardinality is at most k. Moreover, there is a constraint,

$$\sum_{i=1}^{n} x_i \leq k.$$

This constraint, along with the fact that $x_i \geq 0$ for all i, implies the constraint

$$\sum_{i \in T} x_i \leq k$$

for any T such that $|T| \geq k$. Thus, the corresponding matroid polytope is just

$$P_{\mathcal{F}} = \left\{ x \in [0, 1]^n : \sum_{i \in [n]} x_i \leq k \right\},$$

and the separation problem is trivial.

However, in general, including the case of all acyclic subgraphs of a graph, the number of constraints defining the polytope can be exponential (in the size of the graph) and separation is a nontrivial problem.

Separating over matroid polytopes. Theorem 13.4 suggests the following strategy for separation over matroid polytopes. Given $x \in [0, 1]^n$, denote

$$F_x(S) := r_{\mathcal{F}}(S) - \sum_{i \in S} x_i$$

and find

$$S^\star := \operatorname*{argmin}_{S \subseteq [n]} F_x(S).$$

Indeed,

$$x \in P_{\mathcal{F}} \quad \text{if and only if} \quad F_x(S^\star) \geq 0.$$

Furthermore, if $F_x(S^\star) < 0$ then $S^\star$ provides us with a separating hyperplane:

$$\langle y, 1_{S^\star} \rangle \leq r_{\mathcal{F}}(S^\star).$$

This is because

$$F_x(S^\star) < 0 \quad \text{implies that} \quad \langle x, 1_{S^\star} \rangle > r_{\mathcal{F}}(S^\star),$$

but Theorem 13.4 implies that the inequality is satisfied by all points in $P_{\mathcal{F}}$. Thus, in order to solve the separation problem, it is sufficient to solve the minimization problem for F_x. The crucial observation is that F_x is not an arbitrary function – it is submodular, and submodular functions have a lot of combinatorial structure that can be leveraged.

Definition 13.5 (Submodular function). A function $F : 2^{[n]} \to \mathbb{R}$ is called submodular if

$$\forall S, T \subseteq [n], \quad F(S \cap T) + F(S \cup T) \leq F(S) + F(T).$$

As alluded to before, the matroid rank function $r_{\mathcal{F}}$ is submodular; see Exercise 13.4(a).

Theorem 13.6 (The matroid rank function is submodular). *Suppose that* $\mathcal{F} \subseteq 2^{[n]}$ *is a matroid, then the rank function* $r_{\mathcal{F}}$ *is submodular.*

Given the discussion above, we consider the following general problem.

Definition 13.7 (Submodular function minimization (SFM)). Given a submodular function $F : 2^{[n]} \to \mathbb{R}$, find a set $S^{\star}$ such that

$$S^{\star} = \underset{S \subseteq [n]}{\mathrm{argmin}}\, F(S).$$

We have not specified how the function F is given. Depending on the application, it can either be succinctly described using a graph (or some other combinatorial structure), or given as an oracle that, given $S \subseteq [n]$, outputs $F(S)$. Remarkably, this is all we need to develop algorithms for SFM.

Theorem 13.8 (Polynomial time algorithm for SFM). *There is an algorithm that, given an oracle access to a submodular function* $F : 2^{[n]} \to [l_0, u_0]$ *for some integers* $l_0 \le u_0$ *and an* $\varepsilon > 0$, *finds a set* $S \subseteq [n]$ *such that*

$$F(S) \le F(S^{\star}) + \varepsilon,$$

where $S^{\star}$ *is a minimizer of* F. *The algorithm makes* poly $\left(n, \log \frac{u_0 - l_0}{\varepsilon}\right)$ *queries to the oracle.*

Note that, for the application of constructing separation oracles for matroid polytopes, a polynomial running time with respect to $\log \frac{u_0 - l_0}{\varepsilon}$ is necessary. Recall that, in the separation problem, the input also consists of an $x \in [0, 1]^n$ and we considered the function

$$F_x(S) := r_{\mathcal{F}}(S) - \sum_{i \in S} x_i.$$

Given a membership oracle for a matroid, Theorem 13.3 implies an oracle to its rank function, which is submodular by Theorem 13.6. Note that the function F_x is specified by a point $x \in [0, 1]^n$. Even though its range $[l_0, u_0]$ is small, ε has to be of the order of the smallest x_i to recover an optimum ($S^{\star}$) and, hence, to give us a separating hyperplane when the given point is outside the polytope. Thus, logarithmic dependence on the error in Theorem 13.8 implies a polynomial dependence on the bit complexity of x for this separation scheme to yield a polynomial time algorithm.[1]

---

[1] We note that there are alternative combinatorial methods to separate over matroid polytopes using duality and the equivalence between linear optimization and separation; see Exercises 5.14 and 13.6.

Theorem 13.9 (Efficient separation over matroid polytopes). *There is an algorithm that, given a membership oracle to a matroid* $\mathcal{F} \subseteq 2^{[n]}$, *solves the separation problem over* $P_{\mathcal{F}}$ *for a point* $x \in [0, 1]^n$ *with polynomially many (in n and the bit complexity of x) queries to the membership oracle.*

A consequence of this theorem and Theorem 12.5 from Chapter 12 is that we can perform linear optimization over matroid polytopes in polynomial time.

Separating over matroid base polytopes. The maximum cardinality elements of a matroid are called **bases** and the corresponding polytope (convex hull of indicator vectors of bases) is called the **matroid base polytope**. Suppose r is the size of a base of a matroid (from the exchange property it follows that all bases have the same cardinality). The polyhedral description of a matroid base polytope follows from Theorem 13.4 by adding the following equality to $P_{\mathcal{F}}$:

$$\sum_{i=1}^{n} x_i = r. \tag{13.1}$$

Thus, if we have a separation oracle for the matroid polytope, it easily extends to a separation oracle for the matroid base polytope. Note that spanning trees are maximum cardinality elements in the graphic matroid and, hence, the theorem above also gives us a separation oracle for the spanning tree polytope.

13.2.2 Towards an Algorithm for SFM: Lovász Extension

The first idea in solving the (discrete) SFM problem is to turn it to a convex optimization problem. Towards this, we define the **Lovász extension** of $F : 2^{[n]} \to \mathbb{R}$.

Definition 13.10 (Lovász extension). Let $F : 2^{[n]} \to \mathbb{R}$ be a function. The Lovász extension of F is defined to be the function $f : [0, 1]^n \to \mathbb{R}$ such that

$$f(x) := \mathbb{E}\left[F(\{i : x_i > \lambda\})\right],$$

where the expectation is taken over a uniformly random choice of $\lambda \in [0, 1]$.

The Lovász extension has many interesting and important properties. First, observe that the Lovász extension of F is always a continuous function and agrees with F on integer vectors. It is, however, not smooth. Moreover, one can show that

$$\min_{x \in [0,1]^n} f(x) = \min_{S \subseteq [n]} F(S);$$

see Exercise 13.8. Further, the following theorem asserts that the Lovász extension of a submodular function is convex.

Theorem 13.11 (Convexity of the Lovász extension). *If a set function* $F : 2^{[n]} \to \mathbb{R}$ *is submodular then its Lovász extension* $f : [0,1]^n \to \mathbb{R}$ *is convex.*

Thus, we have reduced SFM to the following convex optimization problem:

$$\min_{x \in [0,1]^n} f(x), \tag{13.2}$$

where f is the Lovász extension of the submodular function F. Note that the constraint set is just the hypercube $[0,1]^n$.

13.2.3 Polynomial Time Algorithm for Minimizing Lovás Extension

In the setting of optimizing a convex function f over a hypercube, Theorem 13.1 can be simplified as follows.

Theorem 13.12 (Informal; see Theorem 13.1). *Let* $f : [0,1]^n \to \mathbb{R}$ *be a convex function and suppose the following conditions are satisfied:*

(1) *we are given access to a polynomial time oracle computing the value and the (sub)gradient of* f, *and*
(2) *the values of* f *over* $[0,1]^n$ *lie in the interval* $[l_0, u_0]$ *for some* $l_0 < u_0 \in R$.

Then, there is an algorithm that given $\varepsilon > 0$ *outputs an* ε-approximate solution to $\min_{x \in [0,1]^n} f(x)$ in time $\text{poly}(n, \log(u_0 - l_0), \log \varepsilon^{-1})$.

Given the above theorem, the only remaining step is to present an efficient oracle for computing the values and subgradients of the Lovász extension (which is piecewise linear). This is a consequence of the lemma below.

Lemma 13.13 (Efficient computability of the Lovász extension). *Let* $F : 2^{[n]} \to \mathbb{R}$ *be any function and* $f : [0,1]^n \to \mathbb{R}$ *be its Lovász extension. There is an algorithm that, given* $x \in [0,1]^n$, *computes* $f(x)$ *and a subgradient* $h(x) \in \partial f(x)$ *in time:*

$$O(n T_F + n^2),$$

where T_F *is the running time of the evaluation oracle for* F.

Proof: Without loss of generality, assume that the point $x \in [0, 1]^n$ on which we have to evaluate f satisfies

$$x_1 \leq x_2 \leq \cdots \leq x_n.$$

Then, the definition of f implies that $f(x)$ equals

$$x_1 F([n]) + (x_2 - x_1)F([n] \setminus \{1\})$$
$$+ \cdots + (x_n - x_{n-1})F([n] \setminus [n-1]) + (1 - x_n)F(\emptyset).$$

The above shows that f is piecewise linear and also gives a formula to compute $f(x)$ given x (it requires just $n + 1$ evaluations of F). To compute the subgradient of f at x, one can assume without loss of generality that $x_1 < x_2 < \cdots < x_n$, as otherwise we can perform a small perturbation to reduce to this case. Now, on the set

$$S := \{x \in [0, 1]^n : x_1 < x_2 < \cdots < x_n\},$$

the function $f(x)$ (as demonstrated above) is just a linear function, hence, its gradient can be evaluated efficiently.   ∎

We are now ready to establish a proof of Theorem 13.8.

Proof of Theorem 13.8: As seen in the discussion so far, minimizing a submodular function $F: 2^{[n]} \to \mathbb{R}$ reduces to minimizing its Lovász extension $f: [0, 1]^n \to \mathbb{R}$. Moreover, Theorem 13.11 asserts that f is a convex function. Therefore, one can compute an ε-approximate solution $\min_{x \in [0,1]^n} f(x)$ given just an oracle that provides values and subgradients of f (this follows from Theorem 13.12). If the range of F is contained in $[l, u]$, then so is the range of f. Hence, the running time bound in Theorem 13.8 follows.

Finally, we show how to round an ε-approximate solution $\hat{x} \in [0, 1]^n$ to a set $S \subseteq 2^{[n]}$. From the definition of the Lovász extension, it follows that

$$f(\hat{x}) = \sum_{i=0}^{n} \lambda_i F(S_i)$$

for some sets

$$S_0 \subseteq S_1 \subseteq \cdots \subseteq S_n,$$

and $\lambda \in \Delta_{n+1}$ (the probability simplex in dimension $n + 1$). Thus, for at least one i, it holds that

$$f(S_i) \leq f(\hat{x}),$$

and we can output this S_i, as it satisfies

$$F(S_i) = f(S_i) \leq f(\hat{x}) \leq f(x^\star) + \varepsilon = F^\star + \varepsilon. \qquad \blacksquare$$

13.3 Application: The Maximum Entropy Problem

In this section, we consider the following problem.

Definition 13.14 (Maximum entropy problem). Given a discrete domain Ω, a collection of vectors $\{v_\omega\}_{\omega \in \Omega} \subseteq \mathbb{Q}^n$, and $\theta \in \mathbb{Q}^n$, find a distribution $p^\star$ over Ω that is a solution to the following optimization problem:

$$\max \sum_{\omega \in \Omega} p_\omega \log \frac{1}{p_\omega}$$

$$\text{such that } \sum_{\omega \in \Omega} p_\omega v_\omega = \theta, \qquad (13.3)$$

$$p \in \Delta_\Omega.$$

Here, Δ_Ω denotes the probability simplex, i.e., the set of all probability distributions over Ω.

Note that the entropy function is concave (nonlinear), and Δ_ω is convex, hence, this is a convex optimization problem. However, solving this problem requires specifying how the vectors are given as input.

If the domain Ω is of size N and the vectors v_ω are given to us explicitly, then one can find an ε-approximate solution to Equation (13.3) in time polynomial in N, $\log \varepsilon^{-1}$, and the bit complexity of the input vectors and θ. This can be done for instance using the interior point method,[2] or the ellipsoid method from this chapter.

However, when the domain Ω is large and the vectors are implicitly specified, this problem becomes computationally nontrivial. To take an instructive example, let Ω be the set of all spanning trees T of an undirected graph $G = (V, E)$, and let $v_T := 1_T$ be the indicator vector of the spanning tree T. Thus, all vectors v_T are implicitly specified by the graph $G = (V, E)$. The input to the entropy maximization problem in the spanning tree case is, thus, a graph $G = (V, E)$ and a vector $\theta \in \mathbb{Q}^E$. In trying to apply the above approach to the case of spanning trees in a graph, one immediately realizes that N is

---

[2] For that, one needs to construct a self-concordant barrier function for the sublevel set of the entropy function.

exponential in the size of the graph and, thus, a polynomial in N algorithm is, in fact, exponential in the number of vertices (or edges) in G.

Further, even though an exponential domain (such as spanning trees in a graph) can be specified compactly (via a graph), the output of the problem is still of exponential size – a vector p of dimension $N = |\Omega|$. How can we output a vector of exponential length in polynomial time? We cannot. However, what is not ruled out is an algorithm that, given an element of the domain (say a tree T in G), outputs the probability associated to it in polynomial time (p_T). In the next sections we show that, surprisingly, this is possible and, using the ellipsoid method for convex optimization, we can obtain a polynomial time algorithm for the entropy maximization problem over the spanning tree polytope. What we present here is a sketch consisting of the key steps in the algorithm and the proof; several steps are left as exercises.

13.3.1 Dual of the Maximum Entropy Convex Program

To counter the problems related to solving the entropy maximization problem for exponentially large domains Ω we first use duality to transform this problem into one that has only n variables.

Definition 13.15 (Dual to the maximum entropy problem). Given a domain Ω, a collection of vectors $\{v_\omega\}_{\omega \in \Omega} \subseteq \mathbb{Q}^n$ and $\theta \in \mathbb{Q}^n$, find a vector $y^\star \in \mathbb{R}^n$, the optimal solution to the problem:

$$\min \quad \log\left(\sum_{\omega \in \Omega} e^{\langle y, v_\omega - \theta \rangle}\right) \tag{13.4}$$
$$\text{such that} \quad y \in \mathbb{R}^n.$$

It is an important exercise (Exercise 13.11) to prove that the problems in Equations (13.3) and (13.4) are dual to each other and that strong duality holds whenever θ is in the interior of the polytope corresponding to the convex hull of the vectors $\{v_\omega\}_{\omega \in \Omega}$.

Thus, assuming that strong duality holds, the dual problem (13.4) looks simpler to solve as it is an unconstrained optimization problem in a small number of variables: n. Then, first-order optimality conditions imply that optimal dual solution $y^\star$ leads to a compact representation of the optimal distribution $p^\star$.

Lemma 13.16 (Succinct representation of maximum entropy distribution). *Suppose that $y^\star \in \mathbb{R}^n$ is the optimal solution to the dual to entropy maximization problem (13.4). Then, assuming strong duality holds, the optimal solution $p^\star$ to the entropy maximization problem (13.3) can be recovered as*

$$\forall \omega \in \Omega, \qquad p_\omega^\star = \frac{e^{\langle y^\star, v_\omega \rangle}}{\sum_{\omega' \in \Omega} e^{\langle y^\star, v_{\omega'} \rangle}}. \tag{13.5}$$

Thus, in principle, it seems to be enough to compute $y^\star$ in order to obtain a succinct representation of the maximum entropy distribution $p^\star$.

However, as its objective involves summing up over all the vectors (in cases such as spanning trees in graphs) we need a way to compute this exponential-sized sum in polynomial time. Moreover, while the numerator can be easily evaluated given $y^\star$, the denominator in (13.5) also, essentially, requires an oracle to evaluate the objective function.

Further, we also need a good bound R on $\|y^\star\|_2$. The ellipsoid method depends poly-logarithmically on R, so an exponential in n bound on R might seem sufficient, we note that the dual objective function is exponential in y. Thus, to represent the numbers appearing in it using polynomial in n bits, we need a polynomial (in n) bound on R.

Both a polynomial time evaluation oracle and a polynomial bound on R are nontrivial to obtain and may not hold in general settings. We show, however, that for the case of spanning trees, this is possible.

13.3.2 Solving the Dual Problem Using Ellipsoid Method

Let us denote the objective of the dual program by

$$f(y) := \log \left(\sum_{\omega \in \Omega} e^{\langle y, v_\omega - \theta \rangle} \right).$$

We would like to find the minimum of $f(y)$. For this, we apply the general algorithm for convex optimization based on the ellipsoid method that we derive in Section 13.4. When translated to this setting, it has the following consequence.

Theorem 13.17 (Informal; see Theorem 13.1). *Suppose the following conditions are satisfied:*

(1) *we are given access to a polynomial time oracle computing the value and the gradient of f,*
(2) *$y^\star$ is guaranteed to lie in a ball $B(0, R)$ for some $R > 0$, and*
(3) *the values of f over $B(0, R)$ stay in the interval $[-M, M]$ for some $M > 0$.*

Then, there is an algorithm that given $\varepsilon > 0$ outputs $\hat{y}$ such that

$$f(\hat{y}) \le f(y^\star) + \varepsilon$$

in time $\text{poly}(n, \log R, \log M, \log \varepsilon^{-1})$ *(when an oracle query is treated as a unit operation).*

Note that we do not require the inner ball due to the following fact (Exercise 13.13):

$$\forall y, y' \in \mathbb{R}^n, \quad f(y) - f(y') \leq 2\sqrt{n} \|y - y'\|_2. \tag{13.6}$$

Thus, we can set $r := \Theta\left(\frac{\varepsilon}{\sqrt{n}}\right)$. In general, this does not imply a polynomial time algorithm for the maximum entropy problem as, for specific instantiations, we have to provide and account for an evaluation oracle, a value of R, and M. Nevertheless, we show how to use the above to obtain a polynomial time algorithm for the maximum entropy problem for the case of spanning trees.

13.3.3 Polynomial Time Algorithm for the Spanning-Tree Case

Theorem 13.18 (Solving the dual to the max entropy problem for spanning trees). *Given a graph $G = (V, E)$, numbers $\eta > 0$ and $\varepsilon > 0$, and a vector $\theta \in \mathbb{Q}^E$ such that $B(\theta, \eta) \subseteq P_{ST}(G)$, there is an algorithm to find an ε-approximate solution to*

$$\min_{y \in \mathbb{R}^E} \log \left(\sum_{T \in \mathcal{T}_G} e^{\langle y, 1_T - \theta \rangle} \right) \tag{13.7}$$

in time $\text{poly}(|V| + |E|, \eta^{-1}, \log \varepsilon^{-1})$, *where $\mathcal{T}_G$ is the set of all spanning trees in G.*

Note importantly that the above gives a polynomial time algorithm only if θ is sufficiently inside the polytope P_{ST} (or in other words, when it is far away from the boundary of P_{ST}). If the point θ comes close to the boundary (i.e., $\eta \approx 0$) then the bound deteriorates to infinity. This assumption is not necessary and we give a suggestion in notes on how to get rid of it. However the η-interiority assumption makes the proof simpler and easier to understand.

Proving a bound on R. We start by verifying that the second condition in Theorem 13.17 is satisfied by proving an appropriate upper bound on the magnitude of the optimal solution.

Lemma 13.19 (Bound on the norm of the optimal solution). *Suppose that $G = (V, E)$ is an undirected graph and $\theta \in \mathbb{R}^E$ satisfies $B(\theta, \eta) \subseteq P_{ST}(G)$, for some $\eta > 0$. Then y^*, the optimal solution to the dual to the max entropy problem (13.7), satisfies*

$$\|y^\star\|_2 \leq \frac{|E|}{\eta}.$$

Note that the bound deteriorates as $\eta \to 0$ and, thus, is not very useful when θ is close to the boundary.

Proof of Lemma 13.19: Denote by $m := |E|$ and let $\theta \in \mathbb{R}^m$ be such that $B(\theta, \eta) \subseteq P_{ST}(G)$. Suppose that $y^\star$ is the optimal solution to the dual program. If f denotes the dual objective, we know from strong duality that any upper bound on the optimal primal solution is an upper bound on $f(y^\star)$. Hence, since the maximum achievable entropy of a distribution over $\mathcal{T}_G$ is $\log |\mathcal{T}_G|$, we have

$$f(y^\star) \leq \log |\mathcal{T}_G| \leq \log 2^m = m. \tag{13.8}$$

Recall now that

$$f(y^\star) = \log \left(\sum_{T \in \mathcal{T}_G} e^{\langle y^\star, 1_T - \theta \rangle} \right).$$

Thus, from Equation (13.8) we obtain that for every $T \in \mathcal{T}_G$,

$$\langle y^\star, 1_T - \theta \rangle \leq m.$$

By taking an appropriate convex combination of the inequalities above, it follows that for every point $x \in P_{ST}(G)$, we have

$$\langle y^\star, x - \theta \rangle \leq m.$$

Hence, from the assumption that $B(\theta, \eta) \subseteq P_{ST}(G)$, we conclude that

$$\forall v \in D(0, \eta), \quad \langle y^\star, v \rangle \leq m.$$

In particular, by taking $v := \eta \frac{y^\star}{\|y^\star\|_2}$, we obtain that

$$\|y^\star\|_2 \leq \frac{m}{\eta}. \qquad \blacksquare$$

Efficient evaluation of f. We now verify the first condition in Theorem 13.17. To this end, we need to show that f can be evaluated efficiently.

Lemma 13.20 (Polynomial time evaluation oracle for f and its gradient). *Suppose that $G = (V, E)$ is an undirected graph and f is defined as*

$$f(y) := \log \left(\sum_{T \in \mathcal{T}_G} e^{\langle y, 1_T - \theta \rangle} \right).$$

Then, there is an algorithm that given y outputs the value $f(y)$ and the gradient $\nabla f(y)$ in time poly$(\|y\|_2, |E|)$.

The proof is left as Exercise 13.14. Note that the running time of the oracle is polynomial in $\|y\|$ and not in $\log \|y\|$, as one would perhaps desire. This is a consequence of the fact that even a single term in the sum $e^{\langle y, 1_T - \theta\rangle}$ might be as large as $e^{\|y\|}$ and, hence, it requires up to $\|y\|$ bits to represent.

Proof of Theorem 13.18: We are now ready to conclude a proof of Theorem 13.18 from Theorem 13.17 using the above lemmas.

Proof of Theorem 13.18: We need to verify the conditions: 1, 2, and 3 in Theorem 13.17.

Condition 2 is satisfied for $R = O(\frac{m}{\eta})$ by Lemma 13.19. Given a bound $\|y\|_2 \leq R$, we can now provide a lower and upper bound on $f(y)$ (to verify Condition 3). We have

$$
\begin{aligned}
f(y) &= \log\left(\sum_{T \in \mathcal{T}_G} e^{\langle y, 1_T - \theta\rangle}\right) \\
&\leq \log\left(\sum_{T \in \mathcal{T}_G} e^{\|y\|_2 \cdot \|1_T - \theta\|_2}\right) \\
&\leq \log |\mathcal{T}_G| + \|y\|_2 \cdot O(\sqrt{m}) \\
&\leq m + \frac{m^{3/2}}{\eta} \\
&= \text{poly}\left(m, \frac{1}{\eta}\right).
\end{aligned}
$$

Similarly, we can obtain a lower bound and, thus, for all y such that $\|y\|_2 \leq R$, we have that $-M \leq f(y) \leq M$ with $M = \text{poly}\left(m, \frac{1}{\eta}\right)$.

Condition 3 is also satisfied due to Lemma 13.20. However, it adds a poly(R) factor to the running time (since the evaluation oracle runs in time polynomial in $\|y\|$). Hence, the final bound on the running time (as given by Lemma 13.17) becomes

$$
\begin{aligned}
&\text{poly}(|V| + |E|, \log R, \log M, \log \varepsilon^{-1}) \cdot \text{poly}(R) \\
&= \text{poly}(|V| + |E|, \eta^{-1}, \log \varepsilon^{-1}).
\end{aligned}
$$ ∎

13.4 Convex Optimization Using the Ellipsoid Method

This section is devoted to deriving the algorithm, promised in Theorem 13.1, for solving convex programs

$$\min_{x \in K} f(x)$$

when we have a separation oracle for K and a first-order oracle for f. To this end, we start by generalizing the ellipsoid method from Chapter 12 to solve the feasibility problem for any convex set K (not only for polytopes) and, further, we show that this algorithm, combined with the standard binary search procedure, yields an efficient algorithm under mild conditions on f and K.

13.4.1 From Polytopes to Convex Sets

Note that the ellipsoid method for the feasibility problem for polytopes that we developed in Chapter 12 did not use the fact that P is a polytope, only that P is convex and that a separation oracle for P is available. Indeed Theorem 12.10 in Chapter 12 can be rewritten in this more general form to yield the following.

Theorem 13.21 (Solving the feasibility problem for convex sets). *There is an algorithm that, given a separation oracle for a convex set $K \subseteq \mathbb{R}^n$, a radius $R > 0$ such that $K \subseteq B(0, R)$, and a parameter $r > 0$, gives one of the following outputs:*

(1) *YES, along with a point $\hat{x} \in K$, proving that K is nonempty, or*
(2) *NO, in which case K is guaranteed to not contain a Euclidean ball of radius r.*

The running time of the algorithm is

$$O\left((n^2 + T_K) \cdot n^2 \cdot \log \frac{R}{r} \right),$$

where T_K is the running time of the separation oracle for K.

Note that the above is written in a slightly different form than Theorem 12.10 in Chapter 12. Indeed, there we assumed that K contains a ball of radius r and wanted to compute a point inside of K. Here, the algorithm proceeds until the volume of the current ellipsoid becomes smaller than the volume of a ball of radius r, and then outputs NO if the center of the current ellipsoid does not lie in K. This variant can be seen as an approximate nonemptiness check:

(1) If $K \neq \emptyset$ and vol(K) is "large enough" (determined by r) then the algorithm outputs YES,
(2) If $K = \emptyset$ then the algorithm outputs NO,
(3) If $K \neq \emptyset$, but vol(K) is small (determined by r), then the algorithm can answer either YES or NO.

The uncertainty introduced when K has a small volume is typically not a problem, as we can often mathematically force K to be either be empty or have a large volume when running the ellipsoid method.

13.4.2 Algorithm for Convex Optimization

We now build upon the ellipsoid method for checking nonemptiness of a convex set K to derive a the ellipsoid method for convex optimization. To find the minimum of a convex function $f : \mathbb{R}^n \to \mathbb{R}$ over K, the idea is to use the binary search method to find the optimal value. The subproblem solved at every step is then simply checking the nonemptiness of

$$K^g := K \cap \{x : f(x) \le g\}$$

for some value g. This can be done as long as a separation oracle for K^g is available. One also needs to be careful about the uncertainty introduced in the nonemptiness check, as it might potentially cause errors in the binary search procedure. For this, it is assumed that K contains a ball of radius r and, at every step of the binary search, the ellipsoid method is called with an appropriate choice of the inner ball parameter. Details are provided in Algorithm 13, where it is assumed that all values of f over K lie in the interval $[l_0, u_0]$.

At this point it is not clear that the algorithm presented in Algorithm 13 is correct. Indeed, we need to verify that the choice of r' guarantees that the binary search algorithm gives correct answers most of the time. Further, it is not even clear how one would implement such an algorithm, as so far we have not yet talked about how f is given. It turns out that access to values and gradients of f (zeroth- and first-order oracles of f) suffices in this setting. We call this first-order access to f as well and recall its definition.

Definition 13.22 (First-order oracle). A first-order oracle for a function $f : \mathbb{R}^n \to \mathbb{R}$ is a primitive that, given $x \in \mathbb{Q}^n$, outputs the value $f(x) \in \mathbb{Q}$ and a vector $h(x) \in \mathbb{Q}^n$ such that

$$\forall z \in \mathbb{R}^n, \quad f(z) \ge f(x) + \langle z - x, h(x) \rangle .$$

In particular, if f is differentiable then $h(x) = \nabla f(x)$, but more generally $h(x)$ can be just any subgradient of f at x. We remark that typically one cannot hope to get an exact first-order oracle but rather an approximate one and, for simplicity, we work with exact oracles. An extension to approximate oracles is possible but requires introducing the so-called weak separation oracles, which in turn creates new technical difficulties.

Algorithm 13: Ellipsoid method for convex optimization

Input:
- A separation oracle to a convex set $K \subseteq \mathbb{R}^n$
- A first-order oracle to a function $f : \mathbb{R}^n \to \mathbb{R}$
- An $R > 0$ with the promise that $K \subseteq B(0, R)$
- An $r > 0$ with the promise that a ball of radius r is in K
- Numbers l_0, u_0 with the promise that

$$l_0 \leq \min_{y \in K} f(y) \leq \max_{y \in K} f(y) \leq u_0$$

- A parameter $\varepsilon > 0$

Output: An $\hat{x} \in K$ such that $f(\hat{x}) \leq \min_{x \in K} f(x) + \varepsilon$

Algorithm:

1: Let $l := l_0$ and $u := u_0$
2: Let $r' := \frac{r \cdot \varepsilon}{2(u_0 - l_0)}$
3: **while** $u - l > \frac{\varepsilon}{2}$ **do**
4:    Set $g := \lfloor \frac{l+u}{2} \rfloor$
5:    Define

$$K^g := K \cap \{x : f(x) \leq g\}$$

6:    Run the ellipsoid method from Theorem 13.21 on K^g with R, r'
7:    **if** the ellipsoid method outputs YES **then**
8:       Set $u := g$
9:       Let $\hat{x} \in K^g$ be the point returned by the ellipsoid method
10:    **else**
11:       Set $l := g$
12:    **end if**
13: **end while**
14: **return** $\hat{x}$

13.4.3 Proof of Theorem 13.1

There are two main components to the proof of Theorem 13.1: The first is to show that, given a separation oracle for K and a first-order oracle for f, we can obtain a separation oracle for

$$K^g := K \cap \{x : f(x) \leq g\},$$

and the second component is to show that by using the ellipsoid method to test the nonemptiness of K^g with the parameter r' specified in the algorithm, we are guaranteed to obtain a correct answer up to the required precision. We discuss these two components in separate steps and subsequently conclude the result.

Constructing a separation oracle for K^g. In the lemma below, we show that a separation oracle for the sublevel set

$$S^g := \{x \in \mathbb{R}^n : f(x) \leq g\}$$

can be constructed using a first-order oracle for f.

Lemma 13.23 (Separation over sublevel sets using a first-order oracle).
Given a first-order oracle to a convex function $f : \mathbb{R}^n \to \mathbb{R}$, for any $g \in \mathbb{Q}$, there is a separation oracle for

$$S^g := \{x \in \mathbb{R}^n : f(x) \leq g\}.$$

The running time of this separation oracle is polynomial in the bit size of the input and the time taken by the first-order oracle.

Proof: The construction of the oracle is rather simple: Given $x \in \mathbb{R}^n$, we first use the first-order oracle to obtain $f(x)$. If $f(x) \leq g$, then the separation oracle outputs YES. Otherwise, let u be the subgradient of f at x (obtained using the first-order oracle of f). Then, using the subgradient property, we obtain

$$\forall z \in \mathbb{R}^n, \quad f(z) \geq f(x) + \langle z - x, u \rangle.$$

As $f(x) > g$, for every $z \in S^g$, we have

$$g + \langle z - x, u \rangle < f(x) + \langle z - x, u \rangle \leq f(z) \leq g.$$

In other words,

$$\langle z, u \rangle < \langle x, u \rangle.$$

Hence, u provides us with a separating hyperplane. The running time of such an oracle is clearly polynomial in the bit size of the input and the time taken by the first-order oracle. ∎

By noting that $K^g = K \cap S^g$ we simply obtain that a separation oracle for K^g can be constructed using the respective oracles for K and f.

Bounds on volume of sublevel sets. In this step, we give a lower bound on the smallest ball contained in K^g depending on how close g is to the minimum $f^\star$ of f on K. This is required to claim that the ellipsoid method correctly determines whether $K^g \neq \emptyset$ in various steps of the binary search.

Lemma 13.24 (Lower bound on volume of sublevel sets). *Let* $K \subseteq \mathbb{R}^n$ *be a convex set containing a Euclidean ball of radius* $r > 0$ *and* $f : K \to [f^\star, f_{max}]$ *be a convex function on* K *with*

$$f^\star := \min_{x \in K} f(x).$$

For any

$$g := f^\star + \delta$$

(for $\delta > 0$*), define*

$$K^g := \{x \in K : f(x) \le g\}.$$

Then, K^g *contains a Euclidean ball of radius*

$$r \cdot \frac{\delta}{f_{max} - f^\star}.$$

Proof: Let $x^\star \in K$ be any minimizer of f over K. We can assume without loss of generality that $x^\star = 0$, or $f(0) = f^\star$. Define

$$\eta := \frac{\delta}{f^\star - f_{max}}.$$

We claim that

$$\eta K \subseteq K^g, \tag{13.9}$$

where $\eta K := \{\eta x : x \in K\}$. Since the ball of radius r contained in K becomes a ball of radius ηr in ηK, the claim implies the lemma. Thus, we focus on proving Equation (13.9). For $x \in \eta K$, we would like to show that $f(x) \le g$. We have $\frac{x}{\eta} \in K$ and, hence, from convexity of f we have

$$\begin{aligned}
f(x) &\le (1 - \eta) f(0) + \eta f\left(\frac{x}{\eta}\right) \\
&\le (1 - \eta) f^\star + \eta f_{max} \\
&= f^\star + \eta(f_{max} - f^\star) \\
&= f^\star + \delta \\
&= g.
\end{aligned}$$

Hence, $x \in K^g$, and the claim follows.   ∎

Proof of Theorem 13.1. Given Lemmas 13.23 and 13.24, we are well equipped to prove Theorem 13.1.

Proof of Theorem 13.1: Let $f^\star = f(x^\star)$. First, observe that whenever

$$g \geq f^\star + \frac{\varepsilon}{2},$$

then K^g contains a Euclidean ball of radius

$$r' := \frac{r \cdot \varepsilon}{2(u_0 - l_0)}.$$

Hence, for such a g, the ellipsoid method terminates with YES and outputs a point $\hat{x} \in K^g$. This is a direct consequence of Lemma 13.24.

Let l and u be the values of these variables at the moment of termination of the algorithm. From the above reasoning, it follows that

$$u \leq f^\star + \varepsilon.$$

Indeed,

$$u \leq l + \frac{\varepsilon}{2},$$

and the ellipsoid method can answer NO only for

$$g \leq f^\star + \frac{\varepsilon}{2}.$$

Hence,

$$l \leq f^\star + \frac{\varepsilon}{2}.$$

Therefore, $u \leq f^\star + \varepsilon$ and the $\hat{x}$ output by the algorithm belongs to K^u. Hence,

$$f(\hat{x}) \leq f^\star + \varepsilon.$$

This proves correctness of the algorithm. It remains to analyze its running time. The ellipsoid method runs in $\log \frac{u_0 - l_0}{\varepsilon/2}$ time, and every such execution takes

$$O\left((n^2 + T_{K^g}) \cdot n^2 \cdot \log \frac{R}{r'} \right) = O\left((n^2 + T_K + T_f) \cdot n^2 \cdot \log \left(\frac{R}{r} \cdot \frac{u_0 - l_0}{\varepsilon} \right) \right)$$

time, where we used Lemma 13.23 to conclude that $T_{K^g} \leq T_K + T_f$.   ∎

Remark 13.25 (Avoiding binary search). By taking a closer look at the algorithm and the proof of Theorem 13.1, one can observe that one does not need to restart the ellipsoid method at every iteration of the binary search. Indeed, one can just reuse the ellipsoid obtained in the previous call. This leads to an algorithm with a slightly reduced running time:

$$O\left((n^2 + T_K + T_f) \cdot n^2 \cdot \log \left(\frac{R}{r} \cdot \frac{u_0 - l_0}{\varepsilon} \right) \right).$$

Note that there is no square in the logarithmic factor.

13.5 Variants of Cutting Plane Method

In this section, we present the high-level details of some variants of the cutting plane method that can be used in place of the ellipsoid method to improve results in this and the previous chapter. Recall that the cutting plane method is, roughly, used to solve the following problem: Given a separation oracle to a convex set $K \subseteq \mathbb{R}^n$ (along with a ball $B(0, R)$ containing it), either find a point $x \in K$ or determine that K does not contain a ball of radius $r > 0$, where r is also provided as input.

To solve this problem, a cutting plane method maintains a set $E_t \supseteq K$ and shrinks it in every step, so that

$$E_0 \supseteq E_1 \supseteq E_2 \supseteq \cdots \supseteq K.$$

As a measure of progress, one typically uses the volume of E_t and, thus, ideally one wants to decrease the volume of E_t at every step,

$$\text{vol}(E_{t+1}) < \alpha \text{vol}(E_t),$$

where $0 < \alpha < 1$ is the volume drop parameter. The ellipsoid method achieves $\alpha \approx 1 - \frac{1}{2n}$ and, hence, it requires roughly $O(n \log \alpha^{-1} \log \frac{R}{r}) = O(n^2 \log \frac{R}{r})$ iterations to terminate. It is known that this volume drop rate is tight when using ellipsoids, however, one can ask whether this can be improved to say a constant $\alpha < 1$ when using different kind of sets E_k to approximate the convex body K.

13.5.1 Maintaining a Polytope Instead of an Ellipsoid

Recall that in the cutting plane method, the set E_{t+1} is picked so as to satisfy

$$E_t \cap H \subseteq E_{t+1},$$

where

$$H := \{x \colon \langle x, h_t \rangle \leq \langle x_t, h_t \rangle\}$$

is the halfspace passing through the point $x_t \in E_t$ determined by the separating hyperplane output by the separation oracle for K. In the ellipsoid method E_{t+1} is chosen as the minimum volume ellipsoid containing $E_t \cap H$. One could perhaps argue that this choice of E_{t+1} is not efficient, as we already know that $K \subseteq E_t \cap H$, hence, $E_{t+1} := K \cap E_t$ would be much more reasonable. By following this strategy, starting with E_0 lying in a box $[-R, R]^n$ we produce a sequence of polytopes (instead of ellipsoids) containing K. The crucial question that arises is how to pick a point $x_t \in E_t$ so that no matter what halfspace H through x_t is output by the separation oracle, we can still guarantee that $E_{t+1} := E_k \cap H$ has a significantly smaller volume than E_t. Note that when we pick a point x_t close to the boundary of E_t, H might cut out only a small piece of E_t and, hence, $\mathrm{vol}(E_t) \approx \mathrm{vol}(E_{t+1})$, meaning that no progress is made in such a step. For this reason, it seems reasonable to pick a point x_k that is near the center of the polytope.

It is an exercise (Exercise 13.17) to prove that if x_t is chosen to be the **centroid**[3] of the polytope, then no matter what hyperplane H through x_t is chosen, it holds that

$$\mathrm{vol}(E_t \cap H) \leq \left(1 - \frac{1}{e}\right) \mathrm{vol}(E_t). \tag{13.10}$$

In other words, we obtain a method where $\alpha \approx 0.67$ is a constant. While this sounds promising, this method has a significant drawback: The centroid is not efficient to compute and, even for polytopes, there are no known fast algorithms to find the centroid. Given such a difficulty, there have been many attempts to define alternatives notions of a center of the polytope so as to make it easy to compute and to get a constant $\alpha < 1$. We now give brief overviews of two such approaches.

13.5.2 The Volumetric Center Method

The idea is to use the volumetric center of E_t as x_t. To define it, suppose that E_t is defined by the system of inequalities $\langle a_i, x \rangle \leq b_i$ for $i = 1, 2, \ldots, m$. Let $F : E_t \to \mathbb{R}$ be the logarithmic barrier

$$F(x) = -\sum_{i=1}^{m} \log\left(b_i - \langle a_i, x \rangle\right),$$

and similarly let $V : E_t \to \mathbb{R}$ be the volumetric barrier

$$V(x) = \frac{1}{2} \log \det \nabla^2 F(x)$$

introduced in Definition 11.16 in Chapter 11. Then, the volumetric center x_t of E_t is defined as

$$x_t := \underset{x \in E_t}{\mathrm{argmin}}\, V(x).$$

The intuition for using the volumetric center x_t as the queried point at step t is that x_t is the point around which the Dikin ellipsoid has the largest volume.

---

[3] The centroid $c \in \mathbb{R}^n$ of a measurable, bounded set $K \subseteq \mathbb{R}^n$ is defined to be $c := \int_K x\, d\lambda_n(x)$, i.e., the mean of the uniform distribution over K.

As the Dikin ellipsoid is a decent approximation of the polytope, then one should expect that a hyperplane through the center of this ellipsoid should divide the polytope into two roughly equal pieces and, hence, we should expect α to be small. What can be proved is that indeed, on average (over a large number of iterations),

$$\frac{\text{vol}(E_{t+1})}{\text{vol}(E_t)} \leq 1 - 10^{-6},$$

and, hence, α is indeed a constant (slightly) smaller than 1. Further, the volumetric center x_t of E_t does not have to be recomputed from scratch every single time. In fact, since E_{t+1} has only one constraint more than E_t, we can use Newton's method to compute x_{t+1} with x_t as the starting point. This recentering step can be implemented in $O(n^\omega)$, or matrix multiplication, time. In fact, to achieve this running time, the number of facets in E_t needs to be kept small throughout the iterations, hence occasionally the algorithm has to drop certain constraints (we omit the details).

To summarize, this method, based on the volumetric center, attains the optimal, constant rate of volume drop, hence, it requires roughly $O(n \log \frac{R}{r} \log \frac{1}{\varepsilon})$ iterations to terminate. However, the update time per iteration is $n^\omega \approx n^{2.373}$ is slower as compared to the update time for the ellipsoid method, which is $O(n^2)$ (as a rank one update to an $n \times n$ matrix). See also the method based on analytic center in Exercise 12.6.

13.5.3 The Hybrid Center Method

Given the cutting plane method in the previous section, one might wonder whether it is possible to achieve the optimal, constant volume drop rate and at the same time keep the running time per iteration as low as for the ellipsoid method $\approx n^2$. Lee, Sidford, and Wong showed that such an improvement is indeed possible. To obtain this improvement, consider the following barrier function over the polytope E_t:

$$G(x) := -\sum_{i=1}^{m} w_i \log s_i(x) + \frac{1}{2} \log \det(A^\top S_x^{-2} A + \lambda I) + \frac{\lambda}{2} \|x\|_2^2, \quad (13.11)$$

where $w_1, w_2, \ldots, w_m$ are positive weights and $\lambda > 0$ is a parameter. Similar to Vaidya's approach, the query point is determined as the minimum of the barrier $G(x)$, the **hybrid center**

$$x_t := \underset{x \in E_t}{\arg\min}\, G(x).$$

The use of regularized weighted logarithmic barriers (13.11) is inspired by the Lee-Sidford barrier function used to obtain an improved path-following interior point method mentioned in Section 11.5.2. It can be proved that maintaining x_t and the set of weights w_t such that x_t is the minimum of $G(x)$ over $x \in E_t$ is possible in time $O(n^2)$ per iteration on average. Moreover, such a choice of x_t guarantees a constant volume drop, on average with $\alpha \approx 1 - 10^{-27}$.

13.6 Exercises

13.1   Prove that any two bases of a matroid have the same cardinality.

13.2   Given disjoint sets $E_1, \ldots, E_s \subseteq [n]$ and nonnegative integers $k_1, \ldots, k_s$, consider the following family of sets

$$\mathcal{F} := \{S \subseteq [n] : |S \cap E_i| \leq k_i \text{ for all } i = 1, \ldots, s\}.$$

Prove that $\mathcal{F}$ is a matroid.

13.3   In this exercise, we give two alternate characterizations of a submodular function.

   (a) Prove that a function $F : 2^{[n]} \to \mathbb{R}$ is submodular if and only if for all $T \subseteq [n]$ and $x, y \in [n]$,

   $$F(T \cup \{x, y\}) - F(T \cup \{x\}) \leq F(T \cup \{y\}) - F(T).$$

   (b) Prove that a function $F : 2^{[n]} \to \mathbb{R}$ is submodular if and only if for all $T \subseteq S \subseteq [n]$ and $x \in [n]$,

   $$F(S \cup \{x\}) - F(S) \leq F(T \cup \{x\}) - F(T).$$

13.4   Suppose that $\mathcal{F} \subseteq 2^{[n]}$ is a matroid.

   (a) Prove that its rank function $r_{\mathcal{F}}$ is submodular.
   (b) Prove that the following greedy algorithm can be used to compute the rank $r_{\mathcal{F}}([n])$: Initialize $S := \emptyset$ and iterate over all elements $i \in [n]$, adding i to S whenever $S \cup \{i\} \in \mathcal{F}$. Output the cardinality of S at the end as the rank of $\mathcal{F}$.
   (c) Extend this greedy algorithm to compute $r_{\mathcal{F}}(T)$ for any set $T \subseteq [n]$.

13.5   Prove that for the graphic matroid $\mathcal{F}$ corresponding to a graph $G = (V, E)$, the rank function is

$$r_{\mathcal{F}}(S) = n - \kappa(V, S),$$

where $n := |V|$ and $\kappa(V, S)$ denotes the number of connected components of the graph with edge set S and vertex set V.

13.6 Given a membership oracle to a matroid $\mathcal{F} \subseteq 2^{[n]}$ and a cost vector $c \in \mathbb{Z}^n$, give a polynomial time algorithm to find a $T \in \mathcal{F}$ that maximizes $\sum_{i \in T} c_i$.

13.7 Prove that the following functions are submodular.

(a) Given a matrix $A \in \mathbb{R}^{m \times n}$, the rank function $r : 2^{[n]} \to \mathbb{R}$ defined as

$$r(S) := \text{rank}(A_S).$$

Here, for $S \subseteq [m]$ we denote by A_S the matrix A restricted to rows in the set S.

(b) Given a graph $G = (V, E)$, the cut function $f : 2^V \to \mathbb{R}$ defined as

$$f_c(S) := |\{ij \in E : i \in S, j \notin S\}|.$$

13.8 Prove that for any function $F : 2^{[n]} \to \mathbb{R}$ (not necessarily convex) and for its Lovász extension f, the following hold:

$$\min_{S \subseteq [n]} F(S) = \min_{x \in [0,1]^n} f(x) \quad \text{and} \quad \max_{S \subseteq [n]} F(S) = \max_{x \in [0,1]^n} f(x).$$

13.9 Prove Theorem 13.11.

13.10 For $F : 2^{[n]} \to \mathbb{R}$, define its convex closure $f^- : [0,1]^n \to \mathbb{R}$ to be

$$f^-(x) = \min \left\{ \sum_{S \subseteq [n]} \alpha_S f(S) : \sum_{S \subseteq [n]} 1_S \alpha_S = x, \sum_{S \subseteq [n]} \alpha_S = 1, \alpha \geq 0 \right\}.$$

(a) Prove that f^- is a convex function.
(b) Prove that if F is submodular, then f^- coincides with the Lovász extension of F.
(c) Prove that if f^- coincides with the Lovász extension of F, then F is submodular.

13.11 Prove that for any finite set Ω, and any probability distribution p on it,

$$\sum_{\omega \in \Omega} p_\omega \log \frac{1}{p_\omega} \leq \log |\Omega|.$$

13.12 For a finite set Ω, a collection of vectors $\{v_\omega\}_{\omega \in \Omega} \subseteq \mathbb{R}^n$, and a point $\theta \in \mathbb{R}^n$, prove that the convex program considered in (13.3) is the Lagrangian dual of that considered in (13.4). For the above, you may assume that the polytope $P := \text{conv}\{v_\omega : \omega \in \Omega\}$ is a full-dimensional subset of $\mathbb{R}^n$ and θ belongs to the interior of P. Prove that, under these assumptions, strong duality holds.

13.13 Prove the claim in Equation (13.6).

13.14 Let $G = (V, E)$ be an undirected graph and let Ω be a subset of 2^E. Consider the objective of the dual to max entropy program in (13.4):

$$f(y) := \log \sum_{S \in \Omega} e^{\langle y, 1_S - \theta \rangle}.$$

(a) Prove that, if $\Omega = \mathcal{T}_G$, the set of spanning trees of G, then $f(y)$ and its gradient $\nabla f(y)$ can be evaluated in time polynomial in $|E|$ and $\|y\|$. For this, first show that if $B \in \mathbb{R}^{V \times E}$ is the vertex-edge incidence matrix of G and $\{b_e\}_{e \in E} \in \mathbb{R}^V$ are its columns, then for any vector $x \in \mathbb{R}^E$, it holds that

$$\det\left(\frac{1}{n^2} 1 1^\top + \sum_{e \in E} x_e b_e b_e^\top\right) = \sum_{S \in \mathcal{T}_G} \prod_{e \in S} x_e,$$

where $1 \in \mathbb{R}^V$ is the all-ones vector. *Hint:* Apply the Cauchy-Binet formula.

(b) Prove that, given a polynomial time oracle to evaluate f, one can compute $|\Omega|$ in polynomial time.

13.15 Suppose that $p \in \mathbb{Z}[x_1, \ldots, x_n]$ is a multiaffine polynomial (the degree of any variable in p is at most 1) with nonnegative coefficients. Suppose that L is an upper bound on the coefficients of p. Prove that, given an evaluation oracle for p and a separation oracle for $K \subseteq \mathbb{R}^n$, one can compute a multiplicative $(1 + \varepsilon)$ approximation to

$$\max_{\theta \in K} \min_{x > 0} \frac{p(x)}{\prod_{i=1}^n x_i^{\theta_i}}$$

in time poly$(\log \varepsilon^{-1}, n, \log L)$. You may assume that every point $x \in K$ satisfies $B(x, \eta) \subseteq P$, where P is the convex hull of the support of p and your algorithm might depend polynomially on $\frac{1}{\eta}$. For a multiaffine polynomial, $p(x) = \sum_{S \subseteq [n]} c_S \prod_{i \in S} x_i$.[4]

13.16 In this problem, we derive an algorithm for the following problem: Given a matrix $A \in \mathbb{Z}_{>0}^{n \times n}$ with positive entries, find positive vectors $x, y \in \mathbb{R}_{>0}^n$ such that

$$XAY \quad \text{is a doubly stochastic matrix,}$$

---

[4] The support of p is the family of all sets S such that $c_S \neq 0$.

where $X = \text{Diag}(x)$, $Y = \text{Diag}(y)$ and a matrix W is called doubly stochastic if its entries are nonnegative and all its rows and columns sum up to 1. We denote the set of all $n \times n$ doubly stochastic matrices by Ω_n, i.e.,

$$\Omega_n := \left\{ W \in [0,1]^{n \times n} : \forall i \in [n] \sum_{j=1}^{n} W_{i,j} = 1, \forall j \in [n] \sum_{i=1}^{n} W_{i,j} = 1 \right\}.$$

Consider the following pair of optimization problems:

$$\max_{W \in \Omega_n} \sum_{1 \leq i,j \leq n} W_{i,j} \log \frac{A_{i,j}}{W_{i,j}}. \tag{13.12}$$

$$\min_{z \in \mathbb{R}^n} \sum_{i=1}^{n} \log \left(\sum_{j=1}^{n} e^{z_j} A_{i,j} \right) - \sum_{j=1}^{n} z_j. \tag{13.13}$$

(a) Prove that both problems in Equations (13.12) and (13.13) are convex programs.

(b) Prove that the problem in Equation (13.13) is the Lagrangian dual of that in Equation (13.12) and strong duality holds.

(c) Suppose that $z^\star$ is an optimal solution to (13.13). Prove that, if $y \in \mathbb{R}^n$ is such that $y_i := e^{z_i^\star}$ for all $i = 1, 2, \ldots, n$, then there exists $x > 0$ such that $X A Y \in \Omega_n$.

As an optimal solution to the convex program (13.13) gives us the required solution, we apply the ellipsoid method to solve it. We denote by $f(z)$ the objective of (13.13). For simplicity, assume that the entries of A are integral.

(d) Design an algorithm that given $z \in \mathbb{Q}^n$ computes an ε−approximation to the gradient $\nabla f(z)$ in time polynomial in the bit complexity of A, the bit complexity of z, $\log \varepsilon^{-1}$ and the norm $\|z\|_\infty$.

(e) Prove that $f(z)$ has an optimal solution $z^\star$ satisfying

$$\|z^\star\|_\infty \leq O(\ln(Mn)),$$

assuming that $A_{i,j} \in [1, M]$ for every $1 \leq i, j \leq n$ using the following steps:

(f) Prove that for any optimal solution $z^\star$ and any $i, j \in [n]$

$$\frac{1}{M} \leq e^{z_i^\star - z_j^\star} \leq M.$$

(g) Prove that for any $c \in \mathbb{R}$ and $z \in \mathbb{R}^n$,

$$f(z) = f(z + c \cdot 1_n),$$

where $1_n = (1, 1, \ldots, 1) \in \mathbb{R}^n$.

(h) Give a lower l and upper bound u on the value of $f(z)$ over $z \in B(0, R)$ for $R := O(\ln(Mn))$.

By applying the ellipsoid method we obtain the following theorem.

Theorem 13.26. *There is an algorithm that given an integer matrix $A \in \mathbb{Z}^{n \times n}$ with positive entries in the range $\{1, 2, \ldots, M\}$ and an $\varepsilon > 0$ returns a $\varepsilon-$approximate doubly stochastic scaling (x, y) of A in time polynomial in n, $\log M$ and $\log \varepsilon^{-1}$.*

13.17   Prove the claim in Equation (13.10).

Notes

For a thorough treatment on matroid theory, including a proof of Theorem 13.4, we refer the reader to the book by Schrijver (2002a). A proof of Theorem 13.4 based on the method of iterative rounding appears in the text by Lau et al. (2011). Theorems 13.1 and 13.8 were first proved in the paper by Grötschel et al. (1981). The Lovász extension and its properties (such as convexity) were established by Lovász (1983).

The maximum entropy principle has its origins in the works of Gibbs (1902) and Jaynes (1957a,b). It is used to learn probability distributions from data; see the work by Dudik (2007) and Celis et al. (2020). Theorem 13.18 is a special case of a theorem proved in Singh and Vishnoi (2014). Using a different argument one can obtain a variant of Lemma 13.19 that avoids the interiority assumption; see the paper by Straszak and Vishnoi (2019). Maximum entropy-based algorithms have also been used to design very general approximate counting algorithms for discrete problems in the papers by Anari and Oveis Gharan (2017) and Straszak and Vishnoi (2017). Recently, the maximum entropy framework has been generalized to continuous manifolds; see the paper by Leake and Vishnoi (2020).

The proof of Theorem 13.1 can be adapted to work with approximate oracles; we refer to Grötschel et al. (1988) for a thorough discussion on weak oracles and optimization with them.

The volumetric center-based method is due to Vaidya (1989b). The hybrid barrier presented in Section 13.5.3 is from the paper by Lee et al. (2015). Using their cutting plane method, which is based on this barrier function, Lee et al. (2015) derive a host of new algorithms for combinatorial problems. In particular, they give the asymptotically fastest-known algorithms for submodular function minimization and matroid intersection.

Exercise 13.15 is adapted from the paper by Straszak and Vishnoi (2019). The objective function in Exercise 13.15 can be shown to be geodesically convex; see the survey by Vishnoi (2018) for a discussion on geodesic convexity and related problems.

Bibliography

Allen Zhu, Zeyuan, and Orecchia, Lorenzo. 2017. Linear coupling: an ultimate unification of gradient and mirror descent. Pages 3:1–3:22 of: *8th Innovations in Theoretical Computer Science Conference, ITCS 2017, January 9–11, Berkeley, CA*. LIPIcs, vol. 67.

Anari, Nima, and Oveis Gharan, Shayan. 2017. A generalization of permanent inequalities and applications in counting and optimization. Pages 384–396 of: *Proceedings of the 49th Annual ACM SIGACT Symposium on Theory of Computing*, STOC 2017 June 19–23, Montreal, Quebec.

Apostol, Tom M. 1967a. *Calculus: One-Variable Calculus, with an Introduction to Linear Algebra*. Blaisdell Book in Pure and Applied Mathematics. London: Blaisdell.

Apostol, Tom M. 1967b. *Calculus, Vol. 2: Multi-variable Calculus and Linear Algebra with Applications to Differential Equations and Probability*. New York: Wiley.

Arora, Sanjeev, and Barak, Boaz. 2009. *Computational Complexity: A Modern Approach*. New York: Cambridge University Press.

Arora, Sanjeev, Hazan, Elad, and Kale, Satyen. 2005. Fast algorithms for approximate semidefinite programming using the multiplicative weights update method. Pages 339–348 of: *Proceedings of the 46th Annual IEEE Symposium on Foundations of Computer Science*, FOCS '05, October 23–25, Pittsburgh, PA.

Arora, Sanjeev, Hazan, Elad, and Kale, Satyen. 2012. The multiplicative weights update method: a meta-algorithm and applications. *Theory of Computing*, **8**(6), 121–164.

Arora, Sanjeev, and Kale, Satyen. 2016. A combinatorial, primal-dual approach to semidefinite programs. *Journal of the Association for Computing Machinery*, **63**(2).

Barak, Boaz, Hardt, Moritz, and Kale, Satyen. 2009. The uniform hardcore lemma via approximate Bregman projections. Pages 1193–1200 of: *Proceedings of the Twentieth Annual ACM-SIAM Symposium on Discrete Algorithms, SODA 2009, January 4–6* New York, NY.

Barvinok, Alexander. 2002. *A Course in Convexity*. Providence, RI: American Mathematical Society.

Beck, Amir, and Teboulle, Marc. 2003. Mirror descent and nonlinear projected subgradient methods for convex optimization. *Operations Research Letters*, **31**(3), 167–175.

Beck, Amir, and Teboulle, Marc. 2009. A fast iterative shrinkage-thresholding algorithm for linear inverse problems. *SIAM Journal on Imaging Sciences*, **2**(1), 183–202.

Bonifaci, Vincenzo, Mehlhorn, Kurt, and Varma, Girish. 2012. Physarum can compute shortest paths. Pages 233–240 of: *Proceedings of the Twenty-Third Annual ACM-SIAM Symposium on Discrete Algorithms, SODA 2012, January 17–19*, Kyoto, Japan.

Boyd, Stephen, and Vandenberghe, Lieven. 2004. *Convex Optimization*. Cambridge: Cambridge University Press.

Bubeck, Sébastien. 2015. Convex optimization: algorithms and complexity. *Foundations and Trends in Machine Learning*, **8**(3–4), 231–357.

Bubeck, Sébastien, and Eldan, Ronen. 2015. The entropic barrier: a simple and optimal universal self-concordant barrier. Page 279 of: *Proceedings of the 28th Conference on Learning Theory, COLT 2015, July 3–6*, Paris, France.

Bürgisser, Peter, Franks, Cole, Garg, Ankit, de Oliveira, Rafael Mendes, Walter, Michael, and Wigderson, Avi. 2019. Towards a theory of non-commutative optimization: geodesic 1st and 2nd order methods for moment maps and polytopes. Pages 845–861 of: Zuckerman, David (ed.), *60th IEEE Annual Symposium on Foundations of Computer Science, FOCS 2019, November 9–12*, Baltimore, MD.

Celis, L. Elisa, Keswani, Vijay, and Vishnoi, Nisheeth K. 2020. Data preprocessing to mitigate bias: a maximum entropy based approach. In: *Proceedings of the 37th International Conference on Machine Learning*, ICML 2020, July 13–18, 2020, Virtual Event. *Proceedings of Machine Learning Research* **119**. PMLR 2020.

Chastain, Erick, Livnat, Adi, Papadimitriou, Christos, and Vazirani, Umesh. 2014. Algorithms, games, and evolution. *Proceedings of the National Academy of Sciences*, **111**(29), 10620–10623.

Christiano, Paul, Kelner, Jonathan A., Madry, Aleksander, Spielman, Daniel A., and Teng, Shang-Hua. 2011. Electrical flows, Laplacian systems, and faster approximation of maximum flow in undirected graphs. Pages 273–282 of: *Proceedings of the 43rd ACM Symposium on Theory of Computing, STOC 2011, June 6–8*, San Jose, CA.

Cohen, Michael B., Madry, Aleksander, Tsipras, Dimitris, and Vladu, Adrian. 2017. Matrix scaling and balancing via box constrained newton's method and interior point methods. Pages 902–913 of: *58th IEEE Annual Symposium on Foundations of Computer Science, FOCS 2017, October 15–17*, Berkeley, CA.

Cormen, Thomas H., Leiserson, Charles E., Rivest, Ronald L., and Stein, Clifford. 2001. *Introduction to Algorithms*. Cambridge, MA: MIT Press.

Daitch, Samuel I., and Spielman, Daniel A. 2008. Faster approximate lossy generalized flow via interior point algorithms. Pages 451–460 of: *Proceedings of the 40th Annual ACM Symposium on Theory of Computing, May 17–20*, Victoria, British Columbia.

Dantzig, George B. 1990. A history of scientific computing. Pages 141–151 of: *Origins of the Simplex Method*. New York: Association for Computing Machinery.

Dasgupta, Sanjoy, Papadimitriou, Christos H., and Vazirani, Umesh. 2006. *Algorithms*. New York, NY: McGraw-Hill.

Devanur, Nikhil R., Garg, Jugal, and Végh, Làszló A. 2016. A rational convex program for linear Arrow-Debreu markets. *ACM Transactions on Economics and Computation*, **5**(1), 6:1–6:13.

Diestel, Reinhard. 2012. *Graph Theory*. 4th ed. Graduate Texts in Mathematics, Vol. 173. Berlin, Heidelberg: Springer-Verlag.

Dinic, E. A. 1970. Algorithm for solution of a problem of maximal flow in a network with power estimation. *Soviet Math Dokl*, **224**(11), 1277–1280.

Dudik, Miroslav. 2007. *Maximum Entropy Density Estimation and Modeling Geographic Distributions of Species*. Ph.D. thesis, Princeton University.

Edmonds, Jack. 1965a. Maximum matching and a polyhedron with 0, 1 vertices. *Journal of Research of the National Bureau of Standards*, **69**, 125–130.

Edmonds, Jack. 1965b. Paths, trees, and flowers. *Canadian Journal of Mathematics*, **17**(3), 449–467.

Edmonds, Jack, and Karp, Richard M. 1972. Theoretical improvements in algorithmic efficiency for network flow problems. *Journal of the Association for Computing Machinery*, **19**(2), 248–264.

Eisenberg, Edmund, and Gale, David. 1959. Consensus of subjective probabilities: the pari-mutuel method. *Annals of Mathematical Statistics*, **30**(1), 165–168.

Farkas, Julius. 1902. Theorie der einfachen Ungleichungen. *Journal für die reine und angewandte Mathematik*, **124**, 1–27.

Feige, Uriel. 2008. On estimation algorithms vs approximation algorithms. Pages 357–363 of: *IARCS Annual Conference on Foundations of Software Technology and Theoretical Computer Science*. Leibniz International Proceedings in Informatics (LIPIcs), vol. 2. Dagstuhl, Germany: Schloss Dagstuhl–Leibniz-Zentrum fuer Informatik.

Ford, L. R., and Fulkerson, D. R. 1956. Maximal flow in a network. *Canadian Journal of Mathematics*, **8**, 399–404.

Galántai, A. 2000. The theory of Newton's method. *Journal of Computational and Applied Mathematics*, **124**(1), 25–44. Special Issue: Numerical Analysis 2000. Vol. IV: Optimization and Nonlinear Equations.

Garg, Jugal, Mehta, Ruta, Sohoni, Milind A., and Vishnoi, Nisheeth K. 2013. Towards polynomial simplex-like algorithms for market equilibria. Pages 1226–1242 of: *Proceedings of the Twenty-Fourth Annual ACM-SIAM Symposium on Discrete Algorithms, SODA 2013, January 6–8*, New Orleans, LA.

Garg, Naveen, and Könemann, Jochen. 2007. Faster and simpler algorithms for multicommodity flow and other fractional packing problems. *SIAM Journal on Computing*, **37**(2), 630–652.

Gärtner, Bernd, and Matousek, Jirí. 2014. *Approximation Algorithms and Semidefinite Programming*. Berlin, Heidelberg: Springer.

Gibbs, J. (2010). *Elementary Principles in Statistical Mechanics: Developed with Especial Reference to the Rational Foundation of Thermodynamics*. Cambridge: Cambridge University Press.

Goldberg, A., and Tarjan, R. 1987. Solving minimum-cost flow problems by successive approximation. Pages 7–18 of: *Proceedings of the Nineteenth Annual ACM Symposium on Theory of Computing*, STOC 1987, May 25–27, New York, NY.

Goldberg, Andrew V., and Rao, Satish. 1998. Beyond the flow decomposition barrier. *Journal of the Association for Computing Machinery*, **45**(5), 783–797.

Golub, G. H., and Van Loan, C. F. 1996. *Matrix Computations*. Baltimore, MD: Johns Hopkins University Press.

Gonzaga C. C. (1989) An algorithm for solving linear programming problems in $O(n^3 L)$ operations. Pages 1–28 of: Megiddo, N. (ed.), *Progress in Mathematical Programming*. New York, NY: Springer.

Grötschel, M., Lovász, L., and Schrijver, A. 1981. The ellipsoid method and its consequences in combinatorial optimization. *Combinatorica*, **1**(2), 169–197.

Grötschel, Martin, Lovász, Lászlo, and Schrijver, Alexander. 1988. *Geometric Algorithms and Combinatorial Optimization*. Vol. 2: *Algorithms and Combinatorics*. Berlin, Heidelberg: Springer-Verlag.

Gurjar, Rohit, Thierauf, Thomas, and Vishnoi, Nisheeth K. 2018. Isolating a vertex via lattices: polytopes with totally unimodular faces. Pages 74:1–74:14 of: *45th International Colloquium on Automata, Languages, and Programming, ICALP 2018, July 9–13, Prague, Czech Republic*. LIPIcs, vol. 107.

Hazan, Elad. 2016. Introduction to online convex optimization. *Foundations and Trends in Optimization*, **2**(3–4), 157–325.

Hestenes, Magnus R., and Stiefel, Eduard. 1952. Methods of conjugate gradients for solving linear systems. *Journal of Research of the National Bureau of Standards*, **49**(Dec.), 409–436.

Hopcroft, John E., and Karp, Richard M. 1973. An $n^{5/2}$ algorithm for maximum matchings in bipartite graphs. *SIAM Journal on Computing*, **2**(4), 225–231.

Jaggi, Martin. 2013. Revisiting Frank-Wolfe: projection-free sparse convex optimization. Pages I-427–I-435 of: *Proceedings of the 30th International Conference on International Conference on Machine Learning – Volume 28*, ICML 2013, June 16–21, Atlanta, GA. JMLR.org.

Jain, Prateek, and Kar, Purushottam. 2017. Non-convex optimization for machine learning. *Foundations and Trends in Machine Learning*, **10**(3–4), 142–336.

Jaynes, Edwin T. 1957a. Information theory and statistical mechanics. *Physical Review*, **106**(May), 620–630.

Jaynes, Edwin T. 1957b. Information theory and statistical mechanics. II. *Physical Review*, **108**(Oct.), 171–190.

Karlin, Anna R., Klein, Nathan, and Oveis Gharan, Shayan. 2020. A (slightly) improved approximation algorithm for metric TSP. *CoRR*, **abs/2007.01409**.

Karmarkar, Narendra. 1984. A new polynomial-time algorithm for linear programming. *Combinatorica*, **4**(4), 373–395.

Karp, Richard M., and Papadimitriou, Christos H. 1982. On linear characterizations of combinatorial optimization problems. *SIAM Journal on Computing*, **11**(4), 620–632.

Karzanov, Alexander V. 1973. On finding maximum flows in networks with special structure and some applications. *Matematicheskie Voprosy Upravleniya Proizvodstvom*, **5**, 81–94.

Kelner, Jonathan A., Lee, Yin Tat, Orecchia, Lorenzo, and Sidford, Aaron. 2014. An almost-linear-time algorithm for approximate max flow in undirected graphs, and its multicommodity generalizations. Pages 217–226 of: *Proceedings of the Twenty-Fifth Annual ACM-SIAM Symposium on Discrete Algorithms, SODA 2014, January 5–7*, Portland, OR.

Khachiyan, L. G. 1979. A polynomial algorithm for linear programming. *Doklady Akademii Nauk SSSR*, **224**(5), 1093–1096.

Khachiyan, L. G. 1980. Polynomial algorithms in linear programming. *USSR Computational Mathematics and Mathematical Physics*, **20**(1), 53–72.

Klee, V., and Minty, G. J. 1972. How good is the simplex algorithm? Pages 159–175 of: Shisha, O. (ed.), *Inequalities III*. New York, NY: Academic Press.

Kleinberg, Jon, and Tardos, Eva. 2005. *Algorithm Design*. Boston, MA: Addison-Wesley Longman.

Krantz, S. G. 2014. *Convex Analysis*. Textbooks in Mathematics. Boca Raton, FL: CRC Press.

Lau, Lap-Chi, Ravi, R., and Singh, Mohit. 2011. *Iterative Methods in Combinatorial Optimization*. New York, NY: Cambridge University Press.

Leake, Jonathan, and Vishnoi, Nisheeth K. 2020. On the computability of continuous maximum entropy distributions with applications. Pages 930–943 of: *Proceedings of the 52nd Annual ACM SIGACT Symposium on Theory of Computing, STOC 2020, June 22–26*, Chicago, IL.

Lee, Yin Tat, Rao, Satish, and Srivastava, Nikhil. 2013. A new approach to computing maximum flows using electrical flows. Pages 755–764 of: *Proceedings of the Forty-Fifth Annual ACM Symposium on Theory of Computing. STOC 2013, June 1–4*, Palo Alto, CA.

Lee, Yin Tat, and Sidford, Aaron. 2014. Path finding methods for linear programming: solving linear programs in $\tilde{O}$(vrank) iterations and faster algorithms for maximum flow. Pages 424–433 of: *55th IEEE Annual Symposium on Foundations of Computer Science, FOCS 2014, October 18–21*, Philadelphia, PA.

Lee, Yin Tat, Sidford, Aaron, and Wong, Sam Chiu-wai. 2015. A faster cutting plane method and its implications for combinatorial and convex optimization. Pages 1049–1065 of: *IEEE 56th Annual Symposium on Foundations of Computer Science, FOCS 2015, October*, Berkeley, CA.

Louis, Anand, and Vempala, Santosh S. 2016. Accelerated Newton iteration for roots of black box polynomials. Pages 732–740 of: *IEEE 57th Annual Symposium on Foundations of Computer Science, FOCS 2016, October 9–11, New Brunswick*, NJ.

Lovász, László. 1983. Submodular functions and convexity. Pages 235–257 of: Bachem, A., Korte, B., and Grötschel, M. (eds.), *Mathematical Programming: The State of the Art*. Berlin, Heidelberg: Springer.

Madry, Aleksander. 2013. Navigating central path with electrical flows: from flows to matchings, and back. Pages 253–262 of: *54th Annual IEEE Symposium on Foundations of Computer Science, FOCS 2013, October 26–29, Berkeley, CA*.

Mulmuley, Ketan, Vazirani, Umesh V., and Vazirani, Vijay V. 1987. Matching is as easy as matrix inversion. *Combinatorica*, **7**, 105–113.

Nakagaki, Toshiyuki, Yamada, Hiroyasu, and Toth, Agota. 2000. Maze-solving by an amoeboid organism. *Nature*, **407**(6803), 470.

Nemirovski, A., and Yudin, D. 1983. *Problem Complexity and Method Efficiency in Optimization*. Translated by E. R. Dawson. Chichester: Wiley.

Nesterov, Y., and Nemirovskii, A. 1994. *Interior-Point Polynomial Algorithms in Convex Programming*. Philadelphia, PA: Society for Industrial and Applied Mathematics.

Nesterov, Yurii. 1983. A method for unconstrained convex minimization problem with the rate of convergence $O(1/k^2)$. *Dokl. akad. nauk Sssr*, **269**, 543–547.

Nesterov, Yurii. 2004. *Introductory Lectures on Convex Optimization*. Vol. 87. New York: Springer Science & Business Media.

Orecchia, Lorenzo, Sachdeva, Sushant, and Vishnoi, Nisheeth K. 2012. Approximating the exponential, the lanczos method and an $\tilde{O}(m)$-time spectral algorithm for balanced separator. Pages 1141–1160 of: *Proceedings of the Forty-Fourth Annual ACM Symposium on Theory of Computing*. STOC 2012, May 19–22, New York, NY.

Orecchia, Lorenzo, Schulman, Leonard J., Vazirani, Umesh V., and Vishnoi, Nisheeth K. 2008. On partitioning graphs via single commodity flows. Pages 461–470 of: *Proceedings of the 40th Annual ACM Symposium on Theory of Computing, May 17–20*, Victoria, British Columbia.

Oveis Gharan, Shayan, Saberi, Amin, and Singh, Mohit. 2011. A randomized rounding approach to the traveling salesman problem. Pages 267–276 of: *FOCS'11: Proceedings of the 52nd Annual IEEE Symposium on Foundations of Computer Science*, October 22–25, 2011, Palm Springs, CA.

Padberg, Manfred W., and Rao, M. Rammohan. 1981. *The Russian Method for Linear Inequalities III: Bounded Integer Programming*. Ph.D. thesis, INRIA.

Pan, Victor Y., and Chen, Zhao Q. 1999. The complexity of the matrix eigenproblem. Pages 507–516 of: *Proceedings of the Thirty-First Annual ACM Symposium on Theory of Computing*, STOC 1999, May 1–4, Atlanta, GA.

Peng, Richard. 2016. Approximate undirected maximum flows in $O(m \text{ polylog}(n))$ time. Pages 1862–1867 of: *Proceedings of the Twenty-Seventh Annual ACM-SIAM Symposium on Discrete Algorithms, SODA 2016, January 10–12*, Arlington, VA.

Perko, Lawrence. 2001. *Differential Equations and Dynamical Systems*. Vol. 7. New York, NY: Springer-Verlag.

Plotkin, Serge A., Shmoys, David B., and Tardos, Éva. 1995. Fast approximation algorithms for fractional packing and covering problems. *Mathematics of Operations Research*, **20**(2), 257–301.

Polyak, Boris. 1964. Some methods of speeding up the convergence of iteration methods. *USSR Computational Mathematics and Mathematical Physics*, **4**(12), 1–17.

Renegar, James. 1988. A polynomial-time algorithm, based on Newton's method, for linear programming. *Mathematical Programming*, **40**(1–3), 59–93.

Renegar, James. 2001. *A Mathematical View of Interior-Point Methods in Convex Optimization*. Philadephia, PA: Society for Industrial and Applied Mathematics.

Rockafellar, R. Tyrrell. 1970. *Convex Analysis*. Princeton Mathematical Series. Princeton, NJ: Princeton University Press.

Rothvoss, Thomas. 2017. The matching polytope has exponential extension complexity. *Journal of the Association for Computing Machinery*, **64**(6), 41:1–41:19.

Rudin, Walter. 1987. *Real and Complex Analysis*. 3rd ed. New York: McGraw-Hill.

Saad, Y. 2003. *Iterative Methods for Sparse Linear Systems*. 2nd ed. Philadelphia, PA: Society for Industrial and Applied Mathematics.

Sachdeva, Sushant, and Vishnoi, Nisheeth K. 2014. Faster algorithms via approximation theory. *Foundations and Trends in Theoretical Computer Science*, **9**(2), 125–210.

Schrijver, Alexander. 2002a. *Combinatorial Optimization: Polyhedra and Efficiency*. Vol. 24. Berlin, Heidelberg: Springer-Verlag.

Schrijver, Alexander. 2002b. On the history of the transportation and maximum flow problems. *Mathematical Programming*, **91**(3), 437–445.

Shalev-Shwartz, Shai. 2012. Online learning and online convex optimization. *Foundations and Trends in Machine Learning*, **4**(2), 107–194.

Sherman, Jonah. 2013. Nearly maximum flows in nearly linear time. Pages 263–269 of: *54th Annual IEEE Symposium on Foundations of Computer Science, FOCS 2013, October, 26–29, Berkeley, CA*.

Shor, N. Z. 1972. Utilization of the operation of space dilatation in the minimization of convex functions. *Cybernetics*, **6**(1), 7–15.

Singh, Mohit, and Vishnoi, Nisheeth K. 2014. Entropy, optimization and counting. Pages 50–59 of: *Proceedings of the 46th Annual ACM Symposium on Theory of Computing*, May 31–June 3, New York, NY.

Spielman, Daniel A. 2012. Algorithms, graph theory, and the solution of Laplacian linear equations. In: Czumaj A., Mehlhorn K., Pitts A., Wattenhofer R. (eds), *Automata, Languages, and Programming*. ICALP 2012. Lecture Notes in Computer Science, vol. 7392. Berlin, Heidelberg: Springer.

Spielman, Daniel A., and Teng, Shang-Hua. 2004. Nearly-linear time algorithms for graph partitioning, graph sparsification, and solving linear systems. Pages 81–90 of: *Proceedings of the 36th Annual ACM Symposium on the Theory of Computing*, STOC 2004, June 13–16, Chicago, IL.

Spielman, Daniel A., and Teng, Shang-Hua. 2009. Smoothed analysis: an attempt to explain the behavior of algorithms in practice. *Communications of the Association for Computing Machinery*, **52**(10), 76–84.

Steele, J. Michael. 2004. *The Cauchy-Schwarz Master Class: An Introduction to the Art of Mathematical Inequalities*. New York, NY: Cambridge University Press.

Strang, Gilbert. 1993. The fundamental theorem of linear algebra. *American Mathematical Monthly*, **100**(9), 848–855.

Strang, Gilbert. 2006. *Linear Algebra and Its Applications*. Belmont, CA: Thomson, Brooks/Cole.

Straszak, Damian, and Vishnoi, Nisheeth K. 2016a. Natural algorithms for flow problems. Pages 1868–1883 of: *Proceedings of the Twenty-Seventh Annual ACM-SIAM Symposium on Discrete Algorithms, SODA 2016, January 10–12*, Arlington, VA.

Straszak, Damian, and Vishnoi, Nisheeth K. 2016b. On a natural dynamics for linear programming. Page 291 of: *Proceedings of the 2016 ACM Conference on Innovations in Theoretical Computer Science, January 14–16*, Cambridge, MA.

Straszak, Damian, and Vishnoi, Nisheeth K. 2017. Real stable polynomials and matroids: optimization and counting. Pages 370–383 of: *Proceedings of the 49th Annual ACM SIGACT Symposium on Theory of Computing*, STOC 2017, June 19–23, Montreal, Quebec.

Straszak, Damian, and Vishnoi, Nisheeth K. 2019. Maximum entropy distributions: bit complexity and stability. Pages 2861–2891 of: *Conference on Learning Theory, COLT 2019, June 25–28, Phoenix, AZ*. Proceedings of Machine Learning Research, vol. 99.

Straszak, Damian, and Vishnoi, Nisheeth K. 2021. Iteratively reweighted least squares and slime mold dynamics: connection and convergence. *Mathematical Programming Series A*, 2021.

Teng, Shang-Hua. 2010. The Laplacian paradigm: emerging algorithms for massive graphs. In: Kratochvíl J., Li A., Fiala J., and Kolman P. (eds.), *Theory and Applications of Models of Computation*. TAMC 2010. Lecture Notes in Computer Science, vol. 6108. Berlin, Heidelberg: Springer.

Trefethen, Lloyd N., and Bau, David. 1997. *Numerical Linear Algebra*. Philadelphia, PA: SIAM.

Vaidya, Pravin M. 1987. An algorithm for linear programming which requires $O(((m + n)n^2 + (m + n)^{1.5}n)L)$ arithmetic operations. Pages 29–38 of: *Proceedings of the 19th Annual ACM Symposium on Theory of Computing, May 25–27, New York, NY*.

Vaidya, Pravin M. 1989a. A new algorithm for minimizing convex functions over convex sets (extended abstract). Pages 338–343 of: *30th Annual Symposium on Foundations of Computer Science*, October 30–November 1, *Research Triangle Park, NC*.

Vaidya, Pravin M. 1989b. Speeding-Up linear programming using fast matrix multiplication (extended abstract). Pages 332–337 of: *30th Annual Symposium on Foundations of Computer Science*, October 30–November 1, *Research Triangle Park, NC*.

Vaidya, Pravin M. 1990. Solving linear equations with symmetric diagonally dominant matrices by constructing good preconditioners. Unpublished manuscript, University of Illinois, Urbana-Champaign.

Valiant, Leslie G. 1979. The complexity of computing the permanent. *Theoretical Computer Science*, **8**, 189–201.

van den Brand, Jan, Lee, Yin-Tat, Nanongkai, Danupon, Peng, Richard, Saranurak, Thatchaphol, Sidford, Aaron, Song, Zhao, and Wang, Di. 2020. Bipartite Matching in Nearly-linear Time on Moderately Dense Graphs. Pages 919–930 of: *2020 IEEE 61st Annual Symposium on Foundations of Computer Science (FOCS)*.

Vanderbei, Robert J. 2001. *The Affine-Scaling Method*. In: *Linear Programming*. International Series in Operations Research and Management Science, vol. 114. Boston, MA: Springer.

Vazirani, Vijay V. 2012. The notion of a rational convex program, and an algorithm for the Arrow-Debreu Nash bargaining game. *Journal of the Association for Computing Machinery*, **59**(2).

Vishnoi, Nisheeth K. 2013. $Lx = b$. *Foundations and Trends in Theoretical Computer Science*, **8**(1–2), 1–141.

Vishnoi, Nisheeth K. 2018. Geodesic convex optimization: differentiation on manifolds, geodesics, and convexity. *CoRR*, **abs/1806.06373**.

Wright, Margaret H. 2005. The interior-point revolution in optimization: history, recent developments, and lasting consequences. *Bulletin of the American Mathematical Society (N.S.)*, **42**, 39–56.

Wright, Stephen J. 1997. *Primal-Dual Interior-Point Methods*. Philadelphia, PA: Society for Industrial and Applied Mathematics.

Yudin, D. B., and Nemirovskii, Arkadi S. 1976. Informational complexity and efficient methods for the solution of convex extremal problems. *Ékon Math Metod*, **12**, 357–369.

Zhu, Zeyuan Allen, Li, Yuanzhi, de Oliveira, Rafael Mendes, and Wigderson, Avi. 2017. Much faster algorithms for matrix scaling. Pages 890–901 of: *58th IEEE Annual Symposium on Foundations of Computer Science, FOCS 2017, October 15–17*, Berkeley, CA.

Index